Risk Management and Analysis

VOLUME 2: NEW MARKETS AND PRODUCTS

OTHER TITLES IN THE WILEY SERIES IN FINANCIAL ENGINEERING

INTEREST-RATE OPTION MODELS, Second Edition
Riccardo Rebonato

STRUCTURED SECURITIES FOR INVESTMENT PROFESSIONALS
John C. Braddock

MANAGING CREDIT RISK
John B. Caouette

MANAGING DERIVATIVE RISK
Lillian Chew

DYNAMIC HEDGING
Nassim Taleb

DERIVATIVES FOR DECISION MAKERS
George Crawford and Bidyut Sen

Risk Management and Analysis

VOLUME 2: NEW MARKETS AND PRODUCTS

Edited by Carol Alexander

JOHN WILEY & SONS

Chichester • New York • Weinheim • Brisbane • Singapore • Toronto

Chapters 4, 5, 6, 7 and 9 were previously published in *The Handbook of Risk Management and Analysis.*

Other Wiley Editorial Offices

John Wiley & Sons, Inc., 605 Third Avenue,
New York, NY 10158-0012, USA

WILEY-VCH Verlag GmbH, Pappelallee 3,
D-69469 Weinheim, Germany

Jacaranda Wiley Ltd, 33 Park Road, Milton,
Queensland 4064, Australia

John Wiley & Sons (Asia) Pte Ltd, 2 Clementi Loop #02-01,
Jin Xing Distripark, Singapore 129809

John Wiley & Sons (Canada) Ltd, 22 Worcester Road,
Rexdale, Ontario M9W 1L1, Canada

Library of Congress Cataloging-in-Publication Data

Risk management and analysis. Volume 2: New markets and products/edited by Carol
     Alexander.
          p.   cm. — (Wiley series in financial engineering)
     Includes bibliographical references and index.
     ISBN 0-471-97959-7
     1. Capital markets — Developing countries.   2. Derivative
securities — Developing countries.   I. Alexander, Carol.
II.Series.
HG5993.R57   1998
332'.042 – dc21   98-15961
                                                                                  CIP

British Library Cataloguing in Publication Data

A catalogue record for this book is available from the British Library

ISBN 0-471-97959-7

Typeset in 10/12pt Times by Laser Words, Madras, India
Printed and bound in Great Britain by Biddles Ltd, Guildford and King's Lynn
This book is printed on acid-free paper responsibly manufactured from sustainable forestation,
for which at least two trees are planted for each one used

Contents

List of Contributors

M. DESMOND FITZGERALD
Equitable House Investments Ltd, London, UK

MARK FOX
J.P. Morgan, London, UK

MICHAEL J. HOWELL
CrossBorder Capital, London, UK

IAN KING
American Express Asset Management International, Inc., London, UK

VINCENT LACOSTE
ESSEC, Cergy-Pontoise Cedex, France

EDMOND LEVY
HSBC Midland, London, UK

BLYTHE MASTERS
J.P. Morgan Securities Inc., New York, USA

RICCARDO REBONATO
Barclays Capital, London, UK

L.C.G. ROGERS
University of Bath, Bath, UK

ANDREW STREET
Traded Risk Department, The Financial Services Authority, London, UK

BRYAN THOMAS
Bank of America, Singapore

About the Contributors

M. DESMOND FITZGERALD

M. Desmond Fitzgerald is Chairman and Chief Executive of Equitable House Investments Ltd, a specialized arbitrage and derivatives trading firm. He is also Chairman of Unique Consultants Ltd, a specialized financial training and risk management consultancy firm. Previously he served as Director, Head of Arbitrage at Mitsubishi Finance International plc, as Chief Economist and Head of Planning at Credit Lyonnais-Alexanders, Laing and Cruickshank, and as a senior economist with Chemical Bank. His academic posts have included that of Ernst and Whinney Professor of Finance at the University of Strathclyde, Senior Lecturer and Head of Finance at City University, London, and Associate Professor of Finance at New York University. He has written two standard texts, *Financial Futures* and *Financial Options* and numerous articles in academic and professional journals.

MARK FOX

Mark Fox is a vice president of the Emerging Market Division of J.P. Morgan. He previously worked for eight years at Lehman Brothers as a director of the Emerging Markets Group and European Strategist, also setting up and managing emerging markets portfolios. He has been widely published, including authorship of CFA and ISMA examination texts on emerging markets, and is an associate lecturer on emerging markets for the ISMA Centre at the University of Reading.

MICHAEL J. HOWELL

Michael J. Howell is a founder-director of London-based CrossBorder Capital, an investment advisory firm specializing in global and emerging market asset allocation. Previously Michael was Head of Investment Strategy at ING Barings (1991–1996) and Research Director at Salomon Brothers International (1986–1991). Over the last 15 years Michael has been developing a unique approach to evaluating bond and equity markets based on his analysis of Global Capital Flows and Liquidity. His team has now amassed a database spanning 20 years. Michael has worked both as an academic and as a corporate planner in industry. Michael Howell was educated at Bristol and London Universities, where he graduated with an MA in Economics, specializing in finance and econometrics. He is married with four children.

IAN KING

Ian King is a senior portfolio manager of American Express Asset Management International Inc. with responsibility for all equity investments in emerging markets. He is manager of a number of open- and closed-end investment funds specializing in emerging markets investment, as well as segregated emerging markets portfolios for institutional clients. He is a graduate of Brasenose College, Oxford and a chartered financial analyst.

VINCENT LACOSTE

Vincent Lacoste has been Associate Professor of Finance at the Groupe ESSEC — France for four years. He studied mathematics at the Ecole Normale Superieure in Paris and completed his Ph.D. on statistics and probability while working at the Caisse des Depots. He was Senior Manager for Mitsubihi Finance International plc, in London, for two years, involved with pricing and hedging derivatives on indices, interest rates and commodities. His academic research mainly focuses on interest rate models and optimal hedging strategies. Vincent can be contacted at ESSEC, Finance Department, Av. Bernard Hirsch BP 105, 95021 Cergy-Pontoise Cedex, France. e-mail:lacoste@edu.essec.Fr.

EDMOND LEVY

Edmond Levy is an assistant director in the Specialized Derivatives Group at HSBC Midland, where he is responsible for the development and risk management of foreign products. The group covers a wide range of structured equity and capital market products. Prior to joining the HSBC group, he was at BZW-Barclays Bank and Nomura Bank International plc. Edmond previously lectured in Finance at Liverpool University and Econometrics at Southampton University, where he received his Ph.D.

BLYTHE MASTERS

Blythe Masters is a graduate of Trinity College, Cambridge, with a BA in Economics. She is currently Head of Global Credit Derivatives Marketing and Co-Head of North American Credit Portfolio at J.P. Morgan Securities Inc., based in New York. Ms Masters has been responsible for credit derivatives marketing and product development for the past three years. Her responsibilities include the structuring and distribution of credit derivative products and related credit risk management strategies, both for clients of the bank and internally. She joined J.P. Morgan in 1991, having completed a number of internships in the bank's Interest Rate Swap Group dating back to 1987. She has experience in derivatives marketing and trading (spanning fixed income, commodities and credit markets), as well as structured finance and securitization.

RICCARDO REBONATO

Riccardo Rebonato is Director and Head of Research at Barclays Capital. He is responsible for the modelling, trading, and risk management of European exotic interest-rate products. He holds Doctorates in Nuclear Engineering and Science of Materials/Solid State Physics. Before moving into investment banking he was Research Fellow in Physics at Corpus Christi College (Oxford). He has published papers in several academic journals in finance, and is a regular speaker at conferences worldwide.

L.C.G. ROGERS

Chris Rogers is Professor of Probability at the University of Bath. His MA and Ph.D. degrees are both from the University of Cambridge. He is the author of more than 80 publications, including the famous two-volume work, *Diffusions, Markov Processes, and Martingales*, with David Williams. Many of his papers deal with topics in finance, such as the potential approach to term structure of interest rates, complete models of stochastic volatility (with David Hobson), portfolio turnpike theorems (with Phil Dybvig and Kerry Back), improved binomial pricing (with Emily Stapleton), liquidity effects, and high-frequency data modelling (with Omar Zane). Professor Rogers is an associate editor of several journals, including *Mathematical Finance*, and was the principal organizer of the 1995 programme on Financial Mathematics held at the Isaac Newton Institute in Cambridge.

ANDREW STREET

Andrew Street is Joint Head of the Traded Risk Department in the Financial Services Authority, the UK financial industry regulator. Before the formation of the FSA, Dr Street was Head of the Market Risk Unit within the SFA, which joined with the Bank of England and other regulators to form the SFA in June 1998.

Prior to the SFA, Dr Street was Head of Arbitrage at Mitsubishi Finance International plc (now Tokyo–Mitsubishi International plc). As Executive Director at Mitsubishi he controlled and directed the Equity, Foreign Exchange, Commodity and Bond derivative risk-taking within the firm. He was responsible for initiating and controlling both the proprietary risk-taking of the firm and client-driven new product pricing and risk management. He was promoted to this post in 1993, having previously been the Director of Equity and Commodity Risk Management within Mitsubishi.

His previous experience includes being European Head Trader of Equity Derivatives for Nomura International in London, Senior Equity Derivatives Structurer and Trader at Paribas Capital Markets, and Fixed Income Quantitative Analyst at Barings in the mid-1980s.

His academic background is in Theoretical Nuclear Physics; in particular, numerical solutions to the three-body nuclear problem using finite difference and matrix conversion techniques on supercomputers. His research work took place at Oxford University and the Atomic Energy Research Establishment at Harwell, for which he received his doctorate.

BRYAN THOMAS

Bryan Thomas received a BA in Economics and MBA in Finance and General Management from the University of California, Los Angeles. He worked for three years as a money market trader with Bankers Trust. He then enjoyed ten years with Banque Indosuez, of which three were spent in Paris, learning currency options as the market was developing. He joined Midland Bank, London, where he developed their Tender-to-Contract-Hedge product. In 1993 he became Head of Global Currency Options Development with the Bank of America in London and these responsibilities have taken him to Singapore where he is setting up a new currency options trading desk. Bryan is a frequent speaker at conferences on exotic options.

Preface

In the two years since John Wiley published *The Handbook of Risk Management and Analysis*, interest in the management, modelling and control of financial risks has grown enormously. New geographical markets have emerged as more countries develop derivatives markets and place less restrictions on foreign trade. New products such as credit derivatives and exotic instruments for hedging market risk are being established very rapidly. Financial products such as loans, that traditionally, have been on the banking book only, are now being structured and transformed into tradable instruments.

Currently, experience is of a revolution in risk management to become more quantitative in its approach to all risks. The new, more constraining, regulatory environment has prompted the rapid development of new methods for measuring and modelling financial risk. Financial institutions are setting new standards for risk control that require better pricing models and more stringent validation of all trading models. And recent changes in the rules for calculating risk capital charges have promoted the development of new risk systems, from data management to the internal models for measuring market and credit risk capital.

My initial intention in editing this work was to produce a second edition of the *Handbook*. But the subject has developed and expanded so much that only about one-third of the original book remains. To reflect the division mentioned above, the new book, *Risk Management and Analysis* is published in two volumes: Volume 1: *Measuring and Modelling Financial Risk* and Volume 2: *New Markets and Products*.

New Markets and Products begins with two chapters on emerging markets. The first chapter by Michael Howell analyses the economic characteristics of countries with emerging financial markets and the cross-border debt and equity flows between these and the more developed countries. The emphasis of this chapter is on the financial structure, and the potential for development, of financial sectors in emerging countries. The second emerging markets chapter, by Mark Fox and Ian King, introduces the subject by defining the characteristics of emerging markets. There follows a comprehensive survey, with an historical perspective, of the type of products available to investors. These products range from the Brady bonds already established a decade ago to new instruments such as structured notes that include credit derivatives.

Thereafter, the book covers markets and products of increasing complexity: standard equity and interest rate derivatives; exotic options; swaps (and swaptions); volatility trading and, finally, credit derivatives. As a little precursor, we have a beautiful piece on the origins of Black–Scholes by Chris Rogers. In his own words, "There is nothing original in this chapter, in the sense that a good financial economist would read it and say 'Well, of course'. On the other hand, for those who have not seen this way of thinking of things, there are miraculous revelations ahead; we shall see how martingales, stochastic integration and the notion of equivalent martingale measures leap out of the page." Chris Rogers has made light work of some difficult mathematical concepts that are central to understanding risk-neutral pricing and has brought them to a wide audience.

Chapter 4–7 are reproduced here, with minor amendments, from the original *Handbook*. First, Andrew Street gives an historical overview of equity derivatives markets from a managerial perspective. The next chapter by Riccardo Rebonato presents a mathematical critique and survey of the more standard pricing models for interest rate options. This is a long and comprehensive chapter, covering mathematical tools such as principal components, lattices and PDEs, arbitrage conditions and choice of numeraire, and an analysis of specific models. Chapters 6 and 7 are on exotic options: Edmond Levy presents an excellent mathematical treatment of pricing models for Asian, binary, compound and currency protected options, and although Bryan Thomas looks more superficially at pricing, he also discusses hedging issues concerning these and other exotics such as barriers and lookbacks.

Vincent Lacoste gives a survey of mathematical methods that are fundamental to the pricing and hedging of captions and swaptions in Chapter 8. Starting with the change of numeraire, a general pricing technique that has been pioneered by Helyette Geman, it goes on to discuss hedging swaptions against yield curves and the use of captions for the marking to market of volatility term structures. Chapter 9 by Desmond Fitzgerald, which has already appeared in the *Handbook*, covers the basics of volatility trading. Blythe Masters presents the final chapter on credit derivatives, which focuses on opportunities to exploit and profit from discontinuities in the pricing of credit risk associated with differences between asset classes, maturities, rating categories, debt seniority levels and so on. She surveys the basic principles underlying a number of the more common credit derivatives, illustrating situations where their use produces benefits that can be evaluated without the use of complex mathematical models.

All the authors are acknowledged experts in their field and have been availed upon to find time to write for this book because of their excellent expository skills. I present it with much gratitude to John and Celia Hall for their excellent project management, and with great appreciation for the authors, since they have so little time. My hope is that it may provide some help to the financial risk community in performing the important tasks they currently face.

Carol Alexander

Foreword

Russian bonds falling into an abyss; stock market prices in South East Asia more than halved in less than a month; Latin America on the verge of being sucked into a spiral of devaluations; even the mighty Dow–Jones losing more than 12% in a week on fears about the political future of the American President; rumours of a major US bank filing for protection under Chapter 11 — these are some of today's financial risks.

How much is a particular financial institution exposed to these market risks and through exposures to counterparties? Has it a comprehensive system of limits and controls? Has it qualified personnel with proper authorities, accurate, speedy and robust information systems and adequate capital resources? These are fundamental questions for risk management. On the answers rest the survival chances of the firm.

In what started as a second edition of the well-received *Handbook of Risk Management and Analysis*, Carol Alexander has taken up the challenge of the increasing complexity of today's markets by selecting additional material to cover new aspects of risk modelling and new products, hence the present two-volume edition. As before, the authors are well known not only for their mastery of the subject matter but also for their expository skills. Sound theories and tried methods are explained; new markets and products are clearly described. This is essential reading for the growing community of quantitatively minded risk managers.

Financial risk measurement is based on a two-step process: first, measure the current value of a business; that is, the difference between the values at which assets could be sold and liabilities could be bought (at least in theory); secondly, estimate by how much this current, or so-called mark-to-market value could fluctuate over time as a function of varying market factors and operational changes. The variations are weighted with probabilities to reflect their likelihood.

In practice, this process is fraught with difficulties. Vast areas of business are not valued for fear of relying on model-based values for illiquid products (for example, loans). Many theoretical valuations fall short of taking into account all expected costs such as expected losses because of counterparty risks. Too often, obsolete accounting standards or bizarre tax incentives still obscure or bias the valuation process.

When measuring potential variations over time, the desire of regulators to impose prudential standards has led to simplistic and largely arbitrary rules (as in the case of large exposures measurements) or benchmarks of limited significance (as in the case of Value at Risk (VaR) measurements). Thus, enormous investments in personnel, data bases and calculation tools are being made to obtain results that may satisfy regulators but are otherwise of limited operational value. Indeed, they may at worst give a false sense of security and divert attention from critical issues.

Financial risk management aims to balance risks and returns in accordance with a stated risk management policy, from tactical dynamic hedging decisions to strategic capital allocation decisions. Few institutions have a firm-wide risk policy expressed as a trade-off between risks and returns; perhaps because returns are even more difficult to predict than risks; perhaps because delegation of authority and control is easier when subject to a set of absolute limits; or perhaps because senior management think that the degree of risk-taking should be left to the initiative of individuals. It may also be, however, that these beliefs are remnants of times past and that a modicum of reflection would reveal the advantages of risk management systems based on a pricing of risks.

Such issues and many more have been addressed in these two volumes. General results and state of the art solutions are given, but without pretence to be either comprehensive or final answers. This second edition is a valuable analysis of today's issues but the risk management revolution that started some 12 years ago in the financial markets has still a long way to run. I would not be surprised if a third edition in three volumes became necessary soon.

Jacques Pézier

General Manager
Crédit Agricole Lazard Financial Products Bank

1

Emerging Markets I

MICHAEL J. HOWELL

Many persons have not a distinct perception of the risk of lending to a country in a wholly different state of civilisation. They can hardly imagine the difficulties with which such a country struggles, and the dangers to which it is exposed. They forget that national good faith is a rare and recent thing... [t]he primary conditions of [which] are three — a continuous polity;[1] a fixed political morality; and a constant possession of money... It seems a truism to say that no lender to a country can be safe unless he knows something about that country. But in practice it is a paradox. We lend to countries whose condition we do not know, and whose want of civilisation we do not consider, and therefore, we lose our money. Walter Bagehot, *The Economist*, 1867

1.1 INTRODUCTION

Tomorrow's economies are being built in today's global capital markets. By far the most successful of these economies in the last couple of decades have been those that have endorsed free market economic policies and encouraged financial market reform. Large inflows of portfolio capital have typically followed:

- Private sector cross-border equity investment to the so-called emerging countries has leapt 15-fold since 1989, and debt flows are twenty times larger than they were in 1990.
- There has not been a single year in the last decade when new money exited the emerging stock and bond markets in aggregate.
- In 1993 global investors allocated more new money to the emerging stock markets that they did to the world's two largest equity markets combined, Japan and the United States.

In the wake of these huge cross-border flows, "emerging markets" has become a popular buzz-term with pension plan sponsors and fund management groups. But "emerging" is an ambiguous label. Does it always mean fast-growing? Is it simply a politically correct

Risk Management and Analysis. Vol. 2: New Markets and Products. Edited by Carol Alexander
© 1998 John Wiley & Sons Ltd

way of saying "backward"? Should it refer to prospects for the real economy or to developments in the financial economy?

The description "emerging" plainly suggests dynamism. Indeed, the IFC[2] Emerging Market Share Price Index has sky-rocketed higher over the past decade, delivering a juicy average return of 19.5 per cent a year, in US dollar terms. Mostly in tandem, spreads on high yielding emerging market debt have also narrowed substantially versus benchmark US Treasuries. See Figures 1.1–1.4, and Table 1.1.

However, although the performance of these markets has been awesome, they are a rag-bag of different quality investments from several different continents. Today, around 3,000–3,500 stocks are listed across the 30-plus emerging markets. However, only around 500–1,000 shares in total, or 25–50 stocks per market, dominate overall emerging market trading activity and comprise the bulk of their market capitalizations. We believe that emerging markets have a key place in portfolios, but they must be more tightly defined.

In the six years to 1996, only three times (out of 30 possibilities) does a developed market deliver one of the top five returns; equally, only one makes it into the bottom five places.[3] There is also an echo effect. Out of 54 countries used to compile Table 1.1, Venezuela and Peru both appear four times in six years (as "best" or "worst"), while Bangladesh, Turkey, and Jamaica appear three times each. And, on only one occasion (1995) is it true that at least one "worst" or "best" performer fails to appear in the opposite ranking the next year.

Strangely, despite their cultural and geographic differences, emerging markets share common risk and return characteristics. The remarkable similarity in the pattern of their investment returns probably outweighs these other, more tangible differences, and it necessitates analysing them as a single asset class.

In mature financial markets it has been well documented that investors are rewarded for taking extra systematic risk. Indeed, this is the basis for the CAPM (Capital Asset

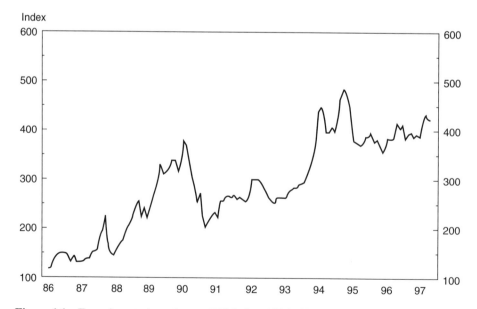

Figure 1.1 Emerging stock markets — IFC index, 1986–97 (US dollar terms). *Source*: IFC

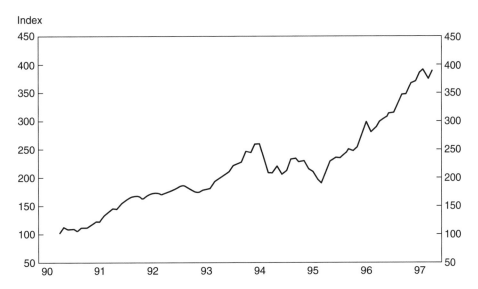

Index

Figure 1.2 Emerging bond markets (Brady bonds)—Salomon Brothers Index, 1990–97. *Source*: Salomon Brothers

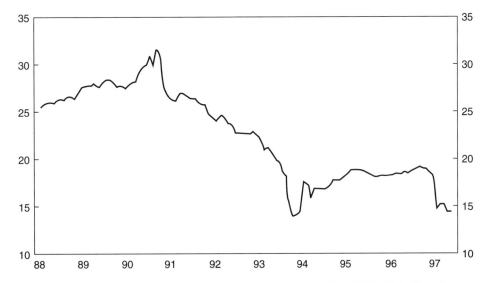

Figure 1.3 Ups and downs—emerging stock market price volatility, 1988–97 (rolling three-year standard deviation). *Source*: CrossBorder Capital

Pricing Model) which uses beta to measure systematic risk. However, Harvey (1994) has shown that there is no relationship between beta and expected returns in several emerging markets.

Bekaert et al. (1996) go on to show that the volatility of the emerging markets still remains above the volatility of developed stock markets, but it has dropped significantly in recent years. Their results highlight a fall to 16 per cent volatility for the IFC index for the five years ending March 1996, compared with 28 per cent in the five years to end-1991.

Per cent

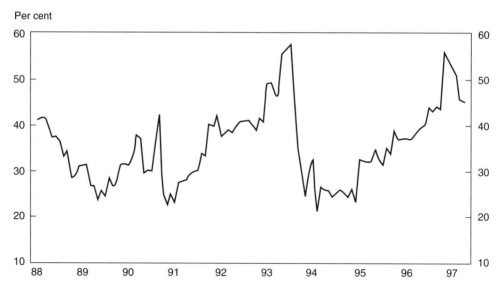

Figure 1.4 Greater integration—cross-correlations between IFC and MSCI world indexes, 1988–97 (rolling three-year percentage correlation coefficient). *Source*: CrossBorder Capital

Table 1.1 Best and worst—stock market winners and losers, 1991–96 (ranked by annual US dollar returns)

Best	1991	1992	1993	1994	1995	1996
1st	Argentina	Jamaica	Poland	Bangladesh	USA	Bangladesh
2nd	Brazil	Venezuela	Turkey	Brazil	Netherlands	Venezuela
3rd	Jamaica	Israel	Zimbabwe	Peru	Peru	Russia
4th	Colombia	Peru	Philippines	Morocco	Zimbabwe	Hungary
5th	Pakistan	Colombia	Hong Kong	Chile	Belgium	China
Worst						
1st	New Zealand	Zimbabwe	Jamaica	Turkey	India	Thailand
2nd	Turkey	Turkey	China	Poland	Pakistan	South Korea
3rd	Indonesia	Greece	Peru	Mexico	Sri Lanka	Pakistan
4th	Finland	Denmark	Venezuela	Hong Kong	Russia	South Africa
5th	Venezuela	Sri Lanka	Bangladesh	Indonesia	Taiwan	Chile

Comparable figures for the MSCI World Index are 10.7 per cent and 18 per cent, respectively. In other words, the volatility of emerging relative to developed stock markets has merely inched lower from 1.55 times to 1.50 times. The general falls in emerging and developed market volatility is probably explained by the increasing integration of world capital markets.

Bekaert and Harvey (1995) confirm that emerging market returns depart from normality. Their higher order moments show both greater positive skewness than developed stock markets, and far greater kurtosis. Summarizing these results, emerging markets have:

- a high *average rate of return*, relative to the mature stock markets;
- a wide *variance* of returns;

- a *fat-tailed (or lepto-kurtonic) return distribution*, indicating the higher frequency of "large" share price rises and "large" share price falls; and
- low cross-correlations between emerging and developed stock markets.

Not only must these four features be explained, but taken together they suggest that emerging financial market investment will be very different from the process of investing in mature financial markets. High relative volatility, low cross-correlations, and P/E multiples that range from single figures for Russia to high double-digits in China, together highlight the lack of integration of emerging markets with world capital markets. They are quite simply different.

One specific difference arising from the third attribute is that emerging market returns are not normally statistically distributed. They are subject to high event risk and have a tendency to "over-shoot" both upwards and downwards. For this reason, the standard deviation is an inadequate measure of investment risk, and the traditional mean–variance approach to optimal asset allocation cannot be safely used. Howell in Euromoney/World Bank (1994) also notes that despite their low cross-correlations with developed stock markets, the high relative volatility of emerging market returns severely limits their ability to reduce overall portfolio risk.[4]

The abnormal return distribution for emerging markets results from the importance of key events:

- *Sudden large and lumpy outflows of Western capital*, mainly associated with the relaxation of controls on outward foreign investment, e.g. the ending of UK Exchange Controls in May 1979 by Mrs Thatcher's in-coming Conservative Government.
- *Sweeping local political change in the emerging countries themselves*, e.g. the fall of the Berlin Wall in November 1989.

Today, footloose global money is polarized in the hands of a few major institutional investors: political power is vested in potentially fragile local consensuses. Future prospects for emerging markets thus greatly depend on latent, unpredictable factors; on the quarterly asset allocation decisions of, may be, as few as twenty global institutions, mainly situated in New York and London;[5] and on continued political reform at the local level. Unfortunately, access to these huddled boardrooms and smoke-filled Cabinet rooms is denied to us.

Of the two, which is the more flaky? What could end the emerging market boom? The immediate answer must be political change, sufficiently strong that it either disrupts or reverses the economic reform process. For example, a revolution in Mexico; a revival of communism in the former Soviet Union; further Tiananmen Square-like incidents in China; or even (unthinkable!) the re-imposition of controls on the outflow of capital by European governments.

But how realistic are such possibilities? The pages of history have turned. Many of the changes we have witnessed since the mid-1980s are plainly irreversible. The Berlin Wall will not be rebuilt. Mexico has become a permanent member of both the OECD, the rich countries' club, and of NAFTA, the North American Free Trade Agreement. Others in the continent will compete to be the next to join. And, much of the mechanism for state planning in China and in Russia has been dismantled once and for all.

Already, a staggering 12 per cent of the world's economically active population live along the banks of China's Yangtze river. Today, Beijing, Shanghai, and Tianjin are mega-cities each with populations in excess of 10 million; Shenyang is close behind. Moreover, at current rates of real growth (around 8 per cent per annum) the effective size of the Chinese economy is roughly doubling every nine years. In PPP[6] terms, Greater China (mainland China, Taiwan, and Hong Kong) is already bigger than the Japanese economy. By the year 2000 it will surpass the combined economic size of Germany plus Japan; it will overtake the 15 EU economies by the mid-2020s, and by the early 2030s, Greater China will be economically more important than North America. The growing economic power of China is one dramatic aspect of the emerging market boom. See Table 1.2.

Overall, the emerging world is outstripping economic growth in the rich industrial countries by a factor of 2–3 times (5.4 per cent versus 2.6 per cent, 1992–96. See Section 1.10.2). Fast growth begets foreign capital. But despite recent vast purchases totalling nearly US$400 billion since 1990, global investors still have a remarkably low exposure to emerging market assets. Figure 1.5 highlights the fact that emerging economies measured by population, land-mass, current output, and resources easily

Table 1.2 The rise of the East—Economic size of Greater China, 1990–2010 (US dollars in billions, at constant 1990 prices and PPP exchange rates). *Source*: CrossBorder Capital and World Bank

	1980	1990	2000E	2010E	2020E	2030E
Greater China	1025.4	2242.4	3220	4625	6650	9525
• United States	4275.6	5522.5	6250	7075	8000	9050
• Japan	1097.5	1642.0	1900	2200	2550	2950
• Germany	877.6	1097.6	1250	1400	1600	1800

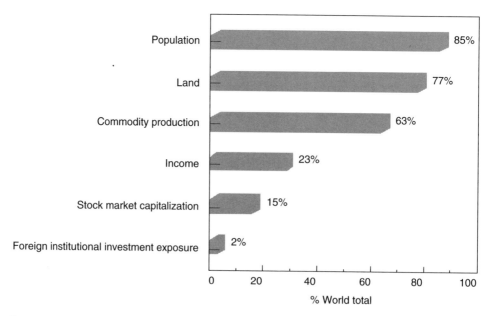

Figure 1.5 The great imbalance—global investors remain underexposed to emerging market investments, 1995. *Source*: CrossBorder Capital

outstrip the measly 2 per cent of Western financial assets currently committed to their capital markets. In other words, as this gap is closed, we should anticipate further strong foreign inflows into emerging stock and bond markets over the coming years.

1.2 GROWING COUNTRIES NOT POOR COUNTRIES

Curiously, most definitions of emerging markets focus on the *level* of development not on its *rate of change*. The vast majority of investors accept the World Bank's (or IFC's) definition of an emerging market as the capital market that serves a poor economy. Here "poor" means an economy where income per head is below US$8,995 in 1995. In itself, this does not sound like a particularly mouth-watering investment opportunity.

For example, South Africa had an income per head of US$3,160 in 1995, compared with Germany's US$27,510—a difference factor of 8.7. Is South Africa, therefore, an emerging market? On the other hand, South Africa's stock market capitalization per head (US$6,519) is very close to Germany's (US$8,433), but both are barely one-fourth of the equivalent US figure (US$33,756). Does this mean that Germany and South Africa have emerging financial markets?

Almost by definition, every poor country wants to get rich. On this basis, so-called emerging markets have significant growth potential. But a huge gap exists between the hope and the reality of growth. Consequently, as an investor interested in growth, this author takes a Marxist view of emerging markets—not Karl Marx, but Groucho. In other words, "emerging markets" constitute a club that any self-respecting country should avoid joining. Simply being poor does not equate with being fast-growing. Certain key conditions are required for strong growth.

Q: Out of 168 countries in the World, how many have enjoyed compound real economic growth of at least 5 per cent per annum in the last decade?

    (a) 52
    (b) 28
    (c) 21
    (d) 14

Surprisingly, the answer is 14 or barely 8 per cent of all countries in the world (that are monitored by the World Bank). Moreover, even this figure includes some minnows which many observers might reasonably exclude, such as tiny Malta and the Maldives. Ireland is the only "rich" country included, and its position probably owes more to massive EC grants than to indigenous economic success. In other words, the term "emerging markets" that is liberally applied to the World's developing, or "poor" economies is a clear misnomer. Only a very small group of countries have, so far, managed to get it right (see Table 1.3).

These countries largely comprised China, the Asian Tiger and Dragon economies of Hong Kong, Malaysia, Singapore, South Korea, Taiwan, and Thailand, together with Chile and Mauritius. Characteristically, this fast-growing group combine high savings ratios with a low incidence of government interference in the economy. While savings ratios across the rich industrial countries (OECD nations) have averaged a little under 20 per cent since 1985, the propensity to save among these fast-growing countries is 10 per cent higher at around 30 per cent. Moreover, within the "fast-growers", government spending and

Table 1.3 The few fast-growers — economies reporting real GDP growth above 5 per cent, annual averages 1985–95

Region:	Asia-Pacific	Africa	Latin America and Caribbean	Europe, Mediterranean and Indian Ocean
	China	Mauritius	Chile	Cyprus
	Hong Kong	Botswana		Ireland
	Singapore			Maldives
	Malaysia			Malta
	South Korea			
	Taiwan			
	Thailand			

taxation both account for less than one-third of GDP (excluding China), compared with between 40 per cent and 50 per cent for the OECD countries.

Inadequate savings can cause high inflation as well as slow growth because an expansionary monetary policy is typically used to fill the financing gap. Therefore, since high taxation is a common cause of low savings, excessive government spending (and hence taxation) often goes hand-in-hand with high inflation, especially in developing countries.

Below we list the common characteristics of "fast-growth" economies (criteria now often enshrined in IMF Structural Adjustment programmes as pre-conditions for further tranches of money) that stand out as quantitative measures of the likelihood of high and sustained growth.

- *Free markets and privatization*, e.g. trade pacts, such as Mercosur and NAFTA, have slashed through the thicket of average 51 per cent tariff rates and non-tariff barriers on 60 per cent of South American trade. The Uruguay Round has roughly halved tariffs on world trade in industrial goods. Between 1980 and 1992, Mexico and Chile privatized 87 per cent and 96 per cent, respectively, of their state-owned firms. And from 1990–95, emerging market privatizations raised US$58.4 billion; US$20.8 billion of which were portfolio purchases.

- *High savings*, e.g. across the successful East Asian economies, national savings rates average around 30 per cent of GDP, compared with less than 20 per cent for the rich industrial countries.

- *Small government, low taxes*, e.g. in China, the state's share has now fallen to only 40 per cent from a peak in 1969 of 89 per cent of overall industrial output, while Russia's private sector, today, provides over 70 per cent of the country's economic activity.

- *Stable money*, e.g. a low rate of domestic inflation and a firm currency encourage risk-taking. Brazil's inflation rate has plunged from 2500 per cent in 1993 to only 8.3 per cent in 1998.

- *Abundant resources*, e.g. the proportion of young persons in higher education. Only 0.6 per cent of Britons are in university-equivalent education, versus 0.7 per cent of Turks, 1.5 per cent of Mexicans, and 2.6 per cent of Koreans. Between 1965 and 1987, Korea's rate of enrolment in secondary education rocketed from 35 per cent to 88 per cent over the same period. Results of cognitive tests, reported by the World

Bank, now show that 78 per cent of 13 year old Koreans can solve a complex task compared with only 40 per cent of similar US schoolchildren.

One measure that neatly satisfies several of these requirements is the so-called *fundamental balance*. It is defined as the sum of a country's current account position plus its net receipts of long-term capital. Long-term capital excludes all short- and medium-term banking flows and most portfolio flows of stocks and bonds. It can be more practically defined as the sum of all foreign direct investment (FDI) by multinational firms and any scheduled repayments of foreign debt.

This single number not only summarizes each country's overall industrial competitiveness and its rate of excess savings in a single statistic, but, partly as a result, it also gauges both their future growth potential and the likely strength of their currencies. Fundamental balances are a convenient index of competitive advantage because countries with trade or current account surpluses must, by definition, have a competitive edge in trade. In addition, economies enjoying sizeable inflows of FDI must, at least in the eyes of the foreign investors, have a future competitive advantage in production.

The fundamental balance method is similar to one that favours economies with high savings ratios, on the basis that high savings mean high rates of investment and/or a vibrant trade sector. However, we prefer to focus on a subset of this savings pool. Specifically, because export industries are likely to enjoy large economies of scale, trade surpluses are likely to promote strong domestic industrial growth. We also prefer FDI over investments made by domestic firms. FDI is particularly important, because it is more likely to incorporate the latest technology and is likely to be associated with more efficient organization and management.

Figure 1.6 highlights the secular growth of FDI into emerging economies since 1986. Multinationals are now investing over US$110 billion in new factories and plants in these

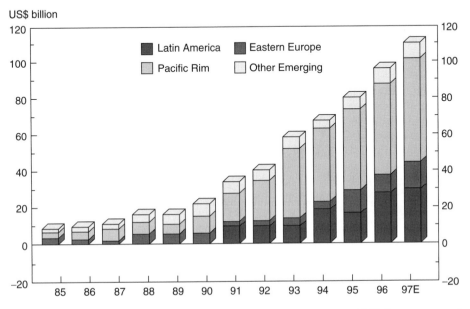

Figure 1.6 The rise and rise of multinational investment—aggregate FDI flows to emerging markets, 1985–97E (US dollars in billions). *Source*: United Nations

countries each year, roughly equivalent to the entire physical transfer of, say, one Ford Motor Company from America to China annually.

We discriminate against large-scale public borrowing. A simple manipulation of the fundamental balance shows that it is roughly equal to the household savings ratio less overall government borrowing, or what we dub "free savings". Therefore, the more the public sector encroaches on the free market, the greater is public borrowing and the smaller is the volume of free savings and the fundamental balance.

Countries with large fundamental surpluses should therefore show above average rates of economic growth; see Figure 1.7. This definition clearly covers both trading economies, such as Singapore, Taiwan, and Hong Kong, that have growth rapidly through export surpluses, as well as countries that have attracted large-scale foreign direct investments, such as Malaysia and China.

A fundamental surplus represents a solid source of long-term demand for a nation's currency. Provided that domestic monetary policy is run prudently (in other words, supply is kept in check), then a fundamental surplus should be linked to a firm or strong exchange rate.

With these five criteria satisfied, poor countries will "emerge". But history shows that economic development does not occur in a straight line. Rather, GDP growth is often exponential. In other words, it follows an S-shaped curve; see Figure 1.8.

The magic of an S-curve is that the first 10 per cent of per capita income occurs over the first third of the development period; during the second third of its lifetime, economies generate the next 80 per cent of their per capita income, leaving the final 10 per cent of income per head to occur over the last third of the development period. Figure 1.8 fits an S-curve to levels of income per head across various countries, using 1995 US dollars.

Projecting forward, assuming 5 per cent–6 per cent annual real growth in the emerging economies, 2 per cent–3 per cent annual real growth in the developed economies, and

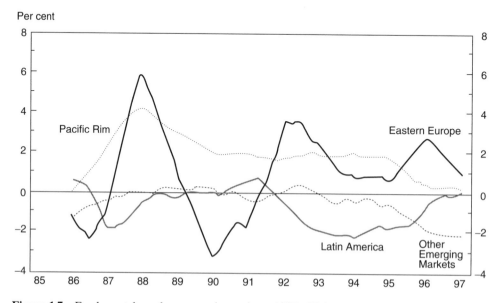

Figure 1.7 Fundamental surpluses — major regions, 1985–97 (per cent of GDP). *Source*: Cross-Border Capital

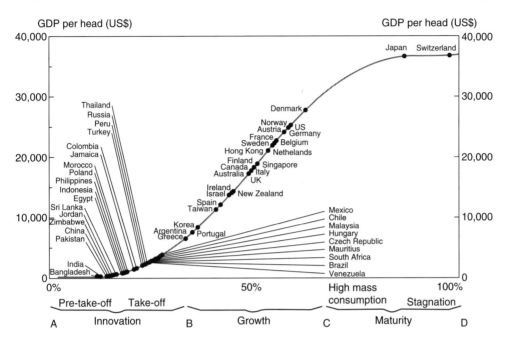

Figure 1.8 S-shaped economic development–GDP per capita, major economies, 1995 (US dollars). *Source*: CrossBorder Capital

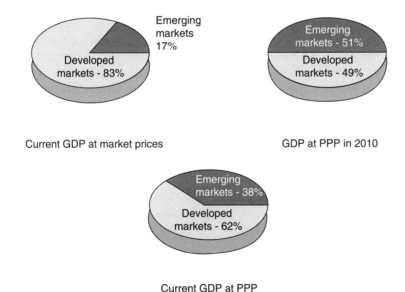

Current GDP at market prices   GDP at PPP in 2010

Current GDP at PPP

Figure 1.9 The world economy in 2010 — GDP in PPP (Purchasing Power Parity) terms and current exchange rates (US dollar terms). *Source*: CrossBorder Capital and World Bank

some move of exchange rates towards their fair-value (i.e. PPP) levels, gives the pie chart shown in Figure 1.9. PPP-based estimates give a higher share for the emerging economies simply because their currencies are currently selling below fair value.

In other words, in less than 15 years time, today's emerging economies will be producing more than half of planetary output, measured at PPP exchange rates. Such is the power of compound growth.

1.3 CROSS-BORDER CAPITAL FLOWS

Thus, the developing world is fast catching up with the rich industrial countries. By population, geography, and mineral wealth they are already much bigger. But by the early years of the next century they should also top the West in GDP terms as well.

Fast growth economies attract foreign capital. Therefore, it should be of no surprise that the direction and composition of capital to emerging markets has changed radically since the 1970s. Gone are the days when bankers and government officials bankrolled what frequently turned out to be shaky or corrupt political regimes. Lord Bauer famously summed up post-war development finance as: "... a system of taking money from poor people in rich countries and giving it to rich people in poor countries".

The role of international agencies in fostering so-called "structural adjustment" largely explains this altered pattern of finance. Buzz words from the 1980s, such as Perestroika (restructuring), Uskoreniye (acceleration of growth), and Glasnost (openness) became institutionalized into the typical four-stage, sequential development programme that was encouraged by the World Bank and the IMF: (i) stabilization; (ii) liberalization; (iii) privatization, and (vi) internationalization.

The New-Speak terms, such as "structural adjustment" and "privatization", are openly encouraged by the IMF and World Bank. "State planning" and "government aid" are Old-Speak phrases that have been quickly and quietly dropped from the official manuals.

And, perhaps, there is no wonder. Growth in the rich industrial countries has slowed to a crawl, under pressure from sprawling state bureaucracies and greying populations. The European Community countries have created no net private sector jobs since the early 1970s, while General Motors, America's largest company, now regularly pays out more in pensions to its retirees than it pays in wages to existing workers. Consequently, generous aid budgets can no longer be afforded, and the purse strings of Western banks remain tightly knotted by on-going balance sheet constraints.

In turn, the practical reality of reduced aid has triggered an intellectual re-assessment. Necessity may be the mother of the thought, but the appalling shortage of private enterprise in these countries seemingly explains their low incomes and slow growth. Generations of the world's poorest people have been weaned on Western aid, leading to a shocking underdevelopment of local institutions and market-places (e.g. the lack of domestic financial markets), and creating what is now dubbed "aid addiction" or the "psychology of dependency". In Africa, for example, aid flows often represent as much as 10 per cent of annual GDP. The 47 sub-Saharan economies produce barely 2.5 per cent of world GDP. More frightening is the fact that of this paltry sum, 40 per cent comes from just two countries: South Africa and Nigeria.

Although official aid has dropped in both absolute and relative importance, more money in total is flowing to the emerging world. Indeed, if this is where future economic growth lies, then it is how it should be. Yet, many still hanker after the old days when aid made up a larger part of a smaller pie. Others, such as MIT economist Paul Krugman, argue that the boom in private sector finance is ill-founded and based solely on a Washington-based conspiracy (the so-called "Washington Consensus"), or smoke-screen, that has painted all emerging markets in a rose-tinted gloss (Krugman (1995)).

The reality is different. Admittedly, many investors have blindly invested in the emerging markets and suffered badly. But one must ask: Would they have made similar mistakes in other investment areas? The critics fail to look at the financing question from the other side. Do emerging market borrowers prefer private funds or government funds? Private lenders typically bring with them other expertise. They can advise, and often steer a project towards a more successful outcome. FDI is the best example of this, because foreign capital will likely have a substantial "crowding in" effect on local investment.

Today, large, transnational pension and mutual funds provide most external finance (ex. FDI) to developing countries. Compared with a 35 per cent share in 1990, private sector financial flows reached a peak of 77 per cent in 1996, over two-thirds coming from portfolio flows of stocks and bonds. However, as Figure 1.9 shows, unlike the flow of FDI, portfolio capital by its very nature is far more volatile. Cross-border equity flows peaked at US$62 billion in 1993. They appear to be growing at a trend rate of around US$10 billion per annum, but with a cycle of plus or minus US$20 billion. Similarly, bond flows reached nearly US$36 billion in 1993. They fell back slightly in both 1994 and 1995, before climbing to a new peak of US$46 billion in 1996.

Much debate centres on whether the forces behinds these foreign flows are primarily (i) "push" factors, e.g. the need for Western investment funds to diversify, or the collapse of domestic returns in the West, or (ii) "pull" factors, e.g. soaring foreign returns, relaxation of local investment controls.

In practice, both push and pull factors have been important. In our view, pull factors have largely determined the strong upward trend in cross-border flows to emerging markets, while the alternating strength of push factors explains the sharp cycle in flows. In other words, periods of low world interest rates, such as 1993, are associated with strong

Table 1.4 Financial flows to developing countries, 1990–96E (US dollars in billions). *Source*: World Bank and CrossBorder Capital

	1990	1991	1992	1993	1994	1995	1996E
Private Flows	**29.8**	**32.0**	**57.1**	**107.2**	**84.8**	**76.7**	**138.6**
Portfolio Flows	15.5	25.9	31.1	98.3	69.2	48.5	96.1
Equities	13.2	15.8	21.2	62.4	39.9	20.0	50.0
Bonds	2.3	10.1	9.9	35.9	29.3	28.5	46.1
Commercial Banks	3.0	2.8	12.5	−0.3	11.0	26.5	34.2
Others	11.3	3.3	13.5	9.2	4.6	1.7	8.3
Official Flows	56.3	65.6	55.5	55.0	45.7	52.9	40.8
Total Financial Flows	**86.1**	**97.6**	**112.6**	**162.2**	**130.5**	**129.6**	**179.4**
Memo items:							
Private Flows as a percentage of Total Flows	**34.6%**	**32.8%**	**50.7%**	**66.1%**	**65.0%**	**59.2%**	**77.3%**
Equity Flows as a percentage of Private Flows	44.3%	49.4%	37.1%	58.2%	47.1%	26.1%	36.1%
Bond Flows as a percentage of Private Flows	7.7%	31.6%	17.3%	33.5%	34.6%	37.2%	33.3%

cyclical portfolio flows to emerging markets. Likewise, periods of rising world interest rates, namely 1994, are linked to slumping portfolio inflows.

Not surprisingly, push factors tend to be underplayed, both by investors and by supra-national institutions, such as the IMF and World Bank. Figure 1.10 shows our estimates of cross-border inflows into the emerging stock markets over the last decade.[7] The trend

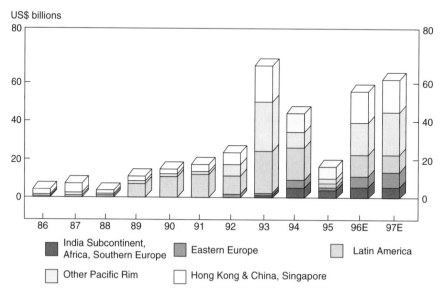

Figure 1.10   Cross-border equity flows to emerging markets, 1986–96 (US dollars in billions). *Source*: CrossBorder Capital

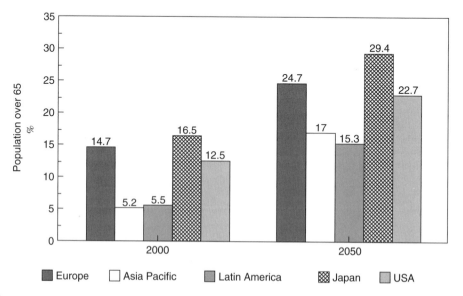

Figure 1.11   Coming demographics pressures will force a change in investment patterns — population aged over 65 years, 2000 and 2050. *Source*: United Nations

rise in foreign equity flows to emerging markets appears to be rising at around US$10 billion per annum, albeit with an average range of plus or minus US$20 billion.

Shifting demographics are a major long-term factor pushing funds out from the rich industrial countries. The average age of the world's population is set to rise dramatically over the next half century. Rich countries face the greatest burden. By the year 2050, nearly 30 per cent of Japan's population will be aged over 65, compared with just over 15 per cent today. Similarly, the number of European retirees is set to jump to roughly 25 per cent of the population. Even in the emerging markets themselves, the proportion of old people will triple over the next half century. To afford to pay these pensions, portfolio managers will have to invest in assets with high prospective returns. This is a key reason for investing in fast-growing emerging economies (see Figure 1.11).

1.4 MARKETS IN EMERGING FINANCIAL ASSETS

There are two ways investors can participate in emerging country growth: (i) invest directly in an emerging market through locally listed stocks and bonds (we include in this category ADRs (American Depository Receipts), GDRs (Global Depository Receipts) and Brady bonds) or (ii) invest indirectly through a major Western company, e.g. Coca-Cola or Unilever, that has a large local involvement (i.e. subsidiary) in emerging countries. We shall focus on the former category.

Over the last decade the emerging debt and equity markets have developed piecemeal and thus largely independently of one another. However, looking ahead, they are more likely to share a common development path, first because of the growing awareness by foreign investors of sovereign risk, and second because the emerging countries are themselves more alert to the need to simultaneously foster industrial and financial development.

The growth of emerging financial markets can, thus, be viewed as three phases:

- International market in low quality sovereign debts, 1988–91 (Phase 1).
- International issuance of privatization shares, 1992–95 (Phase 2).
- General capital market activity, 1996–date (Phase 3).

The creation of Brady bonds in 1988 was the trigger for the first development stage. Admittedly, economic reforms were already well established in several emerging countries, and a few investors already had investments in some emerging markets (notably the "Tiger" economies of South-East and East Asia). Nonetheless, Brady bonds both formalized the link between more domestic reform and more foreign capital and helped to stabilize local currency markets.

The Brady bond programme, eponymous with the former US Treasury Secretary, Nicholas Brady, was initiated by J.P. Morgan in March 1988. The US authorities, at the time, were under pressure from major commercial banks whose balance sheets were haemorrhaging badly following a build-up of foreign sovereign loan defaults. The first issue re-structured defaulted Mexican debt in a novel way by using 20 year US zero coupon bonds to guarantee both the principle and a rolling 18 months of interest payments.

The zeros were bought (with a small US subsidy) by the Mexican authorities. The outlay cost was comparatively low, because zeros sell at a significant discount to parity because they pay no interest. Also, in return for extending the maturity of the local debt and blending in the better quality US Treasury credit, the bankers agreed to write off 35 per cent of the outstanding loans. They not only were able to avoid a damaging total debt write-off, but they now owned a securitized, liquid instrument they could sell on.

The Mexico deal provided a blueprint for a raft of other Brady deals. These covered both other countries, e.g. Argentina, the Philippines, Poland, and Brazil, and other currencies, e.g. Swiss francs, Yen and French francs. However, it is not unreasonable to consider the Brady market today as a mature market, largely in US dollar denominated Latin American debt. Brady bonds still dominate debt trading activity, although their share has dropped from 61 per cent in 1994 to barely 41 per cent during the first quarter of 1997. With help, particularly from sovereign Eurobonds (22.3 per cent of the total) and local market issues (26.4 per cent), overall debt trading has soared. Nearly 85 per cent of overall emerging debt trading involves Latin American issues, with Brazil and Argentina accounting for half. Figure 1.12 shows the recent spectacular rise, using data from the Emerging Markets Traders' Association (EMTA).

Brady bonds are typically analysed using the conventional bond techniques of yield-to-maturity and duration, i.e. interest rate sensitivity. However, to capture the characteristics of the pure emerging market credit, the influence of the US collateral is usually stripped out. The yield of a Brady bond after the US guarantee has been removed is dubbed the "stripped yield", or "swapped stripped yield", in the case of a floating rate bond.

The direction of analysis has also been biased by recent traumas. For example, the 1994/95 Mexican Peso Crisis highlighted the issue of sovereign risk. The size of current account deficits, banking system strength, the quality of capital inflows, and currency over- or under-valuation are all factors now regularly assessed by portfolio managers. In a classic case of slamming the stable door after the horse has bolted, the Mexican authorities now provide weekly Internet updates of key data for investors.

US$ billions

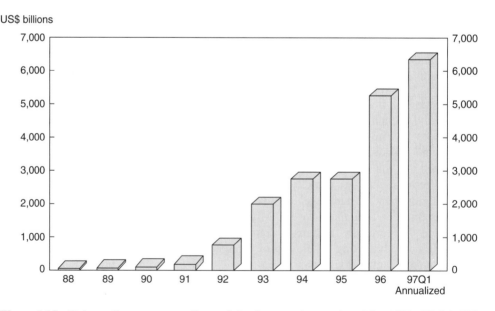

Figure 1.12 Debt trading surges–trading activity in emerging market debt, 1988–97 Q1 (US dollars in billions, annual rate). *Source*: EMTA

A second example is the 1990 US High Yield Crisis which followed Drexel's bankruptcy. Not only did this encourage smaller-sized deals and better covenant protection, it also forced analysts to demand higher EBITDA (earnings before interest expense, taxes, depreciation and amortization) cover for interest payments.

If the heyday of the Brady market was the late 1980s and early 1990s, emerging equities came into their own from around 1992. The spur was unquestionably the depth of the reforms being undertaken across the emerging world. As country after country cut through red tape, encouraged free markets, and reduced government controls, foreign investors fell over each other to buy into the new wave of international offerings of privatization shares, e.g. the 1993 sale of the Argentinean state oil company YPF. The scale of new issuance activity is shown in Figure 1.13. The bulk of these issues became New York listed ADRs. In fact, they grew to be so popular that, according to the New York Stock Exchange, Telmex was the world's heaviest traded stock for two years running in 1994 and 1995.

Because the emerging debt and equity markets have grown up independently, there has, so far, been little cross-asset analysis, e.g. relative yield comparison. P/E multiples are probably the most common tool used to analyse emerging equity markets, with a low multiple the key incentive for investors. However, a P/E multiple by itself says nothing about the further growth potential. Therefore, a better approach is to adjust the P/E by an estimate of future growth.

Our preferred method is to divide the current year P/E multiple by the five-year compound rate of future real growth (i.e. inflation adjusted). For example, if the current P/E is 20 times and five-year real growth is estimated to be 5 per cent per annum, then the P/E growth ratio is 4 (i.e. 20/5 per cent). We have found that P/E growth ratios below around 4.5 offer excellent value.

US Generally Accepted Accounting Practices (GAAP) have become increasingly commonplace across the emerging world.[8] However, in the cases where these still do

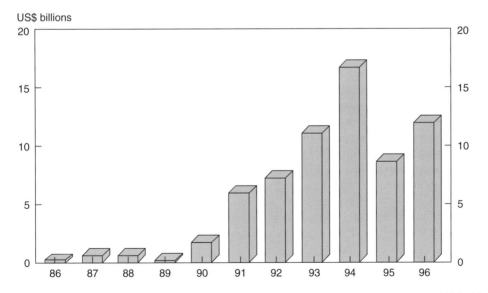

Figure 1.13 Emerging market offerings sky-rocket — international equity new issuance, 1986–96 (US dollars in billions). *Source*: CrossBorder Capital

not apply, we suggest using cash flows rather than earnings. Experience shows that cash flows can eliminate up to 70 per cent of the variations in national earnings definitions.

The first two investment phases we highlighted above must be seen as stepping stones towards more normal capital market activity. Until recently, many emerging countries effectively exported their capital market activity off-shore. New York and London became the key trading and capital-raising centres for Brady bonds and emerging market ADRs and GDRs. Looking ahead, things must change: the easy equity privatizations have been done, and the Brady market will ultimately be overtaken by Eurobonds and, more particularly, local debt markets. For example, in the eyes of many experts, the 1996 Philippine Eurobond issue has already rung the death-knell of the Brady market.

The Eurobond market has for long been out of bounds for most emerging market borrowers, because (i) any loan default effectively closes off access to all international capital markets, and (ii) rating agencies place a "sovereign ceiling" on debt of all corporate issuers, thereby preventing them from receiving a better credit grade than their country of domicile.

Thus, the proliferation of Brady deals re-opened international capital markets for the emerging countries. For example, Mexico's Brady Plan allowed Telmex, the national telephone utility, to raise funds from world bond markets.

Local debt markets are also likely to grow (i) as credit risks narrow, and (ii) as the national monetary authorities attempt to widen and deepen their domestic financial markets. Both factors are more closely related than they appear. A larger balance sheet is a necessary condition for a local Central Bank to become more active. Local credit risks will narrow if the Central Bank actively manages the size and structure of its balance sheet, first to control the rate of domestic credit expansion, and second to maintain an orderly foreign exchange market through the periodic accommodation and sterilization of foreign flows. Successful monetary management will show itself in a low and stable domestic inflation rate, and in a firm exchange rate.

1.5 THE FINANCIAL STRUCTURE OF EMERGING ECONOMIES

Frequently, many pundits confuse the growth of the real economy with the development of financial markets. For example, an emerging economy can have a mature financial system. Equally, a mature economy can have an emerging financial system. Financial development and economic development can be, and often are, separate. Ideally, however, these two spheres should move hand in hand. Investors need to consider carefully which of the two they mean.

Just because an economy grows quickly, does not automatically mean that share prices will go up. In fact, the opposite is very often the case in the short term: strong economies typically have weak financial markets. Looked at another way, share prices go up because investors buy more shares. Before they can buy, these investors must have spare savings resources at the ready. If an economy is too strong, it will absorb these surplus savings and so starve financial markets.

Therefore, a vibrant economy may enjoy bumper profits, but simultaneously share prices could be hard hit by a falling pool of spare savings. Equally, if the economy is too weak, then surplus savings will accumulate and may support share prices, but the appetite of investors for shares will, at the same time, be dampened by poor profit prospects. In short, there is a middle course where economic growth is neither too fast nor too slow, and where savings are neither scarce nor plentiful but just right. Along this path the real economy and financial markets develop roughly hand in hand.

Figure 1.14 highlights this development path. Income per head for 60 countries is plotted along the horizontal axis, and equity market capitalization per head is plotted along the vertical axis.

Three features of the chart should be noted:

1. Economic and financial development proceed closely together, with higher incomes per head being associated with higher market capitalizations per head.

2. The exact relationship is non-linear, so that each 10 per cent rise in per capita income is linked to a 13.7 per cent rise in market capitalization per head.

3. On the basis of the fitted regression line, the US$9,386 per head threshold for "economic emergence" implies an equivalent point of "financial emergence" at US$3,654 per head. And these twin points allow us to pigeon-hole countries into one of four development boxes.

The four quadrants shown in Figure 1.14 define whether an economy is rich or poor, and if the capital market is large or small. The traditional emerging market universe consists of all markets in the top left *and* bottom left quadrants. It should go without saying that this definition contains no references to future growth, and none to either relative stock market size or investment value.

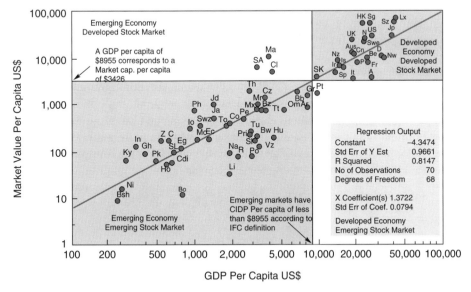

Argentina Ar,Australia Aus, Austria A, Bangladesh Bsh, Barbados Bb, Belgium Be, Bolivia Bo, Botswana Bw, Brazil Bz, Bulgaria Bu, Canada Cn, Chile Cl, China C, Colombia Co,Cote D'Ivoire Cdl, Cyprus Cy, Czech Cz, Denmark D, Ecuador Ec, Egypt Eg, Finland F, France Fr, Germany G, Ghana Gh, Greece Gr, Honduras Ho, Hong Kong HK, Hungary Hu, India In, Indonesia Io, Iran Irn, Ireland Ir, Israel Is, Italy It, Jamaica Ja, Japan Jp, Jordan Jd, Kenya Ky, Lithuania Li, Luxemburg Lx, Malaysia Ma, Mauritius Mr, Mexico Mx, Morocco Mo, Namibia Na, Nepal Np, Netherlands N, New Zealand NZ, Nigeria Ni, Norway Nw, Oman Om, Pakistan Pk, Panama Pn, Peru Pe, Philippines Ph, Poland Po, Portugal Pt, Russia R, Singapore Sg, Slovakia Sl, Slovenia Sv, South Africa SA, South Korea SK, Spain Sp, Sri Lanka SL, Swaziland Swz, Sweden Swe, Switzerland Sz, Taiwan Ta, Thailand Th, Trinidad Tr, Tunisia Tn, Turkey Tu, United Kingdom UK, Uruguay Ur, United States US, Venezuela Vz, Zambia Za, Zimbabwe Z.

Figure 1.14 Economic and financial development, end-1995 (US dollars). *Source*: CrossBorder Capital

In practice, too many investment managers have been innocently caught out either by buying markets in both of these zones, or by purchasing new issues simply on the basis of low P/E multiples and with no reference to future growth.

We noted above that the P/E growth ratio offers one solution. Another option is to use a two-stage selection procedure:

1. Ask which economies or industries will grow the fastest over, say, the next five years (i.e. rising GDP/head)
2. Ask who, if anyone, is going to buy these shares (i.e. rising MC/head). It is not necessarily "cheap" investments that we want, but rather unexploited investments. There has to be buying power.

In fact, we can refine these criteria slightly. To maximize potential share price gains, investors should look not just for a rising market cap/head, but also for a rising market cap/GDP ratio over time. (For example, we would be unhappy if GDP/head jumped by 150 per cent, but market cap/head rose by only 50 per cent.) A "high" market cap-to-GDP ratio should mean that the stock market is liquid. In other words, it has sufficient depth for buyers and sellers to trade shares easily.

Consider the following simple expression:

$$\frac{\text{market cap/head}}{\text{GDP/head}} = \frac{\text{market cap}}{\text{GDP}}$$

The RHS can, in turn, be broken down into two components:

$$= \frac{\text{market cap}}{\text{liquid savings}} \times \frac{\text{liquid savings}}{\text{GDP}}$$

Using this expression, we can better explain financial development. It typically proceeds in two stages, each defined by one of the two terms shown above:

• *Accumulation* — This is driven by rising per capita incomes and involves an increasing ratio between liquid savings and GDP. In other words, as people get richer they save more. Think of this as the "extensive" margin.

• *Portfolio diversification* — This second stage follows on and describes the diversification out of liquid savings into securities. The implied jump in the market cap-to-liquid savings ratio, itself, requires a rising liquid savings-to-GDP ratio. This may be thought of as the "intensive" margin.

In other words, as per capita incomes rise increasingly more-and-more surplus dollars are invested in savings products. When people get richer they typically want to buy their own country's financial assets. *This aspect of economic development is often forgotten by commentators, but in many ways it is one of the most important factors behind strong future returns from emerging stock markets.*

1.6 THE FUTURE SIZE OF EMERGING STOCK MARKETS

Using the above expression and regression results, the future size of the emerging stock markets can be estimated easily. In 1995, the emerging economies had an average per capita income of US$1,198. This compared with US$22,251/head in the developed markets. Using compound growth rates of 5.5 per cent per annum for the emerging

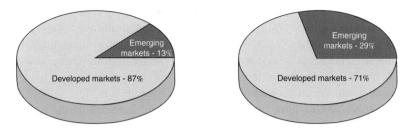

Current market capitalization   Market capitalization in 2010

Figure 1.15   The future size of the emerging stock markets, 2010. *Source*: CrossBorder Capital

economies and 2.5 per cent per annum for the developed countries, per capita incomes should grow to US$2,251 and US$29,755 by 2010, respectively, in real terms.[9] Plugging these numbers into the regression equation yields future stock market capitalizations/head of US$1,077 for the emerging stock markets in 2010, compared with US$590/head today. Similarly, developed stock market capitalization should rise from US$15,203/head today, to US$23,950 in 2010. It follows from these per capita numbers that the emerging markets will comprise 16 per cent of overall world stock market capitalization in 2010, and the developed stock markets will make up 84 per cent. This compares with 13 per cent and 87 per cent, respectively, today.

Rather than use current exchange rates, the above calculations could have used PPPs. As we have seen, PPPs attribute higher incomes to the emerging economies because their market exchange rates are trading well below "fair value". Looking ahead to 2010, the emerging economies should produce just over half of global output in PPP terms, compared with around one-quarter at current exchange rates. Using these PPP estimates of per capita income, it follows that prospective stock market capitalization would change dramatically. On this basis, the emerging markets would make up 43 per cent of world stock market capitalization in 2010, leaving a dismal 57 per cent slice for today's developed stock markets (see Figure 1.15).

However, it would be reasonable to assume that the PPP estimate of future market capitalization is too high and that the estimate using current exchange rates is too low. On the assumption that current exchange rates move half way towards their PPP values by 2010, then emerging stock markets would rise from their current 13 per cent share to a more significant 29 per cent share of the world pie.

1.7   THE GROWING NEED FOR FINANCIAL DEVELOPMENT

A major difference between emerging and developed financial markets arises in the sphere of finance, and in this author's view explains much of their relative risk characteristics. We have just seen that emerging economies typically have underdeveloped financial markets. In short, the depth as well as the breadth of financial markets is lacking. This becomes a particular problem when large foreign investors suddenly wake up to mouth-watering investment opportunities in small, emerging countries.

Paradoxically, over the past decade the concerns of policy-makers in emerging markets have shifted from worrying about the dearth of capital to panicking about the deluge.

Rather than being starved of cash, many developing countries now face the problem of too much money and, more particularly, too much of the wrong sort of money. This has triggered a debate about which is the best development path for the emerging countries. Should countries encourage bank-based financial systems, like Germany, or should they foster stock markets, as in Britain and the United States.

However, it is not the character of the financial system that matters. In fact, both bank finance and equity finance have important roles to play. Rather, it is the type of finance that is key. All financial systems should aim to provide a balance between short-term and long-term funds, with a lot more of the latter than the former.

The problem for emerging markets is that: (i) they are too dependent upon foreign finance, and (ii) much of their recent foreign inflows have consisted of low-quality, short-term flows. As a result, both their currencies and their financial markets have suffered from extreme bouts of volatility. Indeed, nearly every so-called "emerging market crisis" in recent years, from Argentina to Mexico and from Russia to Turkey, has first of all been a currency crisis.

In other words, foreign money can have good as well as bad aspects. Developing countries must have the means to absorb large foreign funds productively: (i) without rapidly driving up their real exchange rate and thereby wrecking the growth prospects of export industries, and (ii) without the extra cash triggering a short-lived economic boom and creating a runaway domestic inflation.

To preserve trade competitiveness, most emerging countries have chosen to manage (i.e. limit) the movement of their currencies, typically versus the US dollar. However, by solving one problem they have created another, potentially worse, problem.

Under managed exchange rate regimes, such foreign liquidity inflows often have multiplicative effects on domestic credit markets which subsequently spill-over into spending, thereby de-railing economic progress. These fierce liquidity swings are a recurrent problem for many emerging countries. The Mexico Peso Crisis in 1994/95 and the Thai Investment Boom between 1993 and 1995 are two recent examples of the indirect damage strong foreign portfolio inflows can do.

This problem for emerging markets is highlighted in the asset composition of their monetary bases (high powered money). In emerging markets the ratio of foreign exchange reserves (a national asset) to the monetary base is substantially higher than in developed economies (140 per cent compared with 70 per cent).[10] In developed economies, other domestic assets, such as government bonds and bills, comprise the bulk of the monetary base. Open market operations are undertaken by the Central Bank in these assets types in order to sterilize the monetary effects of foreign inflows. Plainly, if there are no domestic assets, or only very thin markets exist in them, full sterilization cannot occur and a liquidity boom may be triggered.

The remedy must involve some combination of: (i) more enlightened currency management, e.g. fully flexible exchange rates, or at least a wide target band; (ii) the deepening and widening of the markets in domestic financial assets; and (iii) the limitation of volatile speculative capital inflows.

But, ultimately, more long-term savings are a necessary condition for more stable emerging financial markets. This can be achieved in three broad ways:

- the development of domestic institutional investors, e.g. pension funds, who "have" to invest locally in order to match their liabilities;

- more project finance, where bank finance is tied to specific investments; and
- encouragement of foreign direct investment in plant, machinery and buildings.

To act as a buffer, or cushion, between the supply of foreign savings and the capital demands of local industry, developing countries need to establish their own financial intermediaries, such as banks, insurance companies, and mutual funds, and to deepen their existing bond and bill markets to facilitate better control by their own monetary authorities.

In other words, economic development and financial development should ideally proceed hand in hand. As economies widen out and mature, so the number of investable domestic financial assets should also grow in parallel. This symbiotic relationship is illustrated in Figure 1.14. This chart shows the relationship between GDP/head and equities/head.

This differentiation between the maturity of the domestic financial sector and the development of the real economy allows us both to define more exactly what we mean by an emerging market, as well as providing a useful framework to examine the investment risk for foreign portfolio managers. Two basic types of risk exist:

1. *price risk*, which occurs in the financial market, and measures the ability of investors to successfully capture their required asset prices or capital gains, and
2. *value risk*, which takes place in the real economy, and relates to the investors' ability to successfully capture value, that is profits, dividends, or book values.

Five specific factors govern *price risk*: (i) the likely imposition of capital controls, (ii) the existence of a free market in foreign exchange, (iii) stable financial liquidity, (iv) an efficient settlement system, and (v) rules that prevent insider trading and protect minority shareholders' rights.

In turn, *value risk* is determined by: (i) the existence of political stability, (ii) the pace of economic growth, (iii) stable or rising profit margins, (iv) sound accounting methods, and (v) dependable custodians.

We noted earlier that political risk (e.g. the possible reversal of recent economic reforms) was the major threat to long-term economic and profits growth in the emerging markets, i.e. *value risk*. Similarly, we believe that the key *price risk* for emerging markets centres on the availability of financial liquidity. We do not believe that measures of price volatility capture this risk. Share price volatility is a *consequence* and not a *cause* of risk.

Thus, stable liquidity conditions are a vital but often underestimated requirement of emerging market investing. Liquidity changes either because of the domestic Central Bank, or as the result of large asset shifts by major groups of investors. Therefore, the encouragement of long-term investors, either domestic or foreign, who only slowly change their portfolio structures is crucial to the stability of emerging capital markets. John Maynard Keynes, writing in 1936, wryly noted that:

> Speculators may do no harm as bubbles on a stream of enterprise. But the position is serious when enterprise becomes the bubble on the whirlpool of speculation. When the capital development of a country becomes a by-product of the activities of a casino, the job is likely to be ill-done.

How can this financial liquidity risk be captured? Figure 1.14 shows one measure. This is the quotient between market capitalization and the stock of liquid savings, by market, adjusted for changes in long-term interest rates. Long-term interest rates are inversely

Index

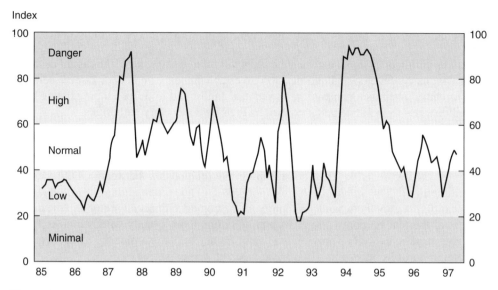

Figure 1.16   Financial liquidity risk, all emerging markets, 1986–97. *Source*: CrossBorder Capital

related to the flow of financial liquidity. The chart is drawn in terms of the number of standard deviations away from a three-year average.

The logic behind this expression is that the market capitalization to liquidity asset ratio measures changes in portfolio structure and, by definition, will fluctuate between set limits. This ratio will peak when the last investor has spent his or her last investment dollar. At this point, the market has reached saturation, because there can be no more buyers and trying to sell around these prices will prove highly risky. Similarly, vice versa.

Mid-1987 and 1994 were high-risk times to invest in emerging equities, according to Figure 1.16, because most investors had already bought. Indeed, these points coincided with sharp falls in market prices. Similarly, late-1990, following the Kuwait Invasion, was a low-risk time to buy emerging market shares because most investors had already jumped back into cash. In all three cases, price volatility jumped *afterwards*.

1.8 CONCLUSION

Today, to be rich you do not have to live in the West or in Japan. Economic power is shifting towards the emerging markets. The case for investing in the emerging markets rests on three aspects:

1. *Economic "catch-up" and faster GDP growth* — emerging economies are growing two to three faster than the rich industrial countries.
2. *Diversification by Western pension funds* — roughly one-third of cross-border investment flows now head towards the emerging countries.

3. *Appearance of active domestic investors* — as the emerging countries get richer they
    will generate more financial savings, the bulk of which will be invested in domestic
    financial markets. Even East Asia's investment industry is still barely one-fifth of
    Britain's, compared with GDP.

The emerging market story is not about swarms of investment bankers waving prospec-
tuses offering low *P/E* new issues. Nor is it about the so-called Washington Consensus,
where policy-makers allegedly exaggerated the virtues of investing in poor countries.
The term "emerging" implies growth. Therefore, investors must look for factors, e.g.
fundamental surpluses, that will sustain rising incomes. Specifically, the emerging market
story is closely linked to political change and the move towards free-market
economics.

In the words of Sir John Templeton, one of the twentieth century's most successful
global investors:

> Avoid investing in those countries with a high level of socialism or government regulation
> of business. Business growth depends upon a strong free-enterprise system ... Governments
> should stop interfering with what people want to do.

In a free capital market, private investors choose which deficits they finance. This competition for funds has triggered a financial beauty contest among emerging market borrowers
and, thereby, underscored the economic reform process as each potential recipient tries
to leap-frog his opponents.

As economy after economy has thrown off its bureaucratic chains and discarded its
socialist shackles, so foreign investors have swarmed in. Such changes compel us to understand better the impact of cross-border capital flows on industry, on financial markets,
and on asset prices. The rise of global money has radically changed our thinking about
investment markets. So much so, it is now widely accepted that:

*   private finance is always better than public finance:
*   when evaluating the best investments, knowing *who is going to buy* (i.e. which
    investors) is as important as analysing *what to buy*; and
*   foreign capital has good as well as bad aspects.

Instead of worrying about a lack of quantity, policy-makers in the emerging countries are
now more concerned about a lack of quality capital. Too much low-quality capital brings
with it the threat of greater financial market volatility which could potentially de-rail
economic development.

Thus policy-makers must look to foster financial as well as industrial development.
One cannot occur successfully without the other. The emphasis must be on encouraging
greater inflows of long-term capital, e.g. FDI, and raising each economy's overall rate
of long-term savings, e.g. more pension funds. Domestic financial institutions should
become more and more significant as a result. For example, in 1910, over 90 per cent of
Australia's (then an emerging economy) largest company, BHP, was owned by foreigners
compared with barely 15 per cent today. It is the growth of domestic savers, the proliferation of domestic savings instruments, and the growth of domestic capital markets that
will characterize the next and most important stage of the emerging market boom.

1.9 APPENDIX 1: SELECTED DATA ON EMERGING MARKETS

	Population (millions)	GDP 1995 (US$bn)	GDP Per Capita (US$)	Bond Market Cap (US$bn)	Equity Market Cap (US$bn)	Equity Market Cap Per Capita (US$)	Liquid Savings (US$bn)	Financial Assets (US$bn)	Financial Assets Per Capita (US$)
Developed Markets									
Australia	18.1	337.9	18,721	98.4	310.1	17,179	207.6	616.1	34,133
Austria	8.1	216.5	26,887	63.6	31.4	3,901	157.4	252.4	31,341
Belgium	10.1	250.7	24,710	242.0	124.7	12,294	184.9	551.6	54,365
Canada	29.6	573.7	19,378	367.1	488.8	16,510	389.6	1,245.4	42,067
Denmark	5.2	156.0	29,890	88.1	75.6	14,483	21.5	185.2	35,478
Finland	5.1	105.2	20,582	34.9	67.4	13,194	18.5	120.8	23,647
France	58.1	1,451.1	24,992	602.4	620.5	10,688	625.5	1,848.5	31,837
Germany	81.9	2,252.3	27,512	1,369.9	728.0	8,892	747.4	2,845.3	34,754
Ireland	3.6	52.8	14,714	25.2	38.2	10,664	52.9	116.4	32,450
Italy	57.2	1,088.1	19,021	888.5	260.7	4,557	300.1	1,449.3	25,336
Japan	125.2	4,963.6	39,641	3,158.6	2,627.6	20,985	4,713.5	10,499.7	83,854
Netherlands	15.5	371.0	24,000	288.8	401.1	25,944	173.9	863.7	55,870
New Zealand	3.6	51.7	14,345	14.3	35.6	9,882	54.1	104.0	28,871
Norway	4.4	136.1	31,253	29.0	61.5	14,118	30.2	120.6	27,703
Spain	39.2	532.3	13,581	179.1	245.0	6,250	430.9	855.0	21,812
Sweden	8.8	209.7	23,751	102.6	252.5	28,599	124.2	479.3	54,286
Switzerland	7.0	286.0	40,633	48.0	436.2	61,963	138.8	623.0	88,505
UK	58.5	1,094.7	18,703	361.4	1,732.4	29,597	1,153.2	3,247.0	55,473
US	263.1	7,100.0	26,984	6,182.2	8,450.2	32,116	4,705.6	19,338.0	73,495
Total	802.3	21,229.5		14,144.1	16,987.5		14,229.7	45,361.3	
Average	42.2	1,117.3	24,173.5	744.4	894.1	17,990.2	748.9	2,387.4	43,961.9
Emerging Markets									
Argentina	34.7	278.4	8,032	57.8	48.9	1,412	47.6	154.3	4,452
Bangladesh	119.8	28.6	239	NA	2.20	18	11.8	14.0	117
Brazil	159.2	579.8	3,641	102.5	258.5	1,623	82.1	443.1	2,783
Chile	14.2	59.2	4,158	15.1	75.3	5,290	29.4	119.8	8,420
China	1200.2	744.9	621	33.3	76.5	64	395.1	504.9	421

Colombia	36.8	70.3	1,909	NA	18.6	505	25.5	44.1	1,198
Czech Republic	10.3	40.0	3,870	NA	19.0	1,839	23.5	42.5	4,114
Egypt	57.8	45.5	787	NA	8.1	140	21.5	29.6	511
Greece	10.5	85.9	8,205	NA	30.7	2,936	48.6	79.4	7,582
Hong Kong	6.2	142.3	22,994	12.0	438.7	70,876	330.9	781.6	126,267
Hungary	10.2	42.1	4,119	NA	4.9	479	8.4	13.3	1,305
India	929.4	319.7	344	83.6	150.7	162	33.3	267.6	288
Indonesia	193.3	190.1	984	2.2	94.9	491	159.9	257.0	1,330
Israel	5.5	87.9	15,917	NA	41.2	7,466	76.0	117.2	21,231
Jamaica	2.5	3.8	1,508	NA	2.3	912	2.6	4.9	1,950
Jordan	4.2	6.4	1,509	NA	2.9	689	2.8	5.7	1,350
Malaysia	20.1	78.3	3,889	39.5	325.5	16,163	162.3	527.3	26,182
Mauritius	1.1	3.8	3,382	NA	1.7	1,507	2.6	4.3	3,802
Mexico	91.8	304.6	3,317	13.3	115.4	1,256	118.4	247.1	2,691
Morocco	26.6	29.5	1,112	NA	5.8	218	3.4	9.2	345
Pakistan	129.9	60.0	462	NA	10.8	83	15.7	26.5	204
Peru	23.8	55.0	2,310	NA	14.5	609	1.0	15.5	651
Philippines	68.6	71.9	1,048	25.2	85.9	1,252	53.1	164.2	2,394
Poland	38.6	107.8	2,793	NA	9.8	253	0.4	10.2	265
Portugal	9.9	96.7	9,740	NA	27.6	2,778	58.0	85.6	8,619
Russia	148.2	331.9	2,240	NA	25.2	170	35.6	60.8	411
Singapore	3.0	79.8	26,726	NA	141.5	47,374	91.9	233.4	78,143
South Africa	41.5	130.9	3,158	NA	271.7	6,553	29.8	301.4	7,271
South Korea	44.9	435.1	9,702	96.7	137.3	3,062	179.8	413.8	9,227
Sri Lanka	18.1	12.6	696	NA	1.8	98	2.9	4.7	260
Taiwan	21.1	244.7	11,595	37.5	321.2	15,221	440.9	799.6	37,894
Thailand	58.2	159.6	2,741	13.7	81.0	1,391	169.7	264.4	4,540
Turkey	61.1	169.5	2,775	8.0	44.6	730	28.4	81.0	1,326
Venezuela	21.7	65.8	3,038	NA	18.0	831	13.0	31.0	1,432
Zimbabwe	11.0	5.9	539	NA	2.5	231	0.4	3.0	271
Total	3,634.0	5,168.4	4,859.9	540.4	2,915.1	5,562.4	2,706.6	6,162.0	10,549.9
Average	103.8	147.7		15.4	83.3		77.3	176.1	

	P/M Rate Times	Market Cap to GNP Ratio (Times)	Financial Assets to GNP Ratio (Times)	P/E Ratio (Times)	Five Year Real GDP Growth (%)	P/E to Growth Ratio (Times)	Annual Inflation (%)	Long-Term Interest Rates (%)	Short-Term Interest Rates (%)	Forex Reserves (US$bn)	Financial Assets as % of Forex
Developed Markets											
Australia	1.49	0.92	1.82	18.0	3.3	5.5	1.3	7.9	6.0	14.4	42.8
Austria	0.20	0.15	1.17	16.1	2.5	6.4	1.5	5.7	3.4	21.1	12.0
Belgium	0.67	0.50	2.20	16.3	2.5	6.5	1.3	5.9	3.2	17.1	32.3
Canada	1.25	0.85	2.17	20.3	2.4	8.5	2.0	6.5	3.2	21.5	57.9
Denmark	3.52	0.48	1.19	18.4	2.5	7.4	1.7	6.5	3.6	14.5	12.8
Finland	3.64	0.64	1.15	14.9	2.5	6.0	0.4	4.9	3.1	11.1	10.9
France	0.99	0.43	1.27	16.6	2.5	6.6	0.9	5.7	3.3	28.7	64.4
Germany	0.97	0.32	1.26	19.3	2.5	7.7	1.4	5.8	3.2	80.2	35.5
Ireland	0.72	0.72	2.21	16.2	2.5	6.5	1.8	6.8	6.2	9.1	12.8
Italy	0.87	0.24	1.33	19.6	2.5	7.8	1.7	7.6	6.9	43.6	33.2
Japan	0.56	0.53	2.12	55.3	3.0	18.4	0.5	2.3	0.6	220.0	47.7
Netherlands	2.31	1.08	2.33	21.5	2.5	8.6	1.9	5.7	3.2	28.3	30.5
New Zealand	0.66	0.69	2.01	14.3	3.5	4.1	1.8	7.8	7.0	4.6	22.5
Norway	2.04	0.45	0.89	16.0	2.5	6.4	3.3	6.1	3.5	27.8	4.3
Spain	0.57	0.46	1.61	18.3	2.5	7.3	2.2	6.8	5.4	60.6	14.1
Sweden	2.03	1.20	2.29	18.8	2.5	7.5	-0.4	7.2	4.1	17.0	28.2
Switzerland	3.14	1.52	2.18	24.6	2.5	9.8	0.6	3.4	1.8	48.2	12.9
UK	1.50	1.58	2.97	16.9	2.5	6.8	2.6	7.5	6.6	35.9	90.4
US	1.80	1.19	2.72	20.4	2.6	7.8	2.8	6.9	5.8	56.2	344.1
Total	NA	NA	NA	NA	NA	NA	NA	NA	NA	759.93	NA
Average	1.52	0.74	1.84	20.09	2.62	7.67	1.54	6.15	4.21	40.00	47.86
Emerging Markets											
Argentina	1.03	0.18	0.55	18.5	4.0	4.6	0.7	8.6	7.1	17.4	8.9
Bangladesh	0.19	0.08	0.49	NA	NA	NA	5.7	NA	7.0	1.7	8.2
Brazil	3.15	0.45	0.76	16.2	4.6	3.5	8.7	NA	21.8	58.1	7.6
Chile	2.56	1.27	2.02	16.8	7.2	2.3	6.1	NA	18.6	16.0	7.5
China	0.19	0.10	0.68	50.3	8.5	5.9	4.0	NA	11.5	114.0	4.4
Colombia	0.73	0.26	0.63	13.0	5.3	2.4	18.5	NA	25.4	9.6	4.6
Czech Republic	0.81	0.48	1.06	16.4	5.4	3.0	6.8	NA	12.1	12.6	3.4
Egypt	0.38	0.18	0.65	NA	4.5	NA	5.4	NA	13.0	17.0	1.7
Greece	0.63	0.36	0.92	23.3	2.8	8.4	6.0	NA	10.5	18.5	4.3
Hong Kong	1.33	3.08	5.49	14.3	5.2	2.8	5.7	NA	6.0	63.8	12.3
Hungary	0.58	0.12	0.32	25.2	5.4	4.7	18.8	NA	21.2	9.8	1.4

India	4.52	0.47	0.84	14.6	6.6	2.2	10.8	NA	6.2	22.7	11.8
Indonesia	0.59	0.50	1.35	19.9	6.9	2.9	5.1	NA	14.4	19.0	13.5
Israel	0.54	0.47	1.33	NA	4.9	NA	10.4	4.3	11.9	15.3	7.7
Jamaica	0.88	0.60	1.29	NA	4.0	NA	25.3	26.9	22.3	0.9	5.5
Jordan	1.04	0.46	0.89	14.3	5.8	2.5	2.5	NA	8.5	1.4	4.1
Malaysia	2.01	4.16	6.73	19.4	7.5	2.6	3.2	NA	7.3	26.1	20.2
Mauritius	0.66	0.45	1.12	NA	NA	NA	8.6	NA	12.1	0.9	4.8
Mexico	0.97	0.38	0.81	16.6	4.0	4.2	24.5	NA	22.1	21.1	11.7
Morocco	1.72	0.20	0.31	NA	4.8	NA	3.9	13.0	9.8	3.7	2.5
Pakistan	0.69	0.18	0.44	13.5	5.8	2.3	13.8	NA	16.3	1.1	24.1
Peru	14.56	0.26	0.28	16.1	5.8	2.8	9.3	NA	5.6	11.1	1.4
Philippines	1.62	1.19	2.28	19.8	6.5	3.0	4.8	NA	10.4	9.7	16.9
Poland	22.01	0.09	0.09	14.2	5.8	2.4	16.6	NA	23.0	17.7	0.6
Portugal	0.48	0.29	0.88	25.0	3.1	8.2	2.5	6.7	5.8	15.5	5.5
Russia	0.71	0.08	0.18	NA	3.0	NA	15.2	NA	33.1	11.1	5.5
Singapore	1.54	1.77	2.92	17.7	6.0	3.0	1.6	6.9	3.4	77.3	3.0
South Africa	9.13	2.08	2.30	14.9	3.9	3.8	9.6	15.1	15.7	1.8	167.5
South Korea	0.76	0.32	0.95	9.3	6.9	1.3	4.3	12.5	13.1	29.9	13.8
Sri Lanka	0.61	0.14	0.37	12.0	4.4	2.7	16.7	NA	10.7	1.9	2.5
Taiwan	0.73	1.31	3.27	27.3	6.4	4.3	1.1	NA	6.8	88.3	9.1
Thailand	0.48	0.51	1.66	9.0	7.9	1.1	4.6	NA	8.3	37.1	7.1
Turkey	1.57	0.26	0.48	18.1	5.1	3.5	78.9	NA	66.1	15.6	5.2
Venezuela	1.38	0.27	0.47	8.6	3.4	2.5	64.9	14.2	18.7	12.5	2.5
Zimbabwe	5.80	0.43	0.50	16.5	5.3	3.1	18.2	17.4	19.8	0.4	7.5
Total	NA	NA	NA	NA	NA	NA	NA	NA	NA	780.60	NA
Average	2.47	0.67	1.30	17.93	5.35	3.44	12.65	12.56	14.99	22.30	11.9

1.10 APPENDIX 2: VALUATION METHODS

1.10.1 Evaluating Emerging Bond Markets — Sovereign Credit Risk

In the early nineteenth century, the British bank Barings & Co. was described as the "Sixth Great Power" because of its vast financial muscle in deciding the fate of nations. Today, Moodies and S&P, the major credit rating agencies, are the world's two superpowers in the eyes of many emerging economies. A thumbs down from Moodies or a green light from S&P can make the difference between economic growth or continued backwardness. They are the modern-day gatekeepers of global finance.

The credit rating agencies undertake a complex evaluation to gauge the likelihood of debt default by each sovereign issuer, i.e. a loss. The analysis is based on a series of factors, such as inflation, income per head, foreign exchange reserves, national balance sheet strength, etc. Our research shows that inflation is probably the key factor behind these credit scores. In other words, economies with low and stable inflation tend to enjoy the highest ratings. Moreover, experience shows that the memory of investors is comparatively short. For example, the United States defaulted against European lenders in the mid-nineteenth century, eliciting the threat from Baron Rothschild that "... they shall never borrow another penny, not a penny".

However, despite their widespread use, these ratings suffer from a number of drawbacks:

- *Compatibility*: Moodies and S&P use different methods of evaluation and different scoring systems. Moreover, they often disagree about credit quality. Which is best?
- *Coverage*: Although more and more countries are now being credit rated, a large number of countries still await a proper evaluation.
- *Sensitivity*: How does a credit rating change if domestic inflation picks up? Does a country's rating improve significantly if income per head rises? Because credit rating is a "black box" process, we cannot easily answer these questions.

Credit risk is probably the most important of a number of factors that affect debt returns. The key influences are:

- credit risk;
- local market risk;
- currency risk; and
- US interest rate risk.

Local market risk is usually measured by historic price volatility, i.e. standard deviation. Currency risk is often seen as being mainly a function of the size of current account deficits and deviations of currencies from their underlying purchasing power parities (PPPs).

Because both the principal and (some) future interest rate payments are collateralized by US dollar zero coupon bonds, the currency risk of a Brady bond (versus a US dollar benchmark) is minimal. Consequently, the stripped Brady spread[11] over US Treasuries is largely determined by the degree of credit and market risk.

Table 1.5 shows the stripped spread of various par bonds. The *Credit Rating Index* shown in the final column is a simple hybrid measure of the two agencies' credit ratings. The index ranges between a maximum value of 100 per cent, for AAA credits, and 0 per cent, for unrated debt. Each step between a higher or lower credit band is given a 5 per

Table 1.5   Major emerging debt markets — stripped spreads and credit ratings, June 1997

Country	Stripped Spread (basis points)	S&P Rating	Moodies' Rating	Credit Rating Index (%)
Argentina	434	BB−	B1	37.5
Brazil	450	B+	B1	35.0
Bulgaria	638	not rated	B3	20.0
Ecuador	745	not rated	not rated	0.0
Mexico	385	BB	Ba2	45.0
Nigeria	652	not rated	not rated	0.0
Peru	344	not rated	B2	30.0
Philippines	174	B	Ba3	35.0
Poland	153	BBB−	Baa3	55.0
Russia*	276	BB−	Ba2	42.5
Venezuela	433	B	Ba2	37.5

*9.5 per cent Eurobond.

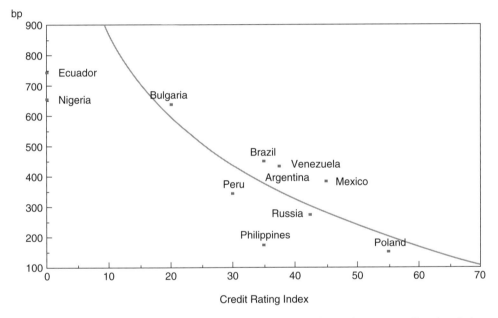

Figure 1.17   "Fair value" for emerging debt markets — stripped spreads versus credit ratings index, June 1997

cent point score on the index. Thus BB (S&P) scores 45 per cent and BBB (S&P) scores 60 per cent. BBB and above are deemed *investment grade*: many investment funds are limited to buying investment grade securities.

The importance of credit ratings can be seen from Figure 1.17. This correlates the *Credit Rating Index* with the stripped yield spread. A logarithmic regression line has been fitted to the data. As credit quality improves, the regression line ultimately becomes asymptotic to the benchmark US Treasury yield. Assuming that credit risk is the major influence on stripped yield spreads, this regression line should represent "fair value". In other words, a sensible investment strategy would be to purchase bond markets above the curve (i.e. where yield spreads lie above "fair value" according to the credit index) and to sell bond markets that lie below the curve. According to Figure 1.17, Brazilian, Mexican and Argentinean Par bonds are "buys", but Philippine, Polish, and Russian bonds are "sells".

1.10.2 Evaluating Emerging Equity Markets — The "Big Bang" Growth Model

Equity markets are typically judged by P/E multiples. Although rules of thumb are common, e.g. 20 times for a "fast growth" stock and eight times for an "ex-growth" stock, the theoretical basis for these calculations comes from the earnings (or dividend) discount model:

$$P = \frac{E}{r - g}$$

where P denotes share prices, E is earnings per share, r is a discount factor, and g represents the growth rate in perpetuity. Re-writing:

$$\frac{P}{E} = \frac{1}{r - g}$$

$$= \frac{1}{r} \times \frac{r}{r - g}$$

Adding one to both sides:

$$= \frac{1}{r} \times \left[1 - \frac{r - g}{r - g} + \frac{r}{r - g} \right]$$

$$= \frac{1}{r} \times \left[1 + \frac{g}{r - g} \right]$$

$$= \frac{1}{r} \times [1 + G]$$

where

$$G = \frac{g}{r - g}$$

The G-factor represents the present value of all future growth opportunities. It can be thought of as "big bang" growth. The stream of future receipts has been reduced to an equivalent single lump sum in today's money. This, of course, is the essence of discounting, but what we have done is to separate out the growth elements, captured by G, from the known value, represented by the existing rate of earnings and capitalized at a rate r.

Re-arranging:

$$\frac{P}{E} = \frac{1}{r} + \frac{G}{r}$$

In words:

$$\text{Price/earnings } (P/E) = \text{Base } P/E + \text{Growth } P/E$$

Two important observations follow from this formula:

1. $1/r$ represents the "base", or "zero growth" P/E. Thus an investment with zero growth potential would not have a zero P/E; rather, its P/E would equal its base P/E of $1/r$. Each unit of present value growth (G) raises the base P/E by $1/r$. The higher is G, the larger the "fair value" multiple an investor should be prepared to pay. And because of the fixed contribution of each investment's base P/E $(1/r)$, the relationship between growth and value is linear but not one-for-one.

2. It is the size of G and not the time profile of the underlying stream of earnings or dividends that matters. In other words, several different earnings streams are capable of generating the same G-factor. Moveover, G-factors can be calculated for earnings and dividends, as well as for sales, investment or aggregate GDP.

The P/E multiple moves up and down according to the extent of growth. It can be "normalized" with respect to growth by forming the "P/E growth" ratio:

$$\frac{P/E}{(1+G)} = \frac{1}{r} = \text{"base or zero-growth } P/E\text{"}$$

Alternatively, this can also be written as:

$$\frac{P}{E(1+G)} = \frac{P}{E^*} = \frac{P}{E + \Delta E}$$

where E^* denotes the present value of all future earnings, and ΔE represents the present value increment in earnings, i.e. $E^* - E$, or $G \cdot E$, and where $1/r$ (the reciprocal of bond yields, which is equivalent to bond prices), the "base" or "zero-growth P/E" can be thought of as being a constant over the long term.

This model is especially useful for analysing emerging markets because it highlights the problem of "fast growth" economies. Consider the value of G, the present value of all future additions to earnings. If an economy is "ex growth", then the value of G will be close to zero, i.e. $\Delta E = 0$. Equally, if an economy enjoys rapid growth, then G will be "large". In this latter case it is likely that the present value of all future growth opportunities will easily exceed current earning, i.e. $\Delta E \gg E$.

This model allows us more insight into the equity valuation process. It follows that the P/E multiple, the favoured tool used by investors in the developed stock markets, will work well if G is close to zero. This would seem a reasonable assumption in the case of the developed economies, which, by definition, are already a long way up the S-shaped development curve.

For emerging markets, where G plainly is not close to zero, the simple P/E is an inappropriate tool. In fact, in those cases of especially fast growth where $\Delta E \gg E$, the $P/\Delta E$ ratio is a more useful valuation measure.

Therefore, we have two extreme valuation cases:

1. Ex-growth $\Rightarrow P/E$.
2. Fast growth $\Rightarrow P/\Delta E$.

Emerging market investors should use the second model (i.e. $P/\Delta E$). However, estimating the present value of all future increments to growth is no easy task. Consequently, we suggest using a "rule of thumb".

Because the $P/\Delta E$ ratio is mathematically equivalent to the P/E divided by some growth rate g, g can be approximated by taking the average annual five-year future

Table 1.6 *P/E* real growth ratios (threshold 4.5 times) — end — May 1997

Country	*P/E*	Five-Year Real Growth	*P/E* Real Growth Ratio
China	50.3	8.5	5.9
Russia	11.5	3.5	3.3
Malaysia	19.4	7.5	2.6
Indonesia	19.9	6.9	2.9
South Africa	14.9	3.9	3.8
Korea	9.3	6.9	1.3
Turkey	18.1	5.1	3.5
India	14.6	6.6	2.2
Brazil	16.2	4.6	3.5
Mexico	16.6	4.0	4.2
Argentina	18.5	4.0	4.6
Poland	14.2	5.8	2.4
Memo:			
US	20.4	2.6	7.8
Japan	55.3	3.0	18.4
UK	16.9	2.5	6.8
Germany	19.3	2.5	7.7

real (i.e. inflation-adjusted) growth rate. We have found that "*P/E* real growth" ratios of 4.5 times or less offer good investment opportunities. Table 1.6 compares the *P/E* real growth ratios for various countries. According to this analysis, the developed stock markets currently offer little value but emerging markets are generally cheap. Korea, India, Poland, Malaysia, Indonesia, and Russia appear especially attractive.

1.11 ENDNOTES

1. Polity — the social and political environment.
2. IFC: International Finance Corporation, a division of the World Bank.
3. That is if Hong Kong and South Africa are classified as "emerging markets".
4. Consequently, we believe that return enhancement rather than risk reduction is the major spur pushing funds internationally.
5. Our data show that the top 20 US portfolio managers out of the largest 150 most active funds account for 60 per cent of all buying and selling decisions in emerging markets.
6. PPP: purchasing power parity.
7. These estimates of equity flows are different from those reported by the World Bank. In both Figures 1.9 and 1.10 we use our own figures. They are based on a different methodology, which tends to place more emphasis on secondary rather than primary flows (new issues).
8. Mobius (1994) describes a case where it took 11,000 man-hours of expert time to restate one Chinese company's three-year accounts into US GAAP.
9. In other words, we have assumed zero price inflation.
10. More dramatically, the foreign reserves to monetary base ratio ranges from 12 per cent for the United States to 605 per cent for Singapore.
11. Stripped spread: The difference in basis points between the stripped yield and the US Treasury yield. The stripped yield is defined as the yield (semi-annualized) of the non-collateralized country cashflows.

1.12 REFERENCES

Bekaert, G., Erb, C.B., Harvey, C.R. and Viskanta, T.E. (1996) "The behaviour of emerging market returns". Paper presented to The Future Of Emerging Market Capital Flows Conference, 23–24 May. New York: University Leonard N. Stern School of Business.

Bekaert, G. and Harvey, C.R. (1995) "Time-varying world market integration". *Journal of Finance*, June, **1**, 403–44.

Euromoney/World Bank (1994) *Investing in Emerging Markets*, Edited by M.J. Howell. Euromoney Publications.

Harvey, C.R. (1994) "The risk exposure of emerging markets", in Euromoney/World Bank, *Investing in Emerging Markets*. Euromoney Publications.

Krugman, P. (1995) "Dutch tulips and emerging markets". *Foreign Affairs*, July/August.

Mobius, M. (1994) *The Investor's Guide to Emerging Markets*. Pitman Publishing.

2

Emerging markets II

MARK FOX AND IAN KING

2.1 INTRODUCTION

2.1.1 The Beginnings of Emerging Markets

Interest in emerging market investment has exploded in the 1990s, both in fixed income and in equities. A consequence of globalization is that it has become harder for investors to find new undiscovered opportunities, and more difficult for investment managers to differentiate their performance and style from their competition. The 1980s was the decade for the opening up of most OECD markets to international investment, both equity and fixed income. In 1984 buying French bonds was regarded as "exotic", but by 1989 France had become mainstream. Meanwhile Italy and Spain began to be purchased as "exotics", but they too became absorbed into the mainstream. The 1990s has become the decade for opening up emerging markets, just as the 1980s was the decade for expanding into more OECD countries.

Capital flows into fixed income emerging markets commenced via a very different route from the route of expansion into new OECD countries in the 1980s, but is now following the familiar pattern. Early fixed income flows came from specialist investors who saw value in the restructured defaulted debt of Mexico and subsequently of other Latin American economies, usually in the form of "Brady" bonds (described further below). As the credit spread on these bonds diminished, their performance became progressively more like that of US Treasury bonds, with less credit play to affect price performance. Early Brady bond investors began to invest instead in local markets in South American countries where higher yields were on offer in exchange for taking currency risk, and the correlations to US Treasuries lower. The pattern of purchasing hard currency emerging debt, either in the form of Brady or Eurobonds, followed by local markets purchases, subsequently was common during the early 1990s.

Two new types of investor have entered emerging markets since those early days, and with them a change in the pattern of investing in emerging markets. The first new entrant was US credit fund managers. Like the early specialist buyers, they purchased hard currency emerging market debt first. They viewed emerging market debt, sovereign

Risk Management and Analysis. Vol. 2: New Markets and Products. Edited by Carol Alexander
© 1998 John Wiley & Sons Ltd

or corporate, as purchasing pure credit, offering them a wider universe than that offered by OECD sovereign and corporate bonds. As their confidence grew they began to take the view that the purest form of credit play on an emerging country, and one that offered greater yield enhancement, was to purchase instruments denominated in the local currency. Local currency offered a more direct sovereign credit view of the competence of economic management as reflected in the currency, as well as default risks priced into spreads on the hard currency bonds. The second group of investors, only really evident since 1993, has been the global fund managers who regard currency risk as a major part of their portfolio allocation. These investors have naturally diversified into local market investment straight away in the same way that they expanded the mix of country bonds within their portfolios in the 1980s. These fund managers sell themselves as currency and interest rate diversification managers, and therefore investment into the local bond markets is the natural path for them rather than credit spread enhancement through the existing hard currency markets.

In the case of equity investors early interest in emerging markets, which began in the 1980s, tended to be through specialist managers, often running single country funds. Geographically, emerging equity markets developed differently from fixed income markets, the early investors being attracted by the high growth that was being achieved in Asia. International interest in Latin America developed much later. Regional funds followed, and finally funds where the portfolio managers had full discretion to choose among markets developed. Use of emerging markets by developed markets portfolio managers came earlier because bond funds have usually been delimited by currency, whereas equity funds are often defined by geographic region. As emerging markets developed in each region they were used by regional managers to diversify their risk in the developed markets.

2.1.2 Defining Emerging Markets

The term "emerging market" is in common usage to cover a wide variety of different forms of risk and has become a blanket term for a broad spectrum of investment activity without due consideration as to the specific nature of the investment type or its risks.[1] Whilst certain characteristics tend to be present in most emerging markets, ultimately the investor has to take a decision in each case as to whether he regards a particular market or country, or an investment strategy being pursued within that country or market, as part of an emerging or developed markets portfolio.

One of the most frequently adopted definitions is that of the World Bank which defines an emerging market as any country where income per capita falls into the lower or middle income category, the upper limit currently being set at US$9,385. This method has the advantage of avoiding the difficulties that arise from using the credit ratings issued by major credit ratings agencies, who can differ widely in their views. However, a single factor definition has dangers. For example, there are a number of small countries, particularly in the Middle East, with very high per capita incomes, but with very underdeveloped political systems and processes that most investors would still describe as emerging. Some investors take the word "emerging" very literally. For them it is not the current state of a country that determines its status, but the speed of change as reflected by GDP growth. Another approach is to look at the countries included in the major emerging markets indices, perhaps limiting the selection of countries to those within one of those indices, although this is arguably simply deferring the decision to a third party.

There is a solid core of countries in Latin America, Eastern Europe, and Asia that fall within a consensus definition of being emerging markets. However, there is also a large band of "crossover" countries where opinions differ widely as to whether the market is emerging or developed. In Europe, Greece and the Czech Republic are classified under both headings by different groups of investors. In the Far East, China is an example of a country whose status is unclear. Its hard currency debt is often traded by developed credit Eurobond desks, whereas local currency debt falls firmly under the "emerging" category. The status of Korea and whether that will change as a result of the 1997 crisis will have to be observed closely. When its Eurobonds were rated A+ most securities houses traded it on their developed credit books. Following the Korean crisis it is unclear how this debt will trade in the future, but for the present its Eurobonds remain on the developed Eurobond desks. Among equity markets, Malaysia appears in both European, Australian and Far East (EAFE) and Morgan Stanley Capital (MSC) indices, and in the IFC emerging markets indices.

In contrast is the historical quirk of sanctions that led to the situation in South Africa where highly developed, liquid bond and equity markets are still traded by emerging markets desks. The country's political and economic situation can be characterized as "emerging", but the markets developed to a high level internally before sanctions preventing foreigners investing there were lifted. The equity market has developed to the extent that its capitalization as a percentage of South Africa's GDP is so large that capital weighted indices give distorted prominence to South Africa (usually around 12 per cent) relative to other emerging countries where equity markets are less developed. In the case of Korea, as the domestic bond market opens to foreigners as part of the IMF package, investors will have to decide how to categorize a market that is four times the size of New Zealand's market, albeit with very variable liquidity, yet we imagine that it will be traded on emerging market desks and invested in by emerging markets fund managers.

In testing whether a market rather than a country is "emerging" the following checklist highlights key indicators to help the investor decide:

1. Limited and inefficiently distributed available information and research on a market, often only obtainable locally.
2. Limited access to the market and variable liquidity.
3. Consequent greater sensitivity to flows.
4. High volatility.
5. Heavy concentration in the hands of a small number of players.
6. Poor settlements procedures.
7. Inadequate regulation.
8. Greater performance sensitivity to political rather than economic considerations relative to developed markets.
9. Greater performance sensitivity to other extraneous considerations such as the commodity or credit cycle.

One characteristic that may surprise by reason of its omission is low capitalization of a market. We have chosen to omit this because a number of the markets are very sizeable and either have suffered from accessibility constraints previously or continue to do so. The above list may appear to present an insurmountable series of barriers as to why anyone would wish to purchase local market debt or equities! Of course the returns can be very high, reflecting the risks involved.

2.1.3 The Size of Emerging Markets[2]

In view of the difficulty in defining which countries fall within the universe of emerging markets, it is obviously not possible to provide an exact definition of the size of the markets; however, we have attempted to provide an approximation. The task is made more difficult by the constantly changing nature of the market, reflecting the fast changing investment climate. In an earlier version of this chapter[3], citing the 1993 *Trading Volumes Survey* compiled by the Emerging Markets Traders Association (EMTA), trading volumes reported were just below US$2trn. Volumes for the third quarter of 1997 alone exceeded US$1.3trn; annual volumes for 1996 were US$5.3trn. Figure 2.1 shows the profile of the market by trading volumes as of the third quarter of 1997.

The change in the profile of the assets traded is as dramatic as the change in volumes. In 1983 Bradys accounted for around 80 per cent of the volumes traded, Eurobonds for around 8 per cent. Bradys now account for 39 per cent, Eurobonds 28 per cent, local markets 26 per cent, and loans for the balance. The EMTA also reported that in the case of three of the most heavily traded countries, Argentina, Brazil, and Mexico, Eurobond trading exceeded Brady trading. The rapid growth in importance of Russia has led to a move in the regional balance of emerging markets away from Latin America. Russian instruments accounted for 13 per cent of traded volumes. Other East European countries, such as Ukraine and Kazakhstan, are also seeing rapid rises in trading activity.

(i) Brady Bonds

The Brady market is still regarded by non-emerging market specialists as the quintessential fixed income emerging asset, but it is gradually diminishing in importance despite its rapid growth in the early 1990s for reasons explored below. Nonetheless, it should not be written off yet. The market is capitalized at around US$100bn; trading volumes in the third quarter of 1997 alone were around US$500mn by face value.

Whilst the Brady market has increased rapidly in size to become a major traded market, there are countervailing forces to its longevity. As described in Section 2.4 on Bradys, several countries have been buying back blocs of their debt and issuing more expensive Eurobonds against them. If these countries continue the progress that they have made in stabilizing their economies and building up their reserves, then their ability and willingness to buy back their Brady debt will increase. Bradys will be withdrawn even for relatively

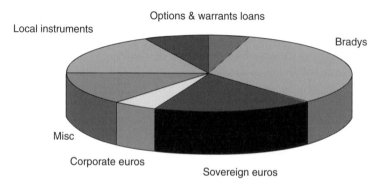

Figure 2.1 Emerging markets trading volumes. *Source:* EMTA

small savings in the cost of their outstanding debt, and the rate of shrinkage in the size of the Brady market due to buybacks will increase. Moreover, there is no obvious source of substantial further new issuance. All the larger countries have now restructured; only a handful of small countries may still do so, with the possibility of issuing Brady bonds against their debt.

(ii) Eurobonds

There has been explosive growth in the issuance of Eurobonds, for reasons fully described in Section 2.5 on Eurobonds below. Figure 2.2 and Table 2.1 show the most recently available statistics on outstanding hard currency international debt (not necessarily Eurobonds), and its growth. In an earlier version of this chapter[3] new Eurobond issuance featured just six countries, compared with the current 20 listed. One major Eurobond market development in the last three years has been the growth of issuance by non-Latin American borrowers, thereby offering much greater diversification amongst emerging market Eurobonds. Latin American issuance still dominates; the countries there were the first to restructure, and also had the largest amount of debt outstanding. However, over time international debt issuance, in particular from Eastern Europe and the former Russian republics, is likely to increase sharply as a proportion of outstandings.

(iii) Local Markets

These too have expanded rapidly in size and diversity in recent years. BIS statistics quote all of the countries in Table 2.1 as having local markets, but there are also many others amongst non-BIS members. A few examples include Kenya and Uganda in Africa, or

Table 2.1 International debt securities outstanding by nationality (US$bn)

S Korea	52.2	Venezuela	8.4
Mexico	51.7	Ex USSR	7.7
Argentina	49.7	India	7.5
Brazil	40.1	Taiwan	5.1
China	16.9	Colombia	4.4
Thailand	14.3	S Africa	4.2
Indonesia	14	Chile	4.1
Hungary	12.3	Israel	2.3
Malaysia	12	Ex-Csz	1.7
Philippines	10.2	Poland	1.1

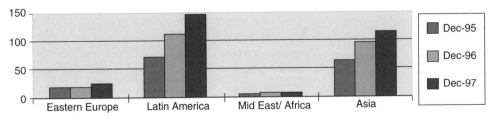

Figure 2.2 Changes in outstanding emerging market debt by region. *Source:* BIS[4]

Lithuania or Estonia in Eastern Europe. In Asia countries such as Vietnam have nascent local markets, and the first local corporate instrument has just been created in Algeria. The markets vary immensely in size from the giant markets of South Korea, Taiwan, and Russia to "markets" consisting in reality of one or two securities that are offered on a primary basis only. The balance of private to government debt also varies immensely. Taking into account all the major markets, our best approximation of the global capitalization of local fixed income markets in emerging countries, including those of South East Asia, would be somewhere in the region of US$2.3trn, comparable with the size of the US Treasury market.[5]

(iv) Equities

For equity markets there is a much sharper distinction to be drawn between investable and non-investable equities. There are a large number of individual equities and whole sectors of markets that are quoted on stock exchanges but can be purchased in theory only. The shares, either held by families or a small closely knit group of owners or foreigners, are not allowed to be invested in by others. Even where there is no formal ban on foreigners, there is often an unofficial policy of never selling the shares to foreigners. The IFC who sponsor the major emerging equity indices therefore have two emerging stock market indices. The IFC Global Composite Index is capitalized at US$1.3trn, but the IFC Investable Composite Index is capitalized at US$800mn. The regional split between the two indices does not vary hugely; the problem of investability exists across emerging markets. Emerging equity markets are more evenly split by region than the fixed income markets. The Investable Index is composed of 41.1 per cent Latin America, 37.67 per cent Asia, and the remainder in Europe, the Middle East and Africa. Within Latin America, Brazil is the largest equity market, capitalized at US$124bn; in Asia, Taiwan is the largest market. In the EAFE area South Africa is three times larger than any other market and has a total weighting in the Index of 12 per cent owing to the historical quirk of South Africa developing a highly successful domestic capital market during the years of isolation due to sanctions. In practice many investors adjust their benchmarks to reduce the weight of South Africa to a more proportional representation of its global importance. The Russian equity market, for example, capitalized at US$34bn, constrained in size only by its relative newness compared with the South African market, is likely to become relatively much larger over time.[6]

2.2 DO EMERGING MARKETS CONSTITUTE A SEPARATE ASSET CLASS?

There is no clear answer as to whether emerging markets should be treated as a separate asset class or not, nor, indeed, of how to determine whether a particular asset group constitutes a separate asset class. Arguably it is not a very important issue, but it has been addressed simply because the question is asked so frequently. We will argue below that there are differences in the way that emerging markets should be treated, but these are questions of degree.

The level of risk typically entailed in an investment will often determine for many investors whether a particular group of assets should be regarded as a separate asset class. Institutional and private investors alike usually regard the portion of their assets invested in emerging markets as high risk/high reward, the success of which is largely dependent upon factors specific to those markets. The evidence shows that it is right to regard emerging markets as considerably more risky than developed markets because of individual market vulnerability either to individual event risk or fallout from events in an unrelated country.

In fact, there is considerable difficulty in assessing volatility in emerging markets as a unified asset class because "emerging markets" covers such an immense range of investments. Developed government bond markets have typically experienced annual volatilities of around 3 per cent–4 per cent. The Brady, loans, and emerging countries' Eurobond markets have been far more volatile over time. For example, the J.P. Morgan Indices for 1997 recorded the volatility of Bradys as 14.43 per cent, for emerging Eurobonds as 13.56 per cent, and for loans as 22.31 per cent. However, emerging local markets were much less volatile than their developed counterparts until the disturbances in Asia during 1997, typically recording volatilities of 1 per cent–1.5 per cent.[6] In 1997, local markets volatility rose sharply to 7.15 per cent. The difficulty in measuring the volatility of emerging markets is further compounded by the very different countries within this category. Not surprisingly, the greatest volatility in local markets was seen in Asia in 1997, whilst Latin America saw relatively little spillover. Even within the Brady market there are massive variances in volatility, Bulgarian Bradys recording the highest volatility of around 27 per cent whilst Poland recorded the lowest amongst the more liquid Bradys at just 7 per cent. However, the overall risks are clearly greater than in developed markets.

The evidence of whether emerging markets do provide higher returns corresponding to the risks is also very difficult to assess because of the wide variance in returns both across asset classes and between countries. The track record of emerging markets in fixed income is very short. International focus on liquid trading of fixed income emerging markets only began in 1990 when Mexican par bonds started trading actively, and the first indices that covered a wide enough group of assets to provide indications across the asset class only began to be compiled in 1993. Table 2.2 shows the results to date.

All that can be deduced with confidence at this stage is that emerging market returns are certainly much more volatile than those of fixed markets. The nature of the markets and the investor base is changing and developing rapidly; 1997 shows some promise of greater maturity in that total returns followed fundamentals. The collapse of Asian currencies rightly had remarkably little effect on the assets of countries that were not directly affected, rather than the general panic that followed the Mexican peso devaluation in 1994 known as the "Tequila Effect".

Many investment managers have "emerging markets" teams either running money dedicated to those markets or advising tactically on when developed portfolios should invest in

Table 2.2 Total returns (%)

	Govt Bonds Global	Broad Brady	Benchmark Eurobonds	Loans	Local Markets
1994	−3.53	−16.31	−16.68	−21.9	−1.77
1995	17.09	21.23	24.43	31.7	10.53
1996	7.58	34.39	19.24	94.7	14.86
1997	1.4	15.75	10.78	3.66	−12.55

Source: J.P. Morgan Indices throughout.[7]

emerging markets. However, there are clear divides within emerging markets, both equity and fixed income, and within fixed income. A distinction needs to be drawn between whether it is the country itself that is emerging, or merely the market. In the Far East several of the countries had ratings for their hard currency debt several notches above investment grade prior to the 1997 crisis, but their local markets were poorly developed, or closed to foreigners. The debt of these countries and countries such as Greece tended to fall into a gap between the emerging and OECD markets desks at many investment banks. South Africa offers another problem. The economy was relatively developed, the bond market very developed, having a fully liquid curve, derivative products, and all the other characteristics of an OECD bond market. However, the anti-apartheid sanctions during the 1970s and 1980s that were lifted only relatively recently mean that most foreigners are still very new to this bond market.

The same team may be managing money against widely differing objectives. At one extreme investors are seeking the maximum possible gain as quickly as possible, taking high risk, often leveraged. At the other end of the spectrum are the fixed income "yield" funds that are especially popular in the United States that are seeking an uplift over US cash rates, but with minimum possible volatility in the Net Asset Value. In between the two are funds seeking to outperform emerging market indices through country, stock, and interest rate environment selection, and non-dedicated funds using emerging markets as diversifiers and enhancers relative to non-emerging market indices. However, the width of the investment objective need not detract from asset homogeneity. Equities are purchased by investors for widely different reasons, but there is a wide consensus that they can be treated as a single asset class.

There are common elements to identifying an emerging market investment, equity, or bond that are not dissimilar to those listed as characteristics of local markets, but of rather wider application:

1. The performance of the asset must be at least partially tied to the fortunes of a country that is not usually associated with global capital investment flows.
2. Whilst the country may have a satisfactory credit rating, there is a greater risk of political instability than is normally expected of a country that is being invested in.
3. Information flows are impaired compared with those of a developed country.
4. Volatility either is greater, or there is a perceived risk that it could be greater, than that for a developed country.
5. It is believed that part of the expected outperformance of the asset relative to similar assets in developed countries is tied to the expected economic outperformance or competitiveness of the developing country.

In practice emerging markets fixed income and equity teams often work much more closely together than their developed markets equivalents. This may be a function simply of the emerging markets teams being smaller, but is also due to the need to share the paucity of information that often characterizes emerging markets. Both emerging equities and bonds share the characteristic of having relatively low correlations with developed indices and with other markets in their universe. Thus, for example, local emerging bond markets have a correlation of −0.01 with global bonds and −0.18 with the US Treasury market. Emerging market indices are rather more highly correlated with their developed market counterparts, with correlations of 0.52 with the S&P 500 and 0.54 with EAFE.[8]

Correlation does not, of course, prove or disprove an asset class. Many mandates are won on the express promise of achieving diversification of returns dependent upon low correlations within a single asset class. In fact, the nature of the risk can vary immensely, from the continuous fluctuations seen in Brady bonds to the discrete risks that can accompany local currency investment, a long period of stability preceding dramatic currency shifts. However, this is also true of different types of equities or bonds.

In the case of equities, the correlation between emerging and developed equity markets has not increased despite anecdotal evidence to the contrary. Despite the globalization of both investment flows and the underlying businesses, the traditional reasons for investing in emerging market equities still hold. Adding emerging markets exposure to a developed markets portfolio reduces the risk characteristics of an equity portfolio. As with fixed income securities, the diversity that exists among emerging stock markets ensures that a high level of diversification can also be achieved among the emerging countries. However, while markets as a whole move with greater independence, stocks within emerging markets tend to offer less diversification versus index performance than their developed market counterparts. This is due to a higher concentration of capitalization and trading among a smaller group of stocks relative to the whole index than occurs in developed markets. Especially in the case of smaller emerging equity markets, a handful of stocks will often dominate the whole market.

The decision as to what constitutes an asset class depends ultimately upon investor and market perception as much as upon statistical evidence. In our view this tips the balance in favour of the treatment of emerging markets as a separate asset class. There is a broad consensus that investment in emerging markets, whatever the objective, requires a specialized process and resources. There is general acceptance of much greater risk for emerging markets bond or equity investment than for OECD investment, and money is allocated accordingly. In practice, expectations of high risk do not always materialize, but as long as the perception remains that different risk tolerance parameters, and performance expectations, should be applied to money allocated to emerging markets, they should be treated as separate.

2.3 NON-PERFORMING LOANS

2.3.1 History

Developed country exposure to emerging countries was originally taken primarily through private sector bank loans. Securitization of emerging market debt came much later. In the 1970s a common misconception among commercial bankers held that nations could never go "bankrupt" in the same manner as private enterprises. It was therefore safe to lend large sums of money to countries rather than corporations because countries would never default. In consequence, massive sums were lent to sovereigns without close scrutiny as to their ability to repay. This belief ignored the experiences of earlier generations of bankers who had suffered sovereign default. The 1980s Mexican debt crisis was in fact the third time this century that Mexico had defaulted. By the late 1980s many countries, including countries in Eastern Europe and Africa, as well as Latin America, found themselves unable to service their accumulated debt.

Once loans became non-performing many banks wished to sell them rather than keep them on their books, and they sought ways of liquidation. Others were willing to buy such loans in the belief either that the defaulting borrower would recommence servicing the loan at a future date, or that the borrower would renegotiate and service the renegotiated debt. Thus a market grew up between banks buying, selling, and swapping defaulted loans with each other. Each deal was unique, and resulted from lengthy negotiation and incurred considerable transactions costs in expenses such as lawyers' fees. Those commercial banks that originally lent money to countries which subsequently defaulted remain the major participants in the loans market.

2.3.2 The Present Market

There is now little activity in syndicated loans compared with the early 1990s because most of the countries that had defaulted have since renegotiated their debt into securitized assets. The handful of countries that have failed to do so, such as Sudan and Iraq, owe relatively small amounts of outstanding debt and are governed by regimes that have shown little interest in negotiating with their bankers or recommencing payment on their loans. Therefore there is much less interest in their debt than in that of the countries that were negotiating and imminently about to recommence servicing their debt.

For a period during the early 1990s the market in syndicated loans became active as investors sought to purchase loans at deep discounts hoping that they would gain value as the prospects for a successful renegotiation and recommencement of the servicing of the debt rose. Until the loans were replaced with tradable securities the loans themselves represented the only way to invest in the debt of a country still in default. However, even at the height of their popularity loans were mostly traded among a relatively small part of the total market because they were subject to sharp price fluctuations on the vaguest of rumours as to how loan negotiations were proceeding, and settlement was extremely difficult. Since the loans were in default their only value was in the probability of future cashflows following a successful renegotiation. While highly volatile, loans did have the attraction of the prospect of large and rapid capital gains for those with the right information and a very low correlation with performing fixed income securities dependent upon more conventional cashflow analysis.

Since loans were, by definition, not securities but contractual obligations between a bank and its borrower, each time a loan was traded it was necessary to maintain the legal link to the original lender. Thus, it was necessary for each new purchaser of loans to establish good title by tracing ownership through a potentially large number of counterparties back to the original lending bank. The result was that loans trades settled late habitually, often many months late, with all the inconvenience that followed.

Loans remain the province of specialists. For those who do trade them, there are a number of special points to consider. Settlement remains very difficult for the reasons explained above. Legal title must be traced successfully back to the original loan between the commercial bank and emerging country or corporate enterprise. Large enough loans to justify trading are usually not standard. Careful specification of the material terms of the loan should be made at the time of trading, ideally with pre-inspection of the loan documentation, although in practice this rarely happens.

When trading in some of the countries close to signing Brady deals substantially increased in volume, the EMTA standardized terms and conditions of loans so far as it could in order to attempt to ease the settlement problems and minimize the need for individual inspection of loan documentation. Thus, if the buyer was buying a "Peruvian Citi Loan according to EMTA terms" he knew what the key terms would be.[9] Generally the individual terms and conditions on any outstanding loans need to be checked carefully.

Poor liquidity should be assumed, and the possibility of counterparty risk must also be taken into account. A failure of title between two earlier counterparties could impact a trade between two subsequent counterparties given the legal nature of trading loans.

2.4 BRADY BONDS

2.4.1 History

Brady bonds are probably the single fixed income asset most closely identified with emerging markets, but also the least understood. They exist solely in emerging markets, resulting from the restructuring of the defaulted debt of emerging market countries under "Brady Plans".

During the 1980s several countries, most notably Mexico, that had been lent large amounts by commercial banks, defaulted on their debt. The amount of money owed to US commercial banks was so large that the default became a threat to the whole commercial banking system and the US government had to intervene. Nicholas Brady, the US Secretary of the Treasury at the time, sponsored a debt restructuring scheme for outstanding Mexican debt modelled upon a floating rate bond structured and brought to the market in March 1988 for Mexico by J.P. Morgan.[10] The unique feature of the bond was that the repayment of the principal and 18 months' worth of the income were secured by holdings of US Treasury zero coupon bonds held in trust until maturity of the bond. Through this structure the investor was given valuable credit enhancement. The borrower gained in that it provided access to the capital markets at a difficult time, and because zeros were used, the cost of buying the insurance was relatively low compared with the capital raised. As a performing security the resulting bond was also much more saleable than a non-performing loan for those banks that wished to cut their exposure to Mexico.

The deal struck between Mexico and its creditor banks, which became known as a Brady deal, allowed Mexico to write off 35 per cent of its outstanding debt in return for extending repayment of the principal over 30 years, the creation of marketable bonds which the banks could sell, and the purchase of US zeros as collateral for some of the bonds, thereby ensuring their marketability. The money for the purchase of the US zeros in that case was provided by Mexico, but the cost partially subsidized by the US Treasury. The exact procedure for issuance and payment of the zeros has varied in each subsequent Brady deal, but is of little significance to investors.

In each subsequent Brady plan the overall level of debt forgiveness has varied, and is a highly sensitive political matter, with each country striving to outdo in the size of the write-down that it has been able to achieve on its debt. Examples are Bulgaria, which achieved 47.1 per cent, and Poland, which achieved 42.5 per cent, but with a greater interest write-off. Vietnam has achieved 53.9 per cent. Note that the overall level of debt forgiveness is an entirely separate matter from the structure and blend of emerging market and US debt within individual bonds.

2.4.2 Structures of Brady Plans

Several different forms of bond structure resulted from the Mexican Brady deal according to the exact requirements of the creditor banks, and since then many other structures have been devised. Bank capital regulatory and taxation environments vary widely across countries. However, all bonds derived from defaulted loans that have been restructured and securitized through Brady plans are known generically as Brady bonds. One barrier to the widespread understanding of Brady bonds has been the seemingly strange names attaching to them. In fact, most of the names are straightforward and logical once the bonds are understood in the context of the debt restructuring negotiations. In the case of Mexico, three bond structures came out of the Brady plan. Some of the other Brady plans have resulted in a much more complicated array of bonds and Brady bonds have many

---

1. Par. At least one tranche of bonds are usually referred to as "par" bonds. These bonds are structured for banks anxious to avoid a capital write-down of the original debt. Forgiveness of debt is in the form of reduced interest payments relative to the amount that would have been paid on the extended period for repayment of the debt. The capital on the loan is repaid at par. Pars are normally fixed rate, but may have features such as a step-up coupon. There is a principal and often a rolling interest guarantee.
Countries include: Argentina, Brazil, Ecuador, Jordan, Mexico, Nigeria, Panama, Peru, Philippines, Poland, Venezuela.

2. Discount. There is frequently a "discount" tranche for those banks anxious to maintain stable margins on their income against loans outstanding in their portfolios, but willing to write off part of the capital value of the loan. These bonds are floating rate, fixing at a margin over Libor. The discount given on the principal can be contrasted with the par payment of the principal in the case of Par bonds. There is a principal and often a rolling income guarantee.
Countries include: Argentina, Brazil, Bulgaria, Dominican Republic, Ecuador, Jordan, Mexico, Panama, Peru, Poland, Venezuela.

3. PDI/IDU/IAN/IAB. The restructuring of the principal debt is usually carried out separately from any outstanding accrued interest, and separate bonds are issued in respect of each part. The bonds that securitize unpaid accrued interest on the original loan carry names such as "PDI" (Past Due Interest), "IDU" (Interest Due Unpaid) in the case of Brazil, "IAB" (Interest Accrued Bonds") in the case of Bulgaria, or "IAN" (Interest Accrued Notes) in the case of Russia. These bonds, together with other variants, tend to be floating rate in nature, reflecting the original covenants in the loans which often reflect penalty payments tied to floating rates plus a margin in the event of a default on paying interest.
Countries include: Brazil, Bulgaria, Dominican Republic, Ecuador, Jordan, Panama, Peru, Poland.

4. FLIRB. A compromise between debt write-offs either entirely through capital or through income is offered by "FLIRB"s (Front Loaded Interest Reduction Bonds). For example, the Brazilian FLIRBs have fixed, rising coupons until 2000, and floating coupon thereafter, following a grace period of several years. As the name suggests, there is a reduction in interest in the front years, the bond converting to a conventional Libor+ floating spread further out. To complicate matters further, in this particular case there is also a sinking fund. Bulgarian FLIRBs are similar in terms of coupon structure, but differ in the grace period and in the latter case there is a rolling interest guarantee, whereas in the former there is a partial capital guarantee. The key point to note here as elsewhere is that there is an identifiable outline structure, but there are endless possible permutations as each bond is the subject of separate negotiation between the sovereign and its creditor banks.
Countries include: Brazil, Bulgaria, Peru, Philippines, Venezuela.

5. NMB/DCB. In some cases banks have been willing to offer fresh loans to countries notwithstanding their current difficulties. Bonds, usually referred to as "New Money" bonds, have been created against these. DCB (Debt Conversion Bonds) do not involve the provision of new money to the emerging country, but are similar to New Money bonds in that they are floating, and amortize. Unlike Discount bonds, they do not have any form of guarantee.
Countries include: Brazil, Mexico, Philippines, Poland, Uruguay, Venezuela.

Figure 2.3   Generic types of Brady bonds

different names. However, all Brady plans tend to include all or many of the bond types set out in Figure 2.3 as part of their structure.

2.4.3 The Brady Market

There are three aspects of Brady bonds within the description above that deserve special attention as they are often overlooked. There is a popular misconception that all Brady bonds are very long dated. First, whilst many Brady bonds have long maturities, there are also many short and medium dated issues. Secondly, there is no set coupon structure to Brady bonds. Bradys can be either floating or fixed rate, or have a step-up structure. For example, in the J.P. Morgan Brady Bond Index of liquid Bradys, 53 per cent are floating rate and 47 per cent have fixed coupons. This does not prevent a common methodology for valuation between them being developed, as described below. Lastly, a common misconception is that all Brady bonds are collateralized with US Treasuries. Whilst this innovation was a distinguishing feature of the original Brady plan, many of the bonds issued under such plans, including one bond issued under the original Mexico plan, do not have US collateral. The absence or presence of US collateral is not a determining factor of whether a bond is a Brady bond, only its genesis within a Brady Plan matters. How much collateral is needed to ensure a successful restructuring is a matter for negotiation in each case.

The vast majority of Brady bonds are US dollar denominated, but there are small amounts of illiquid Brady bonds in a range of other developed currencies such as French francs, Deutschmarks, and Italian lira. Once more the key is the original deal between the lending banks and the borrowers. Most money was lent in US dollars, but banks lent to emerging countries in other currencies as well, and those loans have been converted into Bradys denominated into different currencies according to the original loans. Another limitation of the Brady market is that, despite the addition of Russia, the universe of assets remains very heavily weighted towards Latin America (around 84 per cent of outstanding Bradys).

There is some debate as to how many countries have completed "Brady" plans. This is because a number of countries that defaulted in the 1980s have completed similar forms of restructuring inspired by Brady negotiations, but have not relied specifically upon a Brady-style collateralized bond to complete their negotiations. We have relied upon the widely followed J.P. Morgan Broad Brady Index to show the current composition of the Brady market (Figure 2.4).

There are a number of other countries with very small Brady plans, resulting in fairly illiquid bonds, or that have restructured outstanding debt similar in nature to Brady debt, albeit that the debt was not formally created under a Brady plan. This debt is usually traded by the same desk as Brady bonds and Brady bond portfolios will often be allowed to buy this debt too. The countries with such debt include Bolivia, Colombia, Costa Rica, Croatia, Morocco, Slovenia, and Uruguay.

Prior to the growth in Eurobond issuance by emerging countries and a surge in interest in local markets, Brady bonds were the key fixed income benchmark trading vehicle for emerging markets investors. In Section 2.1 the relative changes in trading volumes that have occurred in emerging market bonds as reported by the EMTA were discussed. It will be seen that between 1991 and 1993 Brady bonds were dominant. However, since then they have been falling off in relative importance as other sources of financing have become available to the rehabilitated countries. The decline in importance of the Brady

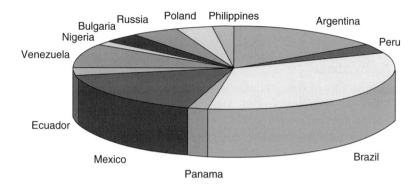

Figure 2.4 Composition of the Brady market

market has been accelerated by a programme of buybacks by several of the issuers. For example, in the third quarter of 1997, before market conditions deteriorated Argentina, Venezuela and Panama issued almost US$7bn in exchanges, Mexico and Brazil having previously carried out large exchange programmes.

The incentive for the buybacks is the anomaly of a wide disparity between the spread offered by the same credit in the same maturity in the Brady and the Eurobond markets that existed for many years. Eurobonds habitually traded on far tighter spreads than the stripped spreads of Bradys[11] of the same countries with similar maturities despite Brady bonds at that time offering far greater liquidity than the equivalent Eurobonds. Only relatively recently have the spreads begun to converge. No really convincing explanation was offered during the time when the anomaly was at its greatest. The anomaly still exists, albeit that it is now much smaller and is acknowledged to be such. The best, but still unconvincing, explanation available was that different investors and market-makers participated in the Brady and Eurobond markets, and were not prepared to be involved in the other market, hence the arbitrage was not exploited. It is the case that some US investors refuse to buy Eurobonds, perceiving them to be illiquid. There continue to be European buyers of Eurobonds, especially private individuals, who for tax reasons do not wish to own paper with a US treasury component that was registered, and are uncomfortable with the longer maturities of many Brady bonds.

The credit spread between Bradys and Eurobonds is a case of a genuine anomaly that has lasted some years, proving that there is still room for market imperfection! As investors and market-makers did not arbitrage the spread differential it was left to the issuers themselves to do so. The issuers have tightened the spread of their Brady bonds through buyback programmes, issuing long dated Eurobonds at tighter spreads to fund their purchases. As the supply of Eurobonds increases, the spread will widen to the point where it is no longer attractive to swap Bradys for Euros. So far, market conditions have been sufficiently favourable to allow several buybacks; however, the strategy is, of course, dependent upon market conditions being sufficiently favourable to be able to complete transactions without undue disturbance.

2.4.4 Analysing Brady Bonds

Those Brady bonds with no US treasury collateral guaranteeing either the principal or the income require no special form of analysis. They are similar to any other single credit bond. The usual measures of duration, average life, convexity, yield to maturity, and spread over benchmark government curves can be applied. In the case of bonds with sinking funds or partial grace periods, the cashflow adjustments can be made as with any other bond with similar features. A comparison of yields between fixed and floating rate bonds can be made in a similar way to that used for other bonds, swapping the cashflows so that either a fixed rate bond can be evaluated relative to Libor, or, as is the more usual convention for Bradys, the floating rate bonds can be swapped to fixed so that spreads over fixed benchmarks can be calculated.

Brady bonds with partial or total US Treasury capital or income guarantees require additional analysis, but this is less complicated than might appear to be the case at first sight. A great deal of misinformed mythology has grown up around the analysis of Brady bonds. For simplicity's sake, all references to Brady bonds in the rest of this section will be taken to mean Bradys with some form of US collateral. The overriding principle is that any measure that can be applied to a conventional bond can be applied twice to a Brady bond, once to the whole bond with the blended US and emerging market credit, and once to the emerging market component stripped of the US collateral. Thus a bond with collateral has a blended yield to maturity for the whole bond, but also a stripped yield to maturity. The stripped yield is calculated as the yield to maturity on the cost of the bond less the net present value of the portion that is in US Treasuries. Expressed properly:

$$\text{stripped yield} = \text{sovereign interest cash flows} + \text{sovereign principal cash flows}$$

$$= \sum_{i=1}^{r} \frac{\text{coupon}_i}{(1 + \text{stripped yield})^i} + \frac{100}{(1 + \text{stripped yield})^r}$$

A cashflow yield can also be expressed as a blended or stripped yield. All other measures such as duration and convexity can also be measured on either a stripped or blended basis, the different measures being taken simply by excluding the value of the US treasury component. In the case of floating Bradys, a comparison between fixed and floating Bradys can be made by swapping cashflows from floating to fixed in exactly the same way as any other bond. If the treasury component has been excluded, then the swapped cashflows are known as "stripped swapped spreads". Stripped swapped spreads allow the comparison on a stripped basis of floating and fixed Bradys in order to ensure a common basis for analysis in order to produce a single stripped yield curve.

Another unusual feature of Brady bonds is not only that there is a blended credit, but that the credit mix is sensitive to market movement and changes over time. All of the above calculations need to be recalibrated every time there is a movement in either the price of the Brady bond or the US Treasury market. As with any other securities, time has an effect upon the calculations, but there is also one effect of time that is unique to blended Brady bonds. The collateral, in the form of zeros, is increasing steadily in value, and the emerging market component of the bonds is falling even in a stationary market environment. Figure 2.5 provides a simple illustration of the changing credit blend of Mexican par bonds from issuance to maturity.

Note that, as in all bond calculations, a discount factor has to be chosen for net present values, and the choice of factor affects the values. In this case prevailing rates at the time of issuance were used. As rates change, the predicted credit mix of the Brady bond will change. As maturity nears, there will be almost no emerging market risk in the

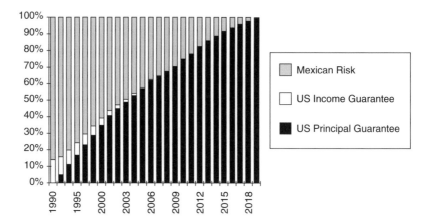

Figure 2.5   Credit risk profile of Mexican par bonds

bond, and most of the credit will be the US Treasury collateral. Over the short term this effect is not significant, but for long-term holders of the debt a misleading impression of excessively favourable performance through spread tightening might be given. In fact, the spread might simply be tightening to reflect the increasing weight of the higher of the two credits within the security.

Changes in the credit blend due to market movements give rise to an additional set of measurements that should be looked at when evaluating Bradys. In the case of a typical single credit bond any movement in price, and therefore yield to maturity, feeds straight through to the calculation of the spread over a government benchmark, the treasury being assumed to be a constant. In this case there are two moving parts. A change in the price of the blended Brady might be due either to a movement in the US Treasury market, which will change the value of the collateral within the bond, or to a movement in the credit spread notwithstanding a constant US Treasury market. An investor will therefore wish to know the sensitivity of a Brady to both the US Treasury market (not least if he is intending to hedge the treasury risk of the Brady) and to changes in the credit spread. Two Brady bonds with the same maturity and coupon for the same country could have different responsiveness to treasuries and to changes in credit spread if the collateral component was different for each bond. It is therefore desirable to consider separately the price change sensitivity of the collateral and of the underlying emerging market credit, i.e. to calculate maturity, duration, and convexity separately for each element. There are thus two durations, convexities, and so on for a blended Brady bond, representing each component of the security.

Table 2.3 summarizes the key measures for assessing Brady bonds with collateral.

While a range of measurements for blended Bradys on a "stripped" basis has been created, owing to the prospectus provisions it is not possible actually to strip Bradys into their component parts. There is an express ban on stripping in the documentation of Bradys, otherwise this would have been done long ago. Indeed, one of the reasons that Brady-for-Eurobond exchanges have succeeded is that the investor is offered an opportunity to acquire pure emerging market risk similar or identical to that contained within the Brady bond without having to pay for the US zero. An exchange is the only means of achieving this.

Table 2.3 Summary of measurements for Brady bonds with collateral

Blended cashflow yield	Yield/Total price of the Brady bond
Blended yield to maturity	Discounted value of all the cashflows/Total price
Swapped yield to maturity	Swapped floating cashflows to fixed for comparison across Bradys
Treasury duration	Sensitivity to interest rate changes
Treasury convexity	First derivative of duration
Blended spread over treasuries	Spread of total bond over benchmark
Stripped cashflow yield	Collateralized or uncollateralized coupon stream/Total price − value of collateral
Stripped yield to maturity	Discounted value of all cashflows, either collateralized or uncollateralized/Total price − value of collateral
Credit or stripped duration	Sensitivity of the bond to changes in credit spread
Credit or stripped convexity	First derivative of credit duration, i.e. changing sensitivity to credit spread as credit spread alters
Stripped spread	Spread of bond based upon yield to maturity of bond stripped of US Treasury collateral component

2.4.5 Evaluating Default Risk

The methodology for the evaluation of default risk in the case of single credit bonds is a long established practice that credit agencies and investors alike have developed over many years, and about which much has been written. In recent years credit analysis has had to evolve to find a way of evaluating bonds backed by letter of credit guarantees, asset backed securities, and even securities backed by pools of other securities. However, none of these structures fits Brady bonds particularly well. Moreover, conventional credit ratings, whilst they do exist for Brady bonds, are not adequate by themselves because they do not capture the extremes of the different credits within the blend of the bond. Stripped spreads fluctuate greatly, but the need to fall back upon the US Treasury component depends upon a discrete rather than continuous risk, i.e. default of the emerging market borrower. A Brady credit structure is very different from the others mentioned; it does not rely upon over-collateralization or cross guarantees, just two credits alongside each other. In order to cope with these peculiarities two forms of analysis have become widely used:

- breakeven payback and
- default probability analysis.

We look at each in turn.

(i) Breakeven payback

This method takes into account the payment being made for a Brady bond over the value of the collateral within it, and then considers the length of time required for the coupon payments to remain current in order to ensure that the investor is paid back for any premium that he has paid over the value of the collateral (Table 2.4).

This method of analysis is less commonly used now than it was, for example in mid-1995, when low Brady bond prices resulted in several Bradys being priced relatively

Table 2.4   Example of breakeven payback

	Price	Value of US Treasury	Emerging Market "Premium"	Breakeven Payback
Argentina Par 03/23*	72.3	22.5	49.8	7.7 years
Poland Par 10/24**	62	20.5	41.5	11.5 years

*Coupon rises annually in 0.25 per cent steps from 5 per cent in 3/96 to a stable 6 per cent from 3/99.
**Coupon rises from 3 per cent to 10/99, 3.5 per cent to 10/00, 3.75 per cent to 10/03, 4 per cent to 10/14, 5 per cent thereafter.

closely to the value of the collateral, and breakevens were as short as one or two coupon payments. Provided an investor believed that the country would be able to meet the next payments, he was buying longer term emerging credit risk as a free option on the value of the collateral. The examples shown here highlight how breakeven analysis can produce counterintuitive answers. The investor pays considerably more for the Argentina par than the Poland par, but gains only two points of additional Treasury collateral. The Poland par has longer emerging market risk when measured by the breakeven payback method than the Argentina par, despite appearances. The breakeven payback methodology also gives a very different answer; indeed, almost an inverse answer, for country risk compared with the more conventionally examined stripped swapped spreads. In the example above Argentina's stripped swapped spread is around 300 basis points (bps) more than Poland's. In other words, the investor is being paid far less to take Poland country risk, or, put another way, the payback period for Poland is much longer.

(ii) Default Probability Analysis

Default probability analysis (DPA) is a large and difficult topic, the implications of which stretch far beyond Brady bonds. However, the application of the various DPA models are of particular interest in this case because of the unique structure of Brady bonds. According to the model and inputs used, at one extreme, as with breakeven analysis, only the AAA Treasury component has a true value, the rest is little more than an option. Breakeven payback analysis is implicitly applying a simple binomial model of either default or no default. At the other extreme, if a model suggests little probability of default, then Bradys may still be very undervalued relative to similarly rated single credit bonds. More sophisticated models seek to attribute a probability of default upon the basis of past statistical experience. Many variables can be built into the model, perhaps the most important being the initial credit rating of the credit being considered.[12] The most thorough analysis of the implications of credit default to date has been carried out as part of the development of RiskMetrics[TM], sponsored by J.P. Morgan and others to which the reader is referred for a more detailed discussion.

2.4.6 Income Guarantees

One feature of some of the blended Brady bonds that makes them more difficult to evaluate is a partial income guarantee. The exact nature of the guarantee varies considerably, and the details need to be checked separately in relation to each bond. Typically the income guarantee period is for the next 6–18 months, rolling forward as each coupon date is successfully met. In the case of the Mexican par bond, for example, there is a rolling guarantee of 18 months' worth of coupon income, which was represented in Figure 2.5

by the middle segment in the columns for the early years. For simplicity's sake, the rolling income guarantee was shown as having diminishing future value, but in fact this representation is questionable. The correct method of evaluation of a rolling guarantee has been the subject of some controversy. The diminishing future value method undervalues the income guarantee. Whilst the guarantee is only for a limited number of payments, it rolls for the life of the bond, so arguably holds a constant future value as long as the coupon is constant.

Another way of evaluating the income option, especially in the case of a floating coupon, is to treat the enhancement of the income as an option, always at the money, but with a changing strike price. The criticism of this treatment, as with all option adjusted spread analysis, is that a future interest rate scenario evaluation is such a subjective exercise, and given that the total value of the underlying option is small (i.e. the number of coupon payments guaranteed), that the exercise is simply not meaningful. The most extreme version of this argument is to ignore the value of the income guarantee.[13] Such a view is somewhat defeatist. Intuitively there is clearly a value to the income guarantee, and some estimate, however subjective and imprecise, is better than systematically undervaluing Bradys with an income guarantee. Most evaluation models used by market participants do attribute some value to the income guarantee, although all agree that the correct value is low.

2.4.7 Trading Strategies Exclusive To Brady Bonds

(i) Nominal Price Range Trading

This is becoming less fashionable as the sophistication of the market is increasing and valuing Brady bonds by spread is becoming the standard. However, price volatility is sometimes still sufficiently high that there are periods when spreads have little meaning and traders will assess relative value by nominal prices. For example, in 1994 Venezuelan and Nigerian par bonds were trading within a two-point range relative to each other, both countries having a high degree of dependency on oil. For some while traders sought to trade that range. Of course this strategy is subject to the obvious hazard that fundamentals cause a shift in the range. Argentina pars versus Brazilian pars is another example of a pair of bonds that are similarly priced at the time of writing, therefore traders are watching the price relationship closely.

(ii) "Drop Dead" Trading

The unique nature of Brady bonds has given rise to a number of strategies that could not be developed for other markets. When the early Brady countries were negotiating their plans the only way that it was possible for investors to take a view on the likely outcome of the negotiations was through the purchase or shorting of loans which would be turned into Brady bonds in the event of a successful outcome, with all the settlement difficulties thereby entailed. For the later countries the market developed when-and-if trading for Bradys, similar in concept to grey market trading in the Eurobond market, but with the twist of a "drop dead" date, i.e. if a plan was not completed by a specific date then all when-and-if trades were cancelled. This addition was necessary because in the case of Eurobonds there is a pre-announced date for the bond to be issued, whereas in the case of Brady negotiations the date for completion as well as the outcome was unknown.

(iii) Trading the Oil Warrants

Several Brady bonds of oil rich countries such as Mexico and Venezuela were issued with attached oil warrants as an additional sweetener for the creditor banks. The usual market convention was to trade and settle any warrants attaching to a particular bond automatically as part of the bond bought and sold. For a brief period one market-maker attempted to accumulate the outstanding oil warrants by accepting delivery of them, but failing to deliver them upon sale of the bond. This practice has since ceased after discussion among the market-makers.

2.5 EUROBONDS

2.5.1 History

Eurobonds are only a viable option for emerging countries that are experiencing some degree of economic success. A country in default on its obligations will find that the international capital markets are generally closed to it until such time as a satisfactory agreement has been reached on the outstanding defaulted debt and a suitable rehabilitation period has ensued. Borrowers have traditionally accorded higher priority to ensuring continued service of their outstanding Eurobonds than of their bank loans. Thus, for example, Venezuela's outstanding Eurobonds never defaulted, although its bank debt required a major Brady restructuring.[14] The policy reasons for this are unclear; the priority seems to have been based on a notion that more opprobrium would follow from a formal default on a quoted and traded bond than "renegotiating" the terms of a bank loan, and that memories of a formal bond default would last longer.[15] Thus, for example, the Eurobond market was closed to Latin American sovereigns between 1988 and the early 1990s when first Mexico and subsequently other Latin countries began to issue debt once more.

Historically the pattern of issuance for countries that have defaulted has been to begin with a relatively short dated issue of fairly limited size to "test the waters". These issues would consequently have limited liquidity, and be almost in the nature of private placements. Gradually longer and larger issues were introduced as investor demand grew. Over time a full credit yield curve was developed, and liquidity rose. Concurrently there was another pattern of issuance for those emerging countries that had not defaulted on their debt, but were regarded as emerging simply because of lack of international familiarity with the local economies. A number of then comparatively highly rated Asian countries issued Eurobonds and Yankees as part of their financing programmes complementing their domestic funding programmes which, at that time, were only accessible to domestic investors. The pattern of issuance was more opportunistic than reflecting a substantial need to raise funds. As the domestic currencies were fixed to the US dollar, or a basket including a large US dollar component, there was little foreign currency risk for the government in issuing US dollar paper.

2.5.2 A Changing Role

In the last three years there has been a radical change in borrowing patterns within the Eurobond market on behalf of emerging market borrowers. Much greater weight has been put on the desirability of creating benchmark bonds, and even curves which are highly visible to borrower and investor alike as a measure of the relative credit judgements between the countries and as a way of measuring progress. A key requirement of a benchmark is liquidity, therefore even the first issues of new sovereign borrowers are comparatively large, typically with a maturity of five years or longer, as shorter dated bonds tend to trade less well due to the bid/offer spread impacting the yield of the bond by a greater amount.

A number of countries who have not needed to raise money have issued bonds solely for prestige and benchmarking issues. The successful launch of a Eurobond issue is seen as an important landmark in the development of an emerging country, signifying the maturing of a country to the point where it can access international capital markets. For this reason there are now a considerable number of smaller countries with just one or two Eurobonds outstanding issued for these reasons, whereas three years ago only the very largest emerging countries had Eurobonds outstanding. The first issues in particular can be priced very attractively for the borrowing country as investors compete strongly to purchase bonds of a new sovereign in order to show diversification within their portfolios.

There are two other factors that have encouraged sovereign Eurobond issuance. While there are examples of Eurobonds being issued by corporates domiciled in a particular country but no issuance by the sovereign (Chile, Taiwan), it is generally easier for corporates to issue, and to achieve tighter spreads, when there is a sovereign benchmark for comparison. Governments have therefore issued Eurobonds in order to assist their own private sector to issue in the Eurobond markets. The second factor arises from the arbitrage, already described in greater depth in the first section, between Brady and Eurobond credit spreads, the latter being historically much tighter than the former. As governments have arbitraged that differential they have needed to issue Eurobonds in order to raise the money to pay for the Brady bonds. This has encouraged both larger and longer issues in order to ensure duration matches the retired Bradys.

In an earlier version of this chapter[3] we indicated that caution should be exercised in respect of liquidity and credit judgement expectations for emerging markets bonds. Both of those provisos are still appropriate, albeit that in neither case do the warnings need to be as strongly expressed as previously. During the 1997 Korean crisis liquidity in the benchmark Eurobonds and Bradys disappeared in a similar fashion. Spreads widened and dealing sizes lessened in both cases, but there was little to choose between them. Unsurprisingly the smaller, less liquid issues of less well known names became completely illiquid. However, this is no different from the behaviour to be expected generally in the Eurobond market in times of severe market disruption. Large liquid benchmarks command premium pricing precisely because they are more likely to retain their liquidity during difficult periods.

It often remains more difficult to analyse corporate credit in emerging countries than in developed countries because of the lack of consistency in reporting standards, but the task is no more difficult than in the case of many lower quality credits in developed markets. In the case of sovereign credit analysis, as we have described elsewhere, political risk is far more important relative to economic risk, but beyond this there is no substantial difference.

2.6 THE ROLE OF CREDIT CURVES

2.6.1 Using Credit Curves

Developed bond markets have benchmark government curves; other credits in the same currency trade at levels of spread to the benchmark curve. The benchmark curve itself is shaped by a mixture of market expectations of fundamental economic and political developments and technical factors in the marketplace. Of increasing importance has been the development of credit curves. The larger non-government credits may have outstanding bonds of several maturities, each trading at a different spread to the equivalent maturity benchmark bond. It thus becomes possible to draw a "credit curve", i.e. a curve of the spreads offered at various maturities by that borrower. The credit curve too will be shaped by a mixture of market expectations, in this case about the expected improvement or deterioration of the credit, and technicals such as supply and demand for the bonds at the various maturities. The same methods can be used to develop generic credit curves showing, for example, what liquid AA or A bonds yield as a spread over the government benchmark at various maturities along the curve. Credit curves provide both a benchmark and an indicator of value for individual bonds against the curve.

The paucity of bonds in different maturities made it almost impossible to produce meaningful credit curves for emerging market debt. Traditional Brady plans often created very short dated or floating rate paper and extremely long maturity bonds. There was almost no paper of intermediate maturity in between. The lack of maturity spread together with technical supply and demand factors affecting individual bonds which might be the sole representative of the 7–10 year sector of the curve made it very difficult to create systematic credit curves providing a true picture of yield enhancement for a given credit along a curve. Historically this was not a cause for concern, emerging market securities traded in a sufficiently volatile manner according to their own dynamics that there was little scientific relationship to curves. A particular piece of information would trigger as large a price reaction in floating rate instruments as in long dated fixed rate bonds.

The creation of benchmark Eurobonds in a number of the countries at various points along the yield curve has led to an improved ability to analyse credit curve shapes in a much more accurate manner. However, it is still the case that for the vast majority of borrowers there are still too few bonds of greatly varying liquidity to be able to construct more than impressionistic curves. Whilst early attempts to apply yield curve spline models of the type in common usage in developed government markets have been made in emerging markets, the gaps in curve issuance and liquidity are still too great to allow more than indicative curves to be created. It is also the case that whilst the gap between Brady and Eurobonds has narrowed considerably, there is still a sufficiently large differential that in the case of some countries there are effectively two credit curves, one for Brady bonds and one for Eurobonds. However, the impetus towards reliable credit curves is strong, given the explosive growth of credit derivatives and asset swapping, both of which employ credit curve modelling as an integral part of pricing credit.

2.6.2 Analysing Credit Curves

Figure 2.6 plots indicative derivative credit curves for Russia and Mexico. Scatter points rather than smoothed curves have been used to demonstrate how few bonds have been used to create these "curves". In the case of Brady bonds, stripped yields are used to compare pure credit.

The shape of the two credit curves is strikingly different. The Mexican curve has a typical positive slope; the greater the duration of the credit exposure the greater the incremental yield offered for exposure to Mexico. At very long maturities the credit curve becomes inverse. This is fairly common behaviour. The difference between, for example, 10- and 30-year credit exposure is relatively theoretical, and the incremental risk is more

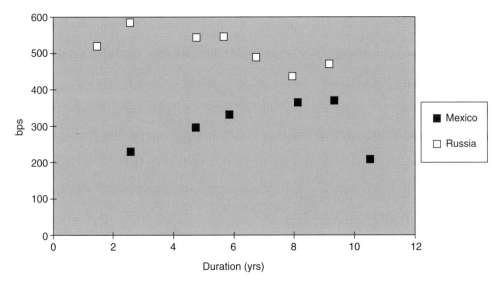

Figure 2.6   Credit spread curves

than counterbalanced by the relative rarity of paper and the desire of investors bullish on a specific credit to buy as long credit duration as they are able to.[12] In the case of Russia the credit curve is flatter, almost random. In this case the curve is a reflection of the relative liquidity as much as any fundamental consideration. For example, the Minfin 5 issue is twice the size of Minfin 6; this degree of additional liquidity commands a significant premium, despite the credit duration of the bond being slightly longer.

2.6.3 Trading Credit Curve Shapes

Credit curve shapes can be exploited in several different ways. The most obvious is simply to take the view that a credit curve within one country is too steep or too flat. A more sophisticated strategy is to arbitrage shapes between credits that the investor perceives to be similar. If, for example, the investor regards Brazil and Argentina as similar, but Brazil has a much flatter credit curve than Argentina, then the investor may chose to put in place a box trade, as given in Table 2.5.

Of course, while the trade may look theoretically attractive the difference may exist for good technical reasons, such as relative supply and liquidity in different parts of the curve. The investor may take the view that in recent years emerging country governments have been increasingly nimble at exploiting inefficiencies in their own credit curves through activities such as the Brady buybacks. If Argentina has a much flatter curve than Brazil because

Table 2.5   Credit curve shape box trade

		Credit Duration	Credit Spread
Short	Brazil Par ZL	7.58 yr	498 bps
Long	Brazil IDU	1.45 yr	358 bps
Short	Arg 10.95% 99	1.73 yr	205 bps
Long	Arg Par	7.55 yr	483 bps

Brazil has far more long dated paper as a result of the size and the structure of its Brady plan, then Argentina may decide to issue more very long dated paper, thereby exploiting the opportunity to roll out the maturity of its debt at relatively little incremental cost.

A third strategy is to take a view on curve shapes driven by technicals versus fundamentals. For example, the fundamentally driven investor may believe that there is a major credit risk at one year, say because of a large roll of short dated debt, but that provided the country survives this, the prospects are very good. However, the curve of the country may have a conventionally shaped positive slope rather than the negative slope that would be implied by this view.

There is also the possibility of exploiting credit curve shapes for hedging arbitrage purposes. If the credit spreads of two countries are highly correlated but the curve shapes very different, then credit exposure in one country at a given duration might be successfully hedged through shorting the credit duration on the other country's credit curve. Dependent upon the relative shapes of the curves, this might offer a cheap alternative to hedging than hedging along the same credit curve.

2.7 LOCAL MARKETS AND EMERGING MARKET CURRENCIES

We have retitled this section from the previous edition to include currencies. Many market participants perceive investing in local emerging markets as driven primarily by currency considerations. Most studies of risk show currency volatility to be the largest source of risk to investing in international bond markets.

2.7.1 The Role of Local Markets in the Investing Cycle

Investment in local bond and money markets has grown sharply in relative importance during the last two years. The nature of involvement with those markets has also changed. Whereas involvement in the local markets would typically represent only the final stage of investment in fixed income emerging markets after Bradys and Eurobonds, many participants who do not purchase Bradys or Eurobonds will buy local markets debt.

As the developed fixed income markets have become more highly correlated the search for new fixed income assets that offer better diversification has driven investors towards local markets. Within Europe, EMU has already led to far less volatility and therefore a reduction in spread trading opportunities between the government bonds of developed countries. Cross market spread traders have therefore looked increasingly towards local emerging markets for diversification. A specific incentive for investing in local bond markets of countries such as the Czech Republic and Hungary is that they are seen as the next convergence play in the process of EMU. Investors have seen massive spread compression, and therefore outperformance, of the debt of countries such as Italy and Spain, and the reduction in volatility of those markets relative to the lower yielding core markets of Europe such as Germany. The Czech Republic, Poland, Hungary, Slovenia, Estonia, and Cyprus have been invited to commence talks to be in the next round to join the EU, and maybe EMU within three years of joining the EU. The local debt markets of those countries could see the same convergence in yields to the much lower yielding core of developed Europe in much the same way as occurred in the less highly rated developed European countries.

Other considerations have also assisted the cause of local markets. There continues to be a substantial constituency of investors who wish to buy only government bonds, even those with lower ratings, notwithstanding that there may be many corporate or supranational issues that are more highly rated, and in the case of the larger corporates may be larger entities than some of the smaller countries. The rationale for this is presumably a belief that governments are inherently less likely to default on their debt or be allowed to fail, regardless of their credit rating. Those investors are increasing the universe of government bonds that they are willing to buy. Several of the major index providers have added emerging market local government bond indices in an effort to create a more truly universal government bond index.

The universe of investable local bond markets has expanded very rapidly. The large number of investors willing to buy local debt has in turn encouraged emerging markets governments to speed up the process of creation and development of the local markets. The list of countries with local markets is long and includes some very exotic names, although many of these markets are still in the earliest stages of development.[5] The stage of development that has to be reached by an emerging country before it is able to sponsor and develop a functioning bond market has become progressively earlier in its economic and business cycle. However, there are still large differences between the liquidity, volatility, and other characteristics of different local markets.[16]

Investment in local bond and money markets tends to lag local equity investment. Within fixed income the sequence of hard currency investment first and local market investment later that used to be the standard has broken down, and indeed reversed. All else being equal, there are good policy reasons why sovereign borrowers might have a natural preference for borrowing in their own rather than another currency. These include the avoidance of currency risk on state borrowing, and the promotion of a domestic financial sector. Both jobs and prestige flow from establishing a local capital market capable of funding government borrowing. While the cost of borrowing will be determined by local market conditions, local currency debt will tend to be more highly rated by the credit agencies than foreign currency debt, the justification for this that is always given is that a government can always print enough of its own currency to avoid a default on its own local debt, an option not available on debt issued in the currency of another country. As many investment mandates employ credit rating agencies as their main limiting factor, the higher rating for locally issued debt enables the borrower potentially to access investors who might not otherwise be able to consider purchase of their debt. Albeit that those investors will have to consider the additional currency risk.

Not all emerging countries, however, have encouraged the growth of local currency bond markets. Some have actively discouraged them and have either banned foreign investment outright or made it very unattractive. Asian countries, in particular, often adopted this policy before the 1997 crisis, fearing that foreign flows into their local markets would detract from their ability to maintain a constant exchange rate against the US dollar. The perception was that the financing needs of both the government and local enterprise could be fully met by domestic portfolio flows, and that foreigners purchasing short dated maturity bonds in particular were doing so only for the purposes of currency speculation. This policy worked for a long time in achieving the objective of a stable exchange rate but allowed progressively greater inefficiencies and currency misvaluations to occur, leading eventually to the large dislocations in Asia during 1997. One of the key requirements of the IMF rescue package for South Korea has been the opening up of the large domestic bond market to foreign investment flows. The mismanagement of the maturity profile of Asian sovereign debt is considered separately in Section 2.10.

It may appear strange that emerging countries that have issued debt in their own currency have continued to fund aggressively through foreign currency borrowings. Yet this option has proved attractive for several countries. Local currency emerging debt markets often commence as small and illiquid (see below). Even though a local currency market may exist, it may not have sufficient capacity to absorb the host government's debt issuance programme. Some countries have maintained barriers seeking to ensure that the local market is only for domestic investors. Emerging countries have been anxious to establish a borrower profile in the high profile international hard currency debt markets, either to create name familiarity or to signal a return to international markets following a period of default or renegotiation of debt. As well as the prestige in demonstrating the ability to access international markets, these issues provide a benchmark for the sovereign credit and against which corporate issues are able to borrow. There have been many instances of corporate borrowers issuing without there being an outstanding sovereign issue from the country in which the corporate is domiciled. However, an outstanding sovereign issue makes pricing and assessing relative value easier for both borrowers and investors.

2.7.2 The Character of Local Emerging Debt Markets

The evolution of local debt markets has followed a strikingly similar pattern across the world. The first and often only issuing credit for some time will be the government or government agencies in a country. Borrowings are usually in the form of Treasury bills at first. Gradually issued maturities lengthen, although initially the size of the longer dated issues tends to be much smaller, and the longer dated bills consequently less liquid. Over time the government begins to issue bonds. These are generally taken to mean securities longer than one year and issued at par with a coupon rather than at a discount, but there is no strict rule about this. Mexico, for example, has issued two year Treasury bills. Over time the bond market grows in depth and liquidity, a full yield curve develops, and eventually derivatives and futures develop as well.

Two forms of common interim development towards the creation of a local market are either bonds linked to, or partially or wholly repayable in, foreign currencies, or index linked bonds. In the past Mexico has issued bonds linked to the US dollar and Greece has issued local bonds linked to the ECU. Many emergent countries experience periods of high inflation and currency weakness, hence the need for the reassuring external link. Examples of index linked bonds can be found in Israel or Chile. In countries such as Chile regulations demanding high levels of pensions savings, most or all of which have to be invested domestically, have also helped to encourage the development of local markets.

Corporate and other non-governmental borrowers will gradually enter the market. The largest and best known names will be first, followed by a broader range of borrowers. Private placement of debt rather than fully public offerings is often the first stage of a non-governmental market developing. Small issues are placed with knowledgeable investors familiar with the credit who are happy to receive the incremental yield offered by the poorly known credit, and are not too concerned about liquidity. Corporate credit assessment of local emerging markets borrowers is often much more difficult than in developed countries. Most corporates will be unrated by the major credit agencies; local credit ratings agencies will apply their own standards. Accounting practices may be very different from those adopted in developed markets, and regulation may be poor or non-existent. Frequently potential buyers of local emerging markets debt will turn to their equity colleagues for help as equity investors are often more familiar with assessing the worth of an enterprise on poor or incomplete information.

There is another type of "emerging" bond market. There are large, liquid bond markets, sometimes of large and reasonably rated countries, that are referred to as "emerging" because it has not yet or is only beginning to open to international investment. For example, South Africa's bond market is far beyond the developmental stage described above. There is a full maturity liquid yield curve, futures, and derivatives. There are many market-makers, and bid/offer spreads are similar to those in developed government bond markets. Local debt is rated as investment grade, at BBB. The market is referred to as "emerging" because for many years foreigners were entitled to buy South African debt but refrained from doing so because of anti-apartheid sanctions applied in many countries. The Korean bond market is capitalized at around US$150bn, twice the size of Ireland's market, and four times the size of New Zealand's. Even when Korea was rated A+ the market was referred to as "emerging". The market was not open to foreigners; only the Korean crisis of November 1997 forced an announcement that in time foreigners would be allowed to buy up to 30 per cent of that market.

As in the case of Korea, many emerging countries have sought to resist external investment in their local bond markets. Malaysia and Taiwan are other examples. There are more subtle forms of restriction than outright bans. Disadvantageous or discriminatory tax treatment is common. Awkward registration, custody, or settlements procedures represent another obstacle. Of course these barriers may not be intentional, merely the result of inefficiency. However, there is often more tardiness in lifting restrictions than can be justified by efficiency arguments. Delays can also be motivated by, for example, a desire to protect the local broking community from outside competition for a longer period in order to provide them with as long a lead time as possible to update to external standards. Overregulation, often not addressing the correct issues, tends to be symptomatic of emerging markets.

2.7.3 Russia — A Case Study

While specific countries have been used as illustrations throughout, there has not been a focus on specific countries, but rather the framework behind country allocation. In the case of local markets, they are as varied as the countries themselves. It was felt appropriate to make an exception and provide a short case study on Russia because it has the potential to become the largest bond market, but is currently a long way from that. The fragmented development of the market across such a large federal state makes it particularly fascinating. Indeed, a number of investment banks with heavy Western involvement that are dedicated solely to exploiting the opportunities offered by the emergent Russian markets have already been set up.

At the federal level there is a large market in federal bills, known as GKOs, estimated at around US$55bn in outstanding. Foreigners first became involved in early 1996, and are estimated to hold up to US$20bn, a rate of growth that is truly remarkable. GKOs are very actively traded. Less well known has been the growth since 1995 of a municipal bills market issued by regions and cities. These are typically six months in maturity, although maturities as long as three years have been issued. The best estimate of the size of the bills market is around US$2bn. Certain cities and regions will be allowed to borrow in their own right on the international markets as well. A further US$2bn market is developing from the securitization of debt owed by various agricultural regions, thus creating a third specialized domestic market. Yet another market is opening up in instruments called "Veksels". Veksels are trade bills, sometimes guaranteed by banks, between enterprises that have been created in order to maintain trade during the massive restructurings of the mid-1990s. It is estimated that there is an astonishing US$12–15bn of these bills in existence. Corporates are in the process of converting these to corporate bonds within the context of more formal debt management programmes rather than the *ad hoc* issuance that has occurred in the past.

The pace of change and of growth of the Russian domestic debt markets should be seen in the context of very poor domestic credit information on the majority of the issuers. Researchers are catching up the marketplace as rapidly as they can but the magnitude of the task is considerable. In the public sector alone there are 21 republics and more than 50 regions, each of which needs to be assessed. As these markets develop it will become possible to develop sectorial relative value models so as to allocate and switch between corporates, agro bonds, and municipal bonds as well as to choose individual credits in the same way that many US managers allocate between mortgages, agencies, and corporates.[17]

2.7.4 Strategic Uses for Investing in Local Markets

Given the considerable difficulties encountered in local markets, it is necessary to consider the right place for local market investment in the spectrum of emerging market fixed income investment. Simple credit judgements on emerging countries can, for example, be far more easily taken through hard currency bonds. There are at least five reasons for utilizing local market securities:

1. An expectation of appreciation of the local currency.
2. Expected slower depreciation of the currency than is factored in by the interest rate differentials between the local bond market and a single or basket of other currency denominated bond markets.
3. Belief that local interest rates will fall due to any of the range of economic factors that can move interest rates.
4. Expected change in the term structure as implied by the yield curve in a particular bond market.
5. Diversification from other bond markets within a portfolio.

None of them is any different from the reasons that might be cited by an investor in OECD bonds for choosing to invest in or overweight one developed bond market versus another. However, there tends to be greater emphasis on the currency component and less on the interest rate element than is the case for developed markets. In keeping with the greater volatility of emerging markets resulting from smaller size as well as genuinely more volatile underlying fundamentals, the effects of any change in the factors that affect bond markets are often exaggerated compared with the effects that similar information would have in developed bond markets.

It should be noted that whilst it is possible to look at local emerging fixed income markets as part of a broader asset diversification strategy, they can also be considered as an investment universe of their own. The diversity of countries and economies is considerable. A study by J.P. Morgan[7] of weekly returns over 16 months for 24 local markets showed great variability in the correlations of different local markets with each other. The highest correlation, however, was only 0.66, whilst many were below 0.1.

2.7.5 Trading and Managing Local Currency Exposure

The differences in styles of currency regime are often thrown into sharper focus in emerging than in developed markets. There are four broad types of currency regime:

- fixed exchange rate, often tied to a hard currency by a currency board (e.g. Bulgaria and Argentina);
- management against a basket (the old regime in Thailand before the Asian crisis);
- a crawling peg against a basket of hard currencies (e.g. Poland and Hungary); or
- a float within a range (often referred to as a "dirty" or "managed" float), or a true float.

The 1997 Asian turmoil provides ample illustration of the risks of a fixed exchange rate without a currency board. For several years many Asian countries sought to maintain a fixed link to the US dollar despite differing inflation, monetary, and trade conditions. Eventually the strain told. In countries willing to adopt currency boards fixed rates have worked well. The price of fixed exchange rates is to allow the developed country to which the emerging currency is tied to set monetary policy. Currency boards have tended to be adopted after currency crises, usually as a last ditch effort to save a country's economy. No currency that has been supported by a currency board has ever been broken by speculative pressure. From an investor's point of view, if a currency board is in place then the only issue becomes the level of incremental yield that he requires to reflect the credit risk of the country, and how successfully the effective abdication of monetary policy to the central bank of the country whose currency is used will be effective in ensuring economic stability.

Regimes that have adopted dirty floats have a track record of tending to fail to depreciate the currency sufficiently to maintain competitiveness, the most well-known example of this being Mexico in 1994. This bias usually results from a mixture of national pride and ensuring that the depreciating currency does not itself institutionalize inflation. A slight lag in the rate of depreciation is acceptable, but the underlying currency must not be allowed to get too overvalued. In this case too a local markets investor has a relatively straightforward task of calculating interest rate differentials between the emerging market and the underlying developed currency or the appropriate weighted basket and determining whether the differential is sufficient reward for the risks taken. However, he must also take into account whether the pace of the crawl is adequate or not and the likelihood of a change in the rate of the crawl. This can work to an investor's advantage as well as disadvantage. If a country's inflation slows down enough to allow a cut in the rate of depreciation, but rate differentials have not yet adjusted to reflect this, then the investor is likely to gain from a fall in interest rates to reflect the new slower rate.

In the case of a genuine free float the nature of the investor's decision is indistinguishable from that which needs to be taken for any developed market weighting, except that emerging currencies tend to be more volatile, and these risks need to be taken into account. Note that the nature of the risk in the case of floating currencies is different from the risk in the case of crawling peg or fixed currencies. Free market risk tends to reflect on a continuous basis, whereas the currency "risk" in the case of fixed or crawling pegs is a discrete one. No fluctuation beyond that allowed occurs for long periods of time until a sudden crisis causes a large one-off move, often followed by a floating period thereafter to establish a new equilibrium rate.

2.7.6 Trading and Managing Local Interest Rate Exposure

The elements of interest rate management in local markets are similar to those in developed markets, although there are certain differences in emphasis. These can be summarized as follows:

1. External influences, including flows, tend to affect domestic emerging bond markets more than their larger developed counterparts.
2. Politics affect sentiment more than in developed markets.
3. Volatility tends to be higher, but not always to the extent that at first appears to be the case. Appearances can be misleading, as nominal rates are often much higher, the nominal movements will often appear very large, maybe hundreds of basis points in a day, but are actually modest in the context of the total. The pattern of moves does, however, tend to be more discontinuous. There will often be prolonged periods of little activity followed by spurts of sudden change, again caused in part simply because the markets are thinner and less liquid, and therefore more responsive to flows.
4. Quantitative analysis is usually much poorer and can be less valuable given the difficulties of discontinuous price action. Even simple trades such as yield curve shape trades can be swamped because, say, there is an announcement of new supply in a particular maturity, or the central bank is forced to raise short rates aggressively to defend the currency. An irregular supply of securities may also lead to strangely shaped yield curves driven by liquidity situations rather than fundamental or quantitative analysis.

Local emerging bond markets are appealing because of low correlations with developed bond markets at a time when correlations amongst the developed markets have been rising steadily and EMU has diminished the potential for diversification among European bonds. This is both because of their vulnerability to local events and because the universe of investors has only a partial overlap. The "Tequila Effect" in 1995 and the damage done to non-Asian countries by the Asian crisis in 1997 demonstrates the degree to which the separate markets are linked to each other by a web of confidence on a short-term basis during volatile markets. However, the low long-term correlations and high potential returns show the longer term appeal that remains.

2.8 EQUITIES

Whereas an emerging market fixed income investment may be in emerging economies or in markets that are emerging it is usually the case that an emerging equity market is an existing asset market in a developing country. Even economies that satisfy the World Bank GDP per capita criterion of being emerging will already have an equity market. What makes such a market a viable investment option for the global emerging markets equity investor is the country's economic development, and the increasing use of the equity market as a means of raising capital for domestic corporations seeking to benefit from the economy's development. As in the case of fixed income investment, the attractions of emerging equity markets centre principally on their potential for higher returns than developed markets. However, in the context of portfolio management there are important diversification benefits that can be gained from an exposure to this asset class.

2.8.1 History

Emerging equity markets did not develop fully as a global asset class until the late 1980s. There were markets before then which certainly would have satisfied most of the established criteria, going back over many decades and even centuries. Yet as an identifiable destination for dedicated equity investment the asset class only developed in the 1980s. Initially a small number of specialist investment houses began to target individual countries, mostly in the emerging Asian economies, through single-country funds. These were usually of the closed-end variety, since in the early stages of the markets' development access to domestic equities was often restricted for foreigners.

The economic and political characteristics that were put in place in the early 1980s and that gave rise to the development of the so-called Asian Tigers centred on pro-business, autocratic regimes promoting strong export growth. Corporations emerged that were able to take advantage of factors specific to emerging economies, namely very low labour costs and a highly motivated workforce. These corporations could produce goods and ship them to the industrialized world much more cheaply than could their developed world competition. As the corporations grew so the economies developed and countries' fiscal revenues increased. This allowed investment in infrastructure which in turn promoted corporate efficiency. At the same time the governments started dismantling state-owned enterprises and transferred ownership of many formerly government-controlled companies to the private sector. This model of privatization has become a staple of emerging economies the world over, and has given rise to vast improvements in efficiency because these companies are run for profit rather than underwritten by a government guarantee that does not promote efficiency.

The path by which the foreign investor came to invest in such markets can broadly be separated into the following distinct steps:

1. Market closed to foreign equity investment.
2. Limited access granted, usually rigidly controlled. Closed-end funds often the only means of gaining access.
3. Foreign portfolio investment permitted in limited size, or growth of a foreign market in shares already listed. So-called "foreign board" shares often trade at a premium to local shares.
4. Increasing liberalization of regulation covering foreign ownership — quotas expanded or foreign shares granted equal voting rights.
5. Complete de-regulation.

Variants of this process have been seen in most emerging equity markets in the last 20 years. However, as in the case of the fixed income markets, the emerging market paradigm has continued to evolve and change. The regimes in many current emerging markets have been more open to rapid capital market expansion, and the process towards fully open capital markets has truncated for many of the newer emerging markets.

There are a number of countries that are considered emerging which have resisted the complete opening of their markets to this day. In Latin America the most notable would be Chile, where restrictions persist on short-term trading by overseas investors. Unsurprisingly, it is usually overseas investors who complain about such a situation, saying that this has not been a good thing for the liquidity of the domestic Chilean market, and limits capital-raising activities for domestic corporations. To circumvent the problem, there have been a plethora of Chilean corporations that have listed American Depository Receipts on international exchanges in a bid to tap wider sources of funding.

In Asia it is still quite common for companies to have two classes of share — one for foreigners and one for locals — and, depending on the environment, it is usually true that the so-called "foreign board" shares trade at a premium to local shares. It is likely that these circumstances will change in the light of the current turmoil in the Asian markets. Foreign ownership restrictions in countries such as Korea have already been lifted in an effort to promote greater capital account flows into the country.

2.8.2 Analysing Emerging Equity Stocks

There are, of course, as many schools of thought as to which method is best in the management of emerging markets portfolios as there are investors. Driven by the fundamental premise that the aim is to construct a portfolio of stocks in emerging countries that will enhance the return of a broader global portfolio whilst diversifying the risk, investors typically adopt one of two approaches. Attribution analysis of emerging markets portfolios has demonstrated that the greatest contribution to the incremental return achieved by the portfolio has come from country allocation. This would therefore appear to favour a top-down investment approach over bottom-up. However, over the long term it appears that the best returns on emerging equity portfolios have been achieved by bottom-up managers. Naturally, this may be a function of the ability of the manager rather than the attributes of the methodology.

(i) Top-down

In the setting of country allocation before stock selection greater emphasis will be placed on the legislature and the political will in a country than for OECD country allocation. One of the key aspects of the successful development of emerging countries is the determination of the incumbent politicians to reform their economy, and there must also be adequate structures in place to allow them to do so. In the recent history of emerging markets it has been noticeable that the politicians responsible for the successful development of their countries have usually had the advantage of a quasi-dictatorial regime to allow them the freedom to push ahead with reforms that are initially unpopular.

It is often the process of reform that leads an investor to a particular market in the first instance, and thereafter is the commitment to reform the administration that will retain the investor's interest. The fundamental attraction of investing in a particular country, however, will be the long-term growth prospects of that country, which should feed through to the long-term growth of equity prices and the equity market.

The stocks that are available in emerging markets are usually representative of a less diverse range of sectors than would be expected in a developed market. As a result it is often the case that emerging markets portfolios are dominated by a few sectors, the most obvious one being the telecommunications sector. In the process of privatization, which is symptomatic of an emerging market in the early stages of development, one of the first companies to be listed on the stock market is the national telephone company. Given its relative size and importance in the infrastructure of an economy, its shares are often the most liquid in a market. They are therefore a natural point of entry into a market for a foreign investor seeking to gain exposure to a country for the first time. It is only once a market has been a destination for foreign capital for some time — occasionally years rather than months — that the attention of investors will move towards more consumer-oriented stocks and away from infrastructure stocks. This parallels the evolution of a burgeoning middle class in a country, with a higher level of disposable income to spend on consumer goods.

(ii) Bottom-up

A bottom-up investor in emerging markets will usually apply certain criteria to a universe of stocks across the whole range of emerging markets, and select stocks accordingly. The country of operation is deemed only to be of secondary importance compared with the company. This method of investment in the asset class is usually favoured by value managers, who carry out a screening process on the universe of stocks, selecting investments on the basis of their valuation. The process is not significantly different between developed and emerging markets, save that special care has to be taken in assessing individual corporate data as local reporting standards may differ from conventions adopted in developed countries.

2.8.3 Trading and Managing Emerging Equity Market Exposure

A number of important practical considerations must be addressed before investing in emerging equity markets. The physical ability to buy and hold shares in a country and the ease of settlement are often not as straightforward as in developed countries. The historical reasons for this are that the lack of activity in a country's shares have not necessitated more up-to-date transactional procedures. Such a lack of activity has obvious implications for the availability of stock, and is also one of the reasons why commissions in emerging equity markets are typically higher than in developed markets.

As in emerging fixed income markets, custody and settlement procedures tend to be more complex. In smaller emerging markets there are usually only a few international banks that have established offices or relationships with local banks to facilitate custody for overseas investors. As the markets develop so the number of custodians proliferate and the cost comes down, but in the early stages the costs can be punitive. There are often variations between countries in settlement times and practices. In many countries at the early stages of development it is not uncommon for a large number of trades to fail because of inadequate procedures in the management of the settlement process, poor communications, etc. It is also true that the penalties that are levied by local regulatory bodies can be much more severe, and buy-ins effected with much greater speed than would be common in developed markets.

Reference has already been made in the opening section to the poorer regulatory environment that often exists in emerging markets. Shareholders' rights, particularly minority shareholder rights, are often not protected adequately in emerging markets. Regulations governing such issues are often not enforced with the same alacrity as in developed markets, and this sometimes means that there is a higher level of insider trading in certain countries. As more foreign investors become involved in investment in particular countries, however, the calls for greater enforcement of securities regulation increase and progress is made to protect shareholder rights.

Once the decision has been made to invest in a particular emerging market, one of the practical obstacles is the availability of stock to buy. Since the capital markets are not used to the same extent as in developed markets, and there is often a large part of industry that remains in the public sector, the equity market of a developing country is usually much smaller as a percentage of the whole economy. This limits the number of companies in which it is possible to invest initially, but as interest grows in the equity market, and as the government and corporations alike realize the availability of another means of raising capital, so equity supply increases.

2.8.4 Strategic Uses for Investing in Emerging Equity Markets

The case for investment in emerging equity markets is not simply one of seeking higher returns, although this is the most important characteristic of the asset class. There are also some very important characteristics of emerging markets that can significantly enhance the risk/reward profile of a diversified global equity portfolio in the portfolio management process.

Although events in emerging economies have precipitated turbulence in the markets in recent years, most notably the so-called "Tequila crisis" at the end of 1994 and the Asian crisis of 1997, the long-term returns on emerging equity markets are still significantly in excess of the long-term returns on developed markets, as shown in Table 2.6. The search for these higher returns has drawn an ever-increasing number of investors into the asset class.

Emerging equity markets display a similar independence of correlations both to developed equity markets and amongst themselves to emerging fixed income markets. Table 2.7 shows the correlations between the major equity asset classes, and Table 2.8 some sample correlations among the larger emerging equity markets.

Table 2.6   Total returns (per cent)

	MSCI EMF (US$)	MSCI World (US$)
1988	34.8	21.2
1989	59.2	14.7
1990	−13.8	−18.7
1991	56.0	16.0
1992	9.0	−7.1
1993	71.3	20.4
1994	−8.7	3.4
1995	−6.9	18.7
1996	3.9	11.7
1997	−13.4	14.2
Average annual return	19.1	9.4

Source: Datastream, weekly data.

Table 2.7   Correlations with MSCI emerging markets free index

	1992	1993	1994	1995	1996	1997
S&P Composite	−0.45	0.89	0.73	0.22	−0.34	−0.33
Nikkei 225	−0.27	0.18	−0.04	0.16	0.75	0.84
FTSE 100	0.28	0.91	0.70	0.38	−0.56	−0.41
MSCI World	−0.17	0.76	0.67	0.43	−0.29	−0.05

Table 2.8 Correlations between MSCI emerging markets indices

	Argentina	Brazil	India	Malaysia	Mexico	Taiwan	Thailand	Turkey	South Africa	EMFS
Argentina										
Brazil	0.81									
India	0.22	0.05								
Malaysia	−0.22	−0.15	0.27							
Mexico	0.51	0.08	0.56	−0.19						
Taiwan	0.67	0.83	0.26	0.11	0.03					
Thailand	−0.58	−0.62	0.48	0.64	−0.03	−0.41				
Turkey	0.57	0.48	−0.21	−0.55	0.25	0.22	−0.68			
South Africa	0.10	0.47	−0.03	0.32	−0.58	0.44	0.09	0.06		
EMFS	0.46	0.43	0.69	0.63	0.32	0.53	0.35	−0.13	0.42	
S&P Composite	0.68	0.82	−0.37	−0.42	−0.14	0.61	−0.83	0.63	0.39	0.63
	Argentina	Brazil	India	Malaysia	Mexico	Taiwan	Thailand	Turkey	South Africa	EMFS

Source: Datastream.
Monthly data, for five years, as at 17 April 1998.

These statistics clearly show that the addition of an exposure to emerging equity markets to a global portfolio will diversify the total portfolio and, because of the historically high returns in the asset class, enhance the total return of the portfolio. Many studies have been carried out to establish the optimum exposure to the asset class for a global portfolio, and efficient frontier work suggests the optimum exposure is 15 per cent of assets. However, given the volatility of the individual markets within the asset class, the perception of the risk of emerging equity market investment usually means that the exposure is lower. Clearly, since the efficient frontier work on risk/reward is based on historical figures, there is some potential justification for this.

The use of historical risk and return data can be used to establish one of the most controversial theories posited about emerging markets. This is that a broadly diversified emerging markets portfolio has a lower level of risk than a developed markets portfolio, per unit of return. Historical analysis of the coefficients of variation of an emerging market and a developed market portfolio will attest to this. The logical explanation is that although individual emerging equity markets have a higher level of systematic risk than individual developed markets, in aggregate, because they move with greater independence of each other, an emerging markets portfolio will have a lower level of overall risk. This phenomenon is known as the heterogeneity of emerging markets.

Another important phenomenon when considering investment in this asset class is that of the homogeneity of emerging markets. This is best exemplified by the trite but apt metaphor "a rising tide lifts all the boats". The evidence is that this works best in emerging markets, especially in least developed markets. Indeed, the degree of distinction made by investors between the companies listed in the market can be treated as a good indicator of the degree of sophistication in a market. Investment performance in such a market is a reflection of the extent to which the fortunes of all the companies are in the hands of the legislators and the economy as a whole rather than the individual companies' management teams. The distribution of share performance away from the mean phenomenon can be used as a "sophistication indicator", as shown in Figure 2.7.

The distribution of stock returns in chart (a) has a lower level of kurtosis and would be more characteristic of the stock returns in a developed market. Chart (b) has a much

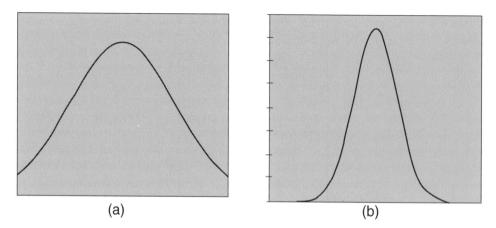

(a)   (b)

Figure 2.7   Equity market sophistication indicator

higher level of kurtosis, indicating that the stock returns are much closer together, and is more representative of an emerging market.

Important portfolio implications arise from this phenomenon. The less developed a market, the fewer the stocks needed to achieve the same level of diversification that would require many stocks in a more developed market. In constructing a portfolio this would mean that a developed market portfolio is likely to have exposure to a comparatively large number of stocks in a smaller number of countries, whereas an emerging markets portfolio would have more countries represented, but with fewer stocks in each.

2.8.5 Benchmarks

Most indices against which emerging markets portfolios are compared are implicitly flawed. The aim of an emerging markets investor is to gain access to a market at an early stage of development. By definition a market capitalization-weighted benchmark will take greater account of a larger market. Therefore, a stock market that has developed more will account for a greater percentage of a given benchmark, and any country allocation that is set with reference to such a benchmark will be obliged to have a higher weighting in the most developed markets.

The most commonly used benchmarks are those produced by Morgan Stanley Capital International (MSCI), the International Finance Corporation (IFC), and the ING Barings Emerging Markets Index team (BEMI). The criterion for inclusion in these indices vary according to a number of factors, such as investability and free float, and all have their respective merits.

2.9 DERIVATIVES

Derivatives have grown rapidly in importance in emerging markets as in all financial sectors. However, emerging markets offer both specific problems and opportunities that make derivatives particularly useful. According to the EMTA, around 8 per cent of total traded volumes in emerging markets are accounted for by debt options and warrants. Additionally, a considerable volume of bonds are tied up in structured notes of the type described below.

2.9.1 Options

Emerging market securities, almost by definition, tend to be more volatile than securities in developed markets; therefore there is a tendency for greater variance in volatility as well. Options are the obvious vehicle to take advantage of the trading opportunities offered. Higher volatility of the underlying securities ensures more attractive economics in using options and overcoming the bid/offer spread, and taking low cost views through options priced comparatively far out-of-the-money. The variance creates more potential for trading volatility itself. Brady bonds in particular lend themselves to options trading because they also satisfy the other key criteria for a successful options market of good liquidity in the underlying security, necessary to ensure smooth deliverability.

In contrast, as we have discussed elsewhere, the nature of the volatility of local markets is discrete rather than continuous. This creates a problem in that the market becomes one sided. Market participants are naturally reluctant to write options most of the time when volatilities are low. However, this pattern opens up greater potential for so-called "exotic" options such as knock-ins or barrier options. These options are only triggered by the occurrence of particular events rather than being constantly open, thereby reducing their cost. For example, a knock-in put option on the Mexican peso might give the buyer the right to put Mexican pesos at any current market price, but only if the Mexican peso trades at a level at least MPS1 below the current level (at the time of writing the peso rate is US\$1=MPS9.08, thus the barrier would be at US\$1=MPS10.08). The buyer of the option is either taking a view or hedging himself against the possibility of a sudden crisis and a sharp, perhaps very short term, collapse of the peso, rather than a gradual depreciation. A scenario such as this is sufficiently within the experience of many local markets participants that it represents a realistic scenario.

2.9.2 Repurchase Agreements

The repurchase agreement, more commonly referred to simply as "repo", has been a major source of developing liquidity for developed markets, and is now a fast growing area of emerging markets. A repo agreement ensures that a market participant will be able to secure a particular security at a future date, thereby enabling him to short the security in the meantime, but confident that he will be able to cover the short at a future date. A reverse repo allows a security to be passed on temporarily, thereby maintaining a longer term position whilst freeing up the balance sheet. Repos and reverse repos achieve the opposite function for the other counterparty. Even among the most liquid emerging market securities, as in all markets, liquidity is prone to disappear during periods of sudden volatility. Such periods occur more frequently in emerging markets than in developed ones. Repo and reverse repo provide the necessary protection to ensure continuous liquidity, even during such periods, and are therefore particularly useful in emerging markets.

2.9.3 Structured Notes

Increasing commercial liquidity in the last three years has resulted in a sharp rise in the number of investors searching for returns over hard currency, particularly US dollar, interbank rates. Typically these investors are confined to hard currency investments and either floating rate or short date fixed maturities. Simultaneously, until the Korean crisis there had been a sharp compression in credit spreads forcing these investors into lower credit quality credits in order to achieve Libor + returns. Emerging market bonds offer a natural underlying vehicle for derivatives structurers to adapt into suitable Libor + structures. Structured notes will often have embedded barrier or knock-out options written into them. For example, a structured note utilizing a bond such as the Republic of Croatia 2002 Eurobond may offer Libor + 200bps, but provide that in the event of Croatia not paying a coupon the buyer of the note will only receive 100− market price of the Croatia 2002 on the date of failing to pay the coupon.

Local market instruments provide even greater opportunity for derivative structures. Varying yield curve shapes due to local factors and the inefficiency of local curves was highlighted in Section 2.7. High local market yields together with local curves can be exploited to achieve US dollar denominated notes offering substantial yields above Libor whilst still ensuring partial or total protection against falls in the domestic currency. The issuer of the note is able partially to hedge the exposure through currency forwards, taking curve risk versus the longer dated underlying security. Also common are notes offering a composite of several emerging market local instruments and currencies, relying upon diversification to achieve maximum yield whilst minimizing currency risk.

Mention should also be made of derivative notes designed around what became collo-quially known as "the currency carry trade". As discussed in Section 2.7 above, one of the currency management techniques common in emerging countries has been to tie the currency to a single developed currency, or a basket of developed currencies. The simplest of these trades was heavily exploited from 1993 until the Asian crisis in 1997. The investor would go long the emerging currency and short the US dollar against it. Provided the peg held, the investor would earn the yield differential without currency risk. For those investors unable to take direct Asian currency exposure, the same trade could easily be captured in a structured note that was US dollar denominated. The same principle worked for any currency tied to a fixed basket of currencies, the short position being the weighted blend of the basket currencies. The sudden collapse of Asian curren-cies in 1997 provided an object lesson in the dangers of currency carry trades, and the risk that investors were taking through the purchase of these notes.

2.9.4 Credit Derivatives

Derivatives on currency and interest rate movements have been used by investors for many years. Derivatives dependent upon credit changes have only become widely exploited since 1995, but volumes have grown very fast. Unsurprisingly emerging markets have participated heavily in this growth. At the heart of credit derivatives is a very simple concept, namely that it is possible to spilt credit risk into much smaller segments than the all-or-nothing view of whether or not a bond will default. The range of credits, and the greater rate of change in credit ratings for emerging credits, sovereign or corporate, than for developed credits makes emerging markets ideal for the growth of credit derivatives.

Examples of credit derivatives would be an option to put a bond that was downgraded more than two notches in a month, or the right of an investor to put a bond should its rating drop below investment grade as his guidelines may not allow him to hold a security rated below this grade. Both of these protect investors from possible situations where they might be forced to sell at exactly the time when markets are likely to be reacting most strongly to adverse news. The purchasers of the riskier side of the derivative will often be emerging markets specialists, frequently local to the country that the derivative is being written on, with a strong positive view on that country. The risk that they take offers a chance to profit from their favourable view, usually through receipt of a premium, often with the ability to take the additional risk off balance sheet.

Section 2.6 highlighted the inefficiencies that are often present in emerging market credit curves. Of course, these represent an opportunity for profit; however, as the box trade shown in Table 2.6 showed, complicated box trades and the ability to take short positions may be needed in order to exploit the anomalies. For investors unwilling or unable to put on the box trade shown as an example in Table 2.6, a derivative note could replicate the trade:

$$\text{redemption value} = 3 \times (\text{slope of 10/5 spread in Brazil}) - (\text{slope of 10/5 year}$$

$$\text{spread in Argentina})$$

Notice that in this example three times leverage was also added. Derivatives are frequently used to achieve leverage which the investor might otherwise have been unable to add to his portfolio.

Credit derivatives will often be embedded into structured notes, but the terms of the note may not make this apparent. Whilst credit derivatives serve a valuable function in splitting the nature of credit risk, or allowing the investor to take targeted credit risk (for example, Greece will be upgraded within a maximum of six months), they also are a trap for the unwary. Consider a note that pays Libor + 250 bps; in the event of the underlying country being downgraded three notches, the investor will receive the underlying. On the face of it these terms are not expressed as a credit derivative, but of course the investor is being paid a spread to take the risky part of the credit derivative. In the event of a three-notch downgrade, the investor is taking all the capital risk of the credit.

2.9.5 Relative Value Trades

One of the most difficult tasks presented by emerging markets, which the next section considers in more detail, is the decision of relative value among the emerging markets. Investors competing against indices can express relative value judgements easily by over- or underweighting countries versus their index. For absolute return investors the task is much more difficult, especially given the difficulties of taking short positions that were discussed in Section 2.9.2. Derivatives enable opinions of relative value to be expressed more easily, again without the need to tie up balance sheet through long and short positions. For example, an investor who is bullish on Russia versus Poland could buy an option that appreciates in value provided the Russia Principals tighten in spread versus the Poland discounts. The option could be dependent upon movements in price rather than yield spread if the investor felt this to be the key relationship. The curve trade illustrated in Section 2.6.3 also required taking short positions; once more an option or a note that rises in value as the view expressed by the investor comes about solves the difficulty.

Derivatives are also useful for non-emerging markets specialists who may wish to take a generic view across a number of emerging countries or a region. An increasingly common guideline in portfolios benchmarked against developed market indices is the ability to invest up to 10 per cent of the portfolio into emerging markets. In the case of many portfolios the sum thus provided may not be adequate to ensure reasonable diversification of holdings within the emerging markets sector of the portfolio. A derivative structured to take account of the performance of either a selected basket of emerging countries, or even of an emerging market index, can allow fully diversified exposure across emerging markets even for relatively small parts of a portfolio.

2.9.6 Equities

Derivatives in emerging equity markets are typically employed in one of two forms. The first is to create a basket of equities, either to replicate an index or to provide exposure to securities that foreigners are unable to buy in the local market. The second is to create warrants on either individual securities or a market. Warrant issues are often issued after a bull run in the underlying stock, when investor attention is particularly focused on that security or market, as the purchaser of warrants is buying volatility, although the view might be a positive or negative view on future direction. The nature of equity risk is less easily divisible into parts than in the fixed income markets, because in the developed markets, derivatives play a less prominent role in the equity markets than in their fixed income counterparts.

2.10 SPECIAL CONSIDERATIONS IN EVALUATING RELATIVE VALUE

There is no difference between emerging markets and other areas of investment in that there are widely differing opinions on how to evaluate relative value. It is the difference in opinion and methodology that, of course, ensures that there is a market. The aim of this section is not to provide a complete primer on investing in emerging markets. Such a work would require a book in its own right and would be controversial because there are so many opinions on the best solution to the problem. Here we highlight only some of the pointers to relative value that are specific to emerging markets.

2.10.1 A Matrix Approach To Regional and Asset Allocation

The most difficult single problem is allocating between the different regions. South America, Eastern Europe, Asia, and Africa are grouped together as "emerging markets", but their cultural and structural diversity is immense. Much of South America is developing industrially for the first time. Eastern Europe has a long history of highly developed industry, but suffered from a constraining governmental system for decades. In contrast, Asia has experienced many years of the greatest economic freedom for development ever seen, but coupled with a high degree of protection for domestic manufacturers and markets. We are aware of at least one fund manager who regards the problem as so insurmountable that he has abandoned emerging markets as an umbrella and only considers asset allocation within each region, and whether he wishes to invest in that region or not. In fact, external debt is much more highly correlated than local debt, not least because the same underlying US Treasury yield curve is used for the vast majority of external debt instruments which are dollar denominated, making it possible to carry out a realistic asset allocation exercise. The complexity of the task is such that asset allocation is probably best carried out by a matrix approach. Table 2.9 illustrates an abbreviated form of such a matrix.

A matrix approach allows account to be taken not only of the varying prospects for regions, but also of the varying characteristics of the forms of security available. For example, when US rates are falling aggressively Bradys will usually be the best performers; conversely, when US rates are rising, local market debt will probably perform best. During strong bullish phases equities and Bradys perform best, whereas local debt

Table 2.9   Asset allocation matrix

	Brady Bonds	Sovereign Eurobonds	Corporate Eurobonds	Local Market Sovereign Debt	Local Market Corporate Debt	Equities
South America						
Mexico						
Argentina						
Brazil						
Eastern Europe						
Poland						
Hungary						
Czech Republic						
Asia						
S. Korea						
Thailand						
Philippines						

will have the most defensive qualities, and so on. A further complication to be taken into account is the limited availability of different asset types in the various markets. For example, Asia is barely represented in the Brady bond market; only the Philippines completed a Brady plan. Eastern Europe too is poorly represented in the Brady market. This, together with a lack of liquid Eurobonds until more recently, led many early Eastern European investors to local markets simply because of a lack of alternative rather than a strong allocation decision towards that sector.

2.10.2 Past Experience

In discussing the lessons of the past there seems to be a widespread consensus among fixed income emerging market participants that credit agencies are of little use in judging relative value. They are perceived as badly lagging indicators, being slow to upgrade and downgrading aggressively only after a country like Mexico or South Korea has run into difficulties. Whilst the full range of economic indicators that are used to make judgements amongst developed countries can be employed, the experiences of Mexico in 1994 and Korea in 1997 have led to much greater emphasis being placed upon the size and maturity structure of a country's outstanding debt than is common in developed countries. Almost by definition, emerging market economies are less rigid than developed economies, and their ability to react to change is much greater. The speed of Mexico's turnaround caught many economists by surprise because they were applying developed country macroeconomic models that respond to events more slowly. There are many other examples, such as Hungary or Brazil in 1994 and Venezuela or Bulgaria in 1997, where the abruptness of the change in economic direction has not been factored into conventional models rapidly enough.

Two other indicators that are widely seen as being of much greater importance in judging emerging countries are the health and development of the financial sector within a country and the opinion of local investors. Excessive lending based upon poor judgement is a common hallmark in emerging countries and can be the first sign of trouble. One recent report[18] has suggested that the traditional measures of health in the financial sector, such as capital adequacy, are of little value in emerging markets, and that a much better measure is the spread banks earn between deposits and loans. This approach fits with the views of many emerging market professionals that observing local activity is one of the most important advance indicators of positive or negative changes, and is much more important than in developed markets. The rationale for this is that in emerging countries information is much more imperfect, and in most emerging countries there is a much greater concentration of wealth and power in the hands of a relatively small number of influential families than is the case in developed markets.

In the early part of this chapter a defining feature of emerging markets was said to be much greater sensitivity to politics than in the case of developed countries. Political science is a subject of its own, but once more a few themes are more dominant in emerging markets than elsewhere. The policy alternatives put forward by opposing politicians tend to be more polarized and their implementation more abrupt than in developed countries. Typically there has been less institutionalization of process and therefore there is scope for individuals to have a larger impact. This can be a negative as well as a positive. Markets can react strongly on trivia, such as the health of one individual, because of a belief that the individual concerned has a completely decisive impact on the policies of that country.[19] Emerging countries have had less time to develop social cohesion than developed countries, and many of them have minority groups pressing either for independence or at least a far greater degree of autonomy, sometimes employing violent means. These events too must be kept under observation.

There are many other special considerations that are specific to certain countries that could be listed, but the purpose here, as throughout this chapter, has been to provide a broad overview of emerging markets.

2.11 ENDNOTES

1. Margaret Price in her book *Emerging Stock Markets* describes the term "emerging market" as having been coined in 1981 by Antoine W. van Agtmael when he served at the IFC.
2. I am grateful to the Emerging Markets Traders Association for allowing me to use their data for this section. Their quarterly *Trading Volumes Surveys* provide far more detailed information than is shown here.
3. Mark Fox, "Emerging markets", in Carol Alexander (Ed.), *The Handbook of Risk Management and Analysis*, Wiley, Chichester, 1996.
4. *International Banking and Financial Market Developments Quarterly*. BIS December 1997. ISSN 1012–9979.
5. Kleiman International Consultants, based in the United States, provide regular survey updates of developments in local emerging markets and new markets as they open.
6. All data in this section are taken from the IFC Emerging Markets Database. Of course, the high volatility of equity markets can change the relative weights and capitalizations rapidly.
7. For consistency, J.P. Morgan statistical and market data have been used throughout as the most comprehensive source available.
8. See "The Emerging Markets Index Plus". *Market Brief*, 19 November 1997. J.P. Morgan.
9. Such was the anxiety to ease the settlements blockages that had occurred, that market participants sometimes took substantial risks for the sake of simplicity. For example, the margin on Ecuador's defaulted loans varied between 0.875 per cent and 2.25 per cent over Libor, but prior to the completion of the Brady plan they were all traded similarly. If Ecuador had paid pro rata on the unpaid interest rather than, in accordance with what has tended to be standard market practice, simply aggregated all the unpaid interest and negotiated it together, then there could have been substantial losers and gainers.
10. The "Aztec" bond totalled US$2.56bn, maturing March 2008. The bond was called in March 1997.
11. See "Analysing Brady bonds" for the explanation of stripped spreads, and why they are the appropriate comparison yardstick compared with Eurobond spreads.
12. The credit rating agencies carry out regular statistical studies of the behaviour of credits at different points in the quality spectrum. The evidence is that the lower the quality of the credit the greater the likelihood of subsequent variation in the credit rating. See, for example, Standard & Poor's *Credit Week*, 15 April 1996.
13. See Ken Telljohann's article "Stripped Yield Madness" (February 1994. Lehman Brothers).
14. Preferential treatment for Eurobonds used to be one of the reasons put forward as to why Eurobonds should trade more expensively than Brady bonds, and why Moodys often gave a one notch higher credit rating to Eurobonds than Brady bonds of the same sovereign borrower, notwithstanding the US collateral. The rating differential has now disappeared. It is unlikely that a borrower would now be able to exercise preference between creditors other than in accordance with any order or precedence set out in the original documentation without a court challenge.
15. The true theoretical shape of yield curves is a far more controversial topic than, for example, the theoretical shape of a government benchmark curve. One theory holds that credit curves should always be steeply inversely shaped at the front end for lower quality credits because the main risk for a bondholder is repayment of principal, and the shorter the bond, the more immediate the major credit risk.

16. For example, despite estimates of 50–60 local markets in emerging countries, J.P. Morgan, whose indices are the most widely used among emerging market participants, include 24 countries in their Emerging Local Market Index as having the true market characteristics to be suitable for inclusion in an index.
17. In the United States municipal bonds normally fall within a separate category because they are taxed differently from other categories of bonds.
18. By Liliana Rojas-Suarez of the Inter American Development Bank. Released January 1998.
19. Some market participants have light-heartedly created "The Five Percent Club". Admission is granted to those whose reported state of health, such as Presidents Suharto of Indonesia or Yeltsin of Russia, have moved equity, bond or currency markets more than 5 per cent.

—— 3 ——
The Origins of Risk-Neutral Pricing and the Black–Scholes Formula

L.C.G. ROGERS

3.1 INTRODUCTION

The theory and practice of finance today requires many skills — computing, applied mathematical, probabilistic, statistical, economic — and it is a sad observation that there are many colleagues working in finance who are expert in their own area, but know little of even the basic ideas from the other areas. This chapter is addressed to those who want to fill in their background a little, and learn something about the fundamental economic ideas that have inspired the development of finance, even though the subject has now become so refined that we may often study it without being aware of its intellectual pedigree. There is nothing original in this chapter, in the sense that a good financial economist would read it and say, "Well, of course". On the other hand, for those who have not seen this way of thinking of things, there are miraculous revelations ahead; we shall see how martingales, stochastic integration and the notion of equivalent martingale measures leap out of the page, for example. These are not just mathematical irrelevancies foisted on the subject by self-satisfied probabilists, they are inevitable consequences of economic thinking. As befits a pedagogical approach, we feel free to cut corners; what follows is rigorous by the standards of physics or applied mathematics, but not rigorous. Indeed, making some of the arguments into proofs would be onerous, if not impossible, but the importance of the ideas is that they guide our thinking.

The fundamental concept is that of an economic *equilibrium*. Imagine a market with many agents, each of whom begins with some assets, and may trade them.[1] The objective of each agent is to maximize his utility, which is some function of the assets held at the end of trading. When two or more agents meet, if there were any mutually advantageous trades available to them, then they would trade, and all benefit. If trading has taken place to the point where no more such mutually advantageous trades are possible, then the market is in equilibrium. The essential insight (due to Arrow and Debreu) is that *in equilibrium, there are equilibrium prices for the different assets in terms of each*

Risk Management and Analysis. Vol. 2: New Markets and Products. Edited by Carol Alexander
© 1998 John Wiley & Sons Ltd

other, and the allocations held by each agent are *what the agents would optimally choose to hold if they were alone in the world, but could buy the different assets at those equilibrium prices.*

This allows us to understand an equilibrium by first studying what an agent would optimally choose to do if faced with certain prices for the assets, and then adjusting those prices so that *the markets clear*, that is, the total amounts of the different assets demanded by the optimally behaving agents are the total amounts present initially in the market.

We follow this recipe in a market evolving randomly in time. To begin with (Section 3.2), we study the possible choices available to an agent, and then we see (in Section 3.4) what the consequences are of optimal behaviour of such an agent. This leads naturally to a notion of equivalent martingale measures, and gives a methodology for pricing contingent claims, even in incomplete markets. Finally, in Section 3.5, we take the simple binomial market and see how these ideas work through in that setting, leading eventually to the Black–Scholes equation when we take a suitable limit. Section 3.3 provides a digression into the background of martingales and equivalent measures, which hopefully many readers will already know. In the Appendix we show how risk-neutral pricing follows from two completely different approaches — an axiomatic approach and the no-arbitrage approach. These two routes to risk-neutral pricing are even shorter than that of Sections 3.2 and 3.4, but less illuminating.

3.2 PORTFOLIO CHOICES

We consider a market developing in time, in which there are n shares, the price at time t of the ith share being denoted S_t^i. There is also a "zeroth share", whose price at time t will be written R_t; we often think of this rather differently, namely as the value at time t of a unit of money invested at time 0 in a deposit account, though this interpretation is not essential. For brevity, we write

$$S_t \equiv (S_t^1, \ldots, S_t^n)^{\mathrm{T}}, \quad \overline{S}_t = (R_t, S_t^1, \ldots, S_t^n)^{\mathrm{T}}$$

where a superscript T denotes transpose. At time t, the agent holds a portfolio

$$\overline{\theta}_t \equiv (\varphi_t, \theta_t^1, \ldots, \theta_t^n)^{\mathrm{T}}$$

where θ_t^i is the number of i-shares held at time t, and φ_t is the number of 0-shares held at time t. The market value of the portfolio at time t is therefore

$$V_t = \overline{\theta}_t \cdot \overline{S}_t \equiv \varphi_t R_t + \sum_{i=1}^{n} \theta_t^i S_t^i \tag{1}$$

What portfolios can the agent choose? Clearly we cannot allow the agent to take $\theta_t^i = \exp(10^6 \cdot t)$. How would he pay for it?! To understand this, suppose that there are two (deterministic) times $T_1 < T_2$, and the agent holds a portfolio process

$$\overline{\theta}_t = \begin{cases} H, & 0 \le t \le T_1 \\ H', & T_1 < t \le T_2 \end{cases}$$

at time t. Thus the value of the portfolio at any time $t \in [0, T_1)$ is just $H \cdot \overline{S}_t$, and the change in value at time T_1 is

$$(H' - H) \cdot \overline{S}(T_1)$$

where we use the equivalent notations $\overline{S}_t \equiv \overline{S}(t)$ to avoid clumsiness. If this difference is zero, then we say that the portfolio is *self-financing*; if the change in value is zero, then no money needs to be added or taken away to finance the change of portfolio! Assuming that the portfolio *is* self-financing, for any $t \in (T_1, T_2]$ the value of the portfolio satisfies

$$V_t = H' \cdot \overline{S}_t$$
$$= H' \cdot (\overline{S}_t - \overline{S}(T_1)) + H \cdot \overline{S}(T_1)$$
$$= H' \cdot (\overline{S}_t - \overline{S}(T_1)) + H \cdot (\overline{S}(T_1) - \overline{S}_0) + H \cdot \overline{S}_0 \qquad (3)$$

where we have used the self-financing condition to pass from the first line to the second. The three terms in the final expression have very simple interpretations: the first is the change in value of the portfolio in the time interval $(T_1, t]$; the second is the change in value in the time interval $[0, T_1]$; and the third is the initial value V_0 of the portfolio.

We can easily generalize to a portfolio that gets changed at the times $T_1 < T_2 < \ldots$. If the agent chooses to hold H_i throughout the time interval $(T_{i-1}, T_i]$, and if the portfolio is self-financing (so none of the changes involves any alteration in the value of the portfolio), then the value at time t will be

$$V_t = V_0 + H_1 \cdot (\overline{S}(T_1) - \overline{S}(0)) + H_2 \cdot (\overline{S}(T_2) - \overline{S}(T_1)) + \cdots + H_k \cdot (\overline{S}(t) - \overline{S}(T_{k-1})) \qquad (4)$$

if $T_{k-1} < t \le T_k$. This can be written more concisely as

$$V_t = V_0 + \int_{(0,t]} \overline{\theta}_u \cdot d\overline{S}_u \qquad (5)$$

The two alternative expressions can be thought of as the *definition* of the integral notation appearing on the right of (5); later, we need to consider what the integral might mean for more complicated portfolio processes $\overline{\theta}$, but for piecewise-constant $\overline{\theta}$ the notational equivalence of (4) and (5) is unmistakeable. Thus we may write

$$V_t - V_0 = \int_{(0,t]} \overline{\theta}_u \cdot d\overline{S}_u$$

Even though we may not yet know how to define the integral appearing on the right of (5) for every $\overline{\theta}$, it is clear that for the piecewise-constant $\overline{\theta}$ being used here it *could* only be defined as (4). The right-hand side of (5) is called the *gains from trade*; it is the change in value of the portfolio arising from the fluctuations in the prices of the assets. Thus we have the key result that for a self-financing portfolio

change in value = gains from trade

This principle holds in complete[2] generality, so that (5) is true whatever the portfolio process $\overline{\theta}$. To make sense of this, we would need to make a definition of the (stochastic) integral appearing on the right of (5), and this is not a minor task because the processes S^i may often have paths of unbounded variation. Could we, perhaps, get by with using only simple piecewise-constant integrands of the type we have looked at so far? We shall soon have an answer to this question.

Is there an easy way to tell when a portfolio is self-financing? This will obviously be important. To understand this, let us suppose initially that $R_t = 1$ for all t. Then for any self-financing portfolio $\bar{\theta}$

$$V_t = \varphi_t + \theta_t \cdot S_t = V_0 + \int_{(0,t]} \theta_u \cdot \mathrm{d}S_u \tag{6}$$

So we see that we can choose *any* θ, and then adjust φ to make the above equation hold. This is intuitively reasonable; we may hold any portfolio of the shares provided we take the money out of our deposit account to pay for it. More generally, if we assume that R grows continuously and define $\tilde{V}_t \equiv V_t/R_t$, $\tilde{S}_t \equiv S_t/R_t$, then we have

$$\tilde{V}_t = \tilde{V}_0 + \int_{(0,t]} \theta_u \cdot \mathrm{d}\tilde{S}_u \tag{7}$$

In words, the change in the *discounted* value of the portfolio is the integral of the portfolio process with respect to the *discounted* asset price processes. If we realize that working with discounted prices is effectively changing the bank account process to be constant, then it is not surprising that we get the same characterization of self-financing portfolio processes as we had at (6). This characterization of the possible wealth processes from self-financing portfolio choice is the starting point for our understanding of the optimal behaviour of an agent.

3.3 SOME NOTIONS AND NOTATIONS FROM PROBABILITY

Everything in this section is quite standard. If the reader is familiar with the contents, then go immediately to the next section.

   As will by now be clear, we are in the business of studying random processes developing in time. The time parameter set, to be denoted $\mathcal{T}$, will always be *either* the set of non-negative integers, $\{0, 1, 2, \ldots\}$ — the "discrete-time" setting — *or* the set of non-negative reals — the "continuous-time" setting. As time passes, an agent gets to know more and more, and his decisions may only be made in the light of information known at the time the decision had to be taken. Thus the choice $\bar{\theta}_t$ of portfolio to be held at time t must depend only on the information available at time t. The "technical" way to say this is that $\bar{\theta}_t$ should be $\mathcal{F}_t$-*measurable*, where $\mathcal{F}_t$ is the σ-field of events known at time t. It is intuitively clear that if an agent is investing in discrete time in 5 assets, then his choice of portfolio to be held on day n should be a function only of the prices of the 5 assets on earlier days, up to and including the $(n-1)$th. In this simple setting this is equivalent to what the "technical" statement says; however, the "technical" statement holds unaltered for much more general situations (continuous time, with an uncountable infinity of available assets, say) in which the notion of "a function of earlier prices" oversteps what the mathematics or the imagination can support!

   A stochastic process $(X_t)_{t\in\mathcal{T}}$ is a family of random variables, and is said to be *adapted* if X_t is $\mathcal{F}_t$-measurable for each $t \in \mathcal{T}$. The classic example is an asset price process; assuming perfect information, the price of an asset at time t is always known at time t! The portfolio $\bar{\theta}_t$ an agent holds at time t is also an adapted process, but it is even a little more; as the discrete-time example above illustrates, the portfolio held on day n had to be decided on day $n-1$, so was known in advance. Such a process is called *previsible*; there is an analogous concept in continuous time, but it is much harder to define, so we shall not even attempt to. Suffice it to say that *previsibility is the natural measurability restriction on portfolio processes*.

Probably the most important class of processes is the class of *martingales*. We give here only the briefest summary of the definitions; for the perfect account of martingale theory in discrete time, see Williams (1991). A martingale is an adapted process $(M_t)_{t \in T}$ with the properties that $\mathbb{E}|M_t| < \infty$ for every t, and

$$M_s = \mathbb{E}_s M_t \equiv \mathbb{E}[M_t | \mathcal{F}_s] \tag{8}$$

for all $s \leq t$ in T. In words, for any $s < t$, the expected value of M_t given $\mathcal{F}_s$ is M_s. The equivalent notations $\mathbb{E}_s Y$ and $\mathbb{E}[Y | \mathcal{F}_s]$ for the *conditional expectation* of a random variable Y given information known by time s are defined by the two properties that $\mathbb{E}_s Y$ is always $\mathcal{F}_s$-measurable, and

$$\mathbb{E}(Y I_F) = \mathbb{E}(\mathbb{E}_s(Y) I_F) \tag{9}$$

for all events $F \in \mathcal{F}_s$. Here, I_F is the random variable which is 1 on the event F, and is 0 otherwise; it is an *indicator* random variable, which indicates whether an event has happened or not. An easy and common example from finance would be where the random variable Y is the payoff of a European call option on a share, and the event F is the event that the price of the share has not dropped below 50 before the option expires. In that case, $Y I_F$ is the payoff of a down-and-out call option, with a knockout barrier at 50.

To rephrase (8) and (9), then, a process $(M_t)_{t \in T}$ is a martingale if for any $s < t$ and any $F \in \mathcal{F}_s$

$$\mathbb{E}[(M_t - M_s) I_F] = 0 \tag{10}$$

and in this form we shall presently meet the martingale condition again.

The only other notion we need to introduce for now is that of a *change of measure*. At one level, this is a formal procedure, and very easy to handle as such. Suppose we are given some non-negative random variable Z, for which $0 < c \equiv \mathbb{E}Z < \infty$. Then we can use it to define a new probability $\mathbb{P}^*$, say, via the recipe

$$\mathbb{P}^*(A) = c^{-1} \mathbb{E}[Z I_A] \tag{11}$$

Note that this is a probability — the countable additivity of $\mathbb{P}^*$ is a consequence of the properties of the integral, and the fact that $\mathbb{P}^*(\Omega) = 1$ follows from the definition of c. It is clear that $\mathbb{P}^*$ is *absolutely continuous* with respect to $\mathbb{P}$ in the sense that if $\mathbb{P}(A) = 0$, then also $\mathbb{P}^*(A) = 0$ — this is a basic property of integrals. The fact that a measure $\mathbb{P}'$ that is absolutely continuous with respect to $\mathbb{P}$ in this sense must have a representation of the form (11) for some random variable Z is a deep and important theorem, the Radon–Nikodym theorem.

As an example of how these things can arise in practice, let us consider a game where you bet on N successive tosses of a coin. This coin lands H with probability p, and lands T with probability $q = 1 - p$. You win 1 each time the coin lands H, you lose 1 each time the coin lands T. Let S_n denote your accumulated gains after the nth toss of the coin, so that $S_0 = 0$, and $|S_n - S_{n-1}| = 1$ for all $n \geq 1$. The situation is extremely simple; there are just 2^N possible outcomes in the sample space, a typical outcome ω being just a sequence of N symbols, H or T. The probability of a particular sequence ω is simply

$$p^j q^{N-j}$$

where j is the number of Hs in the sequence ω. This could equivalently be written as

$$p^{(N+S_N)/2} q^{(N-S_N)/2} \equiv \varphi(p, S_N)$$

say. If we took as our basic probability $\mathbb{P}$ the probability that arises in the situation where $p = 1/2$, we could express the probability $\mathbb{P}_p$ corresponding to a coin with H-probability p via the change-of-measure

$$Z = \frac{\varphi(p, S_N)}{\varphi(1/2, S_N)}$$

In this example, the gains process under $\mathbb{P}$ is actually a martingale, as you are as likely to win 1 as to lose 1 at each toss. If p were different from $1/2$, that is, if the coin were not fair, the gains process would not be a martingale, because you would tend on average to win if $p > 1/2$ or to lose if $p < 1/2$. What we see in this example then is that *by changing measure from $\mathbb{P}_p$ to $\mathbb{P}$, we convert the process S into a martingale!* This is an important technique in finance, which we are going to justify by economic reasoning in the next section, and in two other ways. It is also important to understand that it is *only* a technique; the transformed probability has no "real" status, in that it does not describe how assets behave in the real world;[3] it merely allows us to compute prices and (in some cases) to calculate hedges. The transformed probability can be given various interpretations, as we shall see, and these are illuminating.

3.4 OPTIMAL INVESTMENT

There are many different optimization problems we could pose for the agent, which all lead to broadly similar conclusions. Here is one which is easy to work with. We assume that the agent has a utility function U, which is strictly increasing and strictly concave[4] on $(0, \infty)$, a fixed investment horizon $T > 0$, and aims to

$$\max \mathbb{E} U(V_T)$$

starting from initial wealth V_0. Suppose that the optimal wealth is V_T^*, achieved by using the self-financing portfolio θ^*. If we now consider changing slightly from this optimum θ^* to $\theta^* + \varepsilon\eta$, where ε is very small, the discounted terminal wealth $R_T^{-1}V_T^*$ gets changed to

$$R_T^{-1}V_T = R_T^{-1}V_T^* + \varepsilon \int_{(0,T]} \eta_u \mathrm{d}\tilde{S}_u \equiv R_T^{-1}(V_T^* + \Delta V)$$

from (7). Using the first two terms $U(V_T) = U(V_T^*) + U'(V_T^*)\Delta V + \cdots$ of the Taylor expansion, we find that to first order in ε

$$\mathbb{E} U(V_t) = \mathbb{E}\left[U(V_T^*) + U'(V_T^*) \cdot \varepsilon \int_{(0,T]} \eta_u \mathrm{d}\tilde{S}_u \cdot R_T\right] + o(\varepsilon) \leq \mathbb{E} U(V_T^*)$$

the inequality coming from the fact that V^* is optimal. From this, we learn that

$$\mathbb{E}\left[U'(V_T^*) \cdot R_T \cdot \int_0^T \eta_u \mathrm{d}\tilde{S}_u\right] \leq 0$$

and by arguing similarly for the perturbation $-\eta$ the conclusion is that for any (admissible) perturbation η

$$\mathbb{E}\left[U'(V_T^*) \cdot R_T \cdot \int_0^T \eta_u \, d\tilde{S}_u\right] = 0$$

which we may re-express as

$$\mathbb{E}^*\left[\int_0^T \eta_u \, d\tilde{S}_u\right] = 0 \tag{12}$$

when we define the probability $\mathbb{P}^*$ by

$$\frac{d\mathbb{P}^*}{d\mathbb{P}} = c \cdot U'(V_T^*) \cdot R_T,$$

the constant c being chosen for correct normalization; see (11). By taking especially simple perturbations η, we have a remarkable conclusion. Fixing $t \in (0, T)$, taking some event $F \in \mathcal{F}_t$ and using the perturbation

$$\eta_u = I_{\{t < u \leq T\}} I_F$$

the little change in discounted wealth $\varepsilon \int_{(0,T]} \eta_u d\tilde{S}_u$ becomes $(\tilde{S}_T - \tilde{S}_t)I_F$, statement (12) becomes

$$\mathbb{E}^*\left[(\tilde{S}_T - \tilde{S}_t)I_F\right] = 0$$

and we recognize (see (10)) that

under $\mathbb{P}^*$, discounted price processes are martingales

So, without any contrivance, we have seen that the existence of a probability $\mathbb{P}^*$ equivalent to the original $\mathbb{P}$ under which all discounted asset price processes are martingales *follows from simple ideas of equilibrium!*

Remarks.   (i) In recent years the mathematical finance literature has been full of papers proving various forms of the so-called "Fundamental Theorem of Asset Pricing",[5] which broadly says that in a market there are no arbitrage opportunities if and only if there is an equivalent measure under which all asset price processes are martingales (an EMM). This literature sprang from the original papers of Harrison and Kreps (1979) and Harrison and Pliska (1981), but perhaps the most important issue is why one should think of formulating such a statement in the first place! David Kreps, being a good economist, would undoubtedly have been familiar with the kind of arguments we have just seen, and in the light of this, the formulation of the Fundamental Theorem of Asset Pricing is explained.

It is clear that in equilibrium there can be no arbitrage, and we have just seen that in equilibrium there is an EMM. The fact that these two consequences of equilibrium are equivalent is remarkable and very important (or, depending on your point of view, very unimportant!).

(ii) The optimal portfolio in the general continuous-time setting will not typically be a simple piecewise-constant portfolio, so we really do need a general theory of stochastic integration to underpin the sort of analysis carried out above.

In general, there will be no uniqueness of EMMs; any two agents in the same market would generate an EMM, and these will in general be different. In a *complete* market, which is a market where every contingent claim can be perfectly replicated by suitable trading in the underlying securities, there is of course a unique price for any contingent claim, namely the initial wealth needed to finance the replicating portfolio. We shall study an example of such a market in the next section. The well-established theory of complete markets has been extensively developed in the last 20 years, but incomplete markets (which are much more difficult to handle) have been comparatively neglected. Various mathematicians have made peculiar attempts to define a price of a non-marketed contingent claim in an incomplete market, thereby demonstrating their unfamiliarity with the kinds of arguments sketched above. And indeed, the ideas sketched above need only minor extension to price contingent claims in an incomplete market. Here is how we do it.

If Y is a bounded non-negative contingent claim whose value will be known by time T (for example, the payoff of a European put option), then what would be a fair price p_ε for our agent to pay at time 0 in order to receive εY at time T? If he paid out p at time 0, then his deposit account would be short by an amount pR_T at time T. To offset this, he would be free to go into the market and invest in the assets traded there; the best he could do by trading in the market, his maximized expected utility of terminal wealth, would then be just

$$\sup \mathbb{E}U(V_T + \varepsilon Y - pR_T)$$

As p increases, this expression decreases, and if p were zero, then it would certainly be better than $\mathbb{E}U(V_T^*)$, which is the best he could do if he did not enter into any deal involving Y. So there will be (under mild assumptions) a unique p_ε at which he would be just indifferent to this deal, where

$$\mathbb{E}U(V_T^*) = \sup \mathbb{E}U(V_T + \varepsilon Y - p_\varepsilon R_T)$$

This value of p is the agent's maximal buying price for Y; he would always want to buy Y if it were offered at less than p_ε, and would never pay more than p_ε for Y. Note that the sup is at least what he would achieve if he used the portfolio θ^* and obtained wealth V_T^*, so

$$\mathbb{E}U(V_T^*) \geq \mathbb{E}U(V_T^* + \varepsilon Y - p_\varepsilon R_T)$$

Expanding the right-hand side to order ε we get:

$$\mathbb{E}U(V_T^*) \geq \mathbb{E}\left[U(V_T^*) + U'(V_T^*)(\varepsilon Y - p_\varepsilon R_T)\right] + o(\varepsilon)$$

Rearranging, dividing by ε and letting ε drop to zero, we obtain:

$$\lim_{\varepsilon \downarrow 0} \tfrac{1}{\varepsilon} p_\varepsilon \geq \mathbb{E}^*\left[R_T^{-1}Y\right]$$

If we now consider the analogous argument for buying $-\varepsilon Y$, that is, selling εY, then we obtain:

$$\lim_{\varepsilon \to 0} \tfrac{1}{\varepsilon} p_\varepsilon = \mathbb{E}^*\left[R_T^{-1}Y\right]$$

that is, *the fair time-0 marginal price of a contingent claim is the $\mathbb{P}^*$-expectation of its value discounted back to time 0.* Thus, different agents would have different notions of a fair price for a given contingent claim. There is much more lurking here,[6] but let us leave it now, and look at a simple example.

3.5 THE BINOMIAL MARKET AND THE BLACK–SCHOLES FORMULA

In general, the kind of optimization problem needed to find an EMM by the route described above will not be easy to solve. Here is a very simple example where we can get around the problem altogether.

To start, assume that we are in discrete time, with a deposit account that starts the period worth 1, and a share that starts the period worth 1. At the end of the period the share will be worth u if the period was good, and $d < u$ if the period was bad; the deposit account will be worth $\rho \in (d, u)$ whatever the type of period. Suppose we have an agent who is trying to maximize his expected utility of wealth at the end of the period, in the manner described in the previous section. He will end up with a measure $\mathbb{P}^*$ on the set of possible outcomes, which in this easy example contains just two points, "good" and "bad". If p denotes the probability of "good" under $\mathbb{P}^*$, then we know that the discounted share price process becomes a martingale under $\mathbb{P}^*$, so the expectation of its discounted value at the end of the period must be its value at the beginning of the period:

$$p\frac{u}{\rho} + (1 - p)\frac{d}{\rho} = 1$$

From this, simple algebra leads to the conclusion

$$p = \frac{\rho - d}{u - d} \tag{13}$$

Now we see that *the value of p is unique*; it does not depend on the preferences of the agent.[7]

Now we extend the model, assuming that $u = 1/d$,[8] and consider one period after another, all independent of each other, and all behaving as in the one-period model above. Each period, the share's value gets multiplied by u (on a good period) or by d (on a bad period), and the deposit account's value always gets multiplied by ρ. As before, there is a unique EMM, and under this the log-price process X becomes a random walk with "up" probability given by (13).

We now begin to think of the model with N periods as representing the movement of the asset prices during some fixed time interval $[0, T]$, each period corresponding to $\Delta t \equiv T/N$ units of time. If the compound interest rate of the deposit account is r, then we should therefore express the one-period return of the deposit account as $\rho = \exp(r\Delta t)$, and we similarly write $u = \exp(\Delta x)$, where we think of Δx as small, and we have in mind ultimately to let both Δx and Δt tend to zero appropriately. In these terms, we translate (13) to

$$p = \frac{e^{r\Delta t} - e^{-\Delta x}}{e^{\Delta x} - e^{-\Delta x}} \tag{14}$$

and, in keeping with this way of thinking, we write $X^{(N)}$ for the log-price process; $X^{(N)}$ is a simple random walk, with steps that take values Δx and $-\Delta x$ only, with probabilities p and $1 - p$, respectively, given by (14).

Now consider a contingent claim

$$Y = f(X_{N\Delta t}^{(N)}) \equiv f(X_T^{(N)})$$

At time $t = j\Delta t < T$, when $X_t^{(N)} = m\Delta x$, what is the "fair" price to pay for the contingent claim Y to be delivered at T? It has to be the expected discounted value of the contingent claim:

$$V_N(j\Delta t, m\Delta x) = \mathbb{E}^*[\exp(-(N-j)r\Delta t) \cdot Y] \tag{15}$$

Because we know that the log-price process is a simple random walk, we could rewrite this in terms of an expectation with respect to the binomial distribution: writing $q = 1 - p$ we have

$$V_N(j\Delta t, m\Delta x) = e^{-(N-j)r\Delta t} \sum_{i=0}^{N-j} p^i q^{N-j-i} \binom{N-j}{i} f((m + 2i - N + j)\Delta x)$$

But this can be expressed equivalently (and more usefully) as

$$V_N(j\Delta t, m\Delta x) = e^{-r\Delta t}\{pV_N((j+1)\Delta t, (m+1)\Delta x) + qV_N((j+1)\Delta t, (m-1)\Delta x)\} \tag{16}$$

with the boundary conditions $V_N(N\Delta t, m\Delta x) = f(m\Delta x)$. We can verify (16) directly using Pascal's triangle, or we can preferably interpret it as the Bellman equation of dynamic programming. From this we obtain:

$$
\begin{aligned}
&V_N(j\Delta t, m\Delta x) - e^{-r\Delta t}V_N((j+1)\Delta t, m\Delta x) \\
&= e^{-r\Delta t}\Big(\tfrac{1}{2}[V_N((j+1)\Delta t, (m+1)\Delta x) - 2V_N((j+1)\Delta t, m\Delta x) \\
&\quad + V_N((j+1)\Delta t, (m-1)\Delta x)] + \big(p - \tfrac{1}{2}\big)V_N((j+1)\Delta t, (m+1)\Delta x) \\
&\quad + \big(q - \tfrac{1}{2}\big)V_N((j+1)\Delta t, (m-1)\Delta x)\Big)
\end{aligned} \tag{17}
$$

which looks quite a bit more complicated than (16). But the grouping of the terms is appropriate for what we intend to do next, which is let N go to infinity, while preserving the relation

$$(\Delta x)^2 = \sigma^2 \Delta t$$

If we do this, then from (14) we see that

$$p - \frac{1}{2} \sim \frac{(r - \tfrac{1}{2}\sigma^2)\Delta t}{2\Delta x}$$

So dividing (17) by Δt and letting Δt go to zero, the differencing operations having been grouped appropriately converge to corresponding differential operators, and we get in the limit:

$$-\frac{\partial V}{\partial t} + rV = \frac{\sigma^2}{2}\frac{\partial^2 V}{\partial x^2} + \left(r - \frac{\sigma^2}{2}\right)\frac{\partial V}{\partial x} \tag{18}$$

This formal calculation has led us to the celebrated *Black–Scholes PDE*. We are being rather cavalier in assuming that the discretely defined value functions V_N have a smooth limit for which the analogue (18) of (17) holds, but this is indeed true. The best way to see this is as a consequence of the weak convergence of the random walks $X^{(N)}$ to the process $X_t = \sigma W_t + (r - \sigma^2/2)t$, a Brownian motion with constant drift. As a consequence, the value functions V_N expressed in the form (15) converge pointwise to the limit function

$$V(t, x) = \mathbb{E}[f(X_T)|X_t = x],$$

at least if f is bounded and continuous (as would be the case for a European put option, for example). But now it is an easy matter to deduce that V solves the Black–Scholes PDE (18), since we can write

$$V(T - s, x) = \int \exp(-y^2/2\sigma^2 s)f(x + y + (r - \sigma^2/2)s)\frac{dy}{\sqrt{2\pi\sigma^2 s}}$$

and directly verify from this that V solves (18). Solving the PDE (18) with the boundary condition

$$V(T, x) = (K - e^x)^+$$

gives the Black–Scholes formula for the price of a European put option with strike K.

3.6 APPENDIX: TWO OTHER APPROACHES

In this appendix we present two very different approaches, both of which lead to risk-neutral pricing. Each is quite direct, indeed, arguably simpler than the route we took earlier in Sections 3.2 and 3.4, but does not yield the insight of that (economic) approach. To emphasize this, note that each of the approaches here yields only the *existence* of a risk-neutral pricing measure, but gives no guidance on which to choose when there is more than one.

3.6.1 Axiomatic Approach

We put ourselves in a filtered probability space $(\Omega, (\mathcal{F}_t)_{t \geq 0}, \mathbb{P})$ such that the σ-field $\mathcal{F}_0$ is trivial, and suppose that we have pricing operators $(\pi_{tT})_{0 \leq t \leq T}$ for contingent claims; if Y is some bounded random variable which is $\mathcal{F}_T$ measurable, then the time-t "market" price of Y is

$$\pi_{tT}(Y)$$

This will be a bounded $\mathcal{F}_t$-measurable random variable; any sensible definition of "the market price" at time t would have to be a random variable, because the information contained in $\mathcal{F}_t$ would inevitably affect what the market was willing to pay for Y.

We shall assume that the pricing operators $(\pi_{tT})_{0 \leq t \leq T}$ satisfy certain axioms:

(A1) Each π_{tT} is a bounded positive linear operator from $L^\infty(\mathcal{F}_T)$ to $L^\infty(\mathcal{F}_t)$;

(A2) If $Y \in L^\infty(\mathcal{F}_T)$ is almost surely 0, then $\pi_{0T}(Y)$ is 0, and if $Y \in L^\infty(\mathcal{F}_T)$ is non-negative and not almost surely 0, then $\pi_{0T}(Y) > 0$.

(A3) For $0 \leq s \leq t \leq T$ and each $X \in L^\infty(\mathcal{F}_t)$ we have

$$\pi_{st}(X\pi_{tT}(Y)) = \pi_{sT}(XY)$$

(A4) For each $t \geq 0$ the operator π_{0t} is bounded monotone-continuous — which is to say that if $Y_n \in L^\infty(\mathcal{F}_t)$, $|Y_n| \leq 1$ for all n, and $Y_n \uparrow Y$ as $n \to \infty$, then $\pi_{0t}(Y_n) \uparrow \pi_{0t}(Y)$ as $n \to \infty$.

Axiom (A1) says that the price of a non-negative contingent claim will be non-negative, and the price of a linear combination of contingent claims will be the linear combination of their prices — which are reasonable properties for a market price. Axiom (A2) says that a contingent claim that is almost surely worthless when paid, will be almost surely worthless at all earlier times (and conversely) — again reasonable. The third axiom, (A3), is a "consistency" statement; the market prices at time s for XY at time T, or for X times the time-t market price for Y at time t, should be the same, for any X which is known at time t. The final axiom is a natural "continuity" condition which is needed for technical reasons.

Let us see where these axioms lead us. First, for any $T > 0$ we have that the map

$$A \mapsto \pi_{0T}(I_A)$$

defines a non-negative measure on the σ-field $\mathcal{F}_T$, from the linearity and positivity (A1) and the continuity property (A4). Moreover, this measure is absolutely continuous with respect to $\mathbb{P}$, in view of (A2). Hence there is a non-negative $\mathcal{F}_T$-measurable random variable ζ_T such that

$$\pi_{0T}(Y) = \mathbb{E}[\zeta_T Y]$$

for all $Y \in L^\infty(\mathcal{F}_T)$. Moreover, $\mathbb{P}[\zeta_T > 0] > 0$, because of (A2) again. Now we exploit the consistency condition (A3); we have

$$\pi_{0t}(X\pi_{tT}(Y)) = \mathbb{E}[X\zeta_t\pi_{tT}(Y)] = \pi_{0T}(XY) = \mathbb{E}[XY\zeta_T]$$

Since $X \in L^\infty(\mathcal{F}_t)$ is arbitrary, we deduce that

$$\pi_{tT}(Y) = \mathbb{E}_t[Y\zeta_T]/\zeta_t$$

which shows that the pricing operators π_{st} are actually given by a risk-neutral pricing recipe, with the state–price density process ζ. In practice, the state–price density process is often decomposed as the product of the discount factor $\exp(-\int_0^t r_s ds)$ and the change-of-measure martingale.

3.6.2 No-Arbitrage Approach

The proof that the absence of arbitrage implies that there exists an equivalent measure under which all discounted asset prices are martingales was first given in discrete time by Dalang et al. (1990). The full story for continuous time is much harder; a non-trivial part of the difficulty lies in the fact that the obvious definitions of "no arbitrage" do not work for various reasons, and the framing of the correct definition is a major part of the work of Delbaen and Schachermayer (1997). Here we just give the flavour of the proof of the discrete-time result from Rogers (1994), which has much in common with the ideas of Section 3.4 above.

Suppose we are in a one-period world, and that there are n assets. Also assume for simplicity that there is no discounting: $R \equiv 1$ in the notation of Section 3.2. The changes in the prices of the n assets from the start to the end of the period is denoted by the random vector $X \equiv (X^1, \ldots, X^n)^T$, so that if the agent chooses to hold the portfolio $\theta \in \mathbb{R}^n$ during the period, his gain by the end of the period will just be $\eta \equiv \theta \cdot X$. The no-arbitrage assumption is that there is no θ for which $\mathbb{P}[\eta \geq 0] = 1$ and $\mathbb{P}[\eta > 0] > 0$; in words, you cannot make a gain without also facing some risk of losing. Without loss of generality, we can assume that there is no $a \in \mathbb{R}^n$ for which $\mathbb{P}[a \cdot X = 0] = 1$, for then X would lie in a smaller-dimensional subspace, and we could drop down to that subspace and work there.

The theorem says that if the no-arbitrage assumption holds, then there is a measure $\mathbb{P}^*$ equivalent to $\mathbb{P}$ under which

$$\mathbb{E}^*[X] = 0;$$

the random vector X is a vector of martingale differences.

The idea is to consider the moment-generating function

$$a \mapsto \varphi(a) \equiv \mathbb{E} \exp(a \cdot X), \quad a \in \mathbb{R}^n$$

which we assume without loss of generality is everywhere finite.[9]

Now consider $\alpha \equiv \inf\{\varphi(a) : a \in \mathbb{R}^n\}$. There are two cases to deal with: *either* this infimum is attained, *or* this infimum is not attained.

In the first case, suppose that the infimum is attained at a^*. Then for any non-zero $\theta \in \mathbb{R}^n$ we shall have

$$0 \le \varepsilon^{-1}[\varphi(a^* + \varepsilon\theta) - \varphi(a^*)]$$
$$= \varepsilon^{-1} \mathbb{E}[\exp(a^* \cdot X)(\exp(\varepsilon\theta \cdot X) - 1)]$$
$$\to \mathbb{E}[\exp(a^* \cdot X)\theta \cdot X]$$

and by applying the same argument to $-\theta$ we obtain the conclusion

$$\mathbb{E}[\exp(a^* \cdot X)\theta \cdot X] = 0$$

whatever θ, which is what we were after; the measure whose density with respect to $\mathbb{P}$ is proportional to $\exp(a^* \cdot X)$ will be an equivalent martingale measure.

In the second case, the infimum is not attained, is at least zero (since $\varphi > 0$) and is less than $1 = \varphi(0)$. So there is some sequence of points a_n such that $\varphi(a_n) < \alpha + n^{-1}$. The sequence must be unbounded, otherwise there would be an accumulation point where, by Fatou's lemma, φ would have to be equal to α and the infimum would be attained. By passing to a subsequence, we may suppose that $a_n/|a_n|$ converges to some point γ on the unit sphere. The claim is that

$$\mathbb{P}[\gamma \cdot X > 0] = 0$$

for, if not, there would be some neighbourhood U of γ such that $\mathbb{P}[\theta \cdot X > 0] > 0$ for all $\theta \in U$. Since $a_n/|a_n| \in U$ for large enough n, it would follow that $\varphi(a_n) \to \infty$ as $n \to \infty$, a contradiction. Thus $\mathbb{P}[\gamma \cdot X > 0] = 0$, and so (since X does not lie in a proper subspace) it has to be that $\mathbb{P}[\gamma \cdot X < 0] > 0$, and investing in the portfolio $-\gamma$ gives us an arbitrage. So under the assumption of no arbitrage, the second possibility cannot in fact occur.

3.7 ENDNOTES

1. We might also allow the possibility of other economic activities, such as production; this does not alter the essential features of equilibrium, so we shall omit them and discuss only a *pure exchange* economy.

2. Of course, there have to be *some* restrictions; $\bar{\theta}$ needs to be non-anticipating in a precise sense, and not to grow too wildly — local boundedness is certainly sufficient.

3. Rogers and Satchell (1996) give a stark warning about the difference between real-world and so-called "risk-neutral" probabilities.

4. The strict increase in U is natural, and the strict concavity reflects the agent's risk aversion.

5. The definitive version of this result appears now to have been proved by Delbaen and Schachermayer (1997). We sketch the main ideas of the result in the Appendix (Section 3.6).

6. For example, the result of Jacka (1992) that a contingent claim is attainable if and only if its price is the same with respect to all equivalent martingale measures.

7. This is because the market is complete, and every contingent claim can be replicated perfectly. See any introductory text on finance for the story.

8. With this assumption, the set of possible values for the share at any time is contained in $\{u^n : n \in \mathbb{Z}\}$.

9. If not, we would replace $\mathbb{P}$ by the equivalent measure $\tilde{\mathbb{P}}$ defined by $\tilde{\mathbb{P}} = c \cdot \exp(-|X|^2)\mathbb{P}$, for a suitable normalizing constant c. For this measure, the moment-generating function of X *is* everywhere finite, and the argument proceeds as given.

3.8 REFERENCES

Dalang, R.C., Morton, A. and Willinger, W. (1990) "Equivalent martingale measures and no-arbitrage in stochastic securities market models". *Stochastics and Stochastics Reports*, **29**, 185–201.

Delbaen, F. and Schachermayer, W. (1997) "The fundamental theorem of asset pricing for unbounded stochastic processes". Preprint.

Harrison, J.M. and Kreps, D.M. (1979) "Martingales and arbitrage in multiperiod securities markets". *Journal of Economic Theory*, **20**, 381–408.

Harrison, J.M. and Pliska, S.R. (1981) "Martingales and stochastic integrals in the theory of continuous trading". *Stochastic Processes and their Applications*, **11**, 215–60.

Jacka, S.D. (1992) "A martingale representation result and an application to incomplete financial markets". *Mathematical Finance*, **2**, 239–50.

Rogers, L.C.G. (1994) "Equivalent martingale measures and no-arbitrage". *Stochastics and Stochastics Reports*, **51**, 41–49.

Rogers, L.C.G. and Satchell, S.E. (1996) "Does the behaviour of the asset tell us anything about the option price formula? A cautionary tale". Preprint.

Williams, D. (1991) *Probability with Martingales*. Cambridge University Press.

4
Equity Derivatives

ANDREW STREET

4.1 INTRODUCTION

4.1.1 Aims and Scope of this Chapter

As its title suggests, this chapter will focus on equity derivatives and in particular the new products that have been developed in that area over the last few years. To study in detail the precise pay-off formulae of equity derivatives (EDs from now on) structures and the methods of their mathematical evaluation, whilst important, would be to miss the big picture with regard to derivatives, and the equity variety in particular. It is often said that financial markets are driven by fear and greed, this is as true of derivative markets as of any others. Derivatives only exist because they enhance economic efficiency, they either save money, make money or prevent its loss. This efficiency extends to the ability either to guarantee or insure results, to avoid taxes, to take advantage of specific legislation or to exploit a new category of risk such as volatility or correlation with the enhanced leverage this offers. The world's equity markets and their respective legal frameworks with regard to ownership rights over different classes of shares and dividend rights are far from standardized or non-arbitragable. Each of these markets has specific quirks which can be exploited with derivatives to the advantage of both the issuers and holders of equity financing. Each of these markets has differing liquidities, dealing and settlement terms, dividend policies and general information with regard to the returns available, both actual and prospective. Derivatives can be designed to reduce or overcome a lot of these problems and to take advantage of the potential returns with limited risk. It is often said that derivatives allow the "bundling" and "unbundling" of risk and return. This is not only true of the so-called "emerging markets" such as Thailand and Pakistan but also highly developed stock markets such as the United States or the United Kingdom.

This chapter is broken down into seven further sections. The remainder of this section looks at how the different types of equity derivatives can be classified depending on their structure, use and form. We will then briefly visit the general pricing assumptions of these types of contracts and securities. In Section 4.2 we look at the historical development of

Risk Management and Analysis. Vol. 2: New Markets and Products. Edited by Carol Alexander
© 1998 John Wiley & Sons Ltd

equity derivatives. Section 4.3 deals with the economic utility of equity derivatives for both borrowers and investors. The role of investment banks in the creation of equity derivatives is examined in Section 4.4. Section 4.5 deals exclusively with stock index-based products, including exchange traded OTCs, hybrids and securities. Applications of equity derivatives for single shares and bespoke indices are covered in Section 4.6. The final section looks at the potential future developments for equity derivatives. A glossary of some of the specialist terms used is included in Section 4.8, and references can be found in Section 4.9.

4.1.2 Classification of Equity Derivatives

So what is an equity derivative (ED)? Let us break down the term into its component parts. Equity, in this context, is a share in ownership of a company or corporation. Equities are shares, listed or unlisted on an exchange, which generally carry a voting right at the annual general meeting, an entitlement to a dividend and a pro-rata share in the company's assets at the point of winding up (liquidation) after all other creditors have been paid. Some "equities"; for example, preference shares, are a kind of half-way house between true equities and debt in that they do not carry full voting rights, but have an enhanced entitlement to dividend payments, which may well be fixed in advance and so are not subject in amount to the vagaries of the company's profit cycle. Derivative is a much used and abused word these days; in this context it refers to either a contract or a security whose pay-off or final value is dependent on one or more features of the underlying equity. In many circumstances it is the price of the underlying equity which determines to a large extent the value of the equity derivative, although other factors like interest rates, time to maturity and strike price can play an equally large role. I used the terms "security" and "contract" and it is important that these are explained. A security (e.g. a government bond or "gilt" in the United Kingdom) is an obligation issued by one party to another through the mechanism of listing on a stock exchange. Listing carries with it special obligations through listing conditions which must be satisfied. These conditions vary from exchange to exchange but broadly require production of offering memoranda (which contain such things as details of the issue, audited company accounts and proposed use of funds) and the issue of a fixed number of securities either in definitive or global note form (see glossary). This ensures that new securities cannot be created and destroyed at will, and therefore has consequences for short selling and liquidity squeezes. In general, securities are in finite supply and this has direct consequences for both underlying assets and derivatives themselves. A contract, or more specifically an OTC (literally "over the counter", i.e. privately agreed between two direct counterparts) contract, can be created and destroyed virtually at will and is therefore much less prone to "paper" squeezes which can occur at the time of delivery. In general the underlying equity asset will be a security, whereas the derivative on it may be a contract or a security in its own right. The contract may also be differentiated into standardized, exchange traded contracts and those traded OTC with completely bespoke terms and conditions. These are usually, but not exclusively, agreed under some master document engineered by an industry group such as the International Swap Dealers Association (ISDA).

4.1.3 General Features of Pricing Equity Derivatives

The detailed mechanics of simple and exotic option pricing will be discussed in later chapters in much more detail, but it is worthwhile here to focus upon some practical aspects of equity derivative pricing. Generally most derivative pricing takes place in what is usually called the "Black–Scholes" (see Hull (1993), Cox and Rubenstein (1985) and Wilmott et al. (1994)) universe since this leads to the most readily accessible results (see Special Section Review of Black–Scholes Option Pricing, p. 100). In this universe an instantaneously risk-free portfolio (i.e. a portfolio which yields the risk-free interest rate under all market scenarios when the portfolio is continuously rebalanced) can be constructed out of the derivative, the underlying risky asset and a riskless bond. It is said that the portfolio composed of a special combination of the risky asset and a risk-less discount (or zero bond) "replicates" the value characteristics of the derivative. This requires that asset price volatility is constant, interest rates are constant and have a flat term structure, that the market in the underlying risky asset has infinite liquidity (i.e. a zero bid/offer spread in any size bargain) and that the market price of the asset behaves in an entirely random walk and non-trending manner. If you ask anyone who has traded any market, but especially equity, they will tell you that the real world does not work like that! Some of the conditions of the Black–Scholes universe can be relaxed, but the subsequent differential equations become much more complex to solve with practically no gain in real day-to-day usefulness. The problem of accuracy lies as much with the estimation of parameters, typically forward prices and volatilities, as it does with the dynamics and boundary conditions of the price process. The model produced is at best a good guide which must be used carefully and with insight and experience, it being more important to evaluate carefully the factors that the models cannot cope with and to operate a risk management policy based on relative rather than absolute valuation. An example of the latter is when a three-year call option is hedged by a two-year call option on a volatility calendar spread basis (i.e. a long position in two-year volatility is hedged by selling a vega (volatility) weighted amount of three-year volatility) rather than by a pure delta hedging ("replication") strategy; the possible systematic error is potentially much larger in the latter case, since it is much more likely that systematic valuation errors will cancel in the former case.

The equity underlying has specific valuation problems all of its own. In constructing the forward asset price a dividend yield must be assumed or derived from market prices. Information on prospective dividends is seldom published beyond three to six months of the ex-dividend date and the dividend policies of corporates are notoriously fickle. In a sense they have to be, as the dividend represents one of the balancing items in a company's financial health and is often the first thing to be sacrificed in difficult times. Markets in forward prices are thin (i.e. a wide bid/offer spread) for the equity market indices such as the FTSE 100 or S&P 500 (for which the foregoing problems are reduced somewhat due to the portfolio effect of having many diverse equity dividend flows within it) and virtually non-existent for single stocks. Longer dated option valuation on equity underlyings therefore frequently contains substantial unhedgeable risk which must be priced in as a Black–Scholes extra.

Figure 4.1 is a schematic representation of the forward price of an equity index, i.e. its value today for future delivery (one might pay 1.05 times the spot price today for delivery in a year's time). It is worth noting a few significant features of this figure which have been exaggerated for clarity. During the settlement period or "account" the asset (in this case a basket of stocks representing the "current" stock index) can be bought and sold without any cash flows actually taking place, thus there is no differ-ence in price from spot for the asset traded within the account. The UK stock market

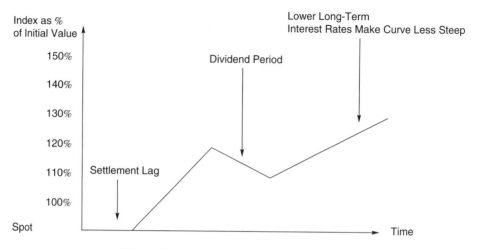

Figure 4.1   Equity index forward price curve

operated a two-week account up until the middle of 1994 when it changed over to rolling ten-day settlement. The French stock market still operates a monthly account for some of its stocks. In general the yield or dividend on the stock index will be less than the prevailing risk-free interest rates; this means that holding the asset will not be self-funding and it will have a negative "cost of carry", i.e. the cost of financing the holding is greater than the dividends received. This is reflected in the positive sloping forward curve. If the dividend flows are concentrated over a particular part of the year, as they are in the French CAC 40 index and the German DAX 30 index or indeed for a single stock, it is possible for the dividend flow to exceed the cost of financing the position over a period of the year. This leads to the negative sloping part of the asset forward curve. If longer-term interest rates are lower than short-term interest rates (i.e. a negative sloping yield curve) the longer-term forward curve will be less steep than the short term.

One further factor with regard to equity forward curves needs to be borne in mind, the mechanism of going "short" the market. "Short" selling is the sale of an asset which one does not already own, it is therefore necessary to borrow the asset to effect the delivery of the sale. This is frequently called stock borrowing/lending or sometimes "repo" (short for "sale and repurchase agreement"), which refers to a contract whereby two parties agree for one to simultaneously buy an asset spot and sell it forward at an agreed price to the other. The net effect is the same as it effectively separates the ownership of an asset (i.e. exposure to price risk) from its "physical" possession or deliverability. The holder (who is not the "owner") of the stock can then deliver the asset in settlement of his sell bargain. The costs of borrowing and lending stock are not constant and are subject to a bid/offer spread. Typically in the United Kingdom the cost is around 0.5 per cent to borrow. There is therefore both an offer and a bid forward asset price curve. In some markets, such as the United Kingdom, there are legal restrictions on borrowing stock, which mean that only a registered market-maker in that particular equity may actually enter the stock loan market to cover a short position. This can lead to distortions in the forward asset price curve and therefore in derivative pricing, particularly on the short side (e.g. put options on individual shares) as we are not dealing in a free and unstratified market.

An even larger problem than establishing the correct forward for the equity asset is deciding on the appropriate volatility or standard deviation of asset price to use in evaluating the equity derivative. Within the model this factor determines the distribution width characteristic of the random walk of the asset price and therefore the range of the possible values for the derivative. If a liquid market in the derivative exists the implied volatility can be back calculated by using the market prices to arrive at a suitable volatility figure, i.e. one that will give market observed prices when inserted in the model. If one is able to buy at the bid and sell at the offer (i.e. act as market-maker in a liquid market) this may be all that is required to run a successful book of options. However when markets are thin or non-existent the problem of parameter estimation generally falls to forecasting techniques from simple weighted mean reverting volatility models to more sophisticated Generalized Auto Regressive Conditional Heteroskedasticity (GARCH) models, based on historical and market implied volatility data. If the market is illiquid and the parameter has to be forecast, any derivative seller is going to want to build in a generous margin of error into his volatility parameter estimation as insurance against getting it wrong and having to hedge the position over a long time horizon.

One further practical problem of equity derivative valuation is the effect of "market impact" on the price of the contingent claim and the related problem of finite bid/offer spread in the underlying asset in a delta hedge ("replication") strategy. Whenever the equity derivative agreement is made the hedge for that risk must in some way be offset in the market. In a simple case the delta equivalent amount of the risky asset is bought or sold.

Consider a call option struck at 100 ("at the money") with the market trading at 99 bid/101 offer in 25/25 lots (25 units on the bid and the offer). If we buy the delta amount of contracts, say 50, we will buy the first lot of 25 at 101 and possibly the next lot of 25 at 102, giving an average price of 101.5. In this case the price is 1.5 above the mean level of the market due to the bid/offer spread and market impact, i.e. the market rallied because we bought it. Our hedge has now cost us 1.5 more than the theory would suggest! We encounter the same problem in a smaller way for the day-to-day rebalances as these are much smaller in size, but become significant when gamma gets large (e.g. near the barrier of an in-the-money barrier option). Also note we have a similar problem on taking the hedge off at expiry or exercise.

Having established some of the more practical aspects of equity derivative pricing above it is worthwhile to examine briefly the concept of the price of a derivative security as being the present value (i.e. discounted back to today's value) of the expected future pay-off of the derivative. Referring to Figure 4.2, we consider a European call option (value C) on an asset, price S, struck at K with expiry time T (i.e. the pay-off at T is $\max(S \text{ (at expiry)} - K, 0)$). The forward price of the asset at time T will be S_T and the width of the probability distribution of the asset price will be $\sigma\sqrt{T}$. If the risk-free rate of interest is R then the value of the derivative is the integral from K to plus infinity of $(S - K)$ multiplied by the normal probability distribution Φ centred on S_T with width $\sigma\sqrt{T}$ over S, discounted by $e^{(T-t)R}$. Equation (1) is given below:

$$C = \frac{1}{e^{(T-t)R}} \int_K^\infty (S - K)\Phi(S_T, \sigma\sqrt{T})\, dS \qquad (1)$$

This concept of the present value of the expected (probabilistic) future value of the derivative pay-off is one of the basic building blocks of derivative pricing and is very

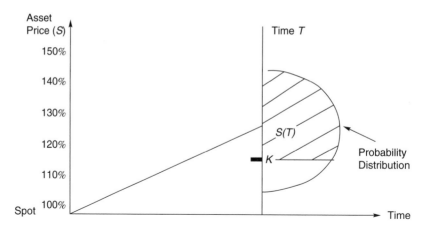

Figure 4.2   Option value as PV of expectation value

useful in looking at more complex pay-off situations where many different scenarios are possible.

Special Section Review of Black–Scholes Option Pricing

Definitions and notations for options in the Black–Scholes universe (Wilmott et al. (1994)):

- $O(S, t)$ is the value of an option at time t with underlying asset price S
- σ is the price volatility of the underlying asset
- K is the exercise price of the option
- T is the expiry
- R is the risk-free interest rate
- Call option (right to buy asset for K) has terminal value $C(S, T) = \max(S - K, 0)$
- Put option (right to sell asset for K), has terminal value $P(S, T) = \max(K - S, 0)$
- Put–call parity ensures $S + P - C = K/e^{(T-t)R}$

Black–Scholes Assumptions:

- The asset price follows log normal random walk
- The risk-free interest rate and volatility are known functions of time
- No transaction costs in hedging portfolio
- No dividends paid during the life of the option
- No arbitrage possibilities, all risk-free portfolios earn the risk-free rate
- Continuous trading of underlying asset
- Underlying asset can be sold short in any size without penalty
- Stochastic differential equation, i.e. the underlying price process of the asset:

$$\frac{\mathrm{d}S}{S} = \sigma \, \mathrm{d}W + \mu \, \mathrm{d}t \tag{2}$$

(where S is the asset price, $\mathrm{d}S$ is a small change in price over time $\mathrm{d}t$, σ is the volatility, $\mathrm{d}W$ is a random variable from a normal distribution, μ is the drift (risk-free rate) and $\mathrm{d}t$ is a small time step)

- Black–Scholes partial differential equation (derived via Ito's lemma and no riskless arbitrage arguments from the above):

$$\frac{\partial O}{\partial t} + \frac{1}{2}\sigma^2 S^2 \frac{\partial^2 O}{\partial S^2} + RS\frac{\partial O}{\partial S} - RO = 0 \tag{3}$$

- A solution for the above differential equation, with the boundary conditions equivalent to the case of a European call option with no dividends, is:

$$C(S,t) = SN(d_1) - \frac{K}{e^{(T-t)R}}N(d_2) \tag{4}$$

$$N(x) = \frac{1}{(2\pi)^{1/2}} \int_{-\infty}^{\infty} e^{-1/2y^2}\,dy \tag{5}$$

$$d_1 = \frac{\ln(S/K) + (R + \sigma^2/2)(T-t)}{\sigma\sqrt{T-t}} \tag{6}$$

$$d_2 = \frac{\ln(S/K) + (R - \sigma^2/2)(T-t)}{\sigma\sqrt{T-t}} \tag{7}$$

- The partial derivatives or option price sensitivities, often known as the "Greeks":

$$\text{Delta } \Delta = \frac{\partial C}{\partial S} \tag{8}$$

$$\text{Gamma } \Gamma = \frac{\partial^2 C}{\partial S^2} \tag{9}$$

$$\text{Theta } \Theta = \frac{\partial C}{\partial t} \tag{10}$$

$$\text{Vega (or Kappa) } \kappa = \frac{\partial C}{\partial \sigma} \tag{11}$$

$$\text{Rho } \rho = \frac{\partial C}{\partial R} \tag{12}$$

Other higher order derivatives exist (e.g. $\partial^2 C/\partial S\,\partial\sigma$) and have esoteric names such as charm, colour, beauty, etc. Dividend sensitivity has come to be known as omega by some market practitioners.

4.2 HISTORICAL DEVELOPMENT

4.2.1 Listed Equity Derivatives

In considering *listed* equity derivatives (these are derivatives which are "listed" or controlled on a recognized exchange) we need to differentiate between those which are traded as contracts, such as futures and options on the FTSE 100 traded on the London LIFFE exchange, and those which are traded as securities and are either settled domestically or through settlement systems such as EuroClear and CEDEL, such as a FTSE 100 index covered warrant issued by an investment bank or a convertible bond issued by a corporation to raise working capital (e.g. The Burton Group $4\frac{3}{4}$ per cent Convertible due 25/08/01).

The FTSE 100 futures and options type equity derivatives are termed exchanged traded contracts or ETCs and are subject to strict regulatory control, daily marking to market and margining on the basis of each counterpart's exposure. Each day payments have to be made to and from the exchange to maintain the financial cover for the risk on open positions. This margin flow consists of two types, initial margin, paid on each opening of a contract and variational margin, paid or received based on the new closing mark to market value of the open positions. The exchange is the counterpart to all contracts and acts as the guarantor of performance under the obligations entered into therein. In the case of options, with their asymmetric risk profile (i.e. the contract is a *right* to the holder and an *obligation* to the seller), only the option premium needs to be paid by the option buyer at the time of purchase. The holder of the option has no further obligations once the premium has been paid. These contracts on stock indices and individual shares are typically shorter dated futures and simple call and put options with standardized terms and conditions.

Since the exchange traded listed equity derivative, an options contract on an equity, was first traded in 1973 (on the Chicago Board Options Exchange), there has been a rapid expansion of exchanges and equity ETCs world-wide. It was in the 1980s that most of Europe gained ETCs on equity indices and increasingly on individual shares. In London in the mid-1980s, LIFFE listed the FTSE 100 futures, then in the early 1990s the FTSE 250. LTOM (the London traded option market, later merged with LIFFE in 1992) listed options on the FTSE 100 index, and by 1992 also listed options on approximately 80 individual equities, most of whom were components of the FTSE 100 index. This exchange was based on the Chicago pattern of pit trading "open outcry" as were the French exchanges called the MATIF (Marché à Terme International de France) and the MONEP (Marché des Options Negotiables de la Bourse de Paris) which lists the CAC 40 futures and options along with options on approximately 20 individual equities. Other exchanges followed, but not all followed the pattern of open outcry pit trading; the German DTB for example is a pure electronic market, where traders communicate only via an electronic data exchange and terminal. This system creates an electronic pit trading environment where bids can be hit and offers taken via a keyboard, mouse and VDU. The derivative contract terms themselves however remain essentially of the same form the world over. A similar system for after-hours trading in London, called Automated Pit Trading (APT), also exists.

The pattern of derivatives exchanges being set up to trade listed future and options contracts on the major large capitalization index of the country's stock market has been one that has been repeated many times over the globe, from Australia's All-Ordinaries Index via Hong Kong's Hang-Seng index to Canada's TSE 35 index. This growth can be linked to several underlying factors in global capital markets:

1. Increasing global investment, diversifying home market portfolios to include overseas exposure so as to increase returns and reduce risk.

2. Significant outperformance of equity markets over fixed income in the 1980s, portfolio weightings therefore tilted more towards equity.

3. Structural changes in capital market regulation and the opening of new markets for investment lead to enhanced opportunities overseas, both in established markets such as Europe and also emerging markets in the Far East and South America.

4. The shift in investment management practices so as to reduce costs and comply with more onerous legislation means a greater emphasis on index tracking, tactical asset

allocation (between cash, equity and bonds; in some cases currency and commodity assets also) and the reduction in costs in trading the market portfolio (as represented by a large market capitalization, broadly based index) via the futures market rather than active management through individual stock selection. Stock selection in overseas markets is made expensive and difficult due to lack of data and non-standard accounting methods.

5. The development of portfolio enhancement techniques such as portfolio insurance, yield enhancement and volatility trading.

6. The explosion of "hedge" funds and other high risk/return collective investments.

7. The development of the over-the-counter derivatives market with the associated hedging needs of the investment banks to hedge their risk.

8. The management of credit risk in overseas investment through properly controlled and margined derivatives exchanges, most of which are based on the Chicago model.

These developments along with other factors have led to the rapid growth of exchange traded futures and options on equity stock indices and individual stocks.

Other forms of listed equity derivative exist, ones that are stock exchange listed securities rather than derivative contracts traded and settled on their own exchange. Most of this type of equity derivative are either *warrants* or *convertible bonds*. These types of financing have their origins in the early Eurobond market of the late 1960s and early 1970s. They became much more prevalent in the early to mid-1980s due to the major equity bull trend in global markets. The Japanese market in particular, up to the end of the 1980s, used debt issues with equity warrants attached and convertibles to finance the remarkable growth of the economy. The Japanese stock market contains one of the largest reservoirs of the types of listed equity derivatives detailed below:

- *Warrants* are essentially options on an underlying share or basket of shares or an equity index, which are listed as securities on an exchange. The warrants may be issued by the company upon whose shares the warrants are exercisable or by a third party, such as an investment bank. The warrants are generally of the call option type and in the case of company issued warrants, frequently lead to the issue of new shares on exercise giving rise to some dilution effects which are not present in warrants issued by third parties (e.g. stock index warrants issued by banks), or indeed in the case of exchange traded contracts. The dilution of the share price on issue of new shares can be calculated by considering the overall value of the company to be a constant at time of issue, plus the exercise premium of the warrants, so that the number of shares in issue multiplied by the share price before exercise is equal to the new total number of shares in issue times the "new" (i.e. diluted) share price plus the amount paid by the warrant holders to exercise their warrants. Dilution can have a large effect on option valuation if the total underlying size of the warrant issue is significant, say 10 per cent of total equity.

  Warrants are frequently issued by corporates alongside a bond issue as a way of encouraging investors to buy the issue (the so-called "Equity Kicker") and for accounting advantages due to the off balance sheet treatment of warrant obligations for tax and accounting purposes. These warrants would frequently be just out-of-the-money (i.e. with a strike price set 5 to 10 per cent above the current share price for each year of the life of the warrant). Not least they offer the funding opportunity of issuing something which will only become a "real" debt for the company if the share price performs well and the warrant holders exercise their rights. Clearly the company would be in a good position to cope with the obligation in those circumstances and would welcome the cash injection from the exercise premium. The buoyant share price would also tend to mitigate dilution effects.

Warrants are traded in a secondary, telephone market and are either settled through domestic arrangements or via EuroClear or CEDEL. This mechanism is very similar to the straight Eurobond market.

- *Convertible bonds (CBs)* are similar in some ways to a bond issue with attached (or "wedded") warrants, except that on exercise the whole bond is surrendered for a fixed number of shares without payment of exercise premium. The convertible bond therefore carries a coupon (annual interest payment) which is lower than a standard plain vanilla bond since the embedded equity option has to be paid for by the investor through reduced interest payments. Convertibles therefore have a hybrid characteristic of both debt and equity. When the underlying share price is low and the embedded equity option is deep out-of-the-money, the convertible bond has a price behaviour similar to a "straight" bond; with a high share price the CB has strong equity price characteristics. The convertible's exercise price is typically (for a five-year issue) set approximately 130 per cent above the spot price and convertibility is usually only available on specific anniversary dates. Company issued CBs do produce dilution as new shares are generally issued. The major benefits to the issuer are similar to warrants: reduced funding costs so long as the share price does not outperform, conversion of debt to equity if it does. Convertibles either trade in price like ordinary bonds, i.e. in percentage of face value (this is true of Euro Converts), or alternatively in absolute price as for French Domestic Convertibles.

More complex hybrid securities were created and listed, generally by investment banks in response to a particular client request. Particular examples are the index linked redemption bonds and the coupon linked redemption bonds, frequently linked to the Nikkei 225 index. These are often termed "structured notes", and can be issued under programmes of issuers such as Medium Term Notes (MTNs) or Euro Commercial Paper (ECP). The listing on a stock exchange is often a requirement for the investor as he is frequently operating under trustee constraints of the type of asset that may be held in a fund. The last five years have seen an increase of this type of bespoke derivative creation, frequently the whole issue is "privately placed" with one client and does not trade in a secondary market in the way a normal, widely distributed security would.

4.2.2 Unlisted or "Over-the-Counter" Equity Derivatives

The development of unlisted or over-the-counter equity derivatives is much harder to trace than the listed EDs since they are by their very nature private transactions between two counterparts. It is probably fair to say that apart from some purely matched transactions the development of OTC equity derivatives followed after the development of the interest rate swap market and stemmed from two main areas: the twin concepts of risk management of a portfolio of risk on an unmatched/active basis by the investment banking intermediary and the repackaging/creation of securities such as covered warrants and structured notes. Both of these ideas have their origins in the fixed income markets, the swap book coming from the back-to-back loan market which in turn was driven by exchange controls. Repackaging and creating securities to satisfy particular investor appetite became more feasible once the techniques of risk control and book running had been established, typified by the growth of asset swaps.

Some of the earliest OTC equity derivatives were options on indices embedded in interest rate swap contracts resulting from the creation of index linked bonds, in particular the Nikkei linked redemption bonds issued in the mid 1980s. These bonds were generally privately placed with Japanese life insurance companies and other institutional investors who effectively wrote long dated options on the index in order to earn an enhanced coupon (interest) on the Euroyen bond. Certain accounting standards in Japan, with regard to the tax treatment of capital gains and income, made this approach particularly attractive. Frequently this technique was also used by traditional fixed income investors to gain equity market exposure whilst not contravening trustee boundaries. These options were frequently repackaged and sold as securities in the form of warrants to European investors.

At this time portfolio insurance techniques using dynamic replication strategies by buying and selling futures contracts according to a notional delta became discredited due to the problem of liquidity at the crucial point of market breakdown. The desire of portfolio managers to buy custom protection to exact dates, strikes and in sufficient size to hedge realistic portfolios became much greater, particularly with funds which closely mimic the index portfolio. OTC index options began to be traded by portfolio managers, particularly out-of-the-money puts and "collar" trades (where put protection is financed by selling a call for a net zero premium).

The increase in the use of tactical asset allocation and greater overseas investment led to an interest in derivatives which allow the switching of equity returns for fixed income returns. The equity returns typically include dividend payments which are often subject to special taxation treatment, which can in some circumstances lead to a payment of more than 100 per cent of the gross dividend declared. These derivatives are called *equity swaps* and have become one of the most popular OTC equity derivatives.

Under certain circumstances an investor would wish to express a particular view of the market, but because of credit considerations, for example the investor wishes to sell options and does not have a credit rating, cannot do so via a pure OTC transaction. He may choose to implement it via a structured investment where a security in the form of a "note" or bond would be specially created with pay-off profiles which linked the payment of interest and/or the final redemption amount to the behaviour of some equity underlying. The OTC option would thus be embedded in the structure, the note structure removing the credit risk for the option buyer. The option is thus termed an *embeddo*. These are frequently known as *structured notes* or *equity linked notes* and became increasingly popular in the early 1990s.

In the next section we will look at the utility of equity derivatives for both investors and borrowers.

4.3 THE UTILITY OF EQUITY DERIVATIVES

In this section we will examine the specific aspects of equity derivatives which make them attractive to both investors and borrowers alike. It is the particular utility of the structures rather than the structures themselves that we examine, specific structural examples will be detailed in Sections 4.5 and 4.6.

4.3.1 The Evaluation of Risk and Return

One of the greatest advances made in mathematical finance was the work done on the evaluation of risk and return (Markowitz (1989)). Essentially statistical analysis of historical data of price evolution allows the mean and moments (usually just the first moment, the width of the distribution at FWHM, the standard deviation) of asset performance to be measured over a suitable time scale. Having corrected for the expected risk-free rate of return, a plot of risk and return can be created for different assets, this is the basis of the Capital Asset Pricing Model (CAPM). The problem arises however as to how stable these statistical measures of risk/return will be in the future, i.e. how good is their predictive power? Not surprisingly over relatively short time periods their predictive power is poor as assets tend to perform relative to business cycles, but improves over longer time horizons. At one end of the quantitative sophistication scale, quantitative tactical asset allocators may well use these data (along with the covariance matrix, which shows how returns on different assets are correlated) to decide the composition (weighting) of their portfolio so as to get their optimal risk/return ratio for the fund. At the other end of the quantitative sophistication spectrum an investor may decide that a particular individual equity looks cheap, as it has underperformed the market for reasons which do not seem to be justified. Both investors are making a value judgement as to the prospective risk/return ratio inherent in their investment. If they include cash as an asset within the portfolio they are effectively creating a replicating portfolio of the type discussed in the special Black–Scholes section earlier, with assumptions as to the prospective variability or volatility in the risky assets. They are in fact synthesizing an option-like pay-off, from which one can infer the implied volatility of the replicating portfolio. If options are available, their prices may be used to benchmark this investment strategy through the comparison of the implied volatility in the replicating portfolio and that implied in the options. The investor is thus clearly faced with a choice as to whether to replicate the desired risk/return portfolio on a prospective basis or to go with the guarantee of performance offered by the option, since purchase of the option effectively allows the investor to lock in the variability of returns at the start rather than suffer the possibility that the risk/return forecast is wrong. Clearly in a situation where the implied volatility of the option is below that of the portfolio, it would seem obvious to go with the guarantee offered by purchase of an option and to keep the balance of funds in risk-free assets. It is thus in this situation cheaper to buy rather than to attempt to replicate the desired pay-off profile. Derivatives can therefore have a great role to play in benchmarking all investment decisions since they offer the certainty of outcome at a price, the price of which may be perceived as rich or cheap to the investor's own analysis and therefore may alter their implementation strategy. This is the essence of the "make or buy" argument of derivatives.

4.3.2 Tax Efficiency

The essence of tax efficiency in derivatives usually comes from their ability to convert income to capital gains or vice versa and in their ability to alter the classification of the security as debt or equity. Thus a simple box spread structure in European options (long call, short put both at strike $K1$, long put, short call both strike at $K2$) which is entirely equivalent to a zero coupon bond may actually be taxed as capital gain rather than income in some tax jurisdictions. In the United Kingdom, for example, the zero bond is a deep discount security and is taxed as income. Clearly the trick with tax efficiency is to use corporate structures in differing tax domiciles, linked by derivatives contracts so that less tax is paid overall by the organization; the linkages are often via an investment bank which may have an active or passive role with respect to the tax authorities. The taxation of dividend income from equities is a good example as often a domestic company holding structure may well benefit from tax rebates which are dependent on having income in that tax state; in a few cases no income in that structure is needed to benefit from enhanced tax rebates compared with foreign investors. This has been particularly true for the German equity market. Dividend swaps or more simply equity swaps allow these dividends to be washed through shell companies. The French market dividend wash requires that the shell company has income to offset.

Conversion of debt interest to dividend payments can also attract significant tax benefits in some jurisdictions. In the United States, payments (Watson et al. (1994)) of interest on instruments that qualify as debt for tax purposes are deductible by the issuer. Payments of dividends on equity stocks are not deductible by the issuer, but corporate holders of equity are generally entitled to deduct a portion of the dividend from their income (typically 70 per cent of the dividend). This leads to various forms of hybrid instruments, many of which are designed not only to be treated as debt for tax purposes, but as equity for financial accounting, regulatory, or rating agency purposes.

There is also industry specific tax legislation which can be exploited using derivative products. In particular the tax treatment of life insurance policies and the contingent liabilities created under these can be used, via a derivative transaction, to lower the costs of longer-term equity investment, especially for the underwriting insurance companies.

4.3.3 Regulatory Efficiency

Regulators such as Securities Exchange Commission (SEC), Securities and Futures Authority (SFA) and Investment Management Regulatory Organization (IMRO) apply capital adequacy rules based on "risk models" which seek to make an organization provide sufficient capital to support its liabilities in the case of extreme market movements or a credit default of a counterpart. These regulatory "hair-cuts" can be reduced by efficient hedging using derivatives and certain regulator treatments can be transformed via a derivative trade either to allow a particular strategy or to reduce its capital costs. In some cases a product has to be sold with a "guarantee" of performance, in which case an organization may well have to buy an option structure from a "AAA" (triple A) rated organization to embed in a product. An example might be the Business Expansion Scheme (BES) structures where the FTSE index performance is provided by an option bought from a third party, highly rated bank. Other examples include the guaranteed minimum performance bonds issued by various building societies, where a minimum rate of interest is guaranteed plus some upside in the equity market. Frequently a regulator may demand that a very small risk within a product or investment strategy be bought in from a third party in much the same way that the reinsurance market takes on board the very low probability, high cost risks of the insurance market.

Another area in which derivatives have a part to play in regulatory efficiency is in the process of mergers and acquisitions (M&A) of companies. Takeovers of companies are governed by legislation and controlled by groups such as the Panel for Takeovers and Mergers (POTAM) in the United Kingdom. There exist trigger levels of *direct* equity ownership which set in train a sequence of events by law, such that a company acquiring say 15 per cent of the total equity of a company is forced either to complete a takeover within a time period or alternatively to back off for a period of time during which no more shares may be bought or sold. Derivatives can be used in these situations to ensure that the total price paid for the acquisition of the company is hedged via option contracts without direct acquisition of shares which would trigger the M&A rules and thus force through the acquisition in a time scale not necessarily of the buyer's choice. Derivatives allow the company to exercise control over the price of the purchase of the target without triggering the takeover rules and thus forcing the bidder's hand.

For pension and mutual funds, derivatives frequently allow regulatory constraints on investments to be met or circumvented. These constraints can be in the generation of a minimum return or a maximum amount of overseas investment or a minimum amount of the fund to be invested in government bonds. Such regulations exist for funds in countries as diverse as Canada, the Netherlands and Japan.

4.3.4 Leverage

Leverage or the ability to gear up or multiply the risk exposure within an investment strategy is probably one of the best known aspects of derivatives products. It is perfectly possible to buy an option for 20 units, have cash of 80 units and still have the same price exposure to an asset as if one had spent 100 units buying the asset. In this case with 100 units one can gear the investment five times since each one times exposure costs only 20 units. Clearly this is risky as one is five times more likely to win or lose a certain amount of return. The point is that derivative products offer choice as to just how risky or not an investment strategy is when one wishes to implement a position. Again one can replicate this leveraged portfolio effect, but the derivative offers a guarantee of pay-off which may in fact be cheaper due to the different financing rates, the costs and difficulty of shorting stock and the overall level of volatility available for purchase in the market.

4.3.5 Implementation of Specific Investment Views

One of the greatest utilities of derivatives is their ability to bundle and unbundle risks. This means that specific investment ideas can be implemented very cleanly without gaining unwanted exposure or losing an exposure which was actually desired. A good example is where an investor may wish to have an equity exposure within an economy, say for example the US stock market, without necessarily having direct exposure to the US dollar. Currency protected options, forwards and futures allow the exposure without the currency risk. The derivative contract is also generally time bounded and so allows an investor to specify a time horizon for his view which is generally not available in traditional equity investment. In general the more specific the risk profile the smaller the risk/return space, with generally a decrease in the overall cost of implementation.

4.3.6 Efficiency and Cost Effectiveness

The efficiency and cost effectiveness of derivatives stems from the ability to trade individual aspects of risk rather than a bundled product, thus an entire portfolio of equities need not be completely liquidated and new stocks bought just to change an aspect of the risk profile. For example if a portfolio is to be made market neutral, selling index futures is much cheaper than selling the individual equities wholesale and then having to buy them back two weeks later. The bid/offer in the futures market for the round turn may be

50 b.p., whereas selling and buying the entire portfolio may well cost 150 b.p. plus taxes such as stamp duty. Particularly in the case of futures markets, the liquidity available frequently outstrips the cash market and makes trades in the market (index) portfolio cheaper than specific, tilted portfolios. The particular bespoke terms of the OTC derivatives contract allow great efficiency in isolating the particular aspect of the risk/return space required by the investor or borrower to suit their views.

The greater liquidity which the futures markets offer over the cash market means that investment strategies can frequently be implemented more speedily and cheaply via a derivatives trade such as a buy or sell programme trade or by staged use of futures and options over a cash flow cycle to manage the liquidity of funds which have investor cash flows over a time period.

One further aspect of OTC derivatives over their exchange traded counterparts is the credit element. As mentioned above the ETCs require margin and maintenance of that margin via a daily mark-to-market process operated by the exchange. If the counterparts are deemed creditworthy by each other they may well buy or sell contracts on the basis of credit, effectively lending or borrowing a sum of money, the interest and/or the principal redemption of which is linked to an equity index, a basket of equity or even a single stock. This is then just an extension of traditional banking business of borrowing and lending money if the equity risk can be effectively hedged. Frequently the returns on this kind of lending are much higher than the traditional business lines and represent one of the main motivations for well-capitalized banks to enter the derivatives markets. For many organizations, it greatly enhances their efficiency if they can finance on credit terms rather than drain working capital from the business where it will be earning higher returns than the interest cost on the bank financing.

For the non-banking counterpart the lack of daily margining of ETCs which OTCs offer considerably simplifies the cash management and administration of derivative positions, which for even simple ETC positions require daily administration.

4.3.7 The Utility of Equity Derivatives for Borrowers

All borrowers are interested in generating funding for the right term at the lowest possible cost. They are also interested in creating, expanding and maintaining a solid secondary market in their paper as this ensures a good market to tap further in the future and may well reduce borrowing costs if managed well, as investors will lower their expected risk premiums if they perceive that it is easier to trade the debts. Derivatives can help in two main ways:

1. The creation of a security with characteristics of particular interest and therefore value to investors which are therefore popular issues and may also attract classes of new investors.
2. The embedded equity option and/or forward elements in the security may well be sold or bought at a price which when hedged out by the derivative provider may provide a subsidy to the issue and thus give cheaper funding. This technique is frequently called volatility arbitrage or forward arbitrage.

The embedding of an option in a security can allow the investor either to buy or to sell volatility on the underlying asset, which opens up exciting possibilities for investors who may not have a direct method of writing options. A recent example of securities of this type has been the boosted coupon note where the investor effectively sells strips of binary options on an equity index for which they receive an enhanced coupon for the number of days during which the index stays within a certain range or "corridor".

Frequently the price of these embedded options in volatility terms and the implied forward interest rates (the effective discount rates for future coupons derived from the yield curve) are fixed at levels which do allow a subsidy to the issue. The whole "wrap" on these securities means that the individual components of the structured note are difficult to separate and price separately, thus making it harder for the investor to truly identify its value. This does not mean that they necessarily represent bad value, but it must be recognized that the structure has a cost of production which must be covered and the investor must be convinced of the correctness of the view embedded in the note.

4.4 THE ROLE OF THE INVESTMENT BANK IN THE CREATION OF EQUITY DERIVATIVES

Investment banks play a key role in the derivative industry, particularly in the creation of new or repackaged securities and as the creators and primary sellers of OTC derivatives contracts. Clearly theirs is a business enterprise driven by the desire to secure profits from this trade, but also clearly they have a duty and a desire to help all elements involved in the trade, both borrowers and investors, to achieve better results since this is the only way that the bank will truly prosper and survive. As mentioned in the introduction, if derivatives did not help business they would not survive, and yet they prosper. Their prosperity is due in no small part to the role of the investment banks and in particular their contribution in the four main areas of Capital, Credit, Risk Aggregation and Technology.

4.4.1 Capital

In creating and hedging OTC derivative transactions the regulatory authorities (such as the Bank of England, the SFA, the Federal Reserve Board, the SEC) require that the participating institution has sufficient capital to meet its obligations in the event of market movement or credit default by one of its counterparts. In the most sophisticated analysis, valuation models and market movement scenarios are used to establish potential losses, the magnitude of these losses determines the amount of capital (in the form of equity and near equity such as subordinated debt) that the institution must have to support its business. The capital requirement is frequently divided into two parts: one is the price risk requirement (market movement) and the other is the credit risk requirement (default of a debtor). These models along with the capital available determine the size of portfolios of derivative positions that can be sustained subject to regulatory approval and licensing. Thus the effective gearing of the balance sheet is determined by how well risks are offset within the models and how small in magnitude the movements in the scenario analysis are, since these ultimately determine the capital usage. The goal of the investment bank is to maximize its return on its capital whilst minimizing the variance (risk) of the profits; it is therefore in its best interest to use all of its capital in very well-hedged, high margin derivatives trades, where the balance sheet leverage is as high as possible without exceeding its regulatory capital requirements.

4.4.2 Credit

The traditional role of banking institutions is the lending of money for term against taking deposits for sight or short-term money. Lending money without collateral is effectively a question of credit and credit risk. Derivative transactions of all kinds can be used to lend money indirectly and thus establish a credit relationship with the counterparty on which a return is earned for the "credit risk". The advantage of derivatives is however that generally a much bigger margin for credit can be achieved than on simple lending business since ostensibly smaller margins on individual trades are more than compensated by the higher volume of trades available for the same capital usage. The banks provide a network of creditworthy institutions through which netting and credit control is effected.

4.4.3 Risk Aggregation

The two main forms of value risk in derivative portfolios are the price movement risk and credit default risk. The network of creditworthy institutions provides hubs of a multi-hub network of transactions with credit default risk. This risk is either bilateral, as in the case of swaps, or asymmetric, as in the case of normal, premium up-front options. The banks provide a valuable service in risk aggregation whereby risks of these types can be offset by running a portfolio of positions which offset in price risk so that only a small portion of the risk, known as the residual, needs to be actively managed. Credit risk is managed by attempting to write business which offsets exposure and via netting agreements (such as the ISDA master) so that payments due to a defaulting counterpart can be offset against those owed in the event of default. In some cases margin or collateral agreements are put in place. The net effect of risk aggregation is to reduce the overall risk in writing business and thus ultimately leads to a lower overall cost and helps to safeguard the banking system.

4.4.4 Technology

The role that technology has to play in the business of derivatives cannot be overstated. The technology, both hardware and software and the mathematics behind them, is essential to the valuation, risk analysis and portfolio evaluation needed in running derivative positions. The risk manager needs real time position analysis to keep him or her informed as to the current risk being run. The trader needs rapid access to pricing models and the parameters such as interest rates, dividend forecasts and estimates of volatility in order to respond to pricing requests from clients. Capital adequacy models along with scenario analysis need to be run every day so that capital adequacy regulations can be observed and reported. This modelling requires enormous processing since it models the performance of non-linear portfolios in many dimensions (such as price movement, interest rate movement, changes in correlation, etc.) and may frequently take hours for a very complex and large portfolio.

Requests from clients for new solutions to problems demand a lot from the product development teams who frequently have to go back to first principles to gain a solution method. Sometimes these may be analytic, but most of the time a numerical solution to the partial differential equations (PDEs) is required (Wilmott et al. (1994)). Often industry standard library routines such as the Numerical Algorithms Group (NAG) library are used to find the fastest and most efficient solutions. These techniques are generally of the finite difference type. For more complex, higher dimensional problems the Monte Carlo techniques are favoured. Monte Carlo is frequently used to provide independent pricing verification through replication of the hedge portfolio of the derivative in a dynamic simulation. These simulation techniques are particularly heavy on computation time since they depend on a large number of iterations for accuracy.

4.5 INDEX PRODUCTS

In this section we shall look at some of the equity derivatives structures in use today. Most of these structures are based on a stock index, although in theory the underlying is not restricted to these; in practice it may be due to liquidity and hedging considerations. The great advantage of most index products is the general availability of extremely liquid exchange traded futures (frequently trading on a bid/offer spread a fraction of that in the cash equities markets) and options for the construction of efficient hedges.

4.5.1 Exchange Traded Equity Derivatives

There has been an explosive growth of exchange traded listed equity derivative index products around the world. Usually the underlying stock index is a broadly based, capital-ization weighted index, the components of which are reviewed periodically by committees and adjusted, often on a quarterly or annual basis (one major exception being the Nikkei 225 index which is a simple average of prices). The typical index of this kind is the S + P 500, an index which represents a very large part of the entire US equity market, which is a capitalization weighted index of the largest 500 stocks in the United States. Listed futures and options exist on this index as do user specified contracts, called "FLEX" options, which are a kind of exchange cleared OTC option. The index and therefore the derivatives on it are used for a range of investment and hedging techniques including index tracking where the use of futures avoids the problems of rebalancing the tracking portfolio as equity weightings change over time. Using futures to track indices has become a very important investment technique owing to its unambiguous performance criteria and low costs and one that has brought much greater liquidity to the futures market itself. Buying and selling a tracking portfolio against the mispriced stock index futures as an arbitrage is also a very popular low risk trading strategy.

The holder or buyer of the futures contract purchases an obligation at a price for the forward purchase of the index, in the case of the S + P 500 in units of the index level multiplied by USD 500. The correct arbitrage price for the future is determined by arbitrage arguments and is equal to the net cost of carry (funding costs less dividends received) of the equivalent index portfolio for the life of the futures contract. The futures contracts are marked-to-market daily by the exchange and a margin cash flow occurs which is equal to the purchase price plus or minus the new settlement price (depending on whether the position is making money or not). This daily cash flow derived from the mark-to-market process is the essential difference between an exchange traded futures contract and a forward contract. The expiry cycles of the futures contract are typically March, June, September and December and contracts may trade out to maturities of two years, although usually liquidity is poor in the back months.

ETC option contracts are usually restricted to simple calls and puts on the index, or in some cases the settlement is in futures contracts rather than being cash settled against the index level at expiry in the same way as the futures contracts. Any variety of option type is generally restricted to the choice of American or European exercise and the expiry cycle is usually like the futures contract with perhaps the addition of contracts on all four nearest months to the spot date.

Investors use ETC futures and options for a range of uses:

1. Hedging downside movement in price by buying puts. This has largely replaced the old replication strategy of portfolio insurance which has been discredited. OTC options are also used for larger trades and to longer time horizons.

2. "Collar" trades whereby downside put protection is purchased by selling an out-of-the-money call. This has the effect of limiting upside gains in reward for limited downside.

3. Yield enhancement of the portfolio by selling out of the money call options.

4. Creating leveraged trading positions to take advantage of market direction movements, sometimes known as "geared futures and options funds".

5. Creating positions in volatility which are market neutral so as to take advantage of changes in the level of volatility.

6. In some markets, for example Germany, the overseas investor may get an enhanced dividend yield through holding deep in the money call options (or futures) over the dividend period rather than actual equity as the derivative will trade at an implied dividend somewhere between the overseas investor rate of 85 per cent and the domestic rate of 156 per cent of announced dividends. It will therefore be cheaper to hold exposure to the market via the derivative over the dividend period rather than the stock.

7. In a takeover situation, a bidder would be able to hedge his overall market risk (systematic) via index products whilst retaining the specific risk of the target company via its shareholding.

8. Index tracking portfolios can use the futures market to manage the regular cash inflow from investors by buying the market via futures in anticipation of full cash investment later. A switch from futures to cash stocks can then be effected at one price, this price is dependent on the futures basis and market liquidity at the time. This switching is known as an "EFP" or exchange for physical.

9. The natural extension of the EFP trade is a programme or portfolio trade where the portfolio is no longer the exact market portfolio but one containing different weightings or "tilts". The price of the programme is the estimate of the unwinding costs of the position against the index futures in the current market conditions. These programmes can be conducted as principal (the bank takes on the risk at a pre-agreed price) or agency (where the execution is best efforts and the fees are commissions plus an incentive fee based on a threshold price for the all-in cost).

10. Global futures markets allow very rapid and cheap deployment of funds in tactical asset allocation since they frequently operate on narrower bid/offers than the cash market and do not require full investment at the time of purchase. This also provides a very efficient method of tracking world indices and switching weighting between countries. When switching weightings between equity and fixed income the greater liquidity of futures provides cost savings.

4.5.2 Over-the-Counter Traded Equity Derivatives

The great advantages of the OTC equity derivative are its complete flexibility as to specification and the ability to operate on a credit basis rather than margin. In general all the features of ETCs can be obtained in OTCs and they can be used as described in the above section. This includes OTC forwards and strips of OTC forwards which are known as equity swaps. However their advantages over the ETCs are bespoke terms and conditions, longer maturities if required and enhanced liquidity which may be offered by a single counterpart handling the whole trade. Moreover many special option types are available OTC which are not available as ETCs. These exotic option types (many of which will be described in more detail in later chapters) such as path dependent options (e.g. barrier options which appear or disappear when the market level crosses the barrier strike), options on more than one asset (e.g. best of two stocks) and options which protect returns in an equity market in a currency not native to that equity market are available over the counter. Not all exotic options are particularly useful with the equity underlying as each asset class has its own unique set of problems. For example the Asian or average rate option is extremely useful in the context of foreign exchange since it mimics the nature of foreign cash flows as they may occur in a business enterprise, e.g. they average exchange rates over a period of, say, three months or a year. So far Asian options have seen little practical interest in the equity sphere, although they are beginning to be incorporated as part of an averaging in and averaging out process in collective investment funds. A brief description of the different kinds of exotic option is given below:

- *Path dependent options* (the value of pay-off is dependent on how the underlying market reaches its final value on the expiry date) include:
  - *Asian* (average strike or average price). Pay-off is the difference between a constant and the arithmetic average of the index.
  - *Lookback* (price lookback or strike lookback). Pay-off is the difference between a constant and the high or low of the asset price over the life of the option.
  - *Delayed strike*. Normal option once the strike price has been set, typically set as an at-the-money option in say one month's time.
  - *Resetting strike*. The option strike price is periodically set to a fixed percentage of the then current market level, freezing the pay-off from the previous period. Known as cliquet or "ratchet" option in France.
  - *Barrier* (up and out, up and in, down and out, down and in). Options which appear or disappear at certain market levels.
  - *Binary* (digital or bet option). Options which pay a fixed amount of money or an amount of an asset and depend on whether the option is in the money or not.
- *MultiAsset* (pay-offs depend on the price performance of more than one risky asset):
  - *Outperformance*. Pay-off is the difference in price of two or more assets.
  - *Best of*. Pay-off is the best performance of one of two or more assets.
- *Currency linked* (pay-offs have an element of risk linked to a FOREX rate):
  - *Quanto* (fixed exchange rate). Pay-off in foreign index has fixed exchange rate in home currency.
  - *Cross option*. Pay-off is the foreign index expressed as a fixed point value in home currency.

- *Compound options*. Options on options, e.g. one month call into a one year put.
- *Special indices*. Options on hybrid indices like the FT World with embedded currency linkage via the index composition.

Equity swaps are bilateral contracts whereby two counterparts are joined so that one party pays an equity index return (either price movement with or without the actual dividends over the period) whilst the other pays a money market return such as a three-month Libor. Depending on the movement of the price index during the period (usually three months) the payment on the equity leg may be either positive or negative. An equity swap can be viewed very simply as counterpart A running an index portfolio on behalf of counterpart B; counterpart A lends B the capital to maintain the position at a rate of interest that B pays to A every quarter. A then buys and maintains the index portfolio. Each quarter any profits are passed from A to B, and losses have to be made good by payment from B to A. The life of an equity swap can range from three months up to about five years and sometimes longer. By swapping the cash flows the currency of returns can be changed, with suitable adjustment to the rates. Indeed both legs of the swap can be pure equity return, e.g. pay FTSE receive S + P 500.

Consider a one-year (four quarterly periods) equity swap on the S + P 500 index versus three-month $US Libor, on a notional amount of $US 10 million. The notional amount is fixed throughout. The starting index level is 100 and three-month $US Libor is 10 per cent at the start. Libor is set in advance and paid in arrears. Counterpart A pays the equity return and receives the money market return from counterpart B. There are no dividends. The cash flows would be as below (in $US):

End of	Index	$US3m Libor	Party A Pays	Party B Pays	Cash Flow
Q1	110	11%	1,000,000	250,000	750,000
Q2	105	8%	−454,454	275,000	−179,454
Q3	115	9%	952,381	200,000	1,152,381
Q4	120	10%	434,783	225,000	659,783

4.5.3 Hybrid Equity Derivatives

Hybrid products are frequently securities which combine an equity derivative with a bond structure to achieve a specific goal as an investment strategy to a particular target market. Below we describe some of the features of more popular hybrid equity derivatives.

(i) Redemption Linked Bond

This is a coupon bond structure where the total redemption amount (the amount due to the investor at maturity), usually 100 per cent of face, is linked via the sale of an option spread to an equity pay-off. As a result the bond has a boosted coupon due to the premium received for the option spread. Consider a two-year bond with annual coupons of 10 per cent. If the investor chooses to sell a 100 per cent–80 per cent two-year put spread (short the at-the-money option) (100 per cent strike) and long the 20 per cent out-of-the-money option (80 per cent strike) for 10 per cent premium, this will boost the coupon on the bond by approximately 5 per cent per year (ignoring compounding). The downside for the investor is of course that he may end up only receiving 80 per cent of his original investment. If he sells two times the spread, he can boost the coupon to 20 per cent per annum but may lose 40 per cent of his investment at maturity. Clearly this strategy can be geared up to five times at which point total loss of principal at maturity is possible. Similar structures can also be constructed using the cash flows of the coupons to produce a coupon linked structure.

(ii) Equity Linked CDs

Certificates of deposit (CDs) are tradable bank debts. Generally these trade as zero coupon bonds, the interest element being the difference between the issue price and the final redemption price (usually 100 per cent). If the redemption amount of the CDs is made a function of a stock index price by selling or buying option spreads on an equity index, the pay-off amounts can be greater than or less than 100 per cent dependent on the final level of the index. This is attractive as in certain circumstances the equity return can be treated as debt interest payments for tax purposes. When these structures are issued by corporates as notes and not CDs they are frequently known by a wide variety of names such as Protected Index Notes (PINS) or Protected Equity Return Certificates (PERCs).

(iii) Business Expansion Scheme (BES) Structures

In the United Kingdom, the government allowed special tax relief at the highest rate to investors in qualifying BESs for investment in start-up businesses in which the minimum investment term is five years. Several schemes were evolved whereby a guaranteed exit price was obtained via a bank guarantee on a property portfolio. As an alternative to receiving a fixed return over the life of the BES some companies offered structures linked to the FTSE index which offered a locking feature whereby if the FTSE index crosses certain price levels during the five-year period these are locked in and paid at the end. These embedded options are forms of barrier options. The minimum return of the original investment is guaranteed, the interest element thus funds the purchase of the embedded option.

(iv) Cliquets in PEA Structures

The French government introduced tax legislation which allowed tax-free investment over a period greater than eight years. This has led to the creation of structured investments which accumulate returns over an eight-year period. These are known as Plan d'Epargne en Actions (PEAs). Unlike traditional cash based PEAs, these specialist derivative structures use zero coupon bonds to guarantee principal return whilst capturing CAC 40 index growth — and storing it away for the requisite eight years — by using various combinations of conventional, "cliquet" and "lock-in " calls. (Cliquet, or ratchet, options capture growth periodically, perhaps slicing the time series annually, whilst lock-ins capture specific levels of performance; for example, lock-in "rungs" may be set at plus 10 per cent, plus 20 per cent and plus 30 per cent growth.)

4.6 SINGLE STOCKS, BESPOKE INDEX PRODUCTS

Many stock index structures described above can be applied to single stock products. The major demand for single stock equity derivatives is for equity linked redemption bonds or "convertibles", particularly in stocks where there is no company issued paper. As discussed previously there are frequently tax advantages in these structures as they mix equity and debt. Notes can be created which allow the investor the choice as to whether he is long or short gamma (long or short options) in the underlying corporate of his choice via this security.

Mergers and acquisitions can give rise to the need for a bidding corporation either to hedge their overall market exposure with respect to their ownership of target shares, or more specifically, to hedge themselves against further price increases in the stock by buying out of the money call options prior to launching the bid. This area of using equity derivatives in corporate finance applications is increasing as knowledge of what can be done legally develops.

As well as single stocks, small baskets of specific stocks may be of use as a derivative underlying in certain circumstances. One example is the hedging of a portfolio of mortgages against default by the borrowers, this is a particular problem since the housing market for repossessed property is poor and represents an inferior way of guaranteeing the value of the investment. One method around this problem is to construct an index from property stocks and purchase a put option on that specific underlying. Thus a poor mortgage environment leads to poor performance by the property sector stocks and hence an increase in value of the hedge.

4.7 FUTURE DEVELOPMENT FOR EQUITY DERIVATIVES

The key feature of derivatives is their role as risk management building blocks in their ability to bundle and unbundle risk. As more investors and borrowers become aware of this capability the growth of volume in exchange traded contracts is inevitable as the volume of global capital flows increases. Enhanced and standardized reporting and accountancy standards across the world will lead to greater uniformity in assessment of risk and returns and therefore a greater proportion of investment will shift to more global equity investment. Increasingly borrowers will capitalize on the ability to lower funding cost by participating in producing structured equity investment to the specific requirements of the investors. Derivatives will play a leading role in opening up new markets since they are capable of removing unwanted risks from early investment. In mainstream investment the drive to lower costs and to justify investment techniques and goals will lead to a much greater emphasis on indexation and other quantitative methods which will naturally lead to a greater use of derivatives, although perhaps principally only via ETCs rather than OTCs.

Packaged investments with guaranteed minimum returns and locking-in returns on a periodic basis, especially when currency protected, will become an increasingly popular way of investment for the smaller investor, especially if encouraged via government legislation for tax shelters such as personal equity plans (PEPs) in the United Kingdom and PEA in France. These products are increasingly being marketed by banks, building societies and other financial institutions.

Structural differences between the tax and regulatory treatment of investments in different domiciles will probably remain for a long time to come and derivatives will continue their role as the primary technique for their exploitation and arbitrage.

The growth and increasing diversity of equity derivatives would seem to be assured for the future as they are not so much individual products but a set of techniques and innovative approaches to real world investment and borrowing goals.

4.8 GLOSSARY OF TERMS

Avoir Fiscal   French domestic holders of cash equity receive an enhanced dividend payment from the state as "holders of physical" shares.

Barrier   Derivative contracts can have appearing or disappearing features which are triggered by the market price crossing the barrier level.

Basis (as in Futures "Basis")   The difference in price between the price of the futures contract and the underlying deliverable.

Borrower   The issuer of debt/equity securities who takes investors' money for use in his business.

Box Spread   Option structure equivalent to a zero coupon bond. Long the market at strike K1, short the market at strike K2 via calls and puts with the same expiry. Value is the present value of K1 minus K2.

Broker   Financial intermediary who introduces two counterparts with an interest in dealing.

Calculation Agent   Third party responsible for ensuring the correct calculation of payments for derivatives contracts at settlement.

Call Option   The holder has the right but not the obligation to buy the underlying asset at the strike price K. The writer assumes an obligation in return for payment of premium. The terminal value at expiry is $Max(S - K, 0)$.

Capital Guarantee Structure   Investment structure usually linked to an equity underlying, where the terminal value has a guaranteed minimum value. Usually achieved by zero coupon bonds and option spreads.

Cash Basket   A portfolio of shares which is a round lot, for example the index portfolio which can be arbitraged against the stock index futures.

Confirmation   Written confirmation of a deal containing details of the agreement, usually a telex.

Convertible Bond   A bond with an embedded option to exchange the bond for a fixed number of underlying shares. Carries a coupon below the market rate to pay for the option.

Corridor Option   Option composed of strips of binary options (cash or nothing) which pays a fixed amount of money for each period that the market is between two values. Sometimes called "boosts".

Debt   Usually in the form of a security, i.e. a bond. The borrowing of money.

Definitive Note   A physical piece of paper representing an obligation which can be physically delivered.

Dividend   Payment to shareholders as return for investment in the corporation.

Equity   A share in the ownership of a company. Usually carries the right to vote at meetings and a share in the dividends.

Equity Derivative   Derivative based on an equity underlying asset.

Equity Linked CD   Tradable bank loan (certificate of deposit) with redemption linked to an equity underlying.

Equity Swap   A bilateral agreement whereby one counterpart agrees to pay an equity return in payment for a money market return, e.g. pay FTSE plus dividends, receive three-month sterling Libor.

EuroClear/CEDEL   Centralized clearing houses for the settlement of Eurobond securities business. Securities accounts are operated like bank accounts on behalf of members.

Exchange Traded Option   Option traded on a derivatives exchange with centralized settlement and margining.

Expiry   The termination time of a derivatives contract, usually when the final pay-off value is calculated and paid.

Forward   Agreement to buy or sell a commodity at some point in the future at a price agreed today. Different from a future as it is not margined and therefore has a greater credit risk.

Forward/Forward   Agreement for the purchase or sale of an underlying in the future agreed for a delayed start date. For example, an interest rate agreement to borrow three-month money in three months time, known as an FRA (forward rate agreement), the interest rate is known as the three-month/three-month forward/forward rate.

Futures Roll   Buying or selling the near month futures contract in favour of the next period futures contract. Rolls the position out to longer maturities.

Global Note   The representation of the obligation under a security held as a single piece of paper against which holdings are matched at EuroClear and CEDEL. If held under a global note the securities cannot be issued in bearer form.

Interest Rate Swap (IRS)   Bilateral agreement to exchange cash flows one leg of which is a fixed coupon, the other leg of which is a floating reference index, e.g. three-month Libor.

Intermediary   A counterparty which stands between two other counterparts, usually to enhance credit quality.

Investor   Counterpart who has long assets and is looking to earn a return by investment.

ISDA   International Swap Dealers Association. Professional body of market participants with responsibility for increasing the overall efficiency of the business by standardization of agreements, etc.

Jelly Roll   Synthetic futures roll using options.

Knock-out Option   Option which disappears, usually worthless, when a barrier price level of the underlying market is breached.

Leverage   The use of derivatives to generate a market exposure greater than one, so that small market movements can produce very large $p + 1$ swings.

Listed Option   Option contract standardized and traded on a derivatives exchange.

Listing   The creation of a security by following stock exchange rules. The security is then included in the official list with closing prices.

Margin (as in profit and initial and variational margin)   Profit margin is the amount of money left after costs have been covered. Initial margin is an amount of money paid on opening a position in an ETC. Variational margin is the amount of money to be paid or received as a result of the daily mark to market of the open ETCs.

Mark-to-Market   The process of evaluating positions at the prevailing market prices to establish $p + 1$ and also margin calls.

Master Document   A legal document where general terms and conditions are agreed.

Maturity   The time period of the life of the derivatives contract.

Mezzanine Finance   Intermediate funding which has characteristics midway between debt and equity. Convertible bonds are an example.

Notional   The underlying size of the deal. The notional value determines the point value of the derivatives pay-off. For example, GBP 10 million notional, strike price of 100, gives a point value of GBP 100,000 per point.

Novation   The mechanism whereby one counterpart to an OTC agreement is changed to another counterpart, so that all other terms and conditions remain the same.

One-off Agreement   A single one-off contract to document a deal rather than as a series of deals under a master agreement.

Option   The right to the holder and an obligation to the seller of a contract either to buy (call) or sell (put) an underlying asset at a fixed price for a premium.

OTC Option   Option traded by private treaty between two counterparts.

Par Bond/Swap   A bond or an interest rate swap whose coupon is equal to the current yield to maturity and therefore has a price equal to 100 per cent for the bond and zero for the IRS. Sometimes known as on-the-run.

Path Dependent Option   Derivatives contract whose final value is dependent on how the market behaved prior to expiry.

Principal   A counterpart to an OTC agreement. The amount of money invested, see also Notional.

Put   The right to sell for the holder and the obligation to buy for the writer at a strike price K for the payment of a premium.

Reference Bank   A bank used to establish a fair price to calculate settlement values for derivative contracts.

Risk Management   The process of establishing the type and magnitude of risk in a business enterprise and using derivatives to control and shape that risk to maximize the business objective.

Screen Price   The price indicated on the dealer screen such as Reuters or Telerate.

SEC (Securities Exchanges Commission)   US official body charged with regulation of many financial products in the United States.

Securitization   The conversion of an asset into a tradeable security, e.g. a mortgage portfolio transformed into a mortgage backed security (MBS).

Security   A tradeable obligation, usually listed on an exchange.

SFA (Securities and Futures Authority)   UK regulatory body responsible for overseeing a large portion of the derivatives business in the United Kingdom.

Spot   The price for immediate delivery of an asset. The shortest delivery period.

Strike Price   The price at which the underlying is bought or sold in an options contract.

Structured Note   Note or bond with pay-off characteristics linked to an equity underlying. A tailor-made investment.

Swapped Deltas   When a option deal is struck, the counterpart may agree to transfer the delta amount of underlying as a hedge for the option; this is swapping deltas.

Unwind   The reversal of an existing contract.

Volatility   The standard deviation of the natural logarithm of the price returns of an asset. The probability factor used in option valuation to determine the range of the random walk of the price process.

Warrant   A security which can be traded and has very similar characteristics to options. Usually longer dated and may be on indices or single stocks.

Zero Coupon Bond (or "Zero")   An obligation which contains only an initial and final cash flow. There are no intermediate cash flows or coupons. Useful as no assumptions have to be made as to the rate at which coupons are reinvested. Frequently used to guarantee a minimum value at maturity in a capital guaranteed product.

4.9 REFERENCES

Bookstaber, R.M. (1991) *Option Pricing and Investment Strategies*. London: McGraw-Hill.
Courtney, D. (1992) *Derivatives Trading in Europe*. London: Butterworths.
Cox, J.C. and Rubinstein, M. (1985) *Options Markets*. New Jersey: Prentice-Hall.

Das, S. (1989) *Swap Financing*. London: IFR Publishing.

Fabozzi, F.J. and Fabozzi, T.D. (1995) *The Handbook of Fixed Income Securities* (4th ed.). New York: Irwin.

Haugen, R.A. (1990) *Modern Investment Theory*. New Jersey: Prentice-Hall.

Hull, J.C. (1993) *Options, Futures, and other Derivative Securities* (2nd ed.). New Jersey: Prentice-Hall.

Hull, J. and White, A. (1991) "Pricing and Hedging Interest-rate Options". Proceeding of the conference, 5–6 September.

Inside The Swap Market (3rd ed.) (1988). London: IFR Books, IFR Publishing Limited.

ISDA Master Agreement, Definitions and Terms (1991, 1993). New York: International Swap Dealers Association Inc.

Markowitz, H.M. (1989) *Mean-Variance Analysis in Portfolio Choice and Capital Markets*. Oxford: Basil Blackwell.

Street, A.M. and Gommo, R.N. (1994) *The Mitsubishi Finance Risk Directory 1995*. London: *Risk Magazine*.

Watson, J. (ed.) (1993) *The Intercapital Equity Derivatives Handbook*. London: Euromoney Books.

Watson, Farley and Williams (Solicitors) (1994) "The US Taxation of Global Derivatives Trading and Hybrid Securities" Private communication.

Wilmott, P., Dewynne, J. and Howison, S. (1994) *Option Pricing: Mathematical Models and Computation*. Oxford: Oxford Financial Press.

5

Interest Rate Option Models:
A Critical Survey

5.1 INTRODUCTION AND OUTLINE OF THE CHAPTER

In every review of the interest rates derivatives markets it appears to be *de rigueur* to present a table, or the ubiquitous bar chart, displaying the exponential-like growth of this type of product in terms of underlying notional, outstanding deals, or some other measure of volume. The correctness of these statistics and the importance of these measures are undeniable; even more significant, however, has been the *qualitative* change in the type of options which have recently begun to be actively traded in the over-the-counter (OTC) markets.

If one chooses, in fact, to describe as "first generation" those options for which the Black model provides a closed-form solution (caps, floors and swaptions), path dependent and barrier options can be reasonably regarded as "second-" and "third-generation" instruments, respectively. These options have been traded more and more frequently, and in ever increasing volumes, either as self-standing instruments (e.g. knock-out caps), or embedded in swaps or structured notes (e.g. indexed-principal swaps or one-way floaters). In either case they have introduced a whole new dimension to the pricing of options dependent on interest rates. On the one hand, they have required the introduction of models capable of pricing instruments crucially dependent on the correlated movements of different portions of the yield curve. On the other hand, they have highlighted the need to manage the risk of these new exotic options in a manner consistent with the pricing and hedging of the first-generation instruments.

The very concept of the "underlying" instrument has undergone a subtle but important transformation: exotic OTC option traders will often hedge their positions in the "third

* Thanks are due to Mike Sherring and Dr Ian Cooper for many useful discussions; to Charles Thompson and Dr Vivian Li for performing some calculations; to Dr Carol Alexander for most helpful editorial comments; and to Dr Thomas Gustavsson, who kindly made available his unpublished thesis. Needless to say, all remaining errors are mine.

Risk Management and Analysis. Vol. 2: New Markets and Products. Edited by Carol Alexander
© 1998 John Wiley & Sons Ltd

generation" instrument using not cash instruments (the old "underlying bond") but the proverbially heady cocktail of actively traded, more elementary *options* (e.g. caps or European swaptions). Whatever the chosen model, it must therefore yield the same price for the plain vanilla hedging options, priced in the market using a different (usually Black's) model.

In this context, the very success of the Black (1976) model for plain vanilla options has been both the blessing and the bane of more sophisticated approaches. It is, in fact, essential to emphasize that expert practitioners are all too aware of the limitations of the Black model, and that their "doctoring" of *the* one unobservable input (the "implied" volatility) can well recover a desired option price; but a priori this procedure does not tell them anything about the "intrinsic" correctness of the model. In other terms, its virtually universal acceptance in the market does not imply a similar acceptance of the underlying assumptions, since distributional features not accommodated by Black's model (notably mean reversion, leptokurtosis, etc.) are incorporated in an *ad hoc* way by adjusting the Black's implied volatility. The indubitable simplicity and intuitive appeal of the Black approach have therefore given rise to a situation where any more sophisticated model has "at least" to recover the Black prices for plain vanilla instruments, if it is to win any acceptance among practitioners. From this point of view the Black approach has become not an equal ranking model, which might see its predictions challenged by a more "realistic" approach, but a benchmark which more advanced methodologies simply cannot ignore.

The need to go beyond Black's closed form formula (to value, for instance, American options) has always been present, but, as pointed out before, option markets have recently seen the appearance of option pay-offs strongly dependent on the imperfect correlation between rates (e.g. yield spread options), on the path followed by the rates (e.g. indexed principal swap), and/or of a discontinuous nature (e.g. knock-out caps). The first class of pay-offs points to two-factor models as the way forward. The second shifts the emphasis towards Monte Carlo approaches. The latter requires, in numeric implementations, a sampling resolution which seriously stretches even one-factor models. The hard lessons learnt by some market practitioners in attempting to risk-manage instruments such as knock-out indexed principal swaps show that even state-of-the-art model implementations are far from being able to provide black-box solutions.

In order to tackle these problems, so many computational procedures (Monte Carlo simulations, finite differences schemes, lattice methodologies, etc.) have been developed, that it is easy to miss their underlying similarities and the common financial reasoning. In this light, the purpose of this chapter is to:

- give a justification for yield curve models
- clarify the constraints that they must satisfy to be financially viable (no arbitrage)
- show how from these common principles the various approaches naturally follow
- review known and present original results on their theoretical and empirical implications
- highlight the caveats and pitfalls the user might encounter.

The model review presented is not meant to be exhaustive; rather, representative examples have been chosen of those classes of models that have so far encountered favour, or aroused interest, among practitioners.

One of the salient messages from this chapter is that the quality of a model should be assessed on the basis not of the a priori appeal of its assumptions (e.g. normal vs. log-normal rates), but of the effectiveness of its hedging performance. This has not only practical but also theoretical appeal, since an option price is, after all, nothing but the cost incurred in running the duplicating hedging portfolio.

Furthermore, I shall stress that the calibration procedure is an integral part of a model specification, and that it makes little sense to talk about the "goodness" or "realism" of a given model; for instance, on the basis of its distributional or economic assumptions, without exploring the ease, robustness and reliability of the parameter estimation procedure.

Financial intuition rather than mathematical rigidness has been stressed throughout; references have been provided to allow the more mathematically inclined readers to find rigorous proofs for the sketchy derivations presented in the text.

I would consider my task more than satisfactorily accomplished if, by the end of the chapter, the reader will not be tempted to paraphrase Oscar Wilde's famous book review: "Good in parts, and original in parts; unfortunately, the good parts were not original, and the original parts were not good."

5.2 YIELD CURVE MODELS: A STATISTICAL MOTIVATION

5.2.1 Statistical Analysis of the Evolution of Rates

The behaviour of the yield curve in its entirety can be described in terms of the evolution of a continuum of spot rates of maturity between $0 + \varepsilon$ and T, where ε is the shortest (instantaneous) lending/borrowing period, and T the longest maturity of interest. All these rates are stochastic variables imperfectly correlated with each other, with the degree of correlation normally decreasing with increasing difference in maturity. If one discretizes the maturity spectrum, and a simple drift/diffusion process is assumed for each rate, one is therefore led to write

$$dr_i(t) = \mu_{r_i}(r_i(t), t) \, dt + \sigma_{r_i}(r_i(t), t) \, dz_i \tag{1}$$

with $i = 1, 2, \ldots, n$ sources of uncertainty (normal Brownian motions). These Brownian motions are not independent, since

$$E[dz_i] = 0 \qquad E[dz_i \, dz_j] = \rho_{ij} \, dt$$

A typical example of the degree of correlation observable among changes in rates of different maturities is shown in Table 5.1 for the UK yield curve in the years 1989–1991.

The next step in the analysis is to realize that, given this high degree of correlation, one could look for orthogonal linear combinations $\{y_j\}$ of the changes in rates (i.e. Δr_i)

Table 5.1 Degree of correlation for changes in UK rates of different maturities (rate $r1$ = three-month rate, rate $r5 = 18$-month rate) for the 1989–1991 period

	$r1$	$r2$	$r3$	$r4$	$r5$
$r1$	1.000	0.915	0.840	0.783	0.732
$r2$	0.915	1.000	0.984	0.955	0.923
$r3$	0.840	0.984	1.000	0.992	0.974
$r4$	0.783	0.955	0.992	1.000	0.994
$r5$	0.732	0.923	0.974	0.994	1.000

$$y_1 = \sum_i \alpha_{1i} \Delta r_i,$$

$$y_2 = \sum_i \alpha_{2i} \Delta r_i,$$

$$\ldots$$

$$y_n = \sum_i \alpha_{ni} \Delta r_i$$

(2)

such that y_1 is the first eigenvector of the variance–covariance matrix, y_2 the second eigenvector constructed to be orthogonal to the first, and so on up to the nth eigenvector. By construction the first new variable y_1 accounts for the maximum amount of the total variability, the second for the maximum amount of the residual variability, and so on up to the nth new variable, by which time 100 per cent of the total variability must be accounted for. This technique, known as Principal Component Analysis (PCA) (see Wilson (1994) for a discussion with up-to-date references to recent empirical work), if applied to the term structure of interest rate of most of the major currencies, produces new variables $\{y_i\}$ such that

(i)   the first principal component is made up by approximately equal weights $\{\alpha_{1i}\}$ of the original variables, and can therefore be intuitively interpreted as the "average level" of the yield curve

(ii) the second is made up by weights $\{\alpha_{2i}\}$ of similar magnitude and opposite signs at the opposite end of the maturity spectrum, and therefore lends itself to the interpretation of being the slope of the yield curve

(iii) the third is made up by weights $\{\alpha_{3i}\}$ of similar magnitude and identical signs at the extremes of the maturity spectrum, and approximately twice as large and of opposite sign in the middle; this feature warrants the interpretation of the third component as the "curvature" of the yield curve.

These results are for instance borne out by the PCA of the rates in the UK market in the years 1989/1992 (see Tables 5.2 and 5.3), where the eight chosen maturity bins span the spectrum from the three-month to the ten-year rate, and the data were sampled with weekly frequency.

    As for the "explanatory power" of these new variables, in most currencies one then finds that the "level" often accounts for up to 80–90 per cent of the total variance, and that the first three principal components taken together often describe up to 95–99 per cent

Table 5.2   Contributions to the overall explained variance of the different principal components for the UK rate data described in the text

Principal Component	Explained Variance (%)	Total Variance (%)
1	92.170	92.170
2	6.930	99.100
3	0.614	99.714
4	0.240	99.954
5	0.031	99.985

Table 5.3 Weights of the original variables (i.e. changes in rates of maturities 1 to 8) needed to produce the first three principal components

Weights	First Principal Component	Second Principal Component	Third Principal Component
1	0.299	−0.768	0.49
2	0.354	−0.333	−0.352
3	0.365	−0.105	−0.389
4	0.367	0.049	−0.259
5	0.364	0.161	−0.196
6	0.361	0.239	−0.005
7	0.358	0.296	0.0258
8	0.352	0.333	0.557

of the intermaturity variability. *The number of independent rates (or linear combinations thereof) needed to describe the whole yield curve can therefore be drastically reduced with little loss of information.*

In establishing a framework for option pricing, some researchers have therefore adopted a two-variable approach. More commonly, however, a single variable has been chosen to describe the whole yield curve. It must be stressed at this point that this does not mean that the yield curve is forced to move in parallel, but simply that only one source of uncertainty is allowed to affect the different rates. The individual rates can be affected by changes in the driving variable to a different extent, in as complex a way as the richness of the model can allow. One-factor models do, however, imply perfect local correlation between movements in rates of different maturities. The relevance of this will be explored next.

5.2.2 A Framework for Option Pricing

In the light of the above, it has been customary, especially in early approaches, to choose one specific rate, usually the short rate, $r(t)$, as a proxy for the single variable (i.e. the level) that PCA indicates can best describe the movements of the yield curve (notice the approximately constant weights for the various maturity rates in the first column of Table 5.3). In this approach, after allowing the stochastic component of its process to be of diffusive nature only (no discontinuous jumps), one is led to write explicitly, or implicitly to assume,

$$dr(t) = \mu_r(r(t), t)\, dt + \sigma_r(r(t), t)\, dz \qquad (1')$$

In this framework, the price of any contingent claim depending on the yield curve as a whole (not only on the short rate) will be a function of calendar time, t, of its pay-off at expiry or maturity, T, and, via Ito's lemma, of the short rate dynamics only. All the rates of maturity intermediate between the maturity of r and T are accounted for in this framework by the process of the short rates, that "drives" the whole yield curve.

This approach, however, is by no means necessary, or unique. The "modern" or "evolutionary" approach, for instance, pioneered by HJM (Heath, Jarrow and Morton (1987)), has taken a continuum of instantaneous forward rates as the building blocks to describe the dynamics of the whole term structure. Equations formally similar to equation (3) above can then be written for each forward rate (and will be derived in following sections). The

PCA mentioned before can provide the volatility inputs for the dynamics of the forward rates (see Section 5.5.4).

Given either approach, the task of pricing contingent claims on instruments dependent on the yield curve movements can in any case be reduced to the following conceptual "ingredients":

(i)   a concrete specification of the process for the driving factor(s) (i.e. for the parameters in equation (3) which describes the dynamics of the short rate);

(ii) a way of translating the deterministic and stochastic movements of the driving variable(s) into the deterministic and stochastic movements of the underlying quantities of interest (bonds, forward rates, etc.);

(iii) a way of relating the possible attainable future values of an asset to its present value, i.e. a discounting procedure.

However, before embarking on the analysis of these different models, a fundamental condition must be imposed concerning point (ii) above, i.e. on the possible "allowable" movements for the prices of the underlying instruments (bonds, etc.) which depend on the yield curve. This fundamental condition must be enforced in order to prevent the possibility of arbitrage (as more precisely defined in the following section) between bonds of different maturities, and, more generally, between any two instruments. So many are the possible equivalent formulations of this no-arbitrage condition (Jamshidian (1990) enumerates 14!), that, once again, it is very easy to miss the underlying common reasoning. Different, albeit equivalent, formulations of no-arbitrage are however useful because enforcing the no-arbitrage condition in a particular form for a specific model can be considerably more straightforward and intuitive than if a different formulation had been chosen. The task of presenting the "classical" (Vasicek (1977)) and "modern"(martingale) formulation of the no-arbitrage condition in such a way as to underline their similarity, and to show how they can be directly applied to different types of implementation, is therefore undertaken in the next section.

5.3 THE NO-ARBITRAGE CONDITIONS

5.3.1 Definition of No-arbitrage in a Complete Market

A rigorous definition of the no-arbitrage condition requires, especially in continuous time, comparatively sophisticated mathematical tools. The attempt will instead be made in this section to point out the financial intuition behind the more rigorous treatments and to highlight those results useful for the practical model implementations presented in later sections. No attempt will be made in this section to re-derive the no-arbitrage results, which are already available, for instance, in Gustavsson (1992), Harrison and Kreps (1979), Harrison and Pliska (1983), or, in a more accessible way, in Rebonato (1996). The most important results will, however, be presented, with a special focus on their relevance for model implementation.

The intuitive idea behind the term "no-arbitrage" is that no riskless strategy of zero set-up cost should yield with certainty a positive return. A rigorous definition requires careful handling of several concepts: a self-financing strategy, an attainable contingent claim, an implicit price system and a complete market. Loosely speaking, the no-arbitrage idea is formalized by (i) showing, within suitable market assumptions, the correspondence between a contingent claim and a zero-set-up cost replicating strategy (whence the attainability condition, the self-financing requirement for the strategy, and the completeness of the market); and (ii) by shifting the no-arbitrage requirement from the contingent claim itself to the replicating portfolio. When this "transfer" is accomplished, one can then translate the intuitive requirement that it should not be possible to gain something for nothing into the condition

$$E_o[\Theta(T)S(T)] > 0 \Rightarrow \Theta(0)S(0) > 0,$$

or, equivalently,

$$\Theta(0)S(0) = 0 \Rightarrow E_o[\Theta(T)S(T)] = 0,$$

where the vector Θ indicates the holdings of the different assets in the strategy, S designates the vector of the asset prices, and $E_o[\cdot]$ indicates expectation taken conditional upon information up to and including time 0. In words, *any contingent claim with strictly positive pay-offs must cost something today; and if a portfolio has zero cost today the expectation of the possible pay-offs of the associated contingent claim is also zero.*

5.3.2 The Condition of No-arbitrage: Vasicek's Approach

In the context of explicit interest rate models, the constraints on the bond price processes were derived as early as 1977 by Vasicek (1977). The derivation, sketched in the following, is extremely simple and intuitively appealing. Its main result, i.e. the maturity independence of the market price of risk, directly leads to the partial differential equation (PDE) approach, which can then be tackled either by explicit analytic solutions, or by the finite differences methods (see Section 5.4.3).

The more modern (martingale) approach has a wider scope, in that it does not start from an explicit process for the short rate, and enjoys greater generality by directly allowing a variety of possible numeraires, as described below. It leads naturally to lattice methodologies (Section 5.4.1) and MC simulations (Section 5.4.2). Due to its greater mathematical complexity it will be dealt with, albeit in a qualitative way, after presenting the Vasicek approach.

The "classic" treatment is well known, and similar in spirit to the Black and Scholes (Black and Scholes (1973)) approach: starting from a general Brownian process for the short rate, $r(t)$, of drift $\mu_r(t)$ and instantaneous variance per unit time $\sigma_r(r, t)^2$,

$$dr(t) = \mu_r(r, t)\, dt + \sigma_r(r, t)\, dz, \tag{1}$$

with dz a standard Brownian motion ($E[dz] = 0$ and $E[dz^2] = 1$).

Ito's lemma yields for the process of a discount bond of maturity T, $P(t, T)$

$$dP(t, T) = [\partial P/\partial r\, \mu_r + \partial P/\partial t + 1/2\sigma_r^2\, \partial^2 P/\partial r^2]\, dt + \sigma_r\, \partial P(t, T)/\partial r\, dz$$

$$\equiv \mu(t, T)\, dt + v(t, T)\, dz \tag{2}$$

A portfolio Π is then created, composed of θ_1 units of bond T_1, and θ_2 units of bond T_2, ($\theta_1 + \theta_2 = 1$, without loss of generality), with the weights so chosen as to cancel the stochastic component of the process for the portfolio:

$$d\Pi = [\theta_1\mu(t, T_1) + (1 - \theta_1)\mu(t, T_2)]\, dt$$

$$+ [\theta_1\, \partial P(t, T_1)/\partial r\, \sigma_r + (1 - \theta_1)\, \partial P(t, T_2)/\partial r\, \sigma_r]\, dz \equiv \mu_\Pi\, dt + \sigma_\Pi\, dz \tag{3}$$

$$\sigma_\Pi = 0 \Rightarrow \theta_1 = (\partial P(t, T_2)/\partial r)/(\partial P(t, T_2)/\partial r - \partial P(t, T_1)/\partial r)$$

$$= v(t, T_2)/[v(t, T_2) - v(t, T_1)] \qquad (3')$$

Since the portfolio return is no longer stochastic, it can only earn, over time dt, the spot rate $r(t)$:

$$d\Pi/\Pi = r(t)\, dt \qquad (4)$$

Therefore, rearranging equation (3) and substituting for θ_1 from equation (3'), one obtains

$$[\mu(t, T_1) - r P(t, T_1)]/v(t, T_1) = [\mu(t, T_2) - r P(t, T_2)]/v(t, T_2) \equiv \lambda(t) \qquad (5)$$

i.e. *the expected return $(\mu - r)$ per unit risk $(1/v)$ is a constant across maturities.* (The result (5) is easily seen to be identical to Vasicek's if one assumes percentage volatility and drift.) Notice that equation (5) imposes a *drift* condition across different discount bonds, which embodies the fact that, in this one-factor universe, investors are "correctly" compensated for their accepting more risk with a longer-maturity bond by an expected return scaled with the riskiness (instantaneous standard deviation) of the bond itself. The maturity-independent quantity $\lambda(t)$ is therefore aptly described as the *market price of risk.*

Furthermore, making use of result (5) one can easily derive the PDE describing the dynamics of a bond of maturity T as a function of the driving factor by equating the coefficients of the drift term:

$$[\partial P/\partial r\, \mu_r + \partial P/\partial t + 1/2\sigma_r{}^2\, \partial^2 P/\partial r^2] = r P + \lambda \sigma_r \partial P/\partial r \qquad (6)$$

Finally, recognizing that no special use has been made in the derivation of the fact that $P(t, T)$ represents a discount *bond* price, one can conclude that the same PDE, supplemented with the appropriate terminal conditions, has to be obeyed by any asset traded in the economy, if arbitrage is to be avoided. Different (one-factor) models will produce PDEs of identical structure to equation (6) above, but with different μ_r and σ_r inputs. This is therefore the fundamental equation that analytic or finite difference methods have set out to solve.

5.3.3 The Condition of No-arbitrage: The Martingale Approach

One of the main advantages of the martingale approach is the direct and natural link afforded between the market price of risk, the discounting procedure (choice of numeraire) and the underlying equivalent measures. It is this link, of great conceptual and practical importance, that ultimately justifies the mathematically rather complex set up, which could otherwise be regarded as an unnecessarily complicated formalism. This and the following three sections report in a concise form those results obtained in Gustavsson (1992) which are of direct relevance to the implementation and analysis of the yield curve models presented further on. For ease of reference, Gustavsson's notation has been retained as much as possible.

Crucial to the treatment is the choice of a numeraire, defined as the common unit on the basis of which the prices of all the N securities can be expressed. Any of the N assets can be chosen as numeraire, as long as it has strictly positive pay-offs at all times and in all states of the world. Assets prices expressed as a function of this numeraire (arbitrarily chosen to be asset 1) can then be written as

$$Z_n{}^*(t) = S_n(t)/S_1(t) \qquad (1)$$

Each distinct choice of numeraire will give rise to a different set of relative prices.

Three theorems then constitute the cornerstones of no-arbitrage pricing: the first gives the necessary and sufficient conditions for the process of relative prices if arbitrage is to be avoided; under the Brownian assumption for the stochastic process, the second provides the explicit martingale form for the relative price processes; the third will enable us to relate processes obtained using different choices of the numeraire. More precisely:

Theorem 1   A complete market is arbitrage-free if and only if there exists a measure Q^*, equivalent to Q, such that the relative prices $Z^*(t)$ become martingales, i.e.

$$E_t^*[Z^*(T)] = Z^*(t) \tag{2}$$

where $E_t^*[\cdot]$ denotes expectation taken at time t with respect to the measure Q^*, contingent on all past and present information up to time t. A few remarks can enhance the financial intuition behind this theorem: saying that a measure Q^* (i.e. loosely speaking, a law associating to events a "probability") is *equivalent* to another measure Q means that events impossible in one measure are also impossible in the other. Therefore no-arbitrage results only stem from the "impossibility regions" of different measures. Furthermore, the statement that, in the new equivalent measure, the relative price process should be a martingale is tantamount to requiring that the expectation of any relative price at any later time should be the same as its price today. This requirement of zero drift might seem surprising, since it seems to imply no expected return from an asset, but, by recalling the definition of $Z^*(T)$ as *ratios* of traded assets, it can be seen that the martingale requirement is equivalent to imposing the *same* return from both assets. But this is very similar to the old Black and Scholes (1973) results, where all assets earn the same (riskless) rate of return. It will become apparent in the next section that it is even more similar, nay identical, to the result obtained using the classic (Vasicek) approach: it will in fact be shown that in the risk-neutral world every bond earns exactly the spot rate. In other words, the change of measure from Q to Q^* tilts the playing field in such a way that the return from each unnormalized asset is the same as the return from the numeraire asset. It can be immediately seen that, since there is no unique choice for the latter, the type and extent of the "tilting" will have to be different for each numeraire choice.

Theorem 2   Under the Brownian assumption for the arrival of information, any martingale $Z^*(t)$ can be represented as

$$dZ_n^*(t) = \sigma_n(t)Z_n^*(t)\,dW^*(t) \tag{3}$$

where $W^*(t)$ is *the* Wiener process in the measure Q^*. (Extension to several processes is straightforward.)

For the sake of concreteness, Theorem 3 will be reported at the end of the section, after introducing actual examples of numeraires.

The importance of these rather abstract beginnings can be appreciated by considering two specific choices for the numeraire, namely (i) by discounting each asset pay-off at time T, $S(T)$, by a discount bond maturing at T, $P(t, T)$, or (ii) by dividing the asset price by a rolled-up-money-market account (for brevity a money-market account in the following), where £1 is reinvested at the prevailing short rate from t up to time T. Both choices correspond to different ways to present-value future cash flows and, implicitly, to construct one's hedged position.

5.3.4 First Choice of Numeraire: The Money Market Account

If one defines the money market account as the value of £1 instantaneously reinvested at the current short term rate

$$B(t) = \exp\left[\int_o^t r(s)\,ds\right] \tag{1}$$

the relative prices with respect to this numeraire are given by

$$Z'_n(t) = S_n(t)/B(t) \tag{2}$$

By Theorem 1, a unique equivalent measure Q' must exist such that the drift of the cash assets and of the money market account are identical, i.e. such that the relative prices are martingales:

$$E'_t[Z'_n(T)] = E'_t[S_n(T)/B(T)] = S_n(t)/B(t) = Z'_n(t) \quad \forall T \geq t \tag{3}$$

Specializing equation (3) to the case where the original asset price is today's price of a bond of maturity T, $P(0, T)$, one readily obtains

$$P(0, T) = E'_t[1/B(T)] = E'_t\left[\exp\left[-\int_o^T r(s)\,ds\right]\right] \tag{4}$$

(since $P(T, T) = 1$), i.e. *today's price of a T-maturity bond is equal to the expectation under Q' of the reciprocal of the money account.* It is instructive to compare equation (4) with the well-known result for a bond price in the case of deterministic interest rates, i.e. with the result that would apply if the future path of the short rate were assumed to be known with certainty at time 0. In this case imposing no-arbitrage implies that $P(t, T) = P(t, s)P(s, T)$. Furthermore, since the instantaneous forward rate, $f(t, T)$ is given by

$$f(t, T) = \partial[\ln(P(t, T))]/\partial T$$

and $r(s) = f(s, s)$ one can write

$$P(0, T) = \exp\left[-\int_o^T r(s)\,ds\right] \tag{4'}$$

where $r(s)$ is now a deterministic quantity. Clearly it is the non-linearity of the discounting operator that brings about the difference between equations (4) and (4').

The crucial importance of result (4) will be appreciated in the context of lattice methodologies. It will suffice for the moment to say that it is by enforcing condition (4) that these numerical procedures ensure that expectations of future option pay-offs are taken with respect to the correct, but a priori unknown, measure Q'.

Moving one step further, from equations (1) and (2) one can obtain that

$$dS_n(t)/S_n(t) = r(t)\,dt + \sigma_n(t)\,dW'(t) \tag{5}$$

i.e. *in the measure Q' the return on any asset is identical* (there is no index n in the drift term) *and is equal to the riskless rate*, thus justifying the name of "risk neutral" for this particular measure. That all the returns should turn out to be identical should come as no surprise, after the qualitative remarks which followed Theorem 1; the specific result that this rate of return must be the riskless rate is specific to the particular choice of numeraire. Result (5) also applies, in particular, to the price of discount bonds, with $P(t, T)$ replacing $S_n(t)$. This result will be of crucial importance in the implementation of lattice methodologies by means of Green's functions.

Furthermore, remembering that the time-t forward rate from time T' to time T'' can be written as

$$f(t, T', T'') = (\ln(P(t, T')) - \ln(P(t, T'')))/(T'' - T') \tag{6}$$

and applying Ito's lemma to $\ln(P(.))$ one easily obtains in the measure Q' for a log-normal bond price process

$$df(t, T', T'') = [v(t, T'')^2 - v(t, T')^2]/(2(T'' - T')) \, dt$$
$$+ [v(t, T') - v(t, T'')]/(T'' - T') \, dw'(t) \tag{7}$$

or, by taking the limit as $T'' \to T'$,

$$df(t, T) = \partial v(t, T)/\partial T \, v(t, T) \, dt - \partial v(t, T)/\partial T \, dw'(t) \tag{8}$$

This expression shows that, *in the measure Q', forward rates are* not *martingales*, and, formally, one could argue that they could be turned into a martingale process by defining a new measure Q^*, where

$$dW^*(t) = dW'(t) - \partial v(t, T)/\partial T \, v(t, T) \tag{9}$$

It is shown in the following section that this *ad hoc* construction exactly creates the measure defined by choosing as numeraire the price of a discount bond.

5.3.5 Second Choice of Numeraire: A Discount Bond

With this choice of numeraire, one can write for the new relative prices

$$Z_n''(t, T) = S_n(t)/P(t, T) \tag{1}$$

By Theorem 1, to any discount bond $P(t, T)$ there corresponds a measure Q'', equivalent to the real-world measure Q, such that relative prices become martingales, i.e.

$$E_t''[Z_n''(u, T)] = E_t''[S_n(u)/P(u, T)] = Z_n''(t, T) = S_n(t)/P(t, T) \quad \forall T \geq u \geq t \tag{2}$$

From definition (1) and equation (2) one can obtain the rate of return on an asset $S(t)$:

$$dS(t)/S(t) = -dP(s, t)/P(s, t) + dZ''(t)/Z''(t) \tag{3}$$

Once again, notice that there is no dependence on the specific asset n on the right-hand side. One can therefore draw the first conclusion that *all assets earn the same percentage return, given by the return on a bond maturing at time t*. This expression can be further clarified by remembering that, since a bond of maturity t and the instantaneous forward rates $f(0, t)$ are linked by

$$P(0, t) = \exp\left[-\int_o^t f(0, s) \, ds\right] \tag{4}$$

Differentiation and substitution in equation (5) gives for Brownian processes

$$dS(t)/S(t) = f(0, t)\,dt + \sigma''(t)\,dW''(t) \tag{5}$$

i.e. the rate of return on any asset in Q'' equals the t-maturity forward rate.

In addition, it is possible to show that, for this choice of numeraire, *forward rates and forward prices are driftless (martingales).* It is clear that financially this way of discounting cash flows corresponds to hedging options by taking positions in *forward* assets, whereas the money market discounting is equivalent to rolling one's positions at the instantaneous short rate. For a single-horizon (European) option, the former approach is clearly more appropriate, since it does not expose the holder to the "reinvestment" risk. This strategy, however, would be unsuitable for multiple-exercise or American options, where no single horizon can be a priori defined. Notice that this subtle distinction, crucial to interest rate options, does not arise in the original Black and Scholes treatment, which can be indifferently cast in either numeraire, since, within that approach, rates are assumed to be deterministic.

5.3.6 The General Link Between Different Measures

Section 5.3.4 has shown that the link between the two measures Q' and Q'' is via a drift transformation like equation (9) in Section 5.3.4. For Wiener processes, this result is actually of general validity, and constitutes the third "cornerstone" (Girsanov's theorem) mentioned in Section 5.3.3. More precisely, it can be shown that, taking any two equivalent measures, Q' and Q, any Wiener process $W'(t)$ in the original measure Q' is transformed into

$$W(t) = W'(t) - \int_o^t q(s)\,ds \tag{1}$$

where $q(s)$ is a suitable function (the Radon–Nikodým derivative). The specific functional form of the function $q(s)$ is, for the purposes of our discussion, less important than the fact that equation (1) describes a *drift* transformation between measures. The link with the "classical" (Vasicek) approach can in fact now be made: the market price of risk equation (5) in Section 5.3.2 is seen to be the change of measure which transforms the *a priori* unknown drift $\mu(t, T)$ in the real world (described by measure Q) into the riskless rate under Q'.

A simple example can perhaps make the above discussion more concrete. Consider the case of the evaluation of a simple caplet of maturity T. With Black's model, which implies discount-bond discounting, each final pay-off is probability-weighted by the log-normal distribution and then discounted by a bond of maturity T. Notice that, given this choice of numeraire, no drift is assumed for the caplet forward rate. Notice also that large pay-offs (corresponding to high realizations of the forward rate, and weighted by their log-normal probability distribution) are discounted using the same discount bond as lower rate pay-offs. Let us consider, on the other hand, a lattice approach, such as the Black–Derman–Troy (BDT) model presented later, which discounts each final pay-off by the actual path followed by the short rate to reach the appropriate state of the world at maturity, i.e. using a rolled-up money market account. By so doing large pay-offs are discounted using larger realizations of the money market account. *Yet lattice approaches give the same value as Black's model for the caplet.* This can only occur because of a different implicit drift associated with the rolled-up numeraire. How the implicit drift of the forward rate can actually be obtained will be shown in Section 5.5.1, but it is important to notice that it is this change in drift that exactly compensates for the different discounting (i.e. numeraire) in the two approaches.

The message of this section can therefore be summarized as follows: the process of discounting pay-offs plays a central role in option pricing, and each numeraire implies a different no-arbitrage measure, under which different quantities have different drifts. In particular, a common choice of numeraire, i.e. a pure T-maturity discount bond, has the computational advantage of implying no drift for the T-maturity forward rate and price, thereby making the evaluation of non-compounded European options very straightforward. The discounting in this measure, however, must be carried out all the way from option expiry to today, without "stopping along the way" to impose, for instance, a compound option exercise condition. It is exactly in order to be able to tackle non-European pay-offs that a different type of numeraire, i.e. the money market account, is employed. The price to be paid is that forward rates are no longer martingales, and their drift must be obtained, either explicitly (e.g. via the HJM evolutionary approach), or implicitly (e.g. via the construction associated with a computational tree such as BDT's). Showing how this is accomplished will be one the central tasks of the sections devoted to these types of models.

5.4 THE IMPLEMENTATION TOOLS

5.4.1 Lattice Approaches: Justification and Implementation

Ho and Lee (1986) (HL in the following) and Black et al. (1990) (BDT in the following) pioneered the use of arbitrage-free computational lattices for the evaluation of interest rate options. Their methodology has enjoyed vast popularity due to the in-built capability of their models to price exactly any received market set of discount bonds, and for the intuitional appeal of their approaches which bear formal, if not very deep, similarities to the Cox–Ross–Rubinstein binomial model. In this section it will be shown how their prescription can be rigorously justified, and that it can afford, combined with the techniques of forward and backward induction, a very efficient computational tool. The results of Section 5.2 will be heavily drawn upon, both to justify the procedures, and to construct the necessary Green's functions.

The starting point for one-factor yield curve lattice models is an exogenous set of discount bond prices $\{P_i(\cdot)\}$ observed in the market. The assumption is also made that the driving factor is the short rate, and that it can be described by a Brownian process. The value of the short rate today, i.e. at time 0 and in state 0, $r(0, 0)$, is known from the price of $P(0, 0, 1\Delta t)$:

$$r(0, 0) = -\ln P(0, 0, \Delta t)/\Delta t \qquad (1)$$

(where $P(i, j, T)$ indicates the price in state i and at time j of a bond of maturity T). It is further assumed that the user knows the time-dependent (absolute or percentage) volatility of the short rate. No explicit knowledge is required about its drift. The short rate itself (HL) or its logarithm (BDT) are then allowed, from today's value, to move up or down with equal probabilities to two, as yet undetermined, states $r(1, 1)$ and $r(1, -1)$ (where, again, the first index denotes the time and the second the state). Given the Brownian assumption, their separation, i.e. $r(1, 1) - r(1, -1)$, can be immediately determined from the knowledge of the volatility at time $t(0)$, $\sigma(0)$, by remembering that the standard deviation of two quantities A and B is simply given by $|A - B|/2$. For the BDT and the

HL case one therefore easily obtains

$$r(1, 1) = r(1, -1)\exp(2\sigma\Delta t) \quad \text{(log-normal (BDT) case)} \tag{2}$$

$$r(1, 1) = r(1, -1) + 2\sigma\Delta t \quad \text{(normal (HL) case)} \tag{2'}$$

respectively. What remains to be determined is the absolute level of the two rates, a unique function, via equations (2) and (2′) of either rate. In order to determine, say, $r(1, -1)$ the following procedure can be employed: construct an additional tree representing bond prices in the same states of the world described by the short rate tree, and extending one extra time step (i.e. in the example treated so far, up to time $2\Delta t$) (see Figure 5.1). If one considers a bond of maturity $2\Delta t$, which therefore pays with certainty £1 in all states of the world at time $2\Delta t$, one can ask for the price of this bond at time $1\Delta t$ in state, say, 1, i.e. for $P(1, 1, 2\Delta t)$. From the results of Section 5.2, if we discount using a market account, this is given by

$$P(1, 1, 2\Delta t) = \mathrm{E}'_{t=\Delta t}\left[\exp-\left(\int_{\Delta t}^{2\Delta t} r(s)\,ds\right)\bigg| r(\Delta t) = r(1, 1)\right] \tag{3}$$

(A slight liberty has been taken with the notation, since "r" denotes the short rate both in the continuous, $r(t)$, and in the discrete, $r(i, j)$, case.) Given the Brownian assumption this expectation is given in discrete time by

$$\mathrm{E}_{t=\Delta t'}[1\exp(-r(1, 1)\Delta t] = \exp(-r(1, 1)\Delta t)\left(1\tfrac{1}{2} + 1\tfrac{1}{2}\right) \tag{3'}$$

where the non-linear function $\exp[\cdot]$ has been taken out of the expectation operator because, at time 1 and in state 1, $r(1, 1)$ is a known quantity. Let us call $P(1, 1, 2\Delta t; r(1, 1))$ and $P(1, -1, 2\Delta t; r(1, -1))$ the value at time 1 of a discount bond maturing at time $2\Delta t$ in the 1 (up) and -1 (down) states of the world, respectively (the parametric argument $r(i, j)$ specifies on which rate(s) the discount bond price depends). The expectation as of today of the price of a $2-\Delta t$ maturity discount bond $P(0, 0, 2\Delta t; r(1, 1), r(1, -1), r(0, 0))$ must then be given by

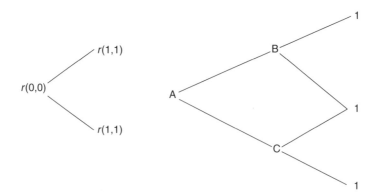

Figure 5.1 $r(0, 0)$ is known at time 0 from equation (1); the value of the short rate in the up state at time $1\Delta t$, $r(1, 1)$, is linked to $r(1, -1)$ by equation (2) or (2′); B is given by $1/2(1 + 1)\exp[-r(1, 1)\Delta t]$; C is given by $1/2(1 + 1)\exp[-r(1, -1)\Delta t]$; A is given by $1/2(B + C)\exp[-r(0, 0)\Delta t]$

$$P(0, 0, 2\Delta t; r(1, 1), r(1, -1), r(0, 0))$$

$$= E'_{t=0}[P(1, 2\Delta t) \exp\left[-\int_{o}^{\Delta t} r(s)\, ds\right] |r(0) = r(0, 0)]$$

$$= \exp[-r(0, 0)\Delta t]1/2\{P(1, 1, 2\Delta t) + P(1, -1, 2\Delta t)\} \tag{4}$$

(Again the equivalence between the continuous, $P(t, T)$, and discrete-time, $P(i, j, T)$, notation should be clear.) The notation employed for the first term in equation (4) emphasizes that the discount bond price $P(0, 0, 2\Delta t)$ depends on $r(0, 0)$, $r(1, -1)$ and $r(1, 1)$. Since, however, $r(0, 0)$ is known from equation (1), since the prices $P(1, \pm 1, 2\Delta t)$ are related to $r(1, 1)$ and $r(1, -1)$ by equation (3), and since the two rates at time 1 $r(1, 1)$, $r(1, -1)$ are linked by the relationships $(2, 2')$ above, the price $P(0, 0, 2\Delta t)$ can be seen to be a function of $r(1, 1)$ (or $r(1, -1)$) only. This function of a single variable can now be equated to the observed market price of a two-year discount bond, thereby uniquely determining the value for $r(1, 1)$ (or $r(1, -1)$). The resulting solution admits close solution for the HL model, or requires a simple numerical algorithm (e.g. Newton–Raphson) for the BDT approach.

It is easy to see that the extension of the rate tree by one time step will introduce a single new unknown and one more equation. All the rates in the various states of the world j at time i are in fact linked by

$$r(i, j + 1) = r(i, j - 1) + 2\sigma\Delta t \quad \text{(HL, normal case)} \tag{5}$$

$$r(i, j + 1) = r(i, j - 1) \exp[2\sigma\Delta t] \quad \text{(BDT, log-normal case)} \tag{5'}$$

and, therefore, given the value of the volatility at time $(i - 1)\Delta t$, they can all be expressed as a function of, say, $r(i, -i)$. The unit pay-offs from a bond maturing at time $i + 1$ can then be discounted to time i using all and only the rates $r(i, j)$ (all a function of $r(i, -i)$), and from time i to time 0 using *already determined rates*. This model value for an $(i + 1)\Delta t$-maturity bond can then be compared with the corresponding market value, and the single unknown, $r(i, -i)$, adjusted accordingly.

By the way lattice methodologies have been described it is clear that the commonly made statement that models like BDT or HL "do not depend on the market price of risk" should actually be rephrased as "do not require an a priori explicit knowledge of the market price of risk". The tree fitting procedure described above, in fact, actually endows the unknown function describing the market price of risk with as many degrees of freedom as there are market discount bonds, and implicitly determines the values of this function which allow exact pricing of the market bonds.

It is also apparent, from the "naive" presentation given above, that fitting further time slices of the interest rate tree as suggested entails traversing the same portions of the lattice over and over again. But, thanks to the no-arbitrage conditions obtained before, there is a way to avoid this duplication of labour. As shown before, in the measure associated with the money market account, all assets, and hence discount bonds, earn the short rate over a time step Δt. To see how this can be of assistance in the construction of the tree, let us define $G(i, j, s, t)$ as the value at time j and state i of a security paying £1 in state s and time $t(t > j)$. These quantities are known in financial literature as Arrow–Debreu prices (see, for example, Jamshidian (1991)), and bear an obvious discrete-time similarity to the Green's functions of physics, which describe the response to the unit (delta) stimulus for linear systems. Notice that the completeness assumption in Section 5.2 ensures the possibility of actually constructing these single pay-off securities by linear combinations of traded assets. A special case of these Arrow–Debreu prices is today's value of a security paying £1 at (s, t), $G(0, 0, s, t)$. Given the assumed market completeness and absence of arbitrage, the price today, $V(0, t)$, of a generic security paying £$v(s, t)$ in state s at a future time t must be given by

$$V(0, t) = \sum_s G(0, 0, s, t) v(s, t); \tag{6}$$

in particular, for a discount bond maturing at time T, equation (6) must reduce to

$$P(0, T) = \sum_s G(0, 0, s, T) \tag{6'}$$

Therefore, *knowledge of the Arrow–Debreu prices completely determines the value of a discount bond*. Furthermore, in the computational trees so far considered, knowledge of the Green's function for time t, $G(0, 0, (\cdot), t)$ immediately determines the value of the Green's function at the next time step, $G(0, 0, (\cdot), t + \Delta t)$. Remembering in fact that *all* assets earn the short rate over time Δt, from Figure 5.2 it is easy to see that the price of a security paying £1 in state j at time $t + \Delta t$ and £0 everywhere else is given by

$$G(0, 0, j, t + \Delta t) = 1/2(0 + 1) \exp[-r(j + 1, t)\Delta t] G(0, 0, j + 1, t)$$
$$+ 1/2(1 + 0) \exp[-r(j - 1, t)\Delta t] G(0, 0, j - 1, t) \tag{7}$$

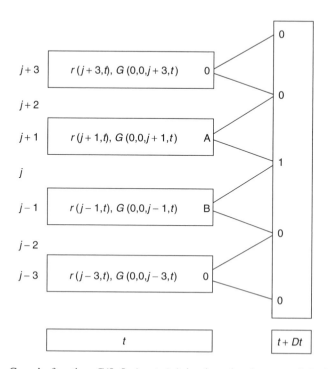

Figure 5.2 The Green's function $G(0, 0, j, t + \Delta t)$ is given by the sum of A $G(0, 0, j + 1, t)$ and B $G(0, 0, j - 1, t)$; A and B are given by $1/2(0 + 1) \exp[-r(j + 1, t)\Delta t]$ and $1/2(1 + 0) \exp[-r(j - 1, t)\Delta t]$, respectively; $G(0, 0, j + 1, t)$ and $G(0, 0, j - 1, t)$ are known

Therefore, *knowledge of the Arrow–Debreu prices and of the short rates at time t completely determines all the Arrow–Debreu prices at time t + Δt*. Furthermore, as shown above, all rates at time t are a unique function, via the volatility, of a single value of the short rate. Therefore, by virtue of equation (6) not only can one express a model bond price as a function of a single unknown rate, as shown before, but the traversing of already fitted portions of the lattice can be avoided by simple multiplication by the appropriate Green's functions. *The computational savings afforded by this technique reduce the number of operations from $O(N^3)$ to $O(N^2)$.*

Once the rate tree has been constructed, the pricing of any security of known terminal pay-off, be it a discount bond or a contingent claim, is easily accomplished by following the backward induction procedure used in the building of the tree: the value at node $(i - 1, j)$ is obtained by averaging the values at nodes $(i, j - 1)$ and $(i, j + 1)$ and discounting them at the short rate prevailing at $(i - 1, j)$. What has been accomplished by the forward induction tree-fitting procedure is to ensure that the short rate process displays the correct drift *for a given choice of the volatility function*. From Section 5.3 one can recall that this drift is a priori unknown, but also that the value of any discount bond is given by the expectation, in the appropriate measure, of the reciprocal of the money market account. By forcing, via the fitting procedure, the model and market price for the discount bond to coincide, one is effectively implicitly imputing *the* drift that, for any given choice of the process variance, characterizes the measure under which *all* expectations (i.e. expectations of *any* future pay-off) have to be taken if arbitrage is to be avoided. Indeed the drift can often be explicitly obtained, either a priori for Gaussian models, or once the tree has been constructed for log-normal models. It will be shown in the following how this can be of more than academic interest, if one is interested, or forced, to carry out a Monte Carlo simulation consistent with a given lattice model.

Notice carefully, however, that the perfect match of model and market prices of discount bonds tells one nothing about the appropriateness of the chosen volatility function. The argument is rather subtle: bond prices depend not only on future expectations of rates, but also on future volatility, via the non-linear expectation operator in equation (4) of Section 5.3.4. A lattice construction of the kind described above therefore creates an expectation of rates (i.e. an implicit drift term for the short rate) which is a function of an unknown quantity, i.e. the chosen volatility function itself. The impasse can only be broken by further forcing correct simultaneous pricing of volatility-dependent instruments, such as caps and floors. It is the correctness of the pricing of the latter, in fact, which ensures that the "correct" (given the model assumptions) contributions to the curvature of the term structure are provided by rate expectations and future volatilities.

This extremely important point will be visited again in the discussion of analytic models, which limit a priori the possible deterministic path followed by the short rate (Section 5.5.3). Further sections will also explore the methodological strengths and weaknesses of lattice approaches with respect to MC (Section 5.4.2) and PDE methods (Section 5.4.3).

5.4.2 Monte Carlo (MC) Approaches

It was pointed out in the introductory section that an increasing number of actively traded OTC interest rate options display path-dependent features. Although skilful, if rather cumbersome, implementations (Hull and White (1993)) often make these problems tractable using lattice methodologies, the most direct and general route towards their evaluation remains the MC approach, first introduced in the option-pricing context by Boyle (1977). Furthermore, recently introduced techniques for MC methodologies (Clewlow and Carverhill (1994)) can give valuable help in the evaluation of the risk statistics that have until recently been very arduous to determine. Further impetus has been given to research into efficient implementations of MC methods by the intellectual and practical appeal of the Heath–Jarrow–Morton (HJM) (evolutionary) approach (see Section 5.5.4), which has so far defied evaluation using recombining lattices.

The idea behind the technique is extremely simple and it amounts to the numerical evaluation of integral (4) in Section 5.3.4: selected stochastic quantities are evolved through time using pre-assigned drifts and volatilities and the Brownian increment dz, which is obtained from a random draw ε from a Gaussian distribution as $dz = \varepsilon\sqrt{\Delta t}$; during the course of each realization, whichever path-dependent statistics are needed to evaluate the final pay-off can be collected; the option value at expiry thus determined is then appropriately discounted to today; the average of a (very) large number of runs is then computed, to give the required expected value of the discounted pay-off. As usual, the conceptually crucial part of the calculation is to ensure that the correct terminal distribution is achieved (i.e. that expectations are taken in the correct measure). Since each different way of discounting implies a different measure, the term "correct" only makes sense once the discounting procedure is specified. In principle, discounting by a discount bond could be employed, as long as quantities such as forward rates or prices were assigned the correct (zero) drift. However, the martingale condition only holds for pay-offs occurring at the bond maturity. Therefore, with this type of discounting no pay-off-sensitive manipulations can be accomplished along the path. In other words, in this framework MC offers no more than a cumbersome (and expensive) way of performing numerically the integral given analytically for European options by Black's result. If, however, one discounted using the money market account, and used the appropriate (non-zero) drifts for forward rates, any intermediate condition can be imposed along the path. The drawback is that the terminal pay-offs must be present-valued (*before* averaging) using the specific path followed by the short rate, and that the forward rate drifts are not known a priori.

After the decision has been taken to tackle a specific problem using MC techniques, several choices still remain to be made: first of all, MC being a technique rather than a model, its "ingredients" (i.e. drifts and variances) must be obtained from the separate choice of a no-arbitrage model. A later section, for instance, will show how to obtain the drift consistent with the BDT model; or, to give a different example, with the HJM approach, also reviewed in the following, the forward rate drifts turn out to be simply related to discount bond variances. In any case, once the desired model has been chosen, specific quantities will have to be evolved over time. One knows, from the results of Section 5.3, that, using a money market account as numeraire, all *assets* grow with a drift equal to the short rate, $r(t)$, and that forward rates display a drift given by equation (8) in Section 5.3.4. In addition, the money market account will have to be reinvested along each path in order to provide the necessary discount factor. To this effect the process for the short rate must also be known. Equation (3′) of Section 5.5.1 or equations (7) and (8) of Section 5.3.4 provide the relevant expressions for the BDT and HJM models, respectively.

The MC technique therefore is yet another route to perform the numerical integration of the final pay-off function times the appropriate probability distribution. In this respect, its similarities with lattice or PDE methodologies (in turn even more closely related) are quite apparent. The methodological differences, however, are the sources of both its strengths and its weaknesses. To begin with, in a binomial lattice methodology the probability of reaching the topmost node after n steps is 0.5^n; for a weekly tree extending out to five years this implies that the topmost path has a probability of occurrence of 5×10^{-79}; in turn, this implies that the highest and lowest values of the short rate sampled by a realistic weekly BDT tree of this maturity can be as high and as low as 10,100 per cent and 0.0060 per cent, respectively, for the example above (GBP curve, May 94, 20 per cent vol.). For this same tree the short rate spacing around the forward rate can be as coarse as 40 b.p. Clearly, a BDT-like lattice methodology affords a very inefficient procedure to take the expectation of any function likely to vary rapidly around the centre of the distribution, as is the case with barrier options. To compound the problem, if one wants to achieve a finer sampling in rate space, one is forced, within a tree framework, to increase the number of time steps as well, thereby paying an n^2 price, despite the fact that the accuracy of the integration is known to depend mainly on the fineness of the r-space sampling, and not on a high number of time steps.

The MC approach is free from all these problems: time steps can be tailor made; the sampling of the distribution is finest around the forward rate (or price, as appropriate); each path has the same probability of occurrence of 1/(number of realizations). Furthermore, it is known that, if one wanted to tackle a multi-factor model, MC is probably *the* method to perform high-dimensional numerical integrations.

These advantages are not without price, at least for "naive" implementations: to begin with, in order to increase by a factor n the accuracy of the MC estimate, n^2 as many simulations have to be carried out. Furthermore, deltas and gammas are arduous to obtain, since they are numerically obtained as differences of noisy quantities. Finally, American early exercise opportunities cannot be evaluated, since at time t the expectation of a pay-off occurring at a later time (obtainable in trees using backward induction) is not available.

The well-known antithetic technique (see, for example, Boyle (1977) or Hull and White (1988)), whereby to each path obtained with the stream of Brownian increments $\{dz_i\}$ the mirror path is added, obtained with the stream $\{-dz_i\}$, can substantially reduce the variance of the estimate. In addition, evaluating using the same stream of random numbers used to price the option of interest another security of analytically known value can provide a way to correct the option estimate (contravariate technique) (Boyle (1977)).

As for deltas or other statistics, a useful procedure consists of using the same series of random numbers to evaluate the option values for two slightly different initial values of the quantity with respect to which differentiation is sought. By this procedure, biases in each individual realization should to a large extent cancel when taking the difference between the "up" and "down" simulation. It is actually not rare to obtain, for relatively simple problems, deltas more accurate than the prices.

These techniques are neither very new nor very complicated. In addition, very recently the Martingale Variate Control (MVC) technique (Clewlow and Carverhill (1994)) has been proposed, which claims to be able to reduce computational time by an order of magnitude; the actual suitability and power of the technique for interest rate options remains to be explored.

Despite these useful ancillary techniques MC procedures are only beginning to achieve great popularity, since, for realistic interest rate applications, a very large number of variables have to be evolved through time: the processes are in fact needed for the short rate and for as many forward rates as resets and pay-off indices affect the pay-offs, plus the "up" and "down" states for all of these quantities. Due to the resulting substantial computation burden, even "clever" implementations therefore often tend to be regarded as "tools of last resort".

5.4.3 PDE Approaches: Finite Differences Schemes and Analytic Solutions

In Section 5.3.2 it was shown that no-arbitrage arguments can lead directly to the PDE obeyed by any contingent claim. Historically this has indeed been the first line of approach to the valuation of interest rate options: as early as 1977 Vasicek introduced a normal mean-reverting model, followed by Cox–Ingersoll–Ross (CIR)'s square-root-volatility process for the mean-reverting rate (Cox et al. (1985)), and Brennan and Schwartz's two-factor model (Brennan and Schwartz (1982)). Lately the approach has enjoyed a renewed interest due to the Longstaff–Schwartz (LS) model (Longstaff and Schwartz (1992)), and to the Hull–White (HW) extended-Vasicek approach (Hull and White (1990a)), reviewed in Sections 5.5.3 and 5.5.2, respectively.

As shown in Section 5.3.2 the common feature of these models is that the set of parameters (e.g. reversion speed, volatility, etc., collectively denoted in the following by $\{\alpha_i\}$), which describe the "real-world" process for the short rate, enter the PDE for an interest rate-dependent instrument together with the market price of risk. Therefore, estimating the $\{\alpha_i\}$ from time-series analysis of rates observed in the "real-world" measure is not sufficient in order to determine the coefficients of the PDE: access is needed to market instruments (e.g. bonds) which price the risk connected with the variability of the underlying factor(s). This is the route followed, among others, by LS: by making use of the time-series estimates of the "real-world" parameters $\{\alpha_i\}$, they obtain an estimate of the market price of risk by cross-sectional best fit to the observed bond prices on a given day.

Alternatively, one can dispense with the time-series analysis altogether, and attempt to determine the non-linear *combinations* of the $\{\alpha_i\}$ and of the market price of risk that cross-sectionally best account for the observed bond prices. Since a discount bond price is given by the expectation of the discounted maturity pay-off

$$P(t, T) = E'_t \left[\exp \left[- \int_t^T r(u)\, du \right] \right]$$

and since the discounting function is non-linear in the short rate, in general the yield of a T-maturity bond will depend not only on expectations of the future rates but also on future volatility. If the model were correctly specified and the "market noise" not too severe it would, of course, be immaterial whether the former or the latter route were followed. In practice, attempting an exclusively cross-sectional estimate of the PDE coefficients has inherent dangers: if the deterministic part of the short rate process is too simple to allow for complex patterns of expectations of rates, an inordinate burden would be put on the shoulders of the volatility component in order to attempt to recover the observed term structure. Humped yield curves have been known to create problems with simple approaches such as CIR or Vasicek. But it should always be remembered that even "rich" models which allow for more complex yield curve shapes can give no guarantee that the correct apportioning will be accomplished by a cross-sectional procedure between yield curvature arising from rate expectations and from future yield volatility.

In order to gain confidence about the reliability of the coefficients, a time-series inspection of their daily cross-sectional estimates is often very useful. Due to the fact that the

$\{\alpha_i\}$ are often estimated in conjunction with the a priori unknown market price of risk, it can be difficult to say anything very precise from the numerical values themselves, but such tell-tale indications as wildly fluctuating estimates over consecutive days can often point to a mis-specified or mis-estimated model.

Once reasonable confidence has been obtained that reliable coefficients have been estimated, if the functional form of the factor's process gives rise to a PDE which admits closed-form solution for the required boundary conditions, the computational advantages are obvious. Less obvious, but just as important, is that considerable computational savings can be accomplished with closed-form models even if numerical methods, such as finite differences, have to be employed to check, for instance, for early exercise opportunities: since at each node both the coefficients and the state variables are known, all quantities, in fact, such as swap rates, which can be expressed as a function of linear combinations of discount bonds, can be evaluated analytically on a node-by-node basis.

The preferred numerical procedures for the integration of the PDE have tended to be linked to finite differences schemes, either in the implicit (IFD) or the explicit (EFD) formulation. In both approaches, a rectangular grid is first set up containing different values of the state variable on one axis, and time on the other (for helpful graphical illustrations of the geometry of the problem see, for example, Press et al. (1990)). The desired initial conditions, $v(., T)$, are first applied at expiry time T. As for the time derivative, it is evaluated as a *forward* difference, i.e. using the known value $v(i, T)$ and the unknown $v(i, T - 1)$. In the EFD scheme, the required first- and second-order space derivatives at node $(i, T - 1)$ (where i denotes the space (rate) co-ordinate and $T - 1$ the time) are then approximated by finite differences computed using the *known* values at nodes $v(i + 1, T)$, $v(i, T)$, $v(i - 1, T)$. In this approach, therefore, a single unknown quantity appears at each node (the value $v(i, T - 1)$ in the time derivative), and locally the PDE can therefore be recast in terms of a linear equation in a single unknown of the form:

$$v(i, T - 1) = A \ v(i - 1, T) + B \ v(i, T) + C \ v(i + 1, T) \qquad (1)$$

This expression lends itself to a suggestive interpretation: if one defines $A' = A \ (1 + r\Delta t)$, $B' = B \ (1 + r\Delta t)$ and $C' = C \ (1 + r\Delta t)$ one can "read" the procedure as implying that the value $v(i, T)$ can move up, straight or down to values $v(i - 1, T)$, $v(i, T)$, $v(i + 1, t)$ with probabilities A', B' and C', respectively. For this interpretation to make sense the three coefficients must all be positive and add up to one. A more careful discussion of the stability issues shows that, for the type of parabolic PDE at hand, these are indeed the conditions (see Ames (1977), Nelson (1990)) for the stability of the numerical procedure. In general, however, the implicit drift of the short rate might be such that, for a given choice of Δt and Δx (where x denotes the "space" (i.e. rate) variable), the above stability conditions might not be satisfied. The problem can be circumvented by allowing the possibility of an upward or downward branching, from (i, j) to $(i + k - 1, j + 1)$, $(i + k, j + 1)$, $(i + k + 1, j + 1)$, with k equal to the smallest integer for which the stability conditions are met. The EFD scheme thus modified is the approach advocated by HW (Hull and White (1990b)) for their extended-Vasicek and extended-CIR approaches.

The IFD scheme, which "simply" differs in that the space derivatives at time $T - 1$ are approximated by a *centred* expression involving $v(i + 1, T - 1)$, $v(i, T - 1)$ and $v(i - 1, T - 1)$, does not suffer from these stability constraints; the appearance of a value, $v(i, T - 2)$, belonging to the time slice being updated implies, however, that no simple expression such as equation (1) is available, and one is forced to solve a linear system of equations; its solution is trivial, since the associated matrix is tri-diagonal, but the appealing intuitional features associated with the EFD scheme are lost. This is certainly one of the reasons why the EFD approach, with the modifications outlined above, has become very popular among practitioners. Despite the formal similarities between this method and lattice approaches, the EFD procedure is intrinsically more "delicate": to begin with, in order to ensure faster convergence and better stability, it is useful to transform the original space (i.e. rate) co-ordinate to a new variable, such that the coefficients of the PDE can be made time-independent (Hull and White (1990b) present a general procedure to accomplish this task). Careful handling of the boundary conditions is in general very important, particularly if more than one state variable is used; in this latter case, a mixture of implicit and explicit approaches (using, for instance, the Hopscotch method (Gourlay and McKee (1979))) is recommended. Furthermore, the "pseudo-probabilities" A', B' and C' can be made time-independent, but are always space-dependent, and have to be determined during the calculation (a lattice approach such as BDT's, instead, simply assumes $\frac{1}{2}$ and $\frac{1}{2}$ probabilities for the up and down states).

On the other hand, the closely linked trinomial tree technology, developed by HW in conjunction with their extended-Vasicek model reviewed later, supplies the user with an additional degree of freedom, with respect to binomial lattice methods, to fit an extra market variable; in particular, the approach can overcome the limitations of the BDT model by allowing the user to specify at the same time both the future volatility of the short rate and the term structure of volatility. Whether this should be regarded as an intrinsically positive feature is a debatable point and is discussed in Sections 5.5.1 and 5.5.2.

5.5 ANALYSIS OF SPECIFIC MODELS

5.5.1 BDT: Model Implications and Empirical Findings

The BDT model (Black et al. (1990)) is a one-factor model algorithmically constructed in such a way as to price exactly any set of market discount bonds without requiring any explicit specification of investors' risk preferences. As a consequence, (plain vanilla) swap rates, which can be expressed as linear combinations of discount bonds, can be priced exactly for any volatility input. Whilst these features are shared by the HL model, the BDT approach further assumes a log-normal process for the short rate. Besides preventing negative rates, this assumption allows the volatility input to be specified as a percentage volatility, thereby following market conventions and making model calibration to cap prices much easier. This latter point is less trivial than it might seem, at least for non-flat term structure, as discussed in connection with the HW model (Section 5.5.2). Therefore, *simultaneous* fitting to the yield curve *and* to cap (or swaption) volatilities is conceptually straightforward and computationally very easy to achieve.

The price to be paid for all these positive features is, on the one hand, numerical (log-normal distributions hinder analytic tractability), and, on the other hand, conceptual: by the very fact that the model is specified algorithmically, it is rather "opaque" as to its implications and hidden assumptions, regarding, for instance, the nature of its mean reversion. It is therefore useful to unravel the implicit features of the BDT model, with a view to understand better the strengths and weaknesses of its performance.

The continuous-time equivalent of the BDT short rate process can be written in the form

$$r(t) = u(t) \exp(\sigma(t)z(t)), \tag{1}$$

where $u(t)$ is the median of the short rate distribution at time t, $\sigma(t)$ the short rate volatility, and $z(t)$ a standard Brownian motion. Unlike the case for the HL model, the median $u(t)$ is not obtainable analytically for log-normal processes. Some insight can, however, be obtained by converting equation (1) to its stochastic incremental form: after applying Ito's lemma to $r = r(t, z(t))$, with $z(t) = [\ln(r(t)) - \ln u(t)]/\sigma(t)$, one easily obtains

$$dy(t) = \{c(t) + a(t)[w(t) - y(t)]\} \, dt + \sigma(t) \, dz \tag{2}$$

with

$$y(t) = \ln[r(t)]$$

$$w(t) = \ln[u(t)]$$

$$c(t) = \partial \ln w(t)/\partial t$$

$$a(t) = \partial \ln[\sigma(t)]/\partial t$$

(Similar expressions are known in the literature; equation (2) above, however, makes explicit the link with the median of the distribution, important for MC implementations; the median, in turn, can be readily obtained from the built tree.) As the expression above shows, if the volatility is assumed to be constant, the model does not display any reversion speed: the logarithm of the short rate evolves by diffusion with a drift which follows the logarithm of the median, as implicitly determined by the forward induction tree-fitting procedure. If, on the other hand, the volatility is decaying with time, for instance according to the simple law

$$\sigma(t) = \sigma(0) \exp(-vt), \quad v > 0 \tag{3}$$

then equation (2) can be rewritten as

$$dy(t) = \{c(t) + v[w(t) - y(t)]\} \, dt + \sigma(t) \, dz \tag{3'}$$

clearly displaying the reversion of the logarithm of the short rate to a time-dependent reversion level, roughly given by the level of the (logarithm of) the forward rates. It is by this feature that the BDT model can simultaneously recover a series of market (Black) cap (or swaption) prices, obtained with a declining implied volatility. The equations obtained above can prove very useful in order to carry out MC simulations consistent with a given BDT implementation. This, in turn, is very important if one wants to risk-manage individual path-dependent options in a portfolio of ordinary options priced using the conventional tree methodology.

From equation (3) and (3') one can see that the assumption of decaying short rate volatility is required to prevent the unconditional variance of the short rate, $\sigma(t)^2 t$, from increasing with t without bounds, which would be inconsistent with the mean-reverting character of the short rate process. By allowing greater flexibility for the $\sigma(t)$ function, the prices of as many caps as desired can be simultaneously and easily obtained. It is important to notice that it is also possible, although slightly more cumbersome, to obtain simultaneous fitting to the prices of a series of options to enter, at different times, the same-maturity swap. It is in general, however, not possible to match at the same time cap and swaption prices; this is no specific shortcoming of the BDT model, but rather reflects the intrinsic limitation of any one-factor model, which, as such, implies perfect instantaneous correlation between different rates: whilst, in fact, a cap is a portfolio of independent options (caplets), a swaption is an option on a portfolio of rates, and, therefore, dependent on the imperfect correlation between them. Yield spread options would be similarly beyond the reach of the BDT approach. Only two-factor models can satisfactorily accommodate this feature.

A feature which is instead specific to the BDT model, as opposed to one-factor models in general, is the fact that the term structure of volatility is completely determined by the specification of the future volatility of the short rate. This simply stems from the fact that the reversion speed, which by and large determines the volatility of rates of different maturities, is not an independent parameter (as, for instance, in the HW model) but is a unique function of the short rate volatility (see equation (2) above). Figure 5.3 shows the volatility of yields of maturities from three months to ten years for a recent market USD curve, for different values of the decay constant v, and for a value of $\sigma(0)$ similar to what is observed at the short end of the cap market. For positive values of the decay constant, as implied by declining Black volatilities, yields of long maturities display less variability than short-maturity yields, in overall agreement with market observations.

With these limitations clearly in mind, it is important to assess the overall "realism" of the model, with a view to the ultimate acid test, i.e. the hedging performance. Within

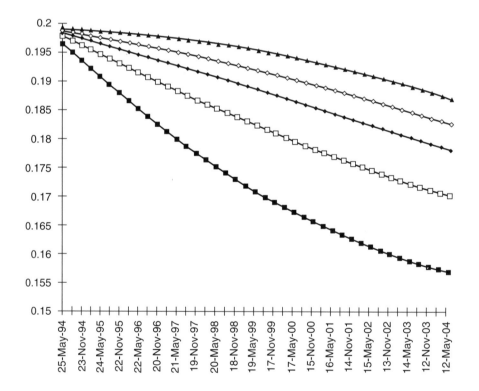

Figure 5.3   Volatility of yields of different maturities (USD 22 February 1994) with decay constant v (top to bottom) = 0, 0.02, 0.04, 0.08, 0.16, and $\sigma_0 = 20$ per cent

the framework of any approach hedging can be accomplished "within the model", i.e. by attempting to neutralize the exposure to the model driving factor(s), or "outside the model", i.e. by obtaining price changes with respect to rate changes virtually not allowed by the model itself, e.g. rigid yield curve shifts. The latter procedure is clearly conceptually inconsistent, but a lot of confidence is needed to embrace the first, since, within the framework of any one-factor model, one could hedge an exposure to a ten-year yield with an overnight deposit! Technically, obtaining in-model hedge parameters is straightforward. By evolving backwards in the tree any two assets, A and B, to time $1\Delta t$, one can obtain their relative sensitivity through their sensitivities to the short rate:

$$\frac{A(\text{up}) - A(\text{down})}{B(\text{up}) - B(\text{down})} = \frac{\{[A(\text{up}) - A(\text{down})]/[r(\text{up}) - r(\text{down})]\}}{\{[B(\text{up}) - B(\text{down})]/[r(\text{up}) - r(\text{down})]\}} \tag{4}$$

Gammas can be similarly obtained by considering the asset prices at time $2\Delta t$, and the corrections for the small theta effect introduced are, in practical applications, both small and straightforward. To see more clearly the conceptual implications of the procedure, one can (Black et al. (1990)) follow the strategy of buying a coupon-bearing bond, selling a call on the bond itself struck at X and purchasing a put, also struck at X. The value of this portfolio must equal the sum of the strike price X and the certain pay-offs from the strategy, i.e. the coupons intervening between today and the option expiry. If the present values of these known cash flows, correctly priced by the model by construction, are denoted as $\{Z(i)\}$, one must be able to write

$$\text{Put}(0) - \text{Call}(0) + \text{Bond}(0) = \sum_i \{Z(i)\}; \tag{5}$$

differentiating each term with respect to the bond price, one obtains

$$\Delta_{\text{call}} - \Delta_{\text{put}} = 1 - \partial \left[\sum \{Z(i)\} \right] \Big/ \partial \text{Bond} \tag{6}$$

The last term on the right-hand side represents the sensitivity of the portfolio of discount bonds to changes in the bond price. This term is absent in any Black-like price model, since, in such a framework, forward bond prices can change without any accompanying change in the discounting. Clearly, the effect becomes significant only when the option expiry is similar to the maturity of the bond.

From equation (4) above, one can easily derive the sensitivity of bond prices (and hence yields) of different maturities to changes in the short rate. In contrast with the term structure of volatilities, these sensitivities in general show little dependence on the decay constant v. They are instead strongly dependent on the shape of the yield curve, as displayed by Figure 5.4 for several market yield curves. Upward sloping term structures (e.g. USD and GBP in 1994) produce an elasticity above 1; the reverse is true for declining yield curves (e.g. ITL and ESP in the last quarter of 1993). This should come as no surprise, given the percentage nature of the BDT volatility. With these sensitivities, one can carry out what is probably one of the most stringent tests of a model's "realism". Armed with the yield sensitivities obtained using equation (4) above and with the foreknowledge of the day-by-day actual experienced changes in the short rate, one can predict the changes in yields of any maturity, and compare the model answers with the market outcome. This analysis, carried out for several currencies for

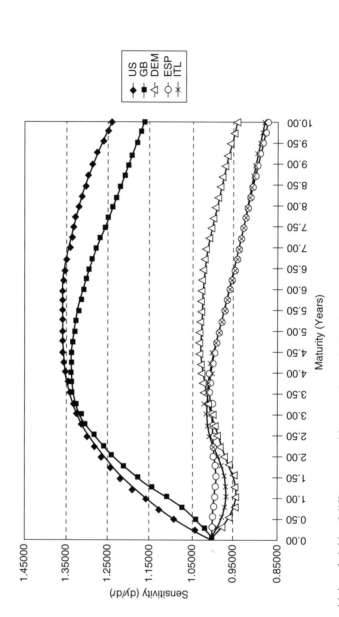

Figure 5.4 Sensitivity of yields of different maturities to a change in the short rate, for the yield curves of USD, GBP, DEM, ITL, ESP (24 February 1994, top to bottom at the right-end extreme). On this date, the GBP and USD yield curves were upward sloping, the DEM curve humped, and the ITL and ESP curve inverted

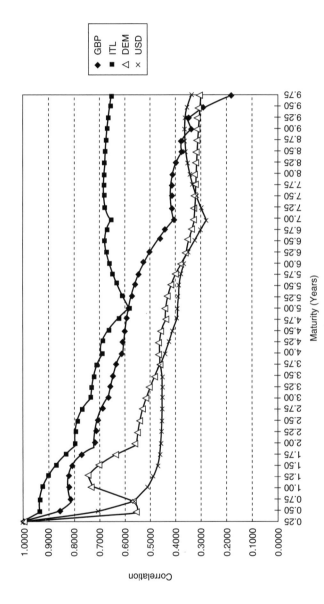

Figure 5.5 Correlation between experienced and model yield changes for increasing yield maturity using a choice of σ_0 and ν to give a good fit to cap prices: top to bottom ITL, USD, DEM, GBP

the period 1990–1993 with decay constant chosen to give an overall acceptable fit to market cap prices, obtained the results summarized in Figure 5.5. The correlation between experienced and predicted yield changes is, by construction, perfect at the short end, and decreases with yield maturity.

Whenever a yield curve displays steepening or flattening the agreement between observed and experienced yield changes is obviously poor, given the one-factor nature of the model. This important test therefore strongly cautions, in such environments, against blind in-model hedging.

The BDT model has therefore been shown to enjoy several positive features (among which the ease of calibration should not be underestimated) but to suffer from two important shortcomings: substantial inability to handle conditions where the impact of a second (tilt) factor could be of relevance; and inability to specify the volatility of yields of different maturities independently of the future volatility of the short rate. The former is unavoidable for any one-factor model; if one felt that the latter could be of relevance for a specific option (e.g. a long-maturity swap with principal determined by a short-maturity index), one could turn to approaches such as the HW model, reviewed in Section 5.5.2.

5.5.2 Extended Vasicek (HW): Model Implications and Empirical Findings

The previous section has highlighted how the mean-reverting features of the BDT model (on which the term structure of volatilities depends) cannot be divorced from the specification of the future volatility of the short rate. Hull and White (HW in the following) circumvent this problem by an approach that naturally combines the "classical" (PDE) approach and lattice methodologies. The process for the short rate, in fact, is explicitly given as

$$dr(t) = a(t)[\theta(t) - r(t)]\, dt + \sigma(t)r^\beta\, dz \tag{1}$$

where the reversion level $\theta(t)$ is always a function of time, β is equal to 0 or $\frac{1}{2}$ to mirror the Vasicek or the CIR approach, respectively, and the volatility and reversion speed functions can, but need not, be time-dependent. The very elegant numerical strategy proposed by HW (1994) for the numerical solution of the accompanying PDE is a version of the Explicit Finite Difference method, modified, as explained in Section 5.4.3, to ensure numerical stability. In an earlier paper, HW (1990b) advocated a procedure whereby the choice was made on a node-by-node basis of whether normal, upward or downward branching should be effected. In a more recent paper (Hull and White (1994)) they have shown that the time step and the level at which switching from normal to modified branching occurs can be determined a priori from the model parameters, thus lightening the computational burden. It should be noticed that, after the switching time step, the resulting tree displays downward branching in the upper (high rates) region, upward branching in the lower region, and normal branching in the middle. Therefore, once switching has occurred, the overall "width" of the tree does not increase, thereby avoiding the wasteful sampling of very high and very low rates occurring with negligible probabilities in conventional (BDT-like) lattice approaches.

As for a comparison with the Vasicek/CIR approach, the salient difference is that, by allowing $\theta(t)$ to change with time, yield curves of arbitrary complex shapes can be exactly fitted. In this respect, therefore, the HW approach (Hull and White (1990a)) shares the same advantages and the same conceptual characteristics as the BDT approach. In addition, if the reversion speed is allowed to be time-dependent, the volatility of the yield of any maturity can be exactly recovered. The price to be paid for this *exact* match is that expressions for bond and bond option prices are no longer analytically obtainable even for the normal (Vasicek, $\beta = 0$) case, and for constant volatility. In earlier papers, Hull and White (1990a, 1993) show in detail the numerical procedure to employ in order to achieve the volatility match. Exact fitting to the term structure of volatilities, however, tends to produce, day by day, $a(t)$ functions that bear little resemblance to each other, and that imply implausible behaviour for the future term structure of volatilities. As Carverhill (1994) shows, the drawback of the BDT approach of imposing a potentially undesirable behaviour to the future behaviour of the short rate, rather than disappearing is shifted to the volatility term structure. In view of these considerations, the precise-fitting approach has been abandoned by practitioners, and by HW themselves in later papers, and the model is normally implemented with constant reversion speed. As a consequence, unlike BDT, it does not exactly reproduce the prices of an arbitrary set of caps. It is therefore customary to estimate, often using a least-square-fit procedure, the value of the reversion speed that best approximates the observed cap prices. If a constant volatility function is also chosen, the fitting is rendered particularly simple by the availability of analytic expressions for bond options: HW (1990a) in fact prove that, for the normal, constant-reversion-speed (a), constant-volatility (σ) model, a call option C expiring at time T and struck at X on a discount bond $P(0, s)$ maturing at time s is given by the Black-like expression

$$P(0, T)[P(T, s)N(h) - XN(h - \sigma_P)] \tag{2}$$

where

$$P(T, s) = P(0, s)/P(0, T)$$

$$\sigma_P = v(0, T)B(T, s)$$

$$v(0, T)^2 = \sigma^2(1 - \exp[-2aT])/(2a)$$

$$B(t, T) = (1 - \exp[-a(T - t)])/a$$

$$P(t, T) = A(t, T)\exp[-B(t, T)r]$$

$$h = (\ln[P(T, s)/X] + \tfrac{1}{2}\sigma_P^2)/\sigma_P$$

$$\ln A(t, T) = \ln[P(0, T)/P(0, t)] - B(t, T)$$

$$- \sigma^2(\exp[-aT] - \exp[at])^2(\exp[2at] - 1)/(4a^3)$$

$$- B(t, T)\partial \ln[P(0, t)]/\partial t$$

Equation (2) highlights the similarity with the Black formula, since $P(0, T)$ plays the role of the discounting bond (the numeraire), and the option struck at X is seen to be a call on the *forward* bond price.

The cap-fitting procedure is, however, not quite as straightforward as one might surmise, both from the technical and from the conceptual point of view. Cap prices and (percentage!) volatilities, in fact, are quoted in the market on the basis of the Black model, which assumes log-normal rates. Since the normal distribution of rates implied by the HW/Vasicek model is fitted to the first two moments of the log-normal distribution, very little price difference is to be found for at-the-money strikes. Moving away from at-the-money strikes, however, the normal assumption begins to play a more important role. For a non-flat term structure of rates and a given strike, however, not all the caplets can be at-the-money. *In matching prices of caps of different maturities it is therefore essential to disentangle the price effects arising from the mean-reverting character of the short rate process* (approximately translated, in a Black framework, by assigning percentage volatilities declining with increasing maturities), *and from the different distributional assumptions*. Large errors in the estimate of the reversion speed can otherwise be made.

More seriously, a declining *percentage* volatility does not automatically imply a declining *absolute* volatility, as displayed by any sharply upward sloping curve. If one takes as a proxy for the absolute volatility the product of the relevant forward rate and its percentage volatility, it is easy to see that commonly observed market yield curves, such as the USD and GBP curves in 1994, coupled even with sharply declining percentage forward rate volatilities, fail to produce a positive (absolute) reversion speed for the normal HW model. Conversely, for declining yield curves, fitting to cap prices which imply a declining percentage volatility will tend to obtain a very strong normal reversion speed. Humped yield curves pose serious problems.

This feature, *per se*, simply indicates that some caution is needed when one is comparing the implications for mean reversion of log-normal and normal models. In the long run, all yield curves should become reasonably flat, and, therefore, a positive mean reversion must prevail in order to price very long caps. If one is interested in intermediate maturities, however, which can still be as long as eight or ten years for recent USD market yield curves, any positive reversion speed could seriously fail to account for their prices.

The situation is clearly illustrated by Figures 5.6 to 5.9. For a textbook case of a flat term structure of interest rates (10 per cent), the HW approach obtains with excellent accuracy the Black cap prices obtained not only with a flat term structure of volatilities (20 per cent, Figure 5.6), but also with a declining volatility (Figure 5.7). Notice that in the first case the optimal reversion speed and absolute volatility turn out to be almost exactly 0 and 0.02 (= 20 per cent · 10 per cent) (This need not a priori have been the case, given the different distributional assumptions). For the second case of a declining percentage volatility, the reversion speed that gives overall best fit is positive (0.0991) and the absolute volatility similar, although not identical, to the product of the Black volatility $\sigma(0)$ (20 per cent) and *the* one rate (10 per cent). It is interesting to note that, in both cases, for at-the-money options the distributional differences play a very minor role.

For a decaying term structure of interest rates the fit to the cap prices obtained using the *same* declining percentage volatility is still acceptable (Figure 5.8), but now the estimated reversion speed is more than five times as large (0.548). Finally, Figure 5.9 shows that for a rising term structure of rates and the same declining term structure of volatilities not only is the fit rather poor, but the estimated "best" reversion speed turns out to be *negative* ($\sigma = 0.0197$, $a = -0.128$).

If one were only interested in these short-to-intermediate maturities, and therefore ready to accept the resulting model inconsistencies with very long maturity instruments, a normal negative reversion speed could be acceptable. From the implementation point of view, however, a negative mean reversion does create additional problems: the trinomial branching switching from "normal" to "upwards" or "downwards", described in detail in Hull and White (1994) and briefly touched upon in Section 5.4.3, totally fails to occur for negative reversion speeds; unfortunately, as discussed in the section devoted to the PDE/trinomial approach, it is indeed the switching that affords a potentially attractive construction in order to avoid the wasteful sampling of rate space effected by a model like BDT.

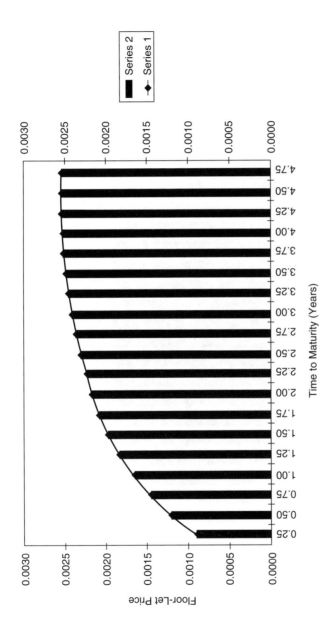

Figure 5.6 Fitting the HW parameters σ and α to log-normal floor prices for at-the-money strikes with flat term structures of interest rates (10 per cent) and of volatilities (20 per cent) for a variety of times to expiry (x-axis in years). The bars indicate the Black floor prices, and the continuous line the HW prices. Optimized reversion speed $a = 0$, $\sigma = 0.02$

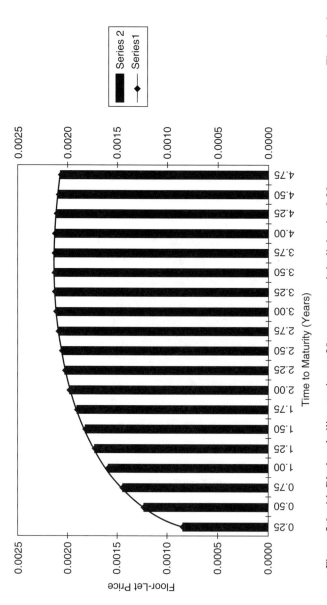

Figure 5.7 Same as Figure 5.6 with Black volatility starting at 20 per cent and declining by 0.20 per cent every quarter. The absolute volatility and the reversion speed were χ^2-optimized to minimize the sum of the squares of the differences between "market" (Black) and model option prices. Optimized reversion speed $a = 0.0991$, $\sigma = 0.02072$

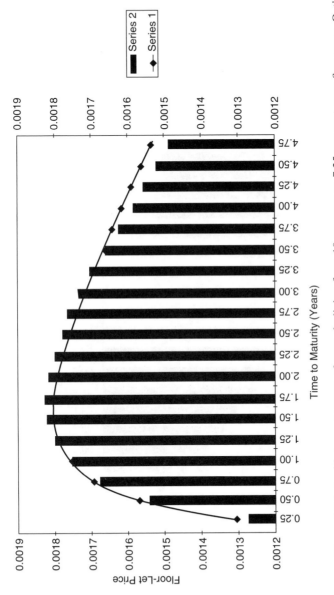

Figure 5.8 Same as Figure 5.7 but with term structure of rates declining from 10 per cent to 7.25 per cent over five years. Optimized reversion speed $a = 0.548$, $\sigma = 0.0231$

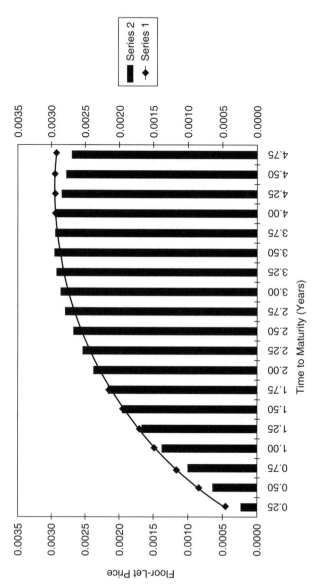

Figure 5.9 Same as Figure 5.8 but with term structure of rates rising from 10 per cent to 16 per cent over five years. Optimized reversion speed $a = -0.1275$, $\sigma = 0.0197$

At the present state of development, the HW approach therefore requires very careful handling. If these shortcomings are recognized, the existence of analytic solutions for bond and bond option prices makes the model of great appeal, if judiciously and carefully implemented. It should be recalled, in fact, that the HW approach is the only one to allow closed-form solutions without having to constrain the deterministic part of the process of the factor: how important this apparently minor point actually is will be fully appreciated after the section on the Longstaff and Schwartz model, and after the final conclusions.

5.5.3 Longstaff and Schwartz: Model Implications and Empirical Findings

The PCA presented in the introductory section indicated that the yield curve dynamics could be very satisfactorily explained by invoking as few as three orthogonal factors, i.e. the average level of the yield curve, its slope, and its curvature. These findings indicated that two-factor approaches should plausibly consider the slope of the yield curve as the second factor. Dybvig (1988) challenged this view by arguing that the level and the slope might well explain 95 per cent of the variance of rates or bond prices; however, if one is interested in the pricing of contingent claims, it might very well be that such an additive second factor has a negligible effect on the value of most options. If this second factor were instead taken to be the variance of the first principal component it could have a small effect on bond prices (virtually none at short maturities), but a significant effect on bond option pricing.

This is the view implicitly taken by Longstaff and Schwartz (1992) (LS in the following) in their two-factor equilibrium model. They derive it by considering a (very) stylized version of the economy, in which interest rates are obtained endogenously, rather than received from the empirical yield curve. In their model agents are faced with the choice between investing or consuming *the* single good produced in the economy. There is a single stochastic constant-return-to-scale technology (i.e. a single production process: identical companies in which investors can purchase shares). If $C(t)$ represents consumption at time t, the goal of the representative agent is to maximize, subject to budget constraints, his/her additive preferences of the form

$$\mathrm{E}_t\left[\int_t^\infty \exp(-\rho s)\ln(C(s))\,\mathrm{d}s\right] \tag{1}$$

Consumption at time s is "discounted" to present the time t by a utility-discounting rate ρ, which present-values the "pleasure" of future consumption $C(s)$. $\mathrm{E}_t[\cdot]$ is the conditional expectation operator, i.e. investors maximize their expectation, subject to information available up to time t, of the discounted future consumption. Consumption or reinvestment decisions have to be made subject to budget constraints that, given the assumptions above, have the form

$$\mathrm{d}W = W\,\mathrm{d}Q/Q - C\,\mathrm{d}t \tag{2}$$

i.e. the infinitesimal change in wealth, W, over time $\mathrm{d}t$ is due to consumption ($-C\,\mathrm{d}t$) and returns from the production process ($\mathrm{d}Q/Q$), scaled by the wealth invested in it (whence the constant-return-to-scale technology assumption).

The returns on physical investment (the only good produced by the economy) are in turn assumed to be described by a stochastic differential equation of the form

$$\mathrm{d}Q/Q = (\mu X + \theta Y)\,\mathrm{d}t + \sigma\sqrt{Y}\,\mathrm{d}Z_1 \tag{3}$$

where dZ_1 is the increment of a Brownian motion, μ, θ and σ are constants, and X and Y are two state variables (economic factors) chosen in such a way that X is the component of the expected returns unrelated to production uncertainty (i.e. to dZ_1), and Y is the factor correlated with dQ. Both X and Y are Wiener processes described by stochastic differential equations

$$dX = (a - bX)\,dt + c\sqrt{X}\,dZ_2 \tag{4}$$

$$dY = (d - eY)\,dt + f\sqrt{Y}\,dZ_3 \tag{5}$$

Given the assumptions made, there is no correlation either between dZ_1 and dZ_2, or between dZ_2 and dZ_3.

If one accepts that the optimal consumption, given the assumption above, is ρW (see Cox et al. (1985) for a proof), direct substitution of equation (4) and of the optimal consumption in the budget constraint equation (3), gives for wealth the stochastic differential equation

$$dW = (\mu X + \theta Y - \rho)W\,dt + \sigma W\sqrt{Y}\,dZ_1 \tag{6}$$

Having obtained the Wiener process followed by the wealth of the representative investor, two results from Cox et al. (1985) can be drawn upon to obtain the partial differential equation obeyed by any contingent claim H:

$$H_{xx}(x/2) + H_{yy}(y/2) + (\gamma - \delta x)H_x + (\eta - (\xi + \lambda)y)H - rH = H_\tau \tag{7}$$

where $x = X/c^2$, $y = Y/f^2$, $\gamma = a/c$, $\delta = b$, $\eta = d/f^2$, r is the instantaneous riskless rate and the market price of risk has been endogenously derived to be proportional to y, rather than exogenously assumed to have a certain functional form.

The set of equations and assumptions described above gives a general equilibrium model for the economy as a whole. Contingent claims are priced in this framework as components of the economy, and their prices are therefore *equilibrium* (rather than "just" no-arbitrage) prices. Whilst this added feature of the LS model is certainly intellectually interesting, it should be kept in mind that their claim of providing a general equilibrium model is only valid within the context of the very stylized economy they assume.

A link between the unobservable quantities X and Y and more directly observable financial quantities can be obtained by remembering that, given the assumed logarithmic form of the utility of wealth function, the instantaneous interest rate is simply equal to the expected return from the production process (dQ/Q) minus the variance of the production returns (notice the similarity with the drift of stock returns in a Black and Scholes world, given by the riskless rate plus a compensation proportional to the standard deviation of the stock returns). Given the definition above, the instantaneous rate is therefore equal to

$$r = \alpha x + \beta y \tag{8}$$

with $\alpha = \mu c^2$ and $\beta = (\theta - \sigma^2)f^2$. Since the stochastic differential equations for x and y are known, Ito's lemma can be applied to obtain the variance of r:

$$V = \alpha^2 x + \beta^2 y \tag{9}$$

Finally, the Wiener processes for r and V can be obtained from equations (9) and (10) by using Ito's lemma, giving

$$dr = [\alpha\gamma + \beta\eta - r(\beta\delta - \alpha\xi)/(\beta - \alpha) - V(\xi - \delta)/(\beta - \alpha)]\,dt + \sigma_{r2}\,dZ_2 + \sigma_{r3}\,dZ_3 \tag{10}$$

$$dV = [\alpha^2 \gamma + \beta^2 \eta - r\alpha\beta(\beta\delta - \alpha\xi)/(\beta - \alpha) - V(\beta\xi - \alpha\delta)/(\beta - \alpha)]\, dt$$
$$+ \sigma_{V2}\, dZ_2 + \sigma_{V3}\, dZ_3 \tag{11}$$

with

$$\sigma_{r2} = \alpha\sqrt{[(\beta r - V)/(\alpha(\beta - \alpha))]}$$
$$\sigma_{r3} = \beta\sqrt{[(-\alpha r + V)/(\beta(\beta - \alpha))]}$$
$$\sigma_{V2} = \alpha\sigma_{r2} \tag{12}$$
$$\sigma_{V3} = \beta\sigma_{r3}$$

Despite the fact that there are no cross-terms (i.e. $[dZ_2\, dZ_3]$) in the products of equations (11) and (12) (due to the assumptions made about the factors X and Y), there exists a non-zero correlation between r and V, which can be easily computed to be

$$\rho_{rV} = E[dr\, dV]/\sigma_r\sigma_V = \alpha^3 x + \beta^3 y/\sqrt{\alpha^2 x + \beta^2 y}\sqrt{\alpha^4 x + \beta^4 y}$$
$$= \alpha^3 x + \beta^3 y/\sqrt{V}\sqrt{\alpha^4 x + \beta^4 y} \tag{13}$$

Therefore, *in the LS model the value of the short rate volatility V is not uniquely determined by the level of the short rate.*

From the results obtained, it is easy to obtain the (unconditional) variances and expectations of r and V in terms of the parameters α, β, γ, δ, η and ξ:

$$E[r] = \alpha\gamma/\delta + \beta\eta/\xi \tag{14'}$$
$$\mathrm{Var}\,[r] = \alpha\gamma/(2\delta^2) + \beta\eta/(2\xi^2) \tag{14''}$$
$$E[V] = \alpha^2\gamma/\delta + \beta^2\eta/\xi \tag{14'''}$$
$$\mathrm{Var}\,[V] = \alpha^4\gamma/(2\delta^2) + \beta^4\eta/(2\xi^2) \tag{14''''}$$

respectively. The crucial importance of these relationships for model calibration will be shown in the following.

As for the joint distribution of the short rate and the variance, it can be shown that, given the absence of correlation between X and Y, it is given by the product of two independent non-central chi-squared distributions.

It is very interesting to examine the one-dimensional distribution $Q(r, t; r_0, V_0)$ resulting from integrating the two-dimensional distribution $q(r, V, t; r_0, V_0)$ over all the possible values of V:

$$\int_{\alpha r}^{\beta r} q(r, V, t; r_0, V_0)\, dV = Q(r, t; r_0, V_0) \tag{15}$$

The result of this integration is shown in Figure 5.10 for several values of t. With t increasing from 0.3 years to one year and to two years one can readily observe a delocalization of the initial value for the short rate of 8.00 per cent. The spreading of the distribution, however, does not increase at the same rate over time, and the rate distribution obtained for five years is virtually indistinguishable from the ten-year distribution. This feature should be contrasted with the type of log-normal distribution assumed, for instance, by the BDT model. In similar models, the burden of avoiding rates becoming too dispersed

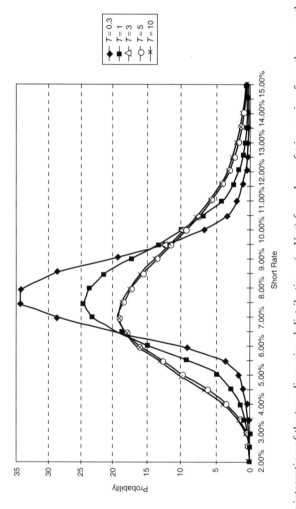

Figure 5.10 Volatility integration of the two-dimensional distribution $q(r, V, t)$ for values of t increasing from three months to ten years. Short rates on the x-axis. Notice how the distribution does not spread out significantly after the first five years

is taken up by imposing a time-dependent (decaying) volatility for the short rate. This *ad hoc* modification is not necessary with the LS model, which obtains more naturally and consistently the same result by virtue of the mean-reverting nature of its rate distribution.

Since any security traded in the LS economy must satisfy the PDE (7), this equation will have to be satisfied, in particular, by a discount bond. When the appropriate boundary condition $P(r, V, T) = 1$ is imposed, and a separation of variables approach is followed, the resulting expression for the value of a discount bond τ years before expiry turns out to be given by

$$P(r, V, \tau) = A^2\gamma(\tau)B^2\eta(\tau)e^{(\kappa\tau + C(\tau)r + D(\tau)V)} \tag{16}$$

with

$$A(\tau) = 2\varphi/[(\delta + \varphi)(e^{\varphi\tau} - 1) + 2\varphi]$$

$$B(\tau) = 2\psi/[(\nu + \psi)(e^{\psi\tau} - 1) + 2\psi]$$

$$C(\tau) = [\alpha\varphi(e^{\psi\tau} - 1)B(\tau) - \beta\psi(e^{\varphi\tau} - 1)A(\tau)]/[\varphi\psi(\beta - \alpha)]$$

$$D(\tau) = [-\varphi(e^{\psi\tau} - 1)B(\tau) + \psi(e^{\varphi\tau} - 1)A(\tau)]/[\varphi\psi(\beta - \alpha)]$$

$$\nu = \lambda + \xi$$

$$\varphi = \sqrt{(2\alpha + \delta^2)}$$

$$\psi = \sqrt{(2\beta + \nu^2)}$$

$$\kappa = \gamma(\delta + \varphi) + \eta(\nu + \psi)$$

As noted above, the market price of risk does not appear by itself, but only in combination with the parameter ξ. An infinity of values λ and ξ can therefore give rise to an identical fit to a given yield curve. Only if one supplemented information obtained from bond prices with information about the "real" (as opposed to risk-adjusted) dynamics of the state variables, would it be possible to estimate, within the context of the model, the market price of risk. Therefore, in order to fit a given yield curve, Longstaff and Schwartz (1994) have proposed the following two similar procedures. In both approaches: (i) a statistical analysis of the time series of the short rate and of the variance of the short rate is first carried out; and (ii) from the constraint that x and y should be greater than zero, one then obtains the condition that

$$\alpha < V/r < \beta \tag{17}$$

and one can therefore choose

$$\alpha = \min[V/r] \tag{18}$$

$$\beta = \max[V/r] \tag{19}$$

where the minimum and maximum are taken over the observed time series; (iii) from the simple system of non-linear equations (14) one can then determine the remaining four parameters. Up to this point the two procedures are identical. As for the evaluation of the further parameter ν related to the market price of risk two strategies can then be followed: (iv) (a) solve analytically with these six parameters and a *guess* value for ν the PDE with the boundary conditions appropriate to discount bonds, compare the model values thus obtained with a market-obtained discount function, and vary the value of ν until the sum of squared deviations is minimized; or (iv) (b) take the first maturity of interest, t_1, solve the PDE above with the boundary condition pertaining to a zero discount bond maturing at time t_1 with a trial value for $\nu(t_1)$, thereby obtaining a model price for the discount bond, $P_{\mathrm{mod}}(\nu(t_1))$; vary this trial value $\nu(t_1)$ until an *exact* match is obtained between the model and the market value; move on to the next maturity, and use the obtained value $\nu(t_1)$ for the numerical integration from time 0 to time t_1, and a trial value $\nu(t_2)$ for the period between t_1 and t_2; vary $\nu(t_2)$ until a match is obtained between observed and model prices. The procedure can be continued until all discount bonds are correctly priced.

It is important to notice that the first strategy is much simpler, since the model discount function can be obtained analytically, as long as ν is constant; however, if this approach is employed one cannot in general recover the observed discount function exactly. On the other hand, the second approach recovers the prices of zero coupon bonds by construction, but is rather laborious due to the need to integrate the PDE (7) numerically. These proposed procedures are far from unique: the LS model allows for a combination of the approaches which are often described as "fundamental" (or historical) and "applied" (or implied), by determining some of the model parameters on the basis of historical data, and the remaining in order to fit whatever market quantity one might desire. If one were to take the purely "historical" estimation route, only ν would remain free to be fitted. At the other extreme as many as six parameters and two state variables could be seen as degrees of freedom, giving rise to a strongly non-linear optimization problem. Finding an unambiguous absolute minimum can be very difficult, and, therefore, a lot of care should be exercised in choosing how many and which parameters should be optimized, and which should be determined from historical statistical series. To illustrate this point, I have performed a test of the ability of the LS model to price correctly the UK gilt market and the swap markets of the United Kingdom, the United States and Germany by best-fitting the six parameters and the two state variables (assumed to be not directly observable). The quality of the fit to the yield curves turned out in general to be very good, as shown in Figure 5.11, even for the case of a very "difficult" yield curve shape.

In the course of this minimization, none of the mathematically unacceptable regions were even encountered in the pre-September 1992 (Black Wednesday) period, despite the fact that no explicit constraint to this effect was put in place. Overall, the variations over time of the coefficients did not seem to be as "wild" as in the analysis of the CIR model, at least in the two sub-periods before and after September 1992. (Strictly speaking, of course, *any* variation of these coefficients, should, from the theoretical point of view, invalidate the model altogether.) After September 1992 (Black Wednesday) all the UK coefficients change radically, which is, after all, not surprising, since the UK yield curve changed drastically both in level and in shape. Needless to say, such a sudden change was in no way compatible with the rate dynamics implied by the model, and should therefore be seen as a "change of universe".

In the procedure described above the short rate was taken to be a completely free parameter in the optimization, and, therefore, the fact that it assumes values very close to the observed short rates is encouraging. On the other hand, since the coefficients were fitted to the market yield curve, and the quality of the fit was always good, the short rate is not really a "free" parameter, since it must, for any reasonable and well-behaved model, be very similar to the shortest fitted yields. The same considerations apply to the

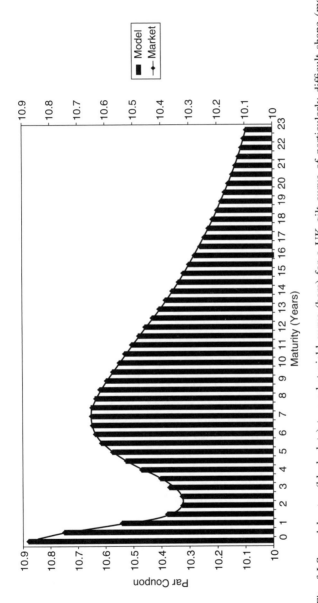

Figure 5.11 Fit of LS model rates (black dots) to market yield curve (bars) for a UK gilt curve of particularly difficult shape (maturities out to 22.5 years on the x-axis)

long yields: their closeness to observed values is, at the same time, both encouraging and, to some extent, ensured by the optimization procedure.

It is very interesting to calculate the degree of correlation between the two driving factors, i.e. the short rate and its variance: this correlation, for all the coefficients obtained, is always very high, sometimes as high as 99 per cent. If it were exactly unity, the model would collapse to a one-factor model. Yet, these very high correlations imply the de-correlations between rates of different maturities of very plausible magnitude. Due to this high degree of correlation between r and V, periods of high short rates are associated with periods of high rate volatility which is, to some extent, a plausible and desirable feature. What is less plausible and desirable, however, is that variance and rates move in step with the closeness implied by the obtained correlations. This feature becomes very important for option hedging. Given the excellent fit to market yield curves obtained by estimating cross-sectionally the model parameters, it is in fact natural to check the realism of the implied yield curve dynamics. To explore this feature the sensitivity of the yield curve to the short rate and the variance can be obtained by differentiating equation (16) with respect to these two state variables using the optimized parameters from the market yield curve for a given day. The "experienced" changes in the short rate and variance over two consecutive days can then be taken to be given by the differences of the respective quantities as obtained after the optimization procedure for the two days. With this information at hand, one can then predict the change in the price of a discount bond of maturity τ, as

$$\Delta F(r, V, \tau) = F(r, V, \tau)[C(\tau)\Delta r + D(\tau)\Delta V] \tag{20}$$

By considering the experienced changes in the discount functions over consecutive days the comparison can then be carried out between model predictions and "reality". Figures 5.12 and 5.13 show the results of some of these tests. For the coefficients obtained using the implied procedure, despite some fortuitously suggestive results, the agreement is in general rather poor, often worse than for the simpler BDT model. The reason for this can be traced to the sensitivity of a discount bond price to the variance of the short rate. This sensitivity is in fact large (roughly as large as the sensitivity to the short rate), but, given the very high degree of correlation between the short rate and its variance, a large experienced change in the former almost necessarily entails a large change in the latter; under these circumstances, the variance contribution to the yield change bears very little resemblance to real life contributions, and can therefore be totally unreliable. In short, the second factor, at least as distilled by the optimization procedure described above, fails convincingly to account for the observed yield variations. The hedging implications of these findings are of course very important: in practical situations one will try to match the sensitivity to the underlying factors of a given instrument with the corresponding sensitivities of two other instruments, judiciously chosen. If the sensitivity to one of the factors is a number of very dubious reliability, the reasonableness and effectiveness of the hedging procedure becomes very questionable. It is also important to point out that the high correlation feature is not specific to the "implied" estimation procedure.

Apart from these calibration issues, in order to bring into play market information from instruments dependent on the volatility of the short rate (such as cap prices), or the degree of correlation between rates of different maturities (such as swaptions), the procedure is not as straightforward as for the discount function. The cap volatility curve could for instance be fitted by means of the following procedure: given a set of parameters (α, β,

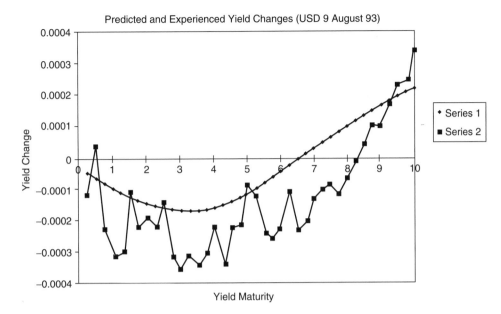

Figure 5.12 An example of a very good prediction (black squares) for a complex pattern of yield changes (USD curve 9 August 1993, maturities out to ten years on the *x*-axis). No one-factor model could reproduce such a complex pattern

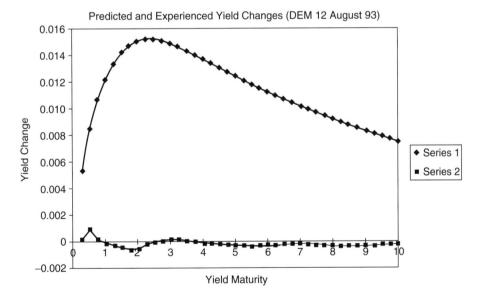

Figure 5.13 An example of a very poor prediction (black squares) for a relatively simple pattern of yield changes (DEM curve 12 August 1993, maturities out to ten years on the *x*-axis). No reasonable one-factor model could produce such big errors for the market yield changes of this particular example

γ, δ, η, ξ and v), however determined, construct a finite difference grid with the terminal pay-off of the cap, and evolve it backwards in time along the three-dimensional (two "space" (r and V) and one time co-ordinate) lattice until time zero is reached; at this time, a two-dimensional array of today's cap values is obtained; for a given (observable) value of $r(0)$ this will collapse to a single vector of cap prices. One can then pick, or interpolate, the volatility V value that gives the correct cap market value. As described, the procedure is suggestively similar to obtaining an "implied volatility" in a Black and Scholes approach.

The problem, however, is that the discount function which describes the model yield curve to be fitted to the market values is a function of the six parameters *and* of the two state variables. The two procedures described above cannot, therefore, be applied independently. The free parameters will specify a yield curve for a given choice of r and V. No "separation of variables" is possible, as it is, implicitly, in the BDT case. The problem is, of course, not insoluble: the degrees of freedom to fit zero coupon bond prices *and* cap volatilities *and* a lot more are all there; what is hard to find, and to my knowledge has not been determined yet, is a procedure to fit both functions in a relatively straightforward way.

The discussion so far has shown that the LS model is very rich and powerful. Ultimately, the success of the model will depend on a successful strategy for the calibration of its many degrees of freedom. Whether fitting all the available market data is desirable is, of course, a different question, whose answer ultimately depends on the confidence the user is prepared to put in a particular model, and on the judgement of the extent to which specific markets (e.g. swaptions) are sufficiently "perfect" (e.g. liquid and/or devoid of institutional frictions) to justify the enforcement of the assumptions that generate the no-arbitrage conditions. Should the user blindly fit a model to these quantities? What should be questioned, the model or the market prices? Is the model indicating trading opportunities?

5.5.4 The HJM Approach

Section 5.3.4 showed that, if the chosen numeraire is the money market account, all assets grow at the riskless rate (equation (5), Section 5.3.4), and forward rates are not martingales but display the drift given by the first term on the right-hand side of equations (7) and (8) of Section 5.3.4, for the discrete and continuous-time case, respectively.

These two equations can be derived within the framework of the Heath et al. (1992) approach, which can therefore be more aptly described as a no-arbitrage condition rather than a specific model. Reasoning similar to the argument that leads from equations (6) to (8) of Section 5.3.4, in fact, requires that, for a log-normal bond price process, the discrete forward rates from time T_1 to time T_2 as seen from the time-t yield curve, $f(t, T_1, T_2)$, should be given by

$$df(t, T_1, T_2) = 1/(2(T_2 - T_1))[v(t, T_2)^2 - v(t, T_1)^2]\, dt$$
$$+ 1/(T_2 - T_1)[v(t, T_1) - v(t, T_2)]\, dz(t) \qquad (1)$$

where $v(t, T)$ is the time-t volatility of a bond of maturity T (see Carverhill (1993) for the equivalence between the price-based and forward-based formulations). Since this equation simply imposes a relationship between the drifts and volatilities of forward rates, and the price volatility functions of discount bond prices, there is no such thing as *the* HJM model;

rather there exist a whole class of models, each characterized by a specific functional form for the volatility functions. It is worthwhile commenting on the complexity and richness of this volatility input. The starting point of any implementation of the HJM approach is the observed yield curve, as described by the collection of discount bonds given at time 0, $P(0, T)$. The link between discount bond prices and instantaneous forward rates $f(0, T)$ (defined as the limit of $f(t, T_1, T_2)$ as T_1 tends to T_2, and denoted, for simplicity, $f(0, T)$) is given by

$$P(0, T) = \exp\left[-\int_0^T f(0, s)\, ds\right] \tag{2}$$

$$f(0, T) = -\partial[\ln P(0, T)]/\partial T \tag{2'}$$

Either the discount bonds or the forward rates can therefore be taken as equivalent building blocks; in either case the approach recovers by construction any given market yield curve. For the valuation of an option depending on n discrete forward rates, $(f(0, t_i, t_i + \tau)$, $i = 1, \ldots, n)$, these will have to be evolved from time 0 to the option expiry. Equations (7) and (8) of Section 5.3.4 show that the values of $2n$ discount bond volatility functions $(v(0, t_i), v(0, t_i + \tau), i = 1, \ldots, n)$ are needed at time 0. Once each forward rate has been evolved over a time step Δt, the $2n$ volatilities at time Δt of discount bonds of maturity $t_i - \Delta t$, $t_i + \tau - \Delta t$ will be required to evolve the forward rates over one further step. In principle, unless some strong volatility constraints are imposed, this approach would leave the user with the task of specifying the price volatilities of discount bonds of continuously changing maturities at each point in the evolution of the forward rates. For practical implementations, the need to specify a functional form for the functions $v(.)$ is therefore clear, and to each particular choice there will correspond *a* particular HJM model. A first and absolutely necessary condition on the function $v(t, \tau)$, in order to prevent infinite drifts, is that $v(t, t) \equiv 0 \forall t$, simply reflecting the certainty of the redemption at par of any discount bond.

A second restriction on the possible functional forms is to impose that the process for the short rate should be Markovian. If this is the case, in fact, HW (Hull and White (1993), see also Carverhill (1992)) prove that the function $v(t, T)$ must be of the form

$$v(t, T) = x(t)[y(T) - y(t)] \tag{3}$$

A further assumption on the volatility functions which, as seen, could in principle depend *both* on calendar time *and* on residual maturity is that of time stationarity, i.e. the requirement that the volatility of the discount bond should depend only on the residual time to maturity, and not on calendar time t. When both these two latter constraints are simultaneously imposed, it is not difficult to prove that the function $v(\cdot, \cdot)$ must have the following functional form

$$v(t, T) = [k(1 - e^{-a(T-t)})]/a \tag{4}$$

whose limit as a tends to zero (i.e. in the absence of mean reversion) is simply

$$v(t, T) = k(T - t) \tag{4'}$$

Inserting (4') in equation (2) of Section 5.5.2 with $B(t, s) = T - s$, and $\sigma(0, T) = kT$, and taking the limit as a tends to zero clearly shows that this particular choice for the volatility function simply gives the continuous-time limit of the HL model, and that the volatilities of spot rates of all maturities, $R(0, T) = -\ln[P(0, T)]/T$, are exactly the same; under this model, therefore, *the whole yield curve can only move strictly in parallel.*

It is interesting to notice that, for choice (4'), the condition of no-arbitrage between bonds is certainly satisfied (by the very construction of the forward rate processes); there still exists the possibility of arbitrage, however, between bonds and the money market account, since rates attain negative values with strictly positive probability in finite time under (4'). This no-arbitrage violation, of course, is no worse than what is found in the HL or extended-Vasicek approaches.

The requirement to make the process for the short rate Markovian (see also the discussion after equation (5) below) is clearly very restrictive, but has the vast computational advantage that any Markov process can always be mapped into a *recombining* lattice, whose number of nodes grows linearly with the number of time steps.

Apart from this special case, an "up" move of all the forwards followed by a "down" move will not, in general, recover the original yield curve. In other words, the accompanying computational tree does not recombine. This feature constitutes the most severe technical drawback connected with the general HJM approach, and it has often forced upon practitioners the use of Monte Carlo techniques. Non-recombining trees have also been proposed, on the basis of the argument that it is the final number of states sampled, rather than the number of time steps, which determines the accuracy of the numerical integration. It has been argued that as few as ten or 12 time steps could give a sufficient sampling for pricing applications, but, in the absence of much published material on the matter, it is difficult to see how a five-year cap with quarterly resets (let alone an option thereon) could be priced using this technique.

Confining oneself to MC approaches, given the choice of numeraire one must be able to discount, prior to the averaging, each pay-off using the value of the money market account obtained in the course of each individual realization. To obtain this quantity one must have access to the value of the short rate at each point in time along the path. The stochastic process for the latter can be shown to be given, for one-factor models, by

$$dr(t) = [\partial f(0, t)/\partial t] \, dt + \left\{ \int_0^t v(\tau, t)\partial^2 v(\tau, t)/\partial t^2 + (\partial v(\tau, t)/\partial t)^2 \right\} dt$$

$$+ [\partial v(\tau, t)/\partial t|_{\tau=t}] \, dz(t) + \left\{ \int \partial^2 v(\tau, t)/\partial t^2 \, dz(\tau) \right\} dt \tag{5}$$

The interpretation of the terms is very interesting: the first clearly reflects the slope of the yield curve as seen from time zero; the third shows that the instantaneous standard deviation of the short rate equals the slope of the price volatility function at the origin, as the running time approaches the maturity; the second term depends on the history of the volatility function up to time t; finally, the fourth depends on the history both of $\sigma(., .)$ and of the Brownian process $z(t)$. From this analysis one can easily see that the process for the short rate is certainly non-Markovian if $v(\tau, t)$ depends on stochastic variables at times earlier than t (see Carverhill (1992)). Furthermore, even if $v(\tau, t)$ only depends on calendar time and time to maturity, the short rate process will still be non-Markovian unless the integrand in the fourth term is identically equal to zero.

For the special choices of the volatility functions mentioned above the short rate processes become

$$dr(t) = \{\partial f(0, t)/\partial t + k^2/(2a)[1 - \exp[-2at]] - ar + af(0, t)\}\, dt + k\, dz \qquad (6)$$

and

$$dr(t) = \{\partial f(0, t)/\partial t + k^2 t\}\, dt + k\, dz \qquad (6')$$

for $a \to 0$ limit. Needless to say, for these choices of the analytic form of the volatility functions, the calibration procedure will not, in general, yield an exact match to the market cap prices.

In the framework of the MC approach, a large number of quantities must therefore be evolved at each time step: as many forwards as caplets in a cap, each in an up and a down state if one needs derivatives, plus the short rate, in the up and down state as well if sensitivity to the discounting is desired; at each reset, one forward, and its accompanying statistics, can be shed, one at a time until the last reset, at which point only the short rate has to be evolved until the option pay-off time. This rather daunting computational task should be compared with a BDT-like tree construction. On the other hand, an option at time t on a bond maturing at time T only requires evolution of the relevant quantities out to option expiry time, thereby saving the wasteful building of the tree out to bond maturity for traditional lattice approaches.

The comparative advantage of the HJM approach is, however, best seen in the case of two-factor models. To begin with, the computational slow-down of Monte Carlo techniques with increasing number of dimensions is less than the speed reduction of finite-difference-based approaches. Furthermore, the analysis carried out in Section 5.3.4 which gives the drift and variance for the forward rates, can be translated almost by inspection into a multi-factor formalism (only the process for the short rate becomes somewhat involved). In addition, the principal component analysis reported in Section 5.2 provides a direct indication of the factors (level and slope) that could be taken to drive the yield curve dynamics. Finally, with appropriate scaling, the loadings (weights) which result from the principal component analysis provide a direct route towards the historical estimation of the volatility functions of the driving factors. Whilst this approach is conceptually straightforward, and bound to make the volatility inputs not only reasonably robust, but also of direct financial appeal (e.g. volatility of the level and of the spread), it will share the shortcomings of historical approaches, in that it will not recover exactly market option prices. The alternative, as usual, is to embrace an "implied" procedure, perhaps after imposing functional constraints on the inputs which embody the gist, if not the numerical output, of the principal component analysis. In this case, however, the calibration to market prices can become very time consuming, especially given the fact that the noise in the price estimates makes the evaluation of the derivatives with respect to the model parameters (needed for Newton–Raphson-like procedures) very arduous.

It is therefore indubitable that the HJM approach has great financial and intellectual appeal, not to mention a certain undeniable elegance; it also fair to say that, at the present stage of computer technology, its practical implementation for actual pricing and risk management applications is at the very boundaries of feasibility.

5.6 CONCLUSIONS OR "HOW TO CHOOSE THE BEST MODEL"

Several different approaches to the pricing of interest rate-dependent options have been reviewed in the preceding sections. The survey has been, by necessity, incomplete, but a few general thoughts should have emerged from the discussion. A distinction was first of all drawn between analytic and algorithmic models, which goes well beyond the greater ease of computation of the former. Starting with analytic approaches, it was shown that the general approach has been to describe the dynamics of the underlying factor(s) by assigning to the drift and variance components of their stochastic processes an explicit functional form in terms of the state variable(s) and of the model parameters. The PDE obtainable from these processes was also shown to contain, in addition to the state variables and the model parameters, the market price of risk. This fact has profound implications for model calibration. It is indeed true, in fact, that statistically and financially well-defined quantities, such as reversion speeds or reversion levels, can be estimated in a conceptually straightforward way. At least some of these quantities, however, only enter the PDE in conjunction with the non-directly observable market price of risk. Two different routes have therefore been followed by researchers and practitioners: the first has been to estimate the financially "observable" quantities pertaining to the factor dynamics (e.g. reversion speeds and reversion levels) from a *time-series* analysis of "real-world" data. Using the estimates thus obtained, *cross-sectional* estimates of the market price of risk can then be carried out via a best fit to the market instruments that price the risk (e.g. bonds). In general, if analytic tractability is to be retained, strong constraints have to imposed on the market price of risk (for the LS model, for instance, it has to be a constant over time). The result of this procedure is that, in general, the pricing of underlying instruments (bonds) implied by the model is not identical to their market values. The severity of the mis-pricing by and large depends on the shape of the yield curve, and will have a different impact for different pricing applications. Earlier models, however, such as Vasicek or CIR, were very seriously deficient in their ability to reproduce any but the simplest yield curve shapes, thus rendering them of little practical use, for instance, for the doubly inflected UK term structure of the early 1990s (see Figure 5.12).

The second approach with analytic models has been to estimate both the parameters in their combinations with the market price of risk and the state variables when not directly observable via a cross-sectional best fit to bond prices. Even with a constant market price of risk this approach has proven capable of recovering, at least for two-factor models such as the LS, complex yield curve shapes with great accuracy. As pointed out in Section 5.5.3, however, the curvature of the yield curve depends both on the expectation of future rates *and* of future volatilities. By an overall best-fit procedure there is therefore no guarantee that, for an imperfectly specified model (and all realistic models by necessity are), the correct (or even a reasonable) apportioning will be found by the minimization procedure of the rate and volatility contribution to the yield curve curvature. To give a concrete example, a model like the CIR, which assumes constant reversion speed and reversion level, can only attempt to account for a humped yield curve with long yields below the current short rate by a very heavy loading on the volatility contribution to the curvature, whilst a more "natural" description of the yield curve shape would plausibly invoke a time-dependent level of reversion.

If cross-sectionally implemented in this fashion, sophisticated two-factor models can therefore be more of a bane than a blessing: as shown in Section 5.5.3, an excellent fit to a given yield curve can in fact give the illusion of a "good" parameterization, whilst in reality a spurious loading can be implying dangerously incorrect sensitivities to the state variables (see Figure 5.12).

A third option is, of course, possible, i.e. to use time series to estimate the financially observable parameters, and to allow for a general time-dependent functional form for the market price of risk, so as to ensure (by construction) perfect fit to the yield curve, whilst retaining, at the same time, control on the financially more transparent quantities. Analytic tractability, however, is in this case lost and, despite the apparently a priori specification of the factors' dynamics, the market price of risk effectively becomes a handy *deus ex machina*, not only "fine tuning" possible imperfections in the statistical estimation of the parameters, but effectively picking up the slack of any model mis-specification. If so implemented, the approach becomes virtually indistinguishable, both conceptually and numerically, from a lattice methodology such as BDT, where the drift is algorithmically constructed so as to price in an arbitrage-free way an exogenous term structure.

At this point, the deciding factor becomes one of numerical efficiency, and, especially for two-factor models, the FD schemes necessary to solve the resulting PDEs do not present significant advantages with respect to n-nomial lattices, or, for that matter, skilful MC implementations.

This brings the discussion naturally to the second (i.e. algorithmic) approach. In view of the above, the high degree of control on the inputs and the capability of recovering exactly a given yield curve have obvious appeal. The numerical burden, however, tends to be severe even for one-factor models. This is particularly true for third-generation discontinuous pay-off (knock-out) options, where the fineness of the index sampling is all important for reliable pricing. But also for continuous pay-off options the hedging requirements can exact a very heavy computational toll. The distinction must in fact be made between in- and outside-model hedging. In the first approach, once the tree has been constructed, the security price is discounted backwards along the tree together with the price of a chosen hedging instrument. By analysing the up and down values one or two time steps before the root (and possibly adjusting for the small theta effect), it has been shown that it is straightforward enough to obtain the desired sensitivities to the driving factor (typically the short rate), and hence the hedge ratio. This approach, however, places a heavy burden on the shoulders of the model itself, since it cannot give any indication about the suitability of the hedging instrument: after all, in the context of a one-factor model in which all rates are instantaneously perfectly correlated, one could hedge a 30-year bond option with an overnight deposit. No sensible user would place such confidence on any of the currently available models. The approach is therefore commonly followed to shock the yield curve by an *exogenously* chosen perturbation of, for instance, forward rates, to rebuild the tree, and to reprice the security accordingly. Taking the difference between the security prices with the different yield curves gives an estimate of the desired sensitivity. Needless to say, this approach is in general conceptually inconsistent with the model used for pricing, since the latter will implicitly assign a virtually zero probability to the imposed shock. It is, however, much less dependent on the implied yield dynamics of a given model, which, as amply shown in the preceding section, is far from being satisfactorily described by any of the available models. As a consequence, the latter is the approach preferred by practitioners, and recommended by many academics.

As pointed out in the introduction, the increased market popularity of products strongly dependent on the imperfect correlation between rates is making the need for a two-factor approach more and more acutely felt: not only are spread-type options becoming increasingly common, but indexed or knock-out instruments (where the principal is determined by an index rate different from the rate determining the pay-off) have also met with great interest. The computational burden can therefore be quite demanding even for one-factor models, especially if discontinuous pay-off options are to be valued. As for algorithmic two-factor models the desiderata are a rather tall order: the joint dynamics of the state variables must, of course, be arbitrage free; the inputs should afford a direct financial interpretation (e.g. they could be volatilities of and correlation between observable financial quantities); the calibration procedure should be not only reasonably fast, but also robust; the lattice should recombine if one wants to avoid falling back on minor variations on the MC theme; once built by forward induction, the lattice structure should be storable by keeping at most $O(n^2)$ parameters (e.g. transition probabilities); the sampling of the state variables should be fine enough to allow realistic pricing and hedging of barrier options.

All the existing two-factor models fall short in some respect of some (or most) of these requirements, which explains why, at the present time, they are often used more as qualitative research tools than as actual pricing methodologies. It is in this latter direction, I believe, that the most challenging and exciting developments of interest rate option pricing will take place in the near future.

5.7 REFERENCES

Ames, W.F. (1977) *Numerical Methods for Partial Differential Equations*. New York: Academic Press.

Black, F. (1976) "The pricing of commodity contracts". *Journal of Financial Economics*, **3**, 167–79.

Black, F., Derman, E. and Toy, W. (1990) "A one-factor model of interest rates and its application to Treasury bond options". *Financial Analysts Journal*, 33–9.

Black, F. and Scholes, M. (1973) "The pricing of options and corporate liabilities". *Journal of Political Economics*, **81**, 637–53.

Boyle, P.P. (1977) "Options: a Monte Carlo approach". *Journal of Financial Economics*, **4**, 323–8.

Brennan, M.J. and Schwartz, E.S. (1982) "An equilibrium model of bond pricing and a test of market efficiency". *Journal of Financial and Quantitative Analysis*, **17**, 301–29.

Brown, H.B. and Schaefer, M.S. (1991) "The term structure of real interest rates and the Cox, Ingersoll and Ross model". Unpublished working paper, London Business School, May.

Brown, S.J. and Dybvig, P.H. (1986) "The empirical implications of the Cox, Ingersoll, Ross theory of the term structure of interest rates". *Journal of Finance*, **41**, 617–29.

Carverhill, A. (1992) "A binomial procedure for term structure options; when is the short rate Markovian?". Working paper, Hong Kong University of Science and Technology, Clear Water Bay, HK, January.

Carverhill, A. (1993) "A simplified exposition of the Heath, Jarrow and Morton model". Working paper, Department of Finance, University of Science and Technology, Clear Water Bay, HK 4 October.

Carverhill, A. (1994) "A note on the models of Hull and White for pricing options on the term structure". Working paper, Department of Finance, University of Science and Technology, Clear Water Bay, HK, July.

Chatfield, C. and Collins, A.J. (1989) *Introduction to multivariate analysis*. London: Chapman and Hall.

Cheng, S.T. (1991) "On the feasibility of arbitrage-based option pricing when stochastic bond price processes are involved". *Journal of Economic Theory*, **53**, 185–98.

Clewlow, L. and Carverhill, A. (1994) "Quicker on the curves". *Risk*, vol. 7, no. 5.

Cox, J.C., Ingersoll, J.E. and Ross, S.A. (1985a) "A theory of the term structure of interest rates". *Econometrica*, **53**, 385.

Cox, J.C., Ingersoll, J.E. and Ross, S.A. (1985b) "An intertemporal general equilibrium model of asset prices". *Econometrica*, **53**, 363.

Dybvig, P.H. (1988) "Bond and bond option pricing based on the current term structure". Working paper, Washington University in St. Louis.

Gourlay, A.R. and McKee, S. (1977) "The construction of Hopscotch methods for parabolic and elliptic equations in two space dimensions with a mixed derivative". *Journal of Computing and Applied Mathematics*, **3**, 201–6.

Gustavsson, T. (1992) "No-arbitrage pricing and the term structure of interest rates". Working paper, Department of Economics, Uppsala University, Economic Studies, **2**.

Harrison, J.M. and Kreps, D. (1979) "Martingales and arbitrage in multiperiod securities markets". *Journal of Economic Theory*, **20**, 381–408.

Harrison, J.M. and Pliska, S. (1981) "Martingales and stochastic integrals in the theory of continuous trading". *Stochastic Processes and their Applications*, **11**, 215–60.

Heath, D., Jarrow, R.A. and Morton, A. (1987) "Bond pricing and the term structure of interest rates: a new methodology". Working paper, Cornell University.

Heath, D., Jarrow, R.A. and Morton, A. (1989) "Bond pricing and the term structure of interest rates: a new methodology". Working paper (revised edition), Cornell University.

Ho, T.S.Y. and Lee, S.-B. (1986) "Term structure movements and pricing interest rate contingent claims". *Journal of Finance*, **41**, 1011–28.

Hull, J. and White, A. (1988) "The use of control variate technique in option pricing". *Journal of Financial and Quantitative Analysis*, **23**, 237–51.

Hull, J. and White, A. (1990a) "Pricing interest-rate derivative securities". *Review of Financial Studies*, **3**, 573–92.

Hull, J. and White, A. (1990b) "Valuing derivative securities using the explicit finite differences method". *Journal of Financial and Quantitative Analysis*, **25**, 87–100.

Hull, J. and White, A. (1993a)"Bond option pricing based on a model for the evolution of bond prices". *Advances in Futures and Options Research*, **6**, 1.

Hull, J. and White, A. (1993b) "Efficient procedures for valuing European and American path-dependent options". *Journal of Derivatives*, Fall issue, 21–31.

Hull, J. and White, A. (1994) "Numerical procedures for implementing term structure models I: single factor models". *Journal of Derivatives*, Fall issue, 7, 16.

Jamshidian, F. (1990) "Bond and option evaluation in the Gaussian interest rate model". Working paper, Financial Strategies Group, Merryll Lynch Capital Markets, World Financial Centre, NY, USA.

Jamshidian, F. (1991) "Forward induction and construction of yield curve diffusion models". Working paper, Financial Strategies Group, Merryll Lynch Capital Markets, World Financial Centre, NY, USA.

Longstaff, F.A. and Schwartz, E.S. (1992a) "Interest rate volatility and the term structure: a two-factor general equilibrium model". *Journal of Finance* **XLVII**, 1259–82.

Longstaff, F.A. and Schwartz, E.S. (1992b) "A two-factor interest rate model and contingent claim valuation". *Journal of Fixed Income* **3**, 16–23.

Merton, R.C. (1973) "Theory of rational option pricing". *Bell Journal of Economics and Management Science*, **4**, 141–83.

Nelson, D.B. and Ramswamy, K. (1990) "Simple binomial approximations in financial models". *Review of Financial Studies*, **3**, 393–430.

Press, W.H., Flannery, B.P., Teukolsy, S.A. and Vettering, W.T. (1990) *Numerical Recipes in C*, 2nd edition, Cambridge, Cambridge University Press.

Rebonato, R. (1996) *Interest-Rate Option Models*, Chichester, John Wiley and Sons.

Vasicek, O. (1977) "An equilibrium characterization of the term structure". *Journal of Financial Economics*, **5**, 177–88.

Wilson, T. (1994) "Debunking the myths". *Risk*, **7**, April, 67–73, and references therein.

6
Exotic Options I

EDMOND LEVY

6.1 INTRODUCTION

This is the first of two chapters covering non-standard derivative contracts provided by a relatively small but growing number of financial institutions. "Exotic" option is now common terminology for an option offering a variation from the standard pay-offs of the European or American call and put options. Broadly, these are contracts whose performances are designed to be aligned more closely to the underlying exposure needs of those seeking to hedge against, or those speculating on, future market conditions. Variations on the standard option can be traced back twenty years or more; however, it is only in the last seven years that we have seen the surge of interest in non-standard derivatives resulting in significant transaction flows. Some are one-off structures designed to meet a client's specific need, but many are recognized financial instruments in their own right. At the time of writing exotic options represent about 5–10 per cent of the total derivatives market and is the fastest growing area in the derivatives business.

Classifying such variations from the conventional option contract is not a straightforward task but we can identify three general lines of development. First, the introduction of path-dependency explicitly in the pay-off. This says that the contract not only depends on what the underlying asset price is on the expiration date but also on how it got there (e.g. Asian options, lookbacks and barrier options). The pay-off of an American-style option also depends on where the asset price is at a point in time which can trigger early exercise; however, in exotic options there is an explicit expression of how *ex ante* the path taken by the asset price will affect the option's pay-off. Second, some exotic contracts have pay-offs that depend on choices made by the holder at points in time prior to the expiration date (e.g. compound options and shout options). Finally, there are those exotic options that are a function of more than one asset price (e.g. quantos and basket options).

This chapter will look at Asian options, binary (or digital) and contingent premium options, and a variety of currency-protected options including currency basket options. Some of the technical detail in the development of pricing formulae has been relegated to appendices to facilitate the presentation.

Risk Management and Analysis. Vol. 2: New Markets and Products. Edited by Carol Alexander
© 1998 John Wiley & Sons Ltd

6.2 ASIAN OPTIONS

Asian options are now an established contract in the armoury of hedging instruments. The Asian option is an example of an option whose pay-off depends on the path of asset prices over a prespecified time horizon. Usually the pay-off of this instrument is a function of the arithmetic average of prices taken at various points in time and hence "average options" is also a frequently used term to describe them. However, other forms of averaging are possible, for example the geometric average.

Two types of Asian options are widely offered — the average rate (or price) option (ARO) and the average strike (or floating average) option (ASO). The average rate option is the more familiar of the two and the more popular in terms of volume of transactions. Briefly, the ARO pays off at maturity the difference (if positive) between the average of prices recorded over a prespecified time interval and a specified strike price. Here the expiry date is normally the same date as the last recording date determining the average. The ASO will pay the difference (if positive) between the asset price on the expiry date and the average of asset prices recorded over a specified time interval. In these structures it is fairly common for the user to specify an expiry date to be later than the last recording date in the average. Usually the two parties to the Asian contract will agree on a reputable source for recording the market price for the underlying asset for each date in the averaging period.

6.2.1 Definition and Uses

At this point it would help to introduce some notation. Let $S(t)$ denote the spot (or cash) price at time t. Suppose the average is defined over the time interval $[t_1, t_N]$ and at points (not necessarily equidistant) on this interval t_i for $i = 1, \ldots, N$. We will denote $A(t)$ as the "running average" to date, and is defined for any timepoint t, $t_m \leq t < t_{m+1}$, by

$$A(t) = \frac{1}{m} \sum_{i=1}^{m} S(t_i)$$

for a corresponding integer $1 \leq m \leq N$, and $A(t) = 0$ for $t < t_1$. Thus $A(t_N)$ represents the simple arithmetic average of N prices. The ARO is characterized by the pay-off function at time t_N given by $\max[A(t_N) - K, 0]$ for a call option, or $\max[K - A(t_N), 0]$ for a put option. The parameter K denotes the specified strike price of the ARO. The ASO is defined as having pay-off at time T of $\max[S(T) - A(t_N), 0]$ for a call and $\max[A(t_N) - S(T), 0]$ for a put where $T(\geq t_N)$ is the expiry date of the ASO.

There are various reasons as to why AROs have become so popular. First, a company's exposure to future price movements is sometimes naturally expressed as exposure to an average of prices in the future. For example, in the absence of a fixed price agreement, the total annual costs of a company will be sensitive to the prices of raw materials used in production over the coming year. However, although a company will have some estimate of its total requirement, it is unlikely that it will know the size and timing of all purchases. More likely, the company will estimate that such costs will be spread evenly (or perhaps with some seasonality) over the year. Such an exposure is better described as a future series of cash flow and total cost will therefore depend on the average (or weighted average) of raw material prices over the year. An ARO call on the price will compensate the company for the difference between the average of prices and a specified strike. Second, averaging is useful as a means to reduce the sensitivity of an option's expiration value to the underlying asset price on the expiration date. Abnormal price movements on the expiration date, arising perhaps from a lack of depth in the market, can lead to distortion of the expiration value of an option. To avoid such effects, some option contracts are expressed as an ARO in which the averaging period is specified as (say) the last ten business days of the option's horizon. A third reason for using AROs is that accounting standards may require translation of foreign currency assets or liabilities at an average of exchange rates over the accounting period. Again an ARO is an obvious choice to reduce the harmful effect that a turbulent currency market might have on a company's balance sheet.

To understand the mechanics of the ARO better let us consider an example of a Japanese exporter to the United States who, concerned with an appreciation of yen versus the US dollar, is seeking to hedge the yen value of expected US dollar receipts. Suppose we are at the end of December and the exporter is planning to establish a hedge for his US dollar exposure for the forthcoming year starting in January of next year. He estimates sales receipts to total 12 million dollars which will be spread evenly each month over the coming year. In the past the exporter always sold his US dollar receipts at month-ends. Suppose the current exchange rate is 90.00 yen to the US dollar and the forward value of yen for the end of December next year is 86.90. Our exporter targets a budget exchange rate of 87.00. To cover his exposure he could purchase a strip of 12 European options with expirations every month-end starting the following January. Each option gives the exporter the right to sell (or put) 1 million US dollars and buy yen at a strike of 87.00. The average premium due on these 12 options might be 2.58 yen per US dollar giving a total premium of 30,960,000 yen for 12 million US dollars cover.

Alternatively the exporter could enter into an ARO put contract. The terms of the ARO contract will specify that the average will be calculated from 12 recordings of the yen per US dollar exchange rate for the last business day of each month from January to December. An agreed source for these recordings (such as the published exchange rate fixing of a central bank or reputable supervisory body) is also specified. Settlement of the contract will be made by comparing the average of fixings with the strike of 87.00. If the average is lower than 87.00 then the exporter will be paid a cash settlement amount in yen of this difference multiplied by 12 million. If on the other hand the average is higher than 87.00 then the settlement amount is zero. Using the same market parameters which determined the premiums for the strip of European put options, the premium for the ARO is 2.11 yen per US dollar or 25,320,000 yen per 12 million US dollars.

In this example, the ARO was 0.47 yen per US dollar cheaper than the strip of European options. In general, the ARO will always be cheaper than the strip. The explanation for this is that there may be occasions when the average is "out-of-the-money" but some of the recordings were "in-the-money". In these instances the ARO will terminate worthless but some of the European options will be exercised. Hence the strip of European options offers a broader exercise criterion and will yield a pay-off which is the same or more than the corresponding ARO. Another way to put this is to note that in general a portfolio of put options on underlying assets is worth more than the option to put the portfolio of such assets.

The difference is directly related to the degree of correlation between the asset prices making up the portfolio. Analogous to basket options (see Section 6.4.3 below), the closer the correlations are to unity the more likely it is that if one option in the portfolio pays off then so will the others (with the same degree of in-the-moneyness). Consequently, if the averaging period is short relative to the option horizon (for instance the last ten days of a 12-month option horizon) we should expect the price of the ARO to be close to the price of a European option of identical strike and expiry date. Notice also that the ARO is a cash-settled agreement. Hence exercise is automatic once all the fixings are determined and their average found to be in-the-money relative to the specified strike. As there is no exchange of currency amounts the exporter has total freedom as to how much of, when and to whom he sells his US dollar receipts.

In this and subsequent examples we consider the US dollar/Japanese yen exchange rate. Suppose the current spot exchange rate is 90.00 yen per dollar, the dollar interest rate is 6 per cent, yen interest rate is 2.5 per cent and annualized volatility for the exchange rate is 13 per cent. Figure 6.1 compares the premium of a US dollar ARO call with that of the strip of European calls at various strikes. In the figure it is assumed that the current date is the end of December and the ARO has fixings every month-end for 12 months starting in January next year. In addition, the ARO is compared to the European call option with expiration end of December next year. In the figure we see clearly that at each strike the relationship ARO < strip < European holds.

The ASO, although less popular, has several uses. Suppose an institution wants to launch a 12-month bond issue whose redemption value is linked to at-the-money (spot) options (puts or calls) on some underlying stock market index. At the indication stage prior to launch it could specify that the strike would be determined by reference to the closing price for the underlying index in (say) a week's time. However, if the institution wanted to avoid the possibility of investors being exposed to market conditions on that particular day (perhaps important economic figures are due to be published around that time) it could alternatively specify the strike to be the average of closing prices for the following two weeks. This alternative specification links the redemption value to an ASO. A second use for the ASO is when a target, that is required to be met, is set based on the average of prices over the coming period but hedges for this period have to be established in advance. If the

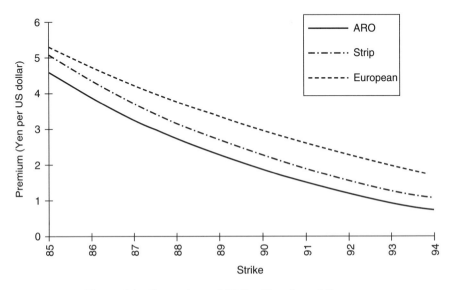

Figure 6.1 Comparison of ARO with strip and European

hedges are placed at the end of the period then there is a mismatch between the target and the hedging vehicle. In this instance an ASO paying the difference between the average over the period and the end-of-period price remedies the mismatch. A similar reason for using ASOs may arise, for example, when a company regularly converts domestic currency receipts from sales in order to pay costs in foreign currency at quarterly intervals. Here the ASO call on the foreign price of a unit of domestic currency will compensate for any difference between the average exchange rate over the quarter and the exchange rate achieved when the foreign currency cost is valued in domestic terms.

When the averaging period is close to the expiry date of the ASO then the premium is close to zero. On the other hand if the averaging period is close to the current date

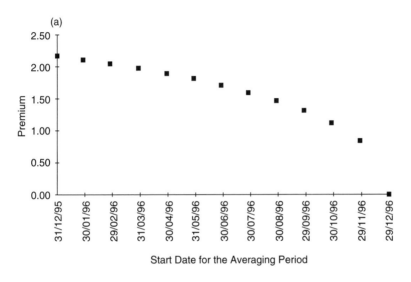

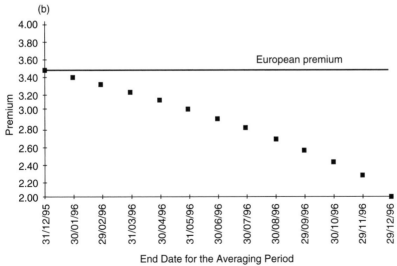

Figure 6.2 (a) Premium for average strike call options, (b) Premium for average strike call options

then the premium for the ASO is close to an at-the-money European option of the same maturity. In Figures 6.2(a) and 6.2(b) we demonstrate these features. In both figures the option horizon is 12 months and the average is determined by 12 points spread evenly over $(t_N - t_1)$. In Figure 6.2(a) the ASO is valued with $t_N = T$ and $(t_N - t_1)$ ranging from zero to 12 months. In Figure 6.2(b), the ASO is valued once more but with $t_1 = 0$ and $(t_N - t_1)$ again ranging from zero to 12 months.

6.2.2 Valuation Approaches

In both AROs and ASOs the terminal value is determined by the average of a history of prices. Option valuation usually assumes asset returns to be normally distributed or, equivalently, that asset prices themselves are log-normally distributed. Because the product of log-normal prices is itself log-normal, the valuation of Asian options determined by a *geometric* average of prices is a relatively simple matter (see Appendix 1). However, the distribution of the *sum* of log-normal components has no explicit representation and complicates the determination of a solution for the (arithmetic) Asian option. In this section we will review various methods that have been proposed for valuing such Asian options.

Define r as the domestic (continuously compounding) interest rate and y the continuous yield on the asset. If the asset is an exchange rate and S is in units of domestic currency per foreign currency, then y is the (continuous) foreign interest rate (denoted r_f in Chapter 7). It is assumed that r and y are constant over the life of the option. In option-pricing, the spot price process assumed is the familiar geometric diffusion

$$dS = \mu S \, dt + \sigma S \, dz \tag{1}$$

where dz is a Wiener process (that is, it is distributed as normal with mean zero and unit variance or $N(0,1)$ for short), and μ and σ are, respectively, the constant drift and volatility parameters. (As indicated in Appendices 1 and 2, a deterministic term structure for interest rates, yields and volatilities can be incorporated into the analysis without too much trouble.) The pay-off on Asian options is based on the future path of spot prices as described by equation (1). Under equation (1) we can express $S(t_i)$ in terms of $S(t_{i-1})$ as:

$$S(t_i) = S(t_{i-1})e^{(\mu-(1/2)\sigma^2)(t_i-t_{i-1})+\sigma\sqrt{t_i-t_{i-1}}Y_i} \tag{2}$$

where Y_i is $N(0,1)$. For $t_i > 0$, when viewed from $t = 0$, $\ln S(t_i)$ is thus normally distributed as $N[\ln S(0) + (\mu - \frac{1}{2}\sigma^2)t_i, \sigma^2 t_i]$.

A popular approach to valuing options is to adopt the risk-neutral transformation of Cox and Ross (1979). This enables us to characterize the solution to the Asian option as:

$$\text{ARO}_C[S(0), K, t] = e^{-rT}E^* \max[A(t_N) - K, 0] \tag{3}$$

for the ARO call and

$$\text{ASO}_C[S(0), K, t] = e^{-rT}E^* \max[S(T) - A(t_N), 0] \tag{4}$$

for the ASO call, where E^* is the expectation operator conditional on $[A(t), S(t)]$ at current time $t = 0$ under the risk-adjusted density function. This means we can treat the process for $S(t)$ now as described by the diffusion (1) with μ replaced by $(r - y)$. Suppose we denote $P[A(t_N) = \omega]$, the conditional density function for $A(t_N)$, by $f^*(\omega)$, then the expectation term in equation (3) can be written as:

$$E^* \max[A(t_N) - K, 0] = \int_K^\infty [A(t_N) - K] f^*(\omega) \, d\omega \qquad (5)$$

For the ASO call we need the joint density of $A(t_N)$ and $S(T)$, $P[S(T) = \xi, A(t_N) = \omega]$. Suppose we denote this by $\gamma^*(\xi, \omega)$, then the expectation term in equation (4) can be written as:

$$E^* \max[S(T) - A(t_N), 0] = \int_0^\infty \int_\omega^\infty [S(T) - A(t_N)] \gamma^*(\xi, \omega) \, d\xi \, d\omega$$

Because the functions $f^*(\omega)$ and $\gamma^*(\xi, \omega)$ are non-standard, to evaluate these integrals most have resorted to numerical procedures or approximation methods.

Of the various numerical procedures advocated, only the Monte Carlo approach will be discussed below. Interested readers should also be aware of Carverhill and Clewlow (1990) (who adopt a Fourier transform approach to evaluate the convolution of density functions) and the extended binomial tree approach of Hull and White (1993). Geman and Yor (1992, 1993) and Geman and Eydeland (1995) have produced some interesting results using Bessel processes. The approximation methods centre on the log-normal distribution making use of the fact that the moments $E^*[A(t_N)^j]$ (for any integer $j > 0$) can be calculated.

(i) Monte Carlo

Monte Carlo is a numerical procedure widely used in option valuation as well as other fields. (See, for example, Hammersley and Handscomb (1964), Rubinstein (1981) and for an application to option valuation see Boyle (1977).) Briefly, the procedure requires one to generate simulations of the price process and hence calculate simulations of the option pay-off. Repeating this procedure several times produces a distribution of option values. The discounted value of the average of these values is an estimate of the value of the option.

In the case of the Asian option the Monte Carlo technique can be easily employed (as demonstrated by Kemna and Vorst (1990) in the case of the ARO). Return to expression (2) and substitute $\mu = r - y$. If we draw outcomes of Y_i (for $i = 1, \ldots, N$) from the standard normal distribution then a sequence of $S(t_i)$ ($i = 1, \ldots, N$) can be constructed. For the ARO, the pay-off $\max[A(t_N) - K, 0]$ must be calculated. Repeat this procedure several times and average all such calculations. Finally taking the present value of this average will produce an estimate for equation (3). To find an estimate for the ASO we should generate an additional random outcome Y_T and calculate $S(T)$ from

$$S(T) = S(t_N)e^{(r-y-(1/2)\sigma^2)(T-t_N)+\sigma\sqrt{T-t_N}Y_T}$$

and hence calculate the pay-off $\max[S(T) - A(t_N), 0]$.

The strength of the paper by Kemna and Vorst is to recognize the high degree of correlation that exists between the (arithmetic) Asian options and their geometric counterparts. As the solution to the geometric versions of the ARO and ASO are known (see Appendix 1) they can be used as control variates for improving the accuracy of the Monte Carlo estimates. That is, for every sequence of Y_i's, as well as calculating the value for the

Asian option (A_M), calculate also the value for the geometric average version (G_M). If the true value for the geometric version is denoted by G, a better estimate for the Asian option is $A^* = A_M + G - G_M$.

(ii) Log-normal Approximations

An alternative approach is to approximate the density functions $f^*(\omega)$ and $\gamma^*(\xi, \omega)$. There are several studies supporting the choice of a log-normal density function as a good approximation. Several authors have independently derived similar approximation methods based on this view (for example, Ruttiens (1990), Vorst (1990), Levy (1990, 1992), Ritchken et al. (1990) and Turnbull and Wakeman (1991)). If $\ln A(t_N)$ is distributed as $N(\alpha, v^2)$ then for the ARO we evaluate equation (5) to give:

$$e^{-rT}E^* \max[A(t_N) - K, 0] = e^{\alpha+(1/2)v^2-rT}N(x_1) - e^{-rT}KN(x_2) \tag{6}$$

where $N(\cdot)$ is the standard normal distribution function, $x_1 = (\alpha - \ln K + v^2)/v$ and $x_2 = x_1 - v$. For the ASO we assume that the covariance of $\ln A(t_N)$ and $\ln S(T)$ is $\rho v \sigma \sqrt{T}$ and make use of a generalization of the exchange of asset option solution in Margrabe (1978) (see Section 6.4.2 below):

$$e^{-rT}E^* \max[S(T) - A(t_N), 0] = S(t)e^{-yT}N(y_1) - e^{\alpha+(1/2)v^2-rT}N(y_2) \tag{7}$$

where $y_1 = [\ln S(t) + (r - y)T - \alpha - \frac{1}{2}v^2 + \frac{1}{2}\Sigma^2]/\Sigma$, $y_2 = y_1 - \Sigma$ and $\Sigma^2 = v^2 + \sigma^2 T - 2\rho v \sigma \sqrt{T}$. The question remains how to determine α, v and ρ.

Suppose we treat $A(t_N)$ as distributed according to the corresponding geometric average $G(t_N) = [S(t_1) \cdot S(t_2) \ldots S(t_N)]^{1/N}$. Thus the parameters α and v become, respectively, the mean and standard deviation of $\ln G(t_N)$. This essentially gives the ARO formula presented in Ruttiens (1990). However, it can be shown that $G(t_N) \leq A(t_N)$ and so the central tendency of the distribution is biased downwards. As a result, with this choice of parameters, the formula for the ARO will undervalue call options. To counter this bias, Vorst (1990) suggests correcting the strike price of the option by this difference so that K is replaced by $K^* = K + E^*[G(t_N)] - E^*[A(t_N)]$.

An alternative and more accurate approach is to correct for both the mean and variance directly by observing that if $\ln A(t_N)$ is $N(\alpha, v^2)$, then from the moment generating function of a normal distribution, $E^*[A(t_N)] = \exp(\alpha + \frac{1}{2}v^2)$ and $E^*[A(t_N^2)] = \exp(2\alpha + 2v^2)$ (see, for example, Hogg and Craig (1970, p. 105)). As both $E^*[A(t_N)]$ and $E^*[A(t_N)^2]$ can be calculated (see Appendix 2), we can determine α and v to be consistent with the mean *and* variance of $A(t_N)$. That is, solve the above equations to give:

$$\alpha = 2 \ln E^*[A(t_N)] - \frac{1}{2} \ln E^*[A(t_N)^2] \tag{8a}$$

$$v = \sqrt{\ln E^*[A(t_N)^2] - 2 \ln E^*[A(t_N)]} \tag{8b}$$

The papers of Levy (1990, 1992) and Ritchken et al. (1990) employ this technique and demonstrate that with α and v chosen in this way, equation (6) provides a good approximation for the ARO. For the ASO, in order to use equation (7), we first need to determine ρ. Levy (1992) suggests we assume a joint bivariate log-normal distribution for $A(t_N)$ and $S(T)$ and evaluate ρ using the following equation:

$$\rho v \sigma \sqrt{T} = \ln E^*[A(t_N)S(T)] - [\alpha + \ln S(t) + (r - y - \frac{1}{2}\sigma^2)T] - \frac{1}{2}(v^2 + \sigma^2 T)$$

Although the mean and variance for $A(t_N)$ are perfectly captured, there will inevitably be differences between the skewness and kurtosis implied by the log-normal fit and those for $A(t_N)$. These differences will become increasingly more apparent as we move to higher levels of volatility (above 20 per cent or so) and/or longer option structures. A method, implemented by Turnbull and Wakeman (1991), to adjust for these effects, is to expand the distribution for $A(t_N)$ around the log-normal. Let $a(\omega)$ be the log-normal distribution, then it can be shown that we can expand $f^*(\omega)$ as:

$$f^*(\omega) = a(\omega) + E_1 \frac{\mathrm{d}a(\omega)}{\mathrm{d}\omega} + E_2 \frac{\mathrm{d}^2 a(\omega)}{\mathrm{d}\omega^2} + E_3 \frac{\mathrm{d}^3 a(\omega)}{\mathrm{d}\omega^3} + \cdots \tag{9}$$

where E_i are terms involving the difference between cumulants (or semi-invariants) implied by the log-normal fit and the true cumulants for $A(t_N)$. For example, E_1 is the difference between the mean of $A(t_N)$ as implied by $a(\omega)$ and the true mean of $A(t_N)$, and E_2 is the difference between the variances. If we substitute equation (9) into equation (5) and evaluate the integral, equation (6) becomes augmented by further terms having $E_i (i = 1, 2, \ldots)$ as coefficients. When α and v are chosen as equation (8), the first two terms are zero (by design), but $E_i (i = 3, 4, \ldots)$ are non-zero. Turnbull and Wakeman take this expansion to E_4 and so correct for differences in skewness and kurtosis.

Levy and Turnbull (1993) show that the log-normal approximation can be further improved by choosing α and v to fit higher moments for $A(t_N)$ but inaccuracies remain at high volatility levels. In a follow-up to this article, Curran (1993) shows that much better results can be obtained by using the risk-neutral distribution of the geometric average, $a(g) = P[G(t_N) = g]$, and evaluating the integral:

$$\int_{K^*}^{\infty} [\mathrm{E}^*[A(t_N)|G(t_N)] - K] a(g) \, \mathrm{d}g$$

where K^* is found so that $\mathrm{E}^*[A(t_N)|G(t_N) = K^*] = K$. Curran shows that this procedure provides estimates for the ARO which are accurate over a wider range of volatilities.

6.2.3 Risk Management of Asian Options

The pay-off of both the ARO and ASO will depend on the progression of the spot price for the underlying asset over the option life. The pricing formulae allow us to measure the instantaneous sensitivity of either option price to the current spot price. Hence, as for European options, at any timepoint we can construct the delta hedge by buying or selling an appropriate amount of the underlying asset in the spot market. The delta hedge is then adjusted dynamically throughout the option's life in line with the progress of the spot price.

As more fixings are recorded more of the average is known and the less is the sensitivity of $A(t_N)$ to the current spot price. In the case of the ARO, this means that both its delta and gamma (the sensitivity of delta to the spot price) diminishes to zero in a discrete fashion. That is, at the moment each fixing is recorded a portion of the outstanding delta hedge will need to be unwound. In Figure 6.3 the delta profile for three ARO calls are compared.

Whether the ARO finishes in-the-money, at-the-money or out-of-the-money, its delta steps to zero. This "delta jump" phenomenon is typical in ARO risk management and is more apparent when N is small relative to the averaging period. A key risk to the trader

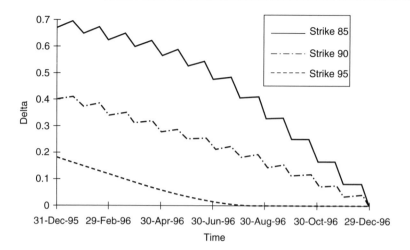

Figure 6.3 Delta profile of ARO calls

here is that he must be able to unwind his residual delta position at a price no worse than the recorded fixing. This risk is analogous to settling European options for cash by calculating its intrinsic value by reference to a predetermined fixing source.

In general, an option trader will aim to minimize the need to rebalance the hedge portfolio by looking for a more stable hedging rule requiring fewer adjustments. For the ARO, a typical strategy would be to choose a European option position that offsets the gamma and volatility exposure. A rule of thumb is to choose a European option with similar strike price to the ARO but with expiration $(t_N - t_1)/3$, that is one-third of the averaging period of the ARO. A more robust hedge would involve a portfolio of European options with similar strikes and expiration dates spread over the averaging period. The rationale behind this is that buying the equivalent strip of European options would cost more than the premium received on the ARO and over-hedges a short ARO position. Alternatively, a weighted strip of European options would minimize the necessary outlay in constructing an initial hedge but maintain gamma and volatility cover. The weights may be chosen by examining the sensitivity of the ARO to changes in (say) $\sigma\sqrt{t_i}$. However, what is suitable initially may require rebalancing at a later date in the light of the progress of recorded fixings. If the expected average remains close to the strike price of the ARO, the trader will have to increase his option cover.

Whereas the delta and gamma of AROs diminish to zero, those for the ASO will converge or (more properly) step to that of the European option with identical expiration date and strike equal to the average. At first, there is likely to be a strong positive correlation between the average and the terminal spot price. However, this correlation will step to zero as more fixings are recorded. Once more delta hedging is possible and, similar to the ARO, this leaves the trader exposed to being able to transact cash hedges at the recorded fixings. If gamma and volatility exposure is a concern then a natural hedging strategy is to regularly purchase at-the-money (spot) options with expiration time T throughout the averaging period. Again, how much is purchased will depend on the progress of the fixings. More importantly, in the case of the ASO the trader is vulnerable to the evolution in implied volatility for these options to a much greater degree than that for hedging AROs. Hence an alternative strategy in constructing an initial hedge is to enter into calendar spreads by buying volatility cover for time T and shorting volatility over the averaging period.

6.3 BINARY AND CONTINGENT PREMIUM OPTIONS

Binary options are also known as bet or digital options. These give the holder the right to receive a prespecified currency amount should the underlying asset price be beyond a specified level (strike) at a point in time (the expiry date). Typically the price of a binary option is quoted per unit of currency. Occasionally they are quoted as a gearing ratio; multiplier paid per unit invested. In practice a reference source, such as a central bank fixing, is agreed to determine the asset price on the expiration date. If this level is above the current asset price then the option is sometimes termed a binary call option. Likewise if the level is below the current asset price then it is termed a binary put option.

Figure 6.4 depicts the price of binary call and put options which pay one dollar for various strikes around the current asset price. In the figure the asset price is assumed to be 100 dollars with annualized volatility (σ) of 15 per cent, its yield (y) is zero, the domestic (continuously compounded) interest rate (r) is 6 per cent, and the term to expiry is three months. Analogous to conventional options, deep-in-the-money call options are those whose exercise and hence pay-out is almost certain. Thus the binary option price will converge to the present value of one dollar payable in three months' time. At the other extreme, where exercise is unlikely, the binary option price will converge to zero.

A contingent premium option is a conventional European option in which the holder pays nothing up front but agrees to pay a prespecified premium at expiry only if the option is in-the-money. These have also been termed pay-later options. Although exercise of the option may be optional, the holder must pay the requisite premium regardless of how deep-in-the-money the option happens to be. Consequently it is possible that, on the expiry date, the holder pays more in premium than he receives in intrinsic value. As

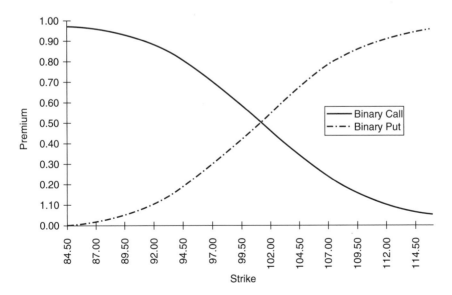

Figure 6.4   Premium for binary options

payment is due only if the option is in-the-money, this payment will always be greater than (and often a multiple of) the premium due on the equivalent European option. Similar to binary options, the terms require a reference source to determine the asset price on the expiry date and hence if payment is due.

Figure 6.5 compares the premiums due on contingent premium options and European options at various strikes. In the figure, the current asset price is 100, $r = 5$ per cent, $y = 0$ per cent, $\sigma = 15$ per cent and term to expiry is 12 months. In Figure 6.6 the expiration value of the contingent premium option at various asset prices is compared to that of the conventional European option. In the figure the strike price for both options is 100.

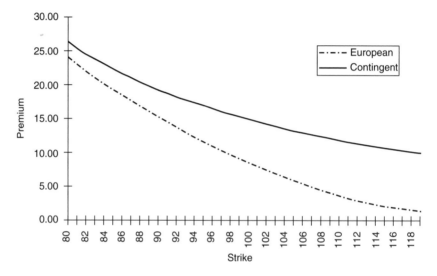

Figure 6.5 Comparison between contingent premium and European call options

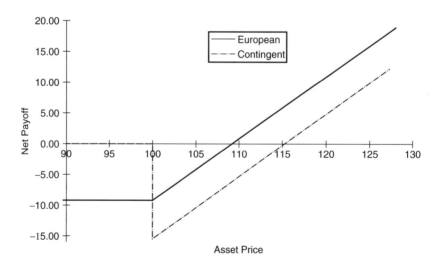

Figure 6.6 Net expiration value of contingent premium and European options

6.3.1 Examples and Uses

Many structures embed one or more binary options. Indeed, the purchase of a contingent premium option can be decomposed into a purchase of a European option and simultaneous sale of a binary option. To see this, look at the pay-off that the contingent premium (call) option offers to the holder:

$$S(T) - K - c \begin{cases} \text{if } S(T) > K \\ \text{otherwise} \end{cases}$$
$$0$$

where $S(T)$ is the asset price at expiry and c is the prespecified premium due on the option. Thus the pay-off is precisely the sum of the pay-off of a European option and sale of a binary call option with strike K and payout c. As the contingent premium option requires no payment up front, c is found so that the binary option here has present value equal to the premium of the European option.

A range-binary option is one where the holder receives a specified currency amount only if the asset price trades at expiry between a lower and upper bound which defines the range. This option can be thought of as a purchase of a binary call (put) option with strike at the lower (upper) bound and sale of a binary call (put) with strike at the upper (lower) bound.

An accrual (sometimes "corridor" or "fairway") option gives the holder the right to receive a prespecified currency amount on expiry for each day the asset price trades within a specified range. The period during which the asset price is monitored to determine payout is often termed the "accrual period". It is easy to see that an accrual option is a portfolio of range-binary options. The portfolio has a range-binary option for each day defining the accrual period. The "maximum payout" is the currency amount paid if the asset price is traded within the range each day in the accrual period. Hence an accrual option will pay the following settlement amount:

$$\text{Settlement} = \frac{\text{Number of accrual days}}{\text{Total days in accrual period}} \times \text{Maximum pay-out}$$

Another use for binary options is in the construction of contingent forward contracts. A contingent forward contract is a forward contract to purchase or sell the underlying asset at an agreed price contingent on the asset price being beyond a specified level on a future date (the expiry date). Suppose the agreed forward price is F and the specified level is B. Typically a contingent forward contract to buy (sell) the asset has B less (greater) than F. In this way there is no commitment to trade if the asset is trading at a price more favourable than B on the expiry date. The structure of this agreement is the purchase of a European call (put) option with strike B and sale of a binary option with strike B and pay-out $F - B$ $(B - F)$.

6.3.2 Valuation and Hedging

The articles of Rubinstein and Reiner (1991) and Turnbull (1992) provide a good discussion on the valuation of binary options and contingent premium options. To value binary options and hence all of the structures mentioned in Section 6.3.1 consider first the European call option. Its value under the geometric diffusion process discussed in Section 6.2.2 is given by the celebrated Black–Scholes formula:

$$C = e^{-rT} E^* \max[S(T) - K, 0] = e^{-yT} S N(x_1) - e^{-rT} K N(x_2) \tag{10}$$

where $x_1 = [\ln(S/K) + (r - y + \frac{1}{2}\sigma^2 T]/\sigma\sqrt{T}$ and $x_2 = x_1 - \sigma\sqrt{T}$. If the asset price is above the strike (K) at expiry then a call option is exercised and the holder pays K units of domestic currency and takes delivery of one unit of the asset. Hence the coefficient of K in equation (10) can be interpreted as the present value of a unit of domestic currency times the (risk-neutral) probability of the asset price being above K at expiry. The pay-off of a binary call option is 1 if $S(T) > K$ and zero otherwise so that its present value can be stated as $C_b = \mathrm{e}^{-rT}P(S(T) > K)$ and, from equation (10), $C_b = \mathrm{e}^{-rT}\mathrm{N}(x_2)$. Similarly, for a binary put option, $P_b = \mathrm{e}^{-rT}\mathrm{N}(-x_2)$. Noting that $\mathrm{N}(-x_2) = 1 - \mathrm{N}(x_2)$ we have $C_b + P_b = \mathrm{e}^{-rT}$, which is the put–call parity condition for binary options.

To value contingent premium call options, we first need to find a value for the expression $\mathrm{e}^{-rT}\mathrm{E}^* \max[S(T) - K - c, 0]$. Let $K^* = K + c$, then equation (10) with K set to K^* is the value for this expression. As contingent premium options are offered at zero premium, solve for c so that $\mathrm{e}^{-rT}\mathrm{E}^* \max[S(T) - K - c, 0] = 0$. That is,

$$c = [\mathrm{e}^{(r-y)T}S\mathrm{N}(x_1) - K\mathrm{N}(x_2)]/\mathrm{N}(x_2)$$

or e^{rT} (premium of option)$/\mathrm{N}(x_2)$. From this discussion we can write down immediately the contingent premium variation for any option, European or other, as the forward value of the option premium divided by the probability of the asset price being at or beyond the strike at expiry. The mark-to-market value of the contingent premium call option (V_c) with agreed payment c is then given by:

$$V_c = (\text{current value of underlying option}) - cC_b(K)$$

that is, a position which is long a European call with strike K and short c binary call options with strike K.

Positions in binary options can be expressed as delta-equivalent positions in the underlying asset. For example, suppose the current asset price is 99.7, $r = 5$ per cent, $y = 0$ per cent, $\sigma = 5$ per cent and term to expiry is three days. A binary call option paying 10 units of domestic currency with strike 100 has value 2.8 and delta 0.75. If the asset price moves to 100.1 its value now is 6.2. Consider the performance of the hedge. At price 99.7 the delta of the binary was 0.75 and so a short position in the binary option requires a hedge of long 7.5 units of the asset. At price 100.1 the loss on the binary position is 3.4 and the profit on the hedge is 3.0. Things are somewhat worse with one day to expiry. At 99.7 the binary is worth 1.4 with delta 0.84 and at price 100.1 the binary is worth 8.4 (5.3 more) with the delta hedge generating a profit of 3.4.

Figure 6.7 shows the delta of the binary option for three days and one day to expiry over a range of asset prices. The reason for the poor performance of delta-hedging is the degree by which delta changes as the underlying asset price moves. We know from European options that the poor performance of a hedge strategy of rebalancing delta hedges at discrete time intervals is directly related to the gamma in the option. Figure 6.8 shows the gamma of the binary option with three days to expiry compared to that of a European option with strike 100. The absolute value of gamma for the binary is greater than that of the European option over most values of the region of asset prices.

A gamma-based hedge for binary options would involve using European options. Consider a portfolio of long a European call with strike K_1 and short a European call with strike $K_2 > K_1$ (having identical expiration to that of the binary option). This has

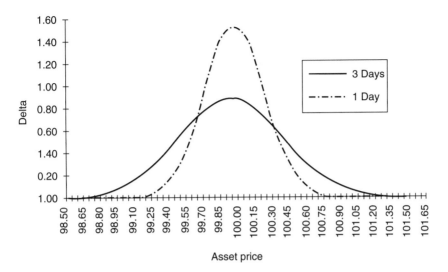

Figure 6.7   Delta of binary options

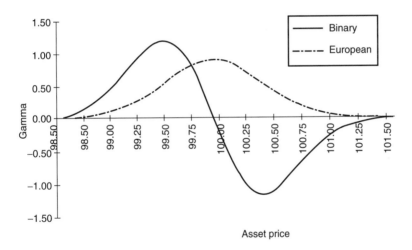

Figure 6.8   Gamma profile for binary and European options

pay-off at expiry given by:

$$
\begin{array}{ll}
K_2 - K_1 & \text{if } S(T) \geq K_2 \\
S(T) - K_1 & \text{if } K_1 \leq S(T) < K_2 \\
0 & \text{if } S(T) < K_1
\end{array}
$$

A purchase of $1/(K_2 - K_1)$ in this portfolio yields one unit of domestic currency on expiry if $S(T) > K_2$. Hence if both K_1 and K_2 are chosen to be close to K then we have an approximation to the binary call with strike K. Indeed if K_1 and K_2 are equidistant around K then as we reduce $(K_1 - K_2)$ the value of the portfolio converges to that of the binary call. To see this, observe that the negative of the partial derivative of the European call option with respect to its strike is precisely the value of a binary call with same strike and time to expiry. This suggests we choose K_1 and K_2 to be close to K and their absolute difference consistent with risk tolerance. For example, to hedge a short position in a binary call, both K_1 and $(K_1 + K_2)/2$ are often chosen to be less than or equal to K. Of course as $(K_1 - K_2)$ reduces so the face amount on the call spread strategy will increase. Hence many institutions will constrain the choice of K_1 and K_2 to be consistent with risk limits on European option trading positions.

6.4 CURRENCY PROTECTED OPTIONS

Contracts on foreign assets often entail a degree of foreign exchange risk which may be unwanted. That is, although the foreign asset price might move favourably such gains could be lost when translated to domestic currency terms. What is needed is the ability to participate in the foreign asset market but with a measure of control on the foreign exchange risk that follows. To answer this, many financial institutions have developed a range of forward and option contracts for investors with differing mixtures of preferences to the foreign asset market exposure and to that of the foreign currency risk. In this section several variations are presented together with their respective pricing formula. The section concludes with a discussion of currency basket options.

6.4.1 Cross-Market Contracts

Forward and option contracts that are cross-market based have been discussed in Derman et al. (1990), Wei (1991) and Reiner (1992). Depending on the nature of the contract, such contracts may be settled as an exchange of cash for delivery of the foreign asset or by an agreed net cash settlement amount. Throughout this section the following notation is used:

T = the number of years to expiry (the delivery date)
S = the current price of the foreign asset (in units of foreign currency)
$S(T)$ = the price of the foreign asset at T
S^* = the fixed price agreed for the foreign asset in foreign currency units
X = the current exchange rate (units of domestic currency per unit of foreign currency)
$X(T)$ = the exchange rate at T
X^* = the fixed exchange rate guaranteed
r = the domestic risk-free interest rate (continuously compounded)
q = the foreign risk-free interest rate (continuously compounded)
y = the dividend yield on the foreign index (continuously compounded)
σ = the annualized volatility of S
ν = the annualized volatility of X
ρ = the instantaneous correlation between movements in S and X

The cross-market contract that is offered will be specified to best meet the investor's outlook and risk preferences. For example, an investor who believes that a foreign equity index will rally and is unconcerned about the foreign exchange risk might desire a contract that pays out:

$$F_1 = X(T)[S(T) - S^*]$$

This is a forward contract to purchase the foreign index at S^* translated at the ruling exchange rate at the expiry date. If a degree of protection is needed in the event the index falls, then a more suitable contract is:

$$C_1 = X(T) \max[S(T) - S^*, 0]$$

This is a call option on $S(T)$ with strike S^* and with pay-off translated to domestic currency at $X(T)$.

If, on the other hand, the investor requires protection on the rate at which his holdings are translated to domestic terms, then the following contracts may be more suitable:

$$F_2 = X^*[S(T) - S^*]$$

$$C_2 = X^* \max[S(T) - S^*, 0]$$

The first, F_2, is a forward contract whose value at expiry in foreign currency terms is as before but this is now translated to domestic terms at a predetermined exchange rate X^*. The option variation C_2 is usually termed a *quanto* call option on the index and sometimes referred to as a *guaranteed exchange rate* contract. The holder of this option receives an option pay-off on $S(T)$ as though it were a domestic asset with price X^*S. The interest differential between the domestic and foreign currencies, $(r - q)$, is an important feature determining the relative value of a quanto option to its European counterpart. When the domestic interest rate is high compared to that of the currency of the asset, then the quanto call option will be cheaper than the option on the asset in foreign terms.

Both F_1 and F_2 will have positive value if the index at expiry is above S^*. Consider, however, the following contracts:

$$F_3 = X(T)S(T) - S^*X^*$$

$$C_3 = \max[X(T)S(T) - S^*X^*, 0]$$

The first, F_3, is a forward contract to take delivery of the foreign asset at S^*X^*, that is at a fixed domestic price. The second is an option to buy the foreign asset at a known strike price in domestic terms. The performance of both contracts will depend *jointly* on $S(T)$ and $X(T)$. The variable $X(T)S(T)$ is the domestic value of the foreign asset at T and either F_3 or C_3 might therefore represent a natural hedge against an open (short) position in the foreign asset when marked-to-market in domestic terms.

Other variations of the cross-market product might be synthetic assets which offer full exposure to the foreign asset but protects the translation exchange rate:

$$F_4 = S(T)[X(T) - X^*]$$

$$C_4 = S(T) \max[X(T) - X^*, 0]$$

The contract F_4 represents a long position in the foreign asset for delivery at expiry but paid for in domestic terms at a predetermined exchange rate. Hence all movements in the domestic value of the foreign asset due solely to fluctuations in the exchange rate are avoided. The option variation is sometimes called the *equity-linked foreign exchange* contract. This is a currency option whose face amount is linked to the value of a foreign asset. It provides unlimited exposure to the foreign asset but attaches a foreign exchange option to the translation risk with strike X^*.

Finally, a complex mixture is a contract that allows the investor exposure to the foreign asset value when converted to domestic currency at a guaranteed exchange rate yet allows the investor to pay for the asset at a predetermined foreign price:

$$F_5 = S(T)X^* - X(T)S^*$$

$$C_5 = \max[S(T)X^* - X(T)S^*, 0]$$

6.4.2 Valuation of Cross-Market Contracts

The valuation of these contracts will depend, in part, on the manner in which the exchange rate and asset price enters the pay-off. For example, the pay-offs in the first case, F_1 and C_1, are just the value of forward and option contracts on $S(T)$ in foreign currency terms converted to domestic terms at the ruling exchange rate. Hence, immediately we should value these by taking the current foreign value of these contracts and converting to domestic terms at the current exchange rate. In the third case, $S(T)$ and $X(T)$ are traded assets and so we can treat the product $S(T)X(T)$ as also traded with forward value consistent with those of $S(T)$ and $X(T)$. In the second case, however, although we know today the conversion rate X^*, $S(T)X^*$ is not a traded security. We need a framework that is consistent with the way forward and option contracts on $S(T)$ and $X(T)$ are valued and which is arbitrage free.

To value these contracts, we will assume the following usual stochastic processes:

$$dS = \mu S \, dt + \sigma S \, dz$$

$$dX = \eta X \, dt + \nu X \, dw$$

where dz and dw are Wiener processes with $E(dz \, dw) = \rho$. All the above cross-market contracts have their values derived from S and X. Thus, in principle, the risks in these securities can be hedged by trading in S and X. Appendix 3 argues that we can value cross-market products as though the returns on the foreign asset S and the exchange rate X satisfy $\mu = (q - y - \rho\sigma\nu)$ and $\eta = (r - q)$, respectively. If we were measuring values in foreign currency terms the risk-neutral expected return on S would be $(q - y)$, but in domestic terms the yield on the foreign asset must be increased by $\rho\sigma\nu$. A common adjustment, therefore, is to define a new yield $y^* = [y + (r - q) + \rho\sigma\nu]$ and treat the new "domestic" asset SX^* as having return $(r - y^*)$. Another way to observe this is to note that, given the assumed processes, Ito's lemma gives

$$d(SX) = (\mu + \eta + \rho\sigma\nu)SX \, dt + \sigma SX \, dz + \nu SX \, dw$$

and hence the expected return on SX is $(\mu + \eta + \rho\sigma\nu)$. Arbitrage ensures that the forward exchange rate earns a rate of return of $(r - q)$ and also that the rate of return on SX is $(r - y)$. Hence it follows that $\eta = (r - q)$ and so, for $(\mu + \eta + \rho\sigma\nu) = (r - y)$ to hold, we require $\mu = (q - y - \rho\sigma\nu)$.

Armed with the risk-neutral returns, we can proceed to value the cross-market instruments as $e^{-rT}E^*(F_i)$ and $e^{-rT}E^*(C_i)$ for each i. The expectations needed are given as follows:

$$E^*[X(T)S(T)] = XSe^{(r-y)T}$$

$$E^*[X(T)S^*] = XS^*e^{(r-q)T}$$

$$E^*[X^*S(T)] = X^*Se^{(q-y-\rho\sigma\nu)T}$$

$$\text{and} \quad E^*[X^*S^*] = X^*S^*$$

Hence $e^{-rT}E^*(F_i)$ are evaluated as:

$$e^{-rT}E^*(F_1) = e^{-rT}[XSe^{(r-y)T} - XS^*e^{(r-q)T}]$$

$$e^{-rT}E^*(F_2) = e^{-rT}[X^*Se^{(q-y-\rho\sigma v)T} - X^*S^*]$$

$$e^{-rT}E^*(F_3) = e^{-rT}[XSe^{(r-y)T} - X^*S^*]$$

$$e^{-rT}E^*(F_4) = e^{-rT}[XSe^{(r-y)T} - X^*Se^{(q-y-\rho\sigma v)T}]$$

$$\text{and} \quad e^{-rT}E^*(F_5) = e^{-rT}[X^*Se^{(q-y-\rho\sigma v)T} - XS^*e^{(r-q)T}]$$

To determine the forward price (f_i) for each cross-market forward, solve for S^* (X^* in the case of F_4) in each of the previous expressions to give net present value of zero:

$$f_1 = Se^{(q-y)T}$$

$$f_2 = Se^{(q-y-\rho\sigma v)T}$$

$$f_3 = (X/X^*)Se^{(r-y)T}$$

$$f_4 = Xe^{(r-q+\rho\sigma v)T}$$

$$\text{and} \quad f_5 = (X^*/X)Se^{(2q-r-y-\rho\sigma v)T}$$

To value the cross-market options we use the generalization of Margrabe (1978). Let S_1 and S_2 be the domestic prices of two assets and let $C(T)$ have pay-off $\max(S_2 - S_1, 0)$ at T, then the current value of C is given by:

$$C = e^{-rT}[E^*(S_2)N(x) - E^*(S_1)N(x - \Sigma\sqrt{T})]$$

where $x = \{\ln[E^*(S_2)/E^*(S_1)] + \frac{1}{2}\Sigma^2 T\}/\Sigma\sqrt{T}$ and Σ^2 is the instantaneous variance of $(dS_2/S_2)/(dS_1/S_1)$. All of the cross-market options above can be viewed as a variation of the exchange of asset option. The risk-neutral expectations have already been derived and hence all that is needed to apply this formula are the appropriate expressions for Σ_i^2 (i denoting one of the five cross-market variations).

In the first case, note that the covariance of $d(XS)/(XS)$ and dX/X is $(v^2 + \rho\sigma v)$ and so $\Sigma_1^2 = (\sigma^2 + v^2 + \rho\sigma v) + v^2 - 2(v^2 + \rho\sigma v) = \sigma^2$. The other expressions are: $\Sigma_2^2 = \sigma^2$, $\Sigma_3^2 = (\sigma^2 + v^2 + \rho\sigma v)$, $\Sigma_4^2 = v^2$ and $\Sigma_5^2 = (\sigma^2 + v^2 - \rho\sigma v)$. Thus, for example, the value of the quanto call option, C_2, is:

$$C_2 = e^{-rT}[X^*Se^{(q-y-\rho\sigma v)T}N(x) - X^*S^*N(x - \sigma\sqrt{T})]$$

with $x = [\ln(S/S^*) + (q - y - \rho\sigma v)T + \frac{1}{2}\sigma^2 T]/\sigma\sqrt{T}$. Likewise, the equity-linked foreign exchange contract, C_4, is given as:

$$C_4 = e^{-rT}[XSe^{(r-y)T}N(x) - X^*Se^{(q-y-\rho\sigma v)T}N(x - v\sqrt{T})]$$

where, $x = [\ln(X/X^*) + (r - q + \rho\sigma v)T + \frac{1}{2}v^2 T]/v\sqrt{T}$. To complete this discussion, note that to value the corresponding put options we may repeat the above but swap S_1 and S_2 or, equivalently, use put-call parity and express these as $P_i = C_i - e^{-rT}E^*(F_i)$ for each $i = 1, \ldots, 5$.

The construction of the cash hedge portfolio is discussed in Appendix 3 in general terms. The argument there follows the spirit of Black and Scholes (1976) to derive the relevant partial differential equation which these contracts must satisfy. In hedging the pay-off on cross-market options, delta-hedging alone is inefficient leaving the portfolio exposed to gamma risk. Hedge portfolios for these products are more likely to contain traded options on the asset and/or options on the exchange rate. A short position in any of the cross-market options is a position which is short the asset volatility or short currency option volatility or short both. However, the correlation term enters with a different sign depending on which variation is being managed. A general rule is to hedge the partial gammas using options on the asset and/or currency options. The net partial delta positions can be offset using cash positions. The correct amount of options will depend on the sign and magnitude of the correlation term. It is only efficient to consider each individual gamma in isolation when the correlation term is absent from the valuation formula or negligible in magnitude. In general one could do better by imposing an estimate of the correlation term and examining the local variation in the hedge portfolio to joint movements in S and X.

Finally, a word of caution. As noted in Reiner (1992), even though we are dealing with a two-asset problem, all the cross-market option formulae could be interpreted as the standard Black–Scholes formula but with modified parameters dependent on the nature of the contract. Indeed the generalized exchange of asset formula could also be given a Black–Scholes interpretation. This follows because the assumed processes imply that in each instance $(dS_2/S_2)/(dS_1/S_1)$ is log-normally distributed. Thus once the appropriate risk-neutral expected return and volatility terms are determined, the problem reduces to that of a single asset process. It is true that the appropriate volatility term is immediately seen from the composite nature of the contract pay-off. That is, the Σ term is just σ for contracts C_1 and C_2 as the "optionality" of these contracts is on the foreign asset. Likewise C_4 is essentially a foreign exchange option so that v is the appropriate volatility term. It is also clear that in contracts C_3 and C_5 both volatility terms must enter together with the covariance term $\rho\sigma v$ (positively for C_3 and negatively for C_5). What is not so obvious are the appropriate "interest rate" terms. To ensure that these are specified correctly, a two-asset frame of reference should be adopted which forces us to consider the appropriate risk-neutral drift terms.

6.4.3 Currency Basket Options

It is rare for companies to be exposed to a single foreign currency and hence a single exchange rate. It is more likely that companies will be exporting to, or sourcing raw materials from, several countries. Likewise, fund managers are unlikely to restrict the diversification of their portfolio to investments within a single currency market. The currency basket option was designed to hedge multi-currency risk with a single instrument. Rather than cover the currency risk with a portfolio of options, the basket option offers the ability to own an option on the portfolio.

The make-up of the basket is tailored to meet the requirements of the purchaser in terms of the range of currencies to be included, the respective currency amounts and the domestic currency value of this basket. For example, a UK company may be exporting to the US and Germany. Suppose this exposure is estimated to require the sale of 4 million US dollars and 6 million Deutschmarks, then the appropriate basket option is defined as the right to: sell USD 4 million, sell DM 6 million and receive a fixed amount of sterling.

The fixed sterling amount plays the part of the strike price of the option. Exercise of the option on the expiry date would depend on whether the transactions yield a better net sterling figure if they were carried out under the option rather than in the spot market. The alternative would be to buy sterling call options against the dollar and Deutschmark. Analogous to the discussion above for Asian options, in purchasing a basket option over the portfolio of individual options the opportunity to exercise some or all is forgone. Hence, the premium for the basket option should never be greater than the total premium outlay on the portfolio of individual options.

To value a basket option, one could treat the value of the basket as having a log-normal distribution and adopt the conventional Black–Scholes valuation model (allowing for risk-neutral returns). The volatility of the basket could be based on estimates from historic data together with a view of its performance over the option horizon. Alternatively, information implied from the option market on the individual exchange rates and cross-exchange rates could be used. The pricing methodology most institutions use is one where the risk inherent in the exotic instrument is identified and, where possible, valued by observing the prices of instruments traded which share a common element of this risk. This is precisely because these instruments are likely to form the foundation for the hedge. This principle is embodied in the following pricing methodology (see also Gentle (1992) and Huynh (1994)).

Define the pay-off of the basket option at time T as:

$$B(T) = \max \left[\sum_{i=1}^{N} A_i X_i(T) - A, 0 \right]$$

where A_i is the foreign currency i amount in the basket of N currency amounts, $X_i(T)$ is the domestic value of one unit of foreign currency i, A is the domestic currency value of the basket to be protected. This can be re-expressed as

$$B(T) = V \max \left[\sum_{i=1}^{N} w_i X_i(T) - k, 0 \right]$$

where $V = \Sigma_i A_i F_i$, F_i is the current forward exchange rate for X_i with delivery T, $w_i = A_i/V$, and $k = A/V$. We make the usual following assumptions for the stochastic process governing the exchange rates X_i:

$$dX_i = \mu_i X_i \, dt + \sigma_i X_i \, dz_i$$

where μ_i and σ_i are constant and dz_i are Weiner processes with $E(dz_i \, dz_j) = \rho_{ij}$. Define the value of the normalized basket at expiry by $P = \Sigma_i w_i X_i(T)$, then we need to develop a distribution for P which is consistent with those for $X_i(T)$ and risk-neutrality.

Similar to the discussion of valuation ideas behind Asian options in Section 6.2.2 above, we can determine a log-normal approximation for P. The first two risk-neutral moments for P are:

$$E^*(P) = \sum_{i=1}^{N} w_i e^{\mu_i + (1/2)\sigma_i^2} = \sum_{i=1}^{N} w_i F_i = 1$$

by construction, and

$$E^*(P^2) = \sum_{i=1}^{N} \sum_{j=1}^{N} w_i w_j E^*[X_i(T)X_j(T)]$$

Using

$$E^*[X_i(T)X_j(T)] = e^{[\mu_i + \mu_j + (1/2)(\sigma_i^2 + \sigma_j^2 + 2\rho_{ij}\sigma_i\sigma_j)]T} = F_i F_j e^{\rho_{ij}\sigma_i\sigma_j T}$$

we have

$$E^*(P^2) = \sum_{i=1}^{N} \sum_{j=1}^{N} w_i w_j \cdot F_i F_j e^{\rho_{ij}\sigma_i\sigma_j T}$$

Hence a log-normal fit for P is to assume $\ln P$ is normally distributed $N(\alpha, \nu^2)$ where $\alpha = -\frac{1}{2} \ln E^*(P^2)$ and $\nu^2 = \ln E^*(P^2)$. The cross-correlations ρ_{ij} can be inferred from the volatility of the corresponding cross-exchange rate (σ_{ij}) as $\rho_{ij} = (\sigma_i^2 + \sigma_j^2 - \sigma_{ij}^2)/(2\sigma_i\sigma_j)$.

As an example, consider a two-currency basket (US dollars and yen) against sterling. Suppose the basket option is defined as the right to receive USD 14.8 million and JPY 1,450 million and pay a fixed amount of sterling in six months' time. Suppose interest rates are 6 per cent, 2 per cent and 8 per cent for dollars, yen and sterling, respectively, and the current exchange rates are USD 1.5000 and JPY 150.00 to the pound. The six-month forwards are then USD 1.4851 and JPY 145.57 giving an "at-the-money" sterling value for the basket of GBP 19.93 million. If volatilities were $\sigma(\text{GBP/USD}) = 9$ per cent and $\sigma(\text{GBP/JPY}) = 13$ per cent with correlation 0.23 (i.e. a USD/JPY volatility of 14 per cent) then the basket option premium is 3.40 per cent on GBP 19.93 million. The individual at-the-money forward option premiums to call dollars and yen are, respectively, 2.44 per cent and 3.52 per cent of the sterling face amount. Hence the basket option would cost GBP 470,000 and the premiums for the individual options would amount to GBP 594,000. Hence the basket option represents about 79 per cent of the cost of the portfolio of options. Figure 6.9 shows how this proportion varies with the correlation between the two exchange rates and with differing degrees of in-the-moneyness (measured relative to

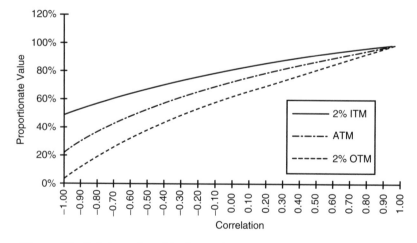

Figure 6.9   Relative value of basket option to portfolio of European options

the forward price). The figure shows that as correlation approaches unity and the option strike moves further in-the-money the saving in premium outlay on the basket option diminishes.

Finally, the standard techniques to hedging options apply to basket options. Traders will both delta- and gamma-manage their positions by trading in the cash and option markets. In the example above, a position long the basket option is one that benefits as volatilities of the X_i's increase but loses value as the correlation between the X_i's increases. The correlation position can be offset by trading options in the relevant cross-exchange rate. In general, the number of currency pair positions in the hedge can be reduced by analysing the statistical make-up of the variance of the basket using principal components or factor analysis.

6.5 APPENDIX 1

In this appendix the geometric ARO and ASO are derived. The geometric average is given by $G(t_N) = [S(t_1) \cdot S(t_2) \ldots S(t_N)]^{1/N}$. Thus $\ln G(t_N) = (1/N)\Sigma_i \ln S(t_i)$. As each $\ln S(t_i)$ is distributed $N(\mu_i, \sigma_i^2)$ then $\ln G(t_N)$ is also distributed as normal $N(\mu_G, \sigma_G^2)$. Hence the ARO call and ASO call are, respectively, given by:

$$e^{-rT}E^* \max[G(t_N) - K, 0] = e^{\mu_G + (1/2)\sigma_G^2 - rT} N(x_1) - e^{-rT} K N(x_2)$$

where $x_1 = (\mu_G - \ln K + \sigma_G^2)/v$ and $x_2 = x_1 - \sigma_G$, and

$$e^{-rT}E^* \max[S(T) - G(t_N), 0] = S(t)e^{-yT} N(y_1) - e^{\mu_G + (1/2)\sigma_G^2 - rT} N(y_2)$$

where $y_1 = [\ln S(t) + (r - y)T - \mu_G - \frac{1}{2}\sigma_G^2 + \frac{1}{2}\Sigma^2]/\Sigma$, $y_2 = y_1 - \Sigma$, $\Sigma^2 = \sigma_G^2 + \sigma^2 T - 2\rho_G\sigma_G\sigma_T$ and $\rho_G\sigma_G\sigma_T$ is the covariance between $\ln G(t_N)$ and $\ln S(T)$. The ARO put and ASO put are, respectively, given by:

$$e^{-rT}E^* \max[K - G(t_N), 0] = e^{-rT} K N(-x_2) - e^{\mu_G + (1/2)\sigma_G^2 - rT} N(-x_1)$$

and

$$e^{-rT}E^* \max[G(t_N) - S(T), 0] = e^{\mu_G + (1/2)\sigma_G^2 - rT} N(-y_2) - S(t)e^{-yT} N(-y_1)$$

It remains only to derive μ_G, σ_G and $\rho_G\sigma_G\sigma_T$.

The mean of $\ln G(t_N)$ is immediately

$$\mu_G = \frac{1}{N} \sum_{i=1}^{N} \mu_i$$

For constant r, y and σ this can be re-expressed as:

$$\mu_G = \ln S(t) + \frac{1}{N} \sum_{i=1}^{N} \left(r - y - \frac{1}{2}\sigma^2\right) t_i$$

and for equidistant fixing intervals from t_1, $t_i = t_1 + (i - 1)(T - t_1)/(N - 1)(i = 1, \ldots, N)$, we have

$$\mu_G = \ln S(t) + \left(r - y - \frac{1}{2}\sigma^2\right)\left(\frac{T - t_1}{2} + t_1\right)$$

The variance of $\ln G(t_N)$ is given by

$$\sigma^2{}_G = \frac{1}{N^2} \left[\sum_{i=1}^{N} \sigma^2{}_i + 2 \sum_{i=1}^{N-1} \sum_{j=i+1}^{N} \rho_{ij} \sigma_i \sigma_j \right]$$

where $\rho_{ij} = \sigma_i / \sigma_j$ is the correlation between $\ln S(t_i)$ and $\ln S(t_j)$ for $i \leq j$. Hence

$$\sigma^2{}_G = \frac{1}{N^2} \left[\sum_{i=1}^{N} \sigma_i^2 + 2 \sum_{i=1}^{N-1} (N - i) \sigma_i^2 \right]$$

when $\sigma_i^2 = \sigma^2 t_i$ we have

$$\sigma^2{}_G = \sigma^2 \frac{1}{N^2} \left[\sum_{i=1}^{N} t_i + 2 \sum_{i=1}^{N-1} (N - i) t_i \right]$$

and for $t_i = t_1 + (i - 1)(T - t_1)/(N - 1)$

$$\sigma^2{}_G = \sigma^2 \left[\frac{(T - t_1)(2N - 1)}{6N} + t_1 \right]$$

As $N \to \infty$ $\sigma_G^2 = \sigma^2[(T - t_1)/3 + t_1]$. Finally, the covariance term $\rho_G \sigma_G \sigma_T$ is given by

$$\rho_G \sigma_G \sigma_T = \text{Cov} \left(\frac{1}{N} \sum_{i=1}^{N} \ln S(t_i), \ln S(T) \right)$$

$$= \frac{1}{N} \sum_{i=1}^{N} \sigma_i^2$$

For $\sigma_i^2 = \sigma^2 t_i$ we have $\rho_G \sigma_G \sigma_T = (\sigma^2/N) \Sigma_i t_i$ and for $t_i = t_1 + (i - 1)(T - t_1)/(N - 1)$

$$\rho_G \sigma_G \sigma_T = \sigma^2 \frac{(T + t_1)}{2}$$

6.6 APPENDIX 2

Although the distribution of $A(t_N)$ is non-standard, closed-form solutions can be readily found for the moments of $A(t_N)$. Indeed Turnbull and Wakeman (1991) describe an efficient algorithm for finding all such moments. Here we provide expressions for the first two moments.

Given that $\ln S(t_i)$ is distributed as $N(\mu_i, \sigma_i^2)$, it follows that the first moment for $A(t_N)$ is given by:

$$E^*[A(t_N)] = \frac{1}{N} \sum_{i=1}^{N} e^{\mu_i + (1/2)\sigma_i^2} = \frac{1}{N} \sum_{i=1}^{N} F_i$$

where F_i denotes the forward price of $S(t_i)$. For constant interest rates and volatility we have

$$E^*[A(t_N)] = \frac{S(t)}{N} \sum_{i=1}^{N} e^{(r-y)t_i}$$

and for $t_i = t_1 + (i-1)(T - t_1)/(N-1)$

$$E^*[A(t_N)] = \frac{S(t)}{N} e^{gt_1} \cdot \frac{1 - e^{ghN}}{1 - e^{gh}}$$

where $h = (T - t_1)/(N - 1)$ and $g = (r - y)$. As the frequency of recordings increases, we have in the limit as $N \to \infty$

$$E^*[A(t_N)] = S(t)e^{gt_1} \cdot \frac{e^{g(T-t_1)} - 1}{g(T - t_1)}$$

The second moment for $A(t_N)$ is given by

$$E^*[A(t_N)^2] = \frac{1}{N^2} \sum_{i=1}^{N} \sum_{j=1}^{N} E^*[S(t_i)S(t_j)]$$

or

$$E^*[A(t_N)^2] = \frac{1}{N^2} \left\{ \sum_{i=1}^{N} E^*[S(t_i)^2] + 2 \sum_{i=1}^{N-1} \sum_{j=i+1}^{N} E^*[S(t_i)S(t_j)] \right\}$$

Noting that $E^*[S(t_i)S(t_j)] = F_i F_j e^{\sigma_i^2}$ for $i \leq j$,

$$E^*[A(t_N)^2] = \frac{1}{N^2} \left[\sum_{i=1}^{N} F_i^2 e^{\sigma_i^2} + 2 \sum_{i=1}^{N-1} \sum_{j=i+1}^{N} F_i F_j e^{\sigma_i^2} \right]$$

For constant interest rates and volatility, we have

$$E^*[A(t_N)^2] = \frac{S(t)^2}{N^2} \left[\sum_{i=1}^{N} e^{(2g+\sigma^2)t_i} + 2 \sum_{i=1}^{N-1} e^{(g+\sigma^2)t_i} \sum_{j=i+1}^{N} e^{gt_j} \right]$$

and for $t_i = t_1 + (i-1)h$

$$E^*[A(t_N)^2] = \frac{S(t)^2 e^{(2g+\sigma^2)t_1}}{N^2} \cdot \left\{ \frac{1 - e^{(2g+\sigma^2)hN}}{1 - e^{(2g+\sigma^2)h}} + \frac{2}{1 - e^{(g+\sigma^2)h}} \right. $$

$$\left. \left[\frac{1 - e^{ghN}}{1 - e^{gh}} - \frac{1 - e^{(2g+\sigma^2)hN}}{1 - e^{(2g+\sigma^2)h}} \right] \right\}$$

Finally as $N \to \infty$ we have

$$E^*[A(t_N)^2] = \frac{2S(t)^2 e^{(2g+\sigma^2)t_1}}{(g + \sigma^2)(T - t_1)^2} \cdot \left[\frac{1 - e^{g(T-t_1)}}{g} - \frac{1 - e^{(2g+\sigma^2)(T-t_1)}}{(2g + \sigma^2)} \right]$$

6.7 APPENDIX 3

Consider a cross-market contract $C(t, S, X)$, valued in domestic terms, whose pay-off at T depends on S and X. Given the stochastic processes assumed for S and X in Section 6.4.2, Ito's lemma states that dC satisfies:

$$dC = (C_t + \mu S C_S + \eta X C_X + \tfrac{1}{2}\sigma^2 S^2 C_{SS} + \tfrac{1}{2}v^2 X^2 C_{XX} + \rho\sigma v S X C_{SX})\,dt$$
$$+ \sigma S C_S\,dz + v X C_X\,dw$$

Suppose we have a position which is short one unit of C. The hedged portfolio, P, is constructed by buying h_S units of S and h_X units of X so that P has value in domestic terms:

$$P = h_X X + h_S S X - C$$

and $dP = h_X\,dX + h_S\,d(SX) - dC$. Applying Ito's lemma and collecting terms gives

$$dP = \phi\,dt + (h_X X + h_S S - X C_X)v\,dw + (h_S X - C_S)S\sigma\,dz$$

where $\phi = h_s(\mu + \eta + \rho\sigma v)SX + h_X\eta X - \lambda$ and $\lambda = C_t + \mu S C_S + \eta X C_X + \tfrac{1}{2}\sigma^2 S^2 C_{SS} + \tfrac{1}{2}v^2 X^2 C_{XX} + \rho\sigma v S X C_{SX}$.

To ensure dP is riskless, choose h_S and h_X so that the coefficients in dP for dz and dw are zero, thus:

$$h_S = (1/X)C_S$$
$$h_X = C_X - (S/X)C_S$$

The portfolio also earns the dividend yield on holdings of S and the foreign interest rate on that of X, so that

$$dP = [\phi + ySC_S + q(XC_X - SC_S)]\,dt$$

However, if P is riskless, to avoid arbitrage we require $dP = rP\,dt$. That is

$$\phi + ySC_S + q(XC_X - SC_S) = r(h_X X + h_S S X - C)$$
$$= rC_X X - rC$$

or

$$rC = C_t + (q - y - \rho\sigma v)SC_S + (r - q)XC_X + \tfrac{1}{2}\sigma^2 S^2 C_{SS} + \tfrac{1}{2}v^2 X^2 C_{XX} + \rho\sigma v S X C_{SX}$$

This is the partial differential equation (PDE) that must be satisfied by all cross-market securities $C(t, S, X)$ (together with their boundary conditions). As with single-asset securities, as time progresses, holdings of S and X must be adjusted to keep the portfolio riskless. In general, for the stochastic processes assumed, the Feynman–Kac theorem (see Karatzas and Shreve (1991)) tell us that the function $C(t, S, X)$ defined by the relation $C(t, S_t, X_t) = e^{-r(T-t)}E_t[C(T, S_T, X_T)]$ solves

$$rC = C_t + \mu S C_S + \eta X C_X + \tfrac{1}{2}\sigma^2 S^2 C_{SS} + \tfrac{1}{2}v^2 X^2 C_{XX} + \rho\sigma v S X C_{SX}$$

Hence by choosing $\mu = q - y - \rho\sigma v$ and $\eta = r - q$ we can solve our PDE for $C(t, S, X)$ using $e^{-r(T-t)}E_t[C(T, S_T, X_T)]$.

6.8 REFERENCES

Black, F. and Scholes, M.S. (1973) "The pricing of options and corporate liabilities". *Journal of Political Economy*, May/June, **81**, 637–54.

Boyle, P.P. (1977) "Options: A Monte Carlo approach". *Journal of Financial Economics*, May, **4**, 323–38.

Carverhill, A.P. and Clewlow, L.S. (1990) "Flexible convolution". *Risk*, April, **3**, 25–9.

Cox, J.C. and Ross, S.A. (1976) "The valuation of options for alternative stochastic processes". *Journal of Financial Economics*, September, **3**, 145–66.

Curran, M. (1992) "Beyond average intelligence". *Risk*, November, **5**, 60.

Derman, E., Karasinski, P. and Wecker, J.S. (1990) "Understanding guaranteed exchange-rate contracts in foreign stock investments". Quantitative Strategies Research Notes, Goldman Sachs, June.

Geman, H. and Eydeland, A. (1995) "Domino effect". *Risk*, April, **8**, 65–7.

Geman, H. and Yor, M. (1992a) "Quelques relations entre processus de Bessel, options asiatiques, et fonctions confluentes hypergéométriques". Comptes Renus Academie Sciences Series 1, 471–4.

Geman, H. and Yor, M. (1992b) "Bessel processes, Asian options and perpetuities". *Mathematical Finance*, **3**, 349–75.

Gentle, D. (1993) "Basket weaving". *Risk*, June, **6**, 51–2.

Hammersley, J.M. and Handscomb D.C. (1964) *Monte Carlo Simulation*. London: Methuen.

Hogg, R.V. and Craig, A.T. (1970) *Introduction to Mathematical Statistics*. 3rd Edition, London: Collier Macmillan.

Huynh, C.B., (1994) "Back to Baskets". *Risk*, May, **7**, 59–61.

Karatzas, I.K. and Shreve, S.E. (1991) *Brownian Motion and Stochastic Calculus*. Graduate Texts in Mathematics 113, Springer-Verlag, 2nd Edition.

Kemna, A.G.Z. and Vorst, A.C.F. (1990) "A pricing method for options based on average asset values". *Journal of Banking and Finance*, March, **14**, 113–29.

Levy, E. (1990) "Asian arithmetic". *Risk*, May, **3**, 7–8.

Levy, E. (1992) "Pricing European average rate currency options". *Journal of International Money and Finance*, **11**, 474–91.

Levy, E. and Turnbull, S.M. (1992) "Average intelligence". *Risk*, February, **5**, 53–9.

Margrabe, W. (1978) "The value of an option to exchange one asset for another". *Journal of Finance*, March, **33**, 177–86.

Reiner, E. (1992) "Quanto mechanics". *Risk*, March, **5**, 59–63.

Ritchken, P., Sankarasubramanian, L. and Vijh, A.M. (1990) "The valuation of path dependent contracts on the average". Unpublished manuscript, School of Business Administration, University of Southern California, September.

Rubinstein, M. and Reiner, E. (1991) "Unscrambling the binary code". *Risk*, October, **4**, 75–83.

Rubinstein, R.Y. (1981) *Simulation and the Monte Carlo Method*. New York: Wiley.

Ruttiens, A. (1990) "Classical replica". *Risk*, February, **3**, 33–6.

Turnbull, S.M. (1992) "The price is right". *Risk*, April, **4**, 56–7.

Turnbull, S.M. and Wakeman, L.M. (1991) "A quick algorithm for pricing European average options". *Journal of Financial and Quantitative Analysis*, September, **26**, 377–89.

Vorst, T. (1990) "Analytic boundaries and approximations of the prices and hedge ratios of average exchange rate options". Unpublished manuscript, Econometric Institute, Erasmus University Rotterdam, February.

Wei, Z. (1991) "Pricing forward contracts and options on foreign assets". Faculty of Management working paper, University of Toronto, May.

7

Exotic Options II

BRYAN THOMAS

This chapter will be oriented towards currency options, reflecting the majority of my options experience. But most of the ideas and many of the formulae can be adapted to other markets.

7.1 BARRIER OPTIONS

7.1.1 Definitions and Examples of Single Barrier Options

Single barrier options are path-dependent. Their value at maturity depends not only on the value of the underlying asset at maturity but also on the traded prices of the asset between inception and expiry. The type of path dependency for barrier options is relatively simple. If the underlying asset ever reaches the barrier during the life of the option, one rule is used to calculate the value at expiry; if the barrier is never reached, another rule applies. Barrier options come in two classes: out and in. Those of the "out" class lapse upon reaching the barrier, and may not be exercised. If the barrier is never reached, they are then equivalent at expiry to a European option of the same type, strike and size. These are generally called knock-out options in preference to the alternative term drop-out options, which seems to be falling out of favour. To enhance the descriptiveness or, in legal terms, to specify which direction spot must move to hit the barrier, knock-out options can be called either down & out options, or up & out options.

This type of option was traded in the unregulated OTC equity options market in the United States prior to 1975, primarily for credit reasons associated with margin rules on equity purchases. Other financial contracts that predate the development of the analytical model contained embedded knock-out options. Once the model was written that described these moribund or relatively rare contracts, the product was introduced into a wide range of markets. In the currency market, barrier options became extremely popular in Japan in the latter part of the "asset bubble" in the late 1980s. Selling currency options was more prevalent than buying options in Japan. This may have been partially due to the accounting treatment that counted any premiums paid as an immediate cost, and any

---

Risk Management and Analysis. Vol. 2: New Markets and Products. Edited by Carol Alexander
© 1998 John Wiley & Sons Ltd

premiums received as profit. To the extent that "Japan plc" had developed a consensus about what range the JPY would be trading in they could profitably sell options. This was observable in terms of options trades and also in intraday changes in implied volatility, which traded lower in Tokyo time due to the excess of supply and tended to rebound once Tokyo closed. This practice generally worked well, but on occasion events in the rest of the world caused the JPY to diverge from the target zone. Astute option writers noticed that this usually happened after a favourable movement, rather than immediately after they sold the option, which created a very favourable environment for the banks that began marketing knock-out options. Knock-out option premiums can never be worth more than the underlying European option whose pay-off dominates that of the knock-out option, as the maximum return is the same, but it can be worth less if it knocks out and the European option ends up back in-the-money. Despite this lower premium, the risk was also lower, particularly the risk that had previously most bothered those option writers. In addition, the possibility of the option knocking out meant that another option could be written sooner, so over a year, the total premium received could be higher. A trader at a bank selling to a Japanese investor early in this period reported that, out of the first 30 knock-out options that investor sold, 28 knocked out, often within the first week. As these were a new product at the time, the bank offering them got a good margin and, hedging them prudently, made quite acceptable profits—though nowhere near what the seller made. Naturally, customers were anxious to be sure they were getting good prices, so they encouraged other banks to develop the capability to offer these products, who in turn marketed them to other clients, always increasing the familiarity with the knock-out options. Eventually the market made some unanticipated moves, the ensuing foreign exchange losses became harder to offset with equity or property profits after the "bubble" burst, and the one-sided nature of the business began to balance out.

The purchase of knock-out options is a strategy that is particularly well suited for proprietary traders or investors having a directional view. They are cheaper than European options, allowing a larger position to be taken risking the same premium. They have a higher delta, so an initial favourable move has a greater positive impact on the option price. They have lower theta and vega, meaning that the position is less effected by the passage of time or an unfavourable volatility move. Hedgers have also found them appealing. With users from both sectors, they are now reported to be the most popular exotic currency option, accounting for over 10 per cent of all currency option trades (by volume) between banks and their clients.

Barrier options of the "in" class must hit the barrier in order to be able to be exercised at expiry. They are generally called knock-in options, or occasionally drop-in options. When more detail is required, the terms used are down & in and up & in options. A position consisting of an "in" barrier option and an "out" barrier option of the same type, maturity, strike and amount is perfectly equivalent to a European option. Either spot hits the barrier, and the "in" option becomes European, or spot does not hit the barrier, allowing the "out" option to be exercised, if desired, at maturity. This relationship is used in almost every pricing model. Knock-out options are traded more frequently than knock-in options, but at the analytic level, the knock-in option is a more fundamental product, so the price of a knock-out option is calculated as the price of a European option less the knock-in.

Thus far we have spoken of whether barriers are "up" or "down" and "out" or "in", but options are also puts or calls. Thus, there are eight permutations; those where spot must be heading in the in-the-money direction to trigger the barrier are called "reverse".

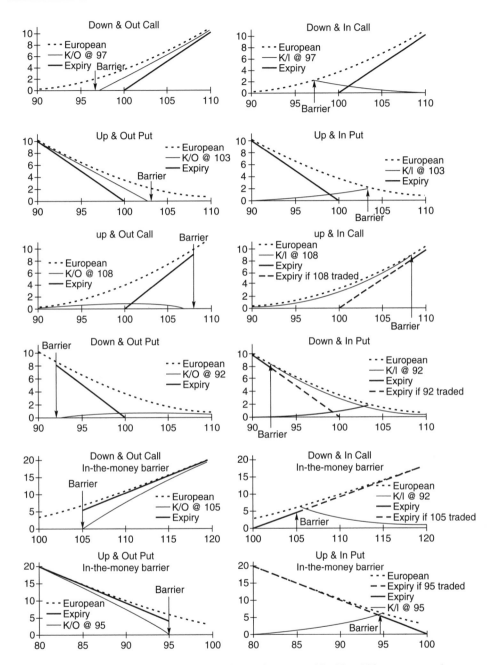

Figure 7.1 Option premiums as a function of spot, with $K = 100$, $r = r_f = 6$ per cent, volatility = 12 per cent and $T = 6$ months

Reverse barrier options must always have their barriers in-the-money, meaning that when spot gets to the barrier, the option is in-the-money. If a reverse knock-out's barrier were out-of-the-money, then it could never be worth anything, as it must have already been knocked out if it were in-the-money at expiry. If a reverse knock-in's barrier were out-of-the-money then it would have the same value as a European option, as it must have already knocked in if it were in-the-money at expiry. The eight types are:

| | Normal | | Reverse | |
	Knock-outs	Knock-ins	Knock-outs	Knock-ins
Calls:	Down & Out Calls	Down & In Calls	Up & Out Calls	Up & In Calls
Puts:	Up & Out Puts	Up & In Puts	Down & Out Puts	Down & In Puts

Of course, if we are considering European or American currency options, every call is a put and vice versa. For a USD/DEM option, a DEM call is a USD put. This applies to barrier options as well. A down & out call on DEM is an up & out put on USD. (Although this terminology is not always agreed between participants, as some prefer to speak of whether the spot rate is going up or down, rather than defining up as the direction that moves a call into-the-money. The presence or absence of the term "reverse", meaning the barrier is reached by spot moving (further) into the money, for a given strike and barrier, is sufficient to remove any possibility of ambiguity.)

For normal barrier options, it is sometimes possible for the barrier to be in-the-money or at-the-money (strike equal to the barrier). If the option is in-the-money, the barrier may be between spot and strike, at the strike, or out-of-the-money. If a normal barrier option is out-of-the-money when dealt, then the barrier must be further out-of-the-money. The risk management characteristics of normal barrier options depend significantly on whether the barrier is out-of-, at-, or in-the-money. Normal barrier options with in-the-money barriers present many of the same risk management challenges as reverse barrier options.

7.1.2 An Analytical Model of Single Barrier Options

A "brute-force" approach to modelling a knock-in option might take an approach like: the integral from now to expiry of the value of a European option with maturity $(T - t)$ and spot = barrier, times the probability of first reaching the barrier at that time, dt. Since the price of a European option itself is an integral, and the function for first passage time isn't simple either, it could be difficult to turn this into a neat analytical formula. Fortunately we are spared all that, thanks to a simple observation illustrated with the following example:

Example 1   Let us consider a GBP call (USD put) struck at 1.5606 K/I @ 1.5300 (that knocks in at 1.5300). For such an option to be worth anything, spot must trade down to 1.5300, then subsequently rise so as to end up above 1.5606 at expiry. The Black–Scholes assumptions do not have belief in trends included. Should spot get to 1.5300 (and we ignore the drift due to interest rate differentials) the market is just as likely to go down to 1.5000 (1.53 divided by 103 per cent) as up to 1.5606 (1.53 times 103 per cent). This is called the reflection principle. For every path leading to the barrier, there are two equiprobable paths leading away from it, one that ends up above and one that ends up below. It is hard to figure out directly the probability of touching the barrier and ending up above 1.5606, but it is easy to figure out the probability of touching the barrier and ending up below 1.50. One cannot end up below 1.50 without having passed the barrier, so the problem thus simplifies into what is the chance of ending up below 1.50, which is contained in the model for a European put. Adjustments must be made for the effect of drift, and the fact that geometric movements from the barrier will mean that the mapping of equiprobable points will be different amounts in-the-money, but the value of the 1.5606 GBP call K/I @ 1.53 is directly related to the value of a European 1.5000 GBP put.

The analytic model is:

$$\Phi S e^{-r_f T} (H/S)^{2\lambda} N[\Psi y] - \Phi K e^{-rT} (H/S)^{2\lambda-2} N[\Psi(y - \sigma\sqrt{T})] \tag{1}$$

where:

$$y = \frac{\ln[H^2/(SK)]}{\sigma\sqrt{T}} + \lambda\sigma\sqrt{T} \qquad \lambda = \frac{r - r_f + \sigma^2/2}{\sigma^2}$$

$\Phi = \{1$ if call; -1 if put$\}$, $\Psi = \{1$ if down barrier; -1 if up barrier$\}$, $H =$ barrier, $S =$ spot, $K =$ strike, $T =$ time to expiry in years, $\sigma =$ annualized volatility, $r =$ domestic rate*, $r_f =$ foreign rate* (*both are continuously compounded interest rates) and N is the normal distribution function.

If r equals r_f then λ is one-half, and the above terms become much simpler. A bit of algebra shows the formula if a down & in call becomes equivalent to an amount K/H of a European put with strike H^2/K. The same formula also applies to up & in puts and European calls. When the interest rate differential is not zero it is possible to derive a more complicated expression for the hedge strike and amount. Unfortunately, it is of limited application, as every day the rate differential becomes less important, so the hedge strike and amount are constantly shifting.

Another interpretation of the formula is that the first term is the value of receiving S, if a call, or the cost of paying S, if a put, conditional upon the market having made the required movement (to the barrier then in-the-money) in a risk neutral framework. The second term is the cost of paying K, if a call, or receiving K, if a put, conditional upon exercise. This same observation can be applied to a European option pricing formula. Although the two probabilities are equal (in the real world) as one doesn't happen without the other, the normal distributions are not evaluated at the same points. This reflects the fact that if the option is worth exercising, S will have an expected value different than its current forward. The way the mathematics works out is elegantly expressed as a change in the risk neutral probability rather than as some other factor to be multiplied by S.

The above models are for normal barriers where the strike is out-of-the-money or at-the-money, for which there is no intrinsic value at the barrier. For non-trivial reverse knock-ins and normal knock-ins where the barrier is in-the-money there is intrinsic value at the barrier. Therefore, if the option should approach the barrier when expiry was near, there would be a large jump in price when the barrier was reached. This makes the equivalence to an option of the other type impossible, as option prices are not discontinuous. There the models for these options are more complicated, but are still analytic models. These were first published in a September 1991 *Risk Magazine* article, "Breaking down the barriers" by Marc Rubenstein and Eric Reiner. Excluding rebates, which will be considered later, they derived four terms that can be variously combined to produce the formulae for all of the possible configurations of single barrier options. One was a European option formula, and another was the "normal" knock-in formula where the barrier is out-of-the-money, like equation (1) above.

Using the interpretation of the option formula as (expected) values multiplied by risk neutral probabilities, an intuitive description of their derivation would be that they determine what pay-offs can occur in what ranges on each type of option, and solve the appropriate integrals. Let us first consider a down & in call option where the barrier is higher than the strike. (The initial spot must be higher than either, else it would have already knocked in!) We can split the pay-off at maturity into two partitions, those where it touches the barrier and ends up between the strike and the barrier, and those where it touches the barrier and ends up above it. The first part can be evaluated as a difference between a European option and some kind of quasi-European option that could be exercised only if it were above the barrier at expiry. The formula for such a "conditional" option is obtained by replacing the strike by the barrier inside the normal probabilities, but leaving the strike untouched outside. This can be seen as an application of the intuitive expected value times risk neutral probability idea. Once a formula exists, it is probable that someone will try to market a product based on it, in the never-ending quest to project a "state-of-the-art" image, or on the assumption that there is a bigger margin in products not already being marketed by the competition. As plenty of firms already have a good understanding of these models and some of them have "rocket scientists" busily trying to come up with something new, it would be surprising if such conditional options hadn't already been marketed. However, they are identical to a portfolio of two other products: a European call option with the strike set at the barrier of the "conditional" option and a binary (digital) option that pays out the difference between the "conditional" strike and the barrier above the barrier.

Using the reflection principle, the second part has many characteristics like a normal knock-in option. Consider the paths that reach the barrier and end up below, which are of course equiprobable (adjusting for drift) with the paths that reach the barrier and end up above, in which we are interested. But, instead of having to move from S to H then H to K, the moment spot gets to the barrier it is already in-the-money, so the H^2/SK in the normal probability is replaced by just H/S. The formulae for the terms are:

$$\Phi Se^{-r_fT}N[\Phi d_1] - \Phi Ke^{-rT}N[\Phi(d_1 - \sigma\sqrt{T})] \qquad \text{(2) European option}$$

$$\Phi Se^{-r_fT}N[\Phi d_3] - \Phi Ke^{-rT}N[\Phi(d_3 - \sigma\sqrt{T})] \qquad \text{(3) "Conditional" option}$$

$$\Phi Se^{-r_fT}(H/S)^{2\lambda}N[\Psi y_1] - \Phi Ke^{-rT}(H/S)^{2\lambda-2}N[\Psi(y_1 - \sigma\sqrt{T})] \qquad \text{(4)}$$

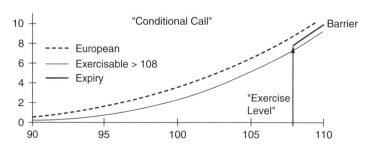

Figure 7.2 A "conditional option, an illustration of equation (3)

Table 7.1

Barrier Option	Barrier vs. Strike	Equation	Φ, Ψ
Knock-in	Out-of-the-money	(1)	1,1 = Down & In Call
			−1, −1 = Up & In Put
Knock-in	In-the-money	(2) − (3) + (4)	1,1 = Down & In Call
			−1, −1 = Up & In Put
Reverse knock-in		(3) + (4) − (1)	1, −1 = Up & In Call
			−1, 1 = Down & In Put
Knock-out	Out-of-the-money	(2) − (1)	1,1 = Down & Out Call
			−1, −1 = Up & Out Put
Knock-out	In-the-money	(3) − (4)	1,1 = Down & Out Call
			−1, −1 = Up & Out Put
Reverse knock-out		(2) − (3) − (4) + (1)	1, −1 = Up & Out Call
			−1, 1 = Down & Out Put

where:

$$d_1 = \frac{\ln[S/K]}{\sigma\sqrt{T}} + \lambda\sigma\sqrt{T} \qquad d_3 = \frac{\ln[S/H]}{\sigma\sqrt{T}} + \lambda\sigma\sqrt{T} \qquad y_1 = \frac{\ln[H/S]}{\sigma\sqrt{T}} + \lambda\sigma\sqrt{T}$$

Putting these terms together allows the creation of the analytic models for all of the varieties of single barrier options (see Table 7.1).

7.1.3 Alternative Modelling Methods

The Black–Scholes assumptions used in deriving the analytical models are somewhat more stressed by the application to barrier options than they are by European-style options. For example, a price jump during the life of a European option could be compensated for by a quiet period later on. But a price jump across a knock-out barrier has more dramatic results, and no chance for later calm to offset those effects. The interest rate or asset yield may not be constant, implying forwards that are closer to or further away from the barrier than the constant rate or yield assumption would imply. Implied volatilities may have a definite skew or smile curve which traders have adapted to in European option markets, but they are unsure how to apply their experience to barrier options. For these and other reasons, various alternative modelling methods have been tried.

The prime candidates for modelling any exotic option are:

- Binomial or trinomial trees
- Monte Carlo simulations
- Construction of a portfolio of European options to duplicate the exotic option
- Numerical methods/analytic approximations

Price lattices like binomial or trinomial trees have a disadvantage for computing accurate prices for barrier options. With a number of iterations that would provide a perfectly acceptable price for an American-style option, the price between the node just inside the barrier and the node just outside is quite wide. This means that, given a strike price, volatility, maturity and number iterations, a fairly wide range of different barriers would produce exactly the same price, in contrast to the results of the analytical model and intuition. Arbitrarily increasing the number of iterations is not an effective way of overcoming this problem, as the results do not converge monotonically to the desired result.

However, by carefully selecting the number of iterations so that the barrier is just barely beyond a node, a result near the analytic result can be achieved.

It is not worth implementing a lattice to replicate the analytic result. The purpose is usually to introduce a feature that cannot be properly reflected in the closed form solution. If the forward curve is non-linear, which would be caused by a sloping yield curve in one of the markets, then the different interest rates at each iteration could be reflected, improving the quality of the assessment of the probability of the barrier being reached. If the desire was to evaluate the impact of the volatility term structure or the volatility smile curve, then a trinomial lattice would be required.

In an article entitled "Pricing and hedging with volatility smiles", that appeared in *Risk Magazine* (January 1994), Bruno DuPire described how, using the prices of European options for a whole range of strikes and maturities, one could derive the instantaneous volatility for any future time and spot level within that range. That set of derived future spot-dependent volatilities could be used either to populate a trinomial lattice or in a Monte Carlo simulation for the purpose of pricing a barrier option. (The variance reduction techniques, described in the previous chapter, antithetic and control variate, should be used in implementing an efficient Monte Carlo simulation.)

Using Bruno DuPire's idea, it is possible to recalculate all of the future instantaneous volatilities if the implied volatility of one of the European option volatilities is slightly perturbed (0.01 per cent). A particular barrier could be repriced, allowing the calculation of the sensitivity of the premium of the barrier option to that European option, which can be used to determine how much of that European option to include in the hedge. If the process is repeated for all of the European options used as inputs in the derivation of the future instantaneous volatilities, then the option portion of the hedge portfolio could be derived. (This does not determine the spot/forward hedge required, which must be found by other means, such as looking inside the lattice. Changing the initial spot slightly and repricing the option is not the right way to proceed, as a change in spot implies a change in volatilities as well.) Obviously, the resulting hedge portfolio will consist of the options chosen as original inputs. In markets where liquidity is concentrated on standard strikes and maturities, as with exchange traded options, this is helpful. However, for OTC currency options, more work needs to be done to make sure of selecting the right options as inputs.

Bruno DuPire's idea is quite interesting in that it allows the different volatilities of different strikes (the smile curve) to be taken into account when pricing and hedging, and allows for changes in volatility, albeit in a deterministic fashion. (The price, and therefore implied volatility, of any European option may be calculated for any future time and spot level.) Whilst this is an improvement on the Black–Scholes assumptions, and should help explain many of the observed short-term shifts in volatility associated with short-term spot movements, being deterministic, it does not fully seem to reflect the full range of changes that can occur to volatility. The level of spot has a profound and significant impact on volatility levels, but it is not the only influence. It could be sufficient to explain the behaviour of volatility when a currency devalues, but would not be powerful in explaining the shifts that occur when some major political change impacts volatility levels, such as what happened to USD/JPY volatility when the LDP lost power in 1993. To model stochastic volatility properly, a two factor (at least) model would be required. The work Bruno DuPire has done should be used as a new starting point, as previous attempts at modelling using stochastic volatility only managed to explain about half of the observed volatility differences between strikes.

7.1.4 Risk Management of Single Barrier Options

(i) Pricing

Unless the counterparty (customer or other dealer) specifically requests a strategy, it is market practice to quote both bid and offer for the requested option and amount. The price could be "live", meaning not referring to a particular spot market price and only valid for the brief time it takes to respond (or even less if the quoter says "Change!"). When quoting a "live" price, the option dealer is exposed to unfavourable changes in the spot market, as it might move at the same time the option is dealt. Accordingly, "live" prices may be somewhat wider to this risk, and are not made immediately prior to scheduled releases of economic data. Most barrier option dealing by dealers with their clients is on the basis of "live" prices.

Alternatively, the price could be quoted on a specific spot reference level, which would be approximately the market when the quote was requested. The dealer would calculate the delta and propose bid and ask prices for the option, based on his also transacting the delta hedge with the counterparty. This makes the market more efficient, as the barrier option bid–ask spread can be shrunk by the delta times the spot market bid–ask spread. Another benefit is that this allows the seeker of the quote the flexibility of comparison shopping. Three banks can be queried, and the responses, even if not simultaneous, will be comparable, and the best can be selected. If the seeker of the quote is in a hurry to transact the option before spot has a chance to move, he can set his spot hedge first, and then search for the best option price. Unlike the OTC market for European-style currency options, the prices are not quoted in volatility terms (like 9.5 per cent to 9.8 per cent), because this could result in either inverted quotes (the bid being higher than the offer) on some barrier options or an inability to actually quote the desired price. (Sometimes the maximum or minimum of the function of premium of a barrier option for its volatility can occur near market volatilities. Considering the other risks in managing the option, the dealer might want to add or subtract a margin to that extremum, which could only be achieved by using a complex number component in the volatility. As this degree of complexity is unwelcome, it is simpler to use price spreads.)

Besides reflecting all of the market parameters required to price a European option, the price of a barrier option should reflect the expected cost of hedging. The analytical model ignores transaction costs, but the real world doesn't. An estimation of the particular transaction costs of a barrier option should be focused on the barrier event:

- how likely is the barrier to be reached?
- is the required action at the barrier a stop loss or take profit order? and
- the expected size of the order at the barrier

As options with out-of-the-money barriers have less sensitivity to volatility than the underlying European option, and the size of the order at the barrier decreases with the passage of time, the width of the bid–ask spread can be similar to or slightly wider than the underlying European option. As buying a knock-out option would generate an easy-to-manage take profit order, the bid is usually close to the theoretical level that would be obtained by using the same inputs as pricing the underlying European option using the market parameters appropriate for the bid side. The offer side may be found by adding a spread, thus using the "extra" spread to protect against the risk of the stop loss order.

The size of the order that must be executed at the barrier increases for barrier options, whether "reverse" or "normal" with in-the-money barriers. Because of this increasing risk, they usually have a bid–ask spread that is two to three times wider than the underlying European option. For barriers that are very far in-the-money, and with little time remaining, the spread can be even wider.

Table 7.2

Option Type (Barrier)	Delta	Gamma	Vega	Theta	Rho
European	0–100	positive	positive	negative	$\sim$ delta$^*T$
K/Out (OTM)	higher	lower	lower	lower	lower
K/In (OTM)	negative	lower	lower	lower	lower
K/Out (ATM)	$\sim$ 100	$\sim$ 0	$\sim$ 0	0– $\sim$ S/N fwd pts	0– $\sim$ delta$^*T$
K/In (ATM)	negative	$\sim$ same	$\sim$ same	negative	variable
K/Out (ITM)	>100	negative	negative	positive	0– $\sim$ delta$^*T$
K/In (ITM)	negative	higher	higher	more negative	variable
Reverse K/Out	lower or −	lower or −	lower or −	less negative or +	variable
Reverse K/In	0–higher	0–higher	0–higher	0–more negative	variable

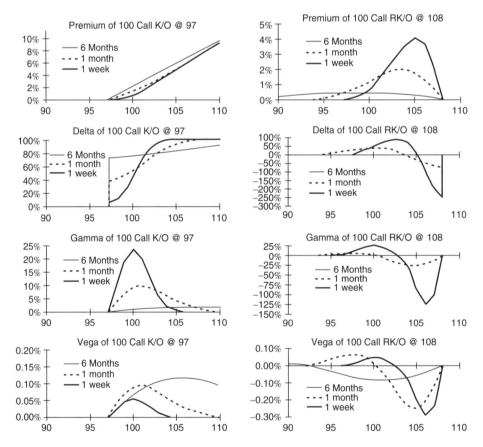

Figure 7.3

(ii) Derivatives

Table 7.2 may serve as a synthesis of several sets of graphs. The barrier option derivatives are compared to the underlying European option when possible.

The experienced option trader is very familiar with matching derivatives to hedge a complicated options position, although he knows he will have to start paying attention to positions by strike as they approach expiry. The same process can be applied to barrier option positions, although it is more important to note how the derivatives shift with spot movement and time to be able to pick a hedge whose derivatives will continue to provide a good match for the barrier options under changing market conditions and some passage of time. If the volume of OTC dealing far outweighs the barrier positions, and the opportunities provided by continuous dealing in those markets mean that it is trivial to adjust the position, then matching local derivatives is sufficient.

(iii) Hedging

As described in the analytical model section, a normal knock-in option has a strong equivalence to a European option of the other type (put vs. call). Hedging down & in calls with European puts and hedging up & in puts with European calls is therefore quite tempting. The strategy works perfectly if the barrier is never reached, but what is important is how well this works when the spot gets to the barrier, which is covered in the next section.

Hedging knock-outs can be broken down into covering the European component, and using the European hedge for the knock-in part. This is not the most common method. As normal knock-outs have less gamma than European options, there is a stronger tendency to rely on delta hedging. To the extent that the vega risk is unwanted, a partial hedge using the underlying European option can be used. The vega position will shift as spot moves nearer to or farther away from the barrier. Most currency options markets have a smile curve (the implied volatilities for different strikes with the same maturity) that is neither flat nor symmetric. Typically, if spot moves towards the side that has the higher volatilities, market volatilities will increase, at least temporarily. Being short a knock-out with only a delta hedge creates a short vega position which decreases when the market moves towards the barrier. If the barrier is on the same side as the part of the smile curve with the higher volatility, then such moves would benefit the delta hedged knock-out position, increasing the willingness of market-makers to be content with just delta hedging.

Another hedging technique is the use of static hedges, constructed with European options that match reasonably well the current and future values of a barrier option in a wide range of spot and volatilities, up to the point where the barrier is reached. This eliminates the necessity to continually rebalance the hedge. As the delta gaps when the option knocks-in or knocks-out, the static hedge must be "costlessly unwound" at that point. If a spot hedge is executed at the barrier level, then this is approximately achievable, if one ignores bid–ask spreads and the effect of any volatility smile curve. The static hedge for a normal knock-in option, like a down & in call or a up & in put, for which the barrier is out-of-the-money, can be derived from the pricing formula. It is straightforward if the rates for each currency are identical. The static hedge for a down & in call is a put, and for an up & in put is a call. The strike of the static hedge is H^2/SK, and the amount required is K/H. When the rates are not identical, the calculation is more difficult and less useful, as the passage of time will change the hedge strike and amount. If the barrier is never reached,

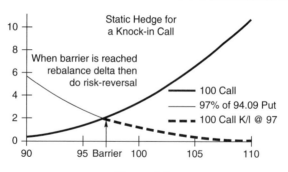

Figure 7.4

this option finishes out of the money, so the hedge would have worked perfectly. More importantly, if one assumes that the volatility smile is always flat, and the interest rates are always identical, then whenever the barrier is reached, the value of the static hedge will match the cost required to buy the European option that the knock-in option has become.

As a knock-out option can be considered as a portfolio of a long European option and a short knock-in option, the static hedge for a normal knock-out option with an out-of-the-money barrier is simply long the underlying European option and short the static hedge for the knock-in option.

Static hedges for barrier options with in-the-money barriers are less common. In fact the solution may be considered more difficult to manage than the original problem. The problem is replicating the way the intrinsic value gaps at the barrier. Although the premium as a function of spot is continuous prior to the moment of expiry, the fact that it gets ever steeper near the barrier as expiry approaches makes it difficult to find a simple static hedge. Consider the case of an up & out call, a 1.50 USD call/DEM put RKO @ 1.60, so spot USD/DEM was somewhere below 1.60. If, close to expiry, spot is near the strike, then the option will behave rather like a European-style 1.50 USD call, because the barrier is unlikely to be reached. Therefore, the 1.50 USD call is a good candidate for inclusion in the static hedge. If only one other option is sought to complete the hedge, the choice is dependent upon time to maturity. Since the up & out call begins to decrease in value as spot approaches the barrier, the sale of some option is indicated. Using an iterative process and least-squared-errors decision rule to find the strike and amount of the option to be sold, assuming 10 per cent volatility, DEM interest rates of 5.5 per cent and USD interest rates of 6 per cent, the results were:

Days remaining	30	15	7	3
Strike	1.5675	1.5780	1.5850	1.5900
Amount	2.615	3.8	5.545	8.32

Of course, any of these would still require an order to be executed at the barrier, and the hedging options "costlessly" unwound. Although any one of these hedges is a good "gamma" hedge on the day it is set, over a wide range of prices, the fit worsens with the passage of time. Therefore, it is necessary to use more than two options in the static hedge.

Assuming that the barrier is far enough in-the-money so the underlying European option would have little time value at that point, then the best static hedge using three options includes the underlying European option and a large spread, the short leg just before the barrier with the long leg equidistant on the other side of the barrier. The amount of the

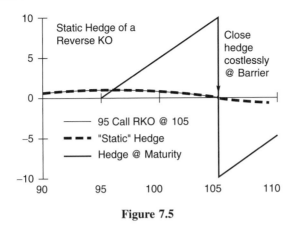

Figure 7.5

spread required is twice the intrinsic value drop at barrier divided by the width between the spread strikes. The closer the spread strikes are to the barrier, and therefore the larger the size of the spread, the better the static hedge matches the reverse knock-out option. Such a large, tight spread by itself is the static hedge for a binary option. Thus, if there were, contrary to current market conditions, a liquid market in binary options, the static hedge would be long the underlying European, and short a binary option struck at the barrier with a pay-off of twice the drop in intrinsic value at the barrier. It has to be twice as large because prior to expiry a binary option is worth half of its pay-off when spot is at the strike (assuming equal interest rates and ignoring the present value effect). Thus the ever steepening decline to barrier is well matched by the binary option.

Should the barrier be not so remote from the strike of a reverse knock-out option, then a fourth option would have to be added to the static hedge, to offset the time value of the underlying European option at the barrier. Changing the size of the binary-like portion of the static hedge is not sufficient, as the time value to be offset must decline as expiry approaches. Instead, an option of similar type, well out-of-the-money, should be sold. To offset the time value, it should have the same kind of relation to the underlying strike as the hedge option for a normal knock-in option, i.e. hedge strike $= H^2/K$, and size $= S/H$ if the interest rates are equal.

(iv) Barrier Events

The analytic model assumes that the hedge is costlessly exited at the barrier, which is easier said than done. The risk of not achieving this can be mitigated by a variety of means. Even before a barrier option is traded, it is important to establish unambiguous legal terms covering the barrier event. Who is responsible for monitoring the market and what are their duties? Most dealers' terms specify that they determine whether or not an option has reached the barrier. This seems to work with clients, but is perhaps a hindrance to interbank dealing. The concept of a partial barrier event is included in some banks' terms, if they are working a take profit order, to manage a sold knock-in or purchased knock-out, but if they only manage to execute part of the order at the barrier, then they would declare that it had only partially knocked-in or knocked-out. For stop loss orders, a partial fill usually means that the rest must be done at a worse price, so barrier events that create stop loss orders do not give rise to partial barrier events. There is an inherent contradiction between the views that could be taken between two dealers having opposite positions in the same barrier option. There have been some attempts to co-ordinate the execution of the two orders, but this is not yet become market standard practice.

When a dealer sells a normal knock-out option with an out-of-the-money barrier to a hedger, they often try to solicit a take profit order in the spot market at the barrier from the client. This can be in the client's interest, because, should the option get far enough out-of-the-money to reach the barrier, then they can usually set a forward hedge at better terms than initially available, even counting the cost of the premium. Some dealers have been known to offer an incentive if the client agrees to make this order irrevocable for the life of the option, usually by lowering the cost of the option by a pip. It is worthwhile for the dealer to do this, as the easy-to-manage take profit order for the size of the option will more than offset the risky stop loss order for the size of the delta. It is also in the client's interest to do this, if he is a hedger, as he will be protected against the possibility of a violent move occurring that would hit the barrier when they are not watching the market, thereby removing their hedge and then rebounding to levels where a hedge is required. As their order would have been filled at the barrier, they could instead use it as the basis to set a favourable forward hedge for their commercial exposure. Such a procedure for the use of knock-out options for hedging can be demonstrated to be less risky than using European options. Given competitive prices, the expected return from each strategy is equal, but at the point the barrier is reached, the hedger using a European option should sell it and replace it with a forward hedge, as he now has substantial gain on his commercial position that is only minimally hedged by the option which is now well out-of-the-money. The amount he will receive by selling the European option depends on the time it takes to reach that level, and what volatility is at that time. Why should the hedger spend extra for the European option at inception, when the reward for that incremental expenditure is the risky value potentially received when the option is resold?

For in-the-money barriers giving rise to stop loss orders, as the delta near the barrier rises as expiry approaches, it can be a good idea to avoid Monday expiries. A gap across the barrier could be caused by some weekend event. Although these are rare, they have happened; remember the Plaza Accord and the Russian coup. If this should happen just prior to expiry when the delta is highest, it could be very expensive. If you are not happy with the gap risk, maybe your client is not happy with the prospect of the option knocking-out so close to expiry. Give him a call and see if he wants to square up his position.

If that does not work, consider dealing in other barrier options with the same (or a nearby) barrier, that will mitigate the size of the order you will have to place. Purchasing an overnight option struck at the barrier in the amount of the stop loss order can protect you, but at a probable high cost.

Concerns of gaps across the barrier aside, using a simple delta neutral hedging strategy relying only on the spot market has an advantage over the more complex hedging strategies using options if the market gets to the barrier, as the transaction costs of unwinding the hedge will be lower.

7.1.5 Barrier Options Combinations

(i) Ladder Options and Step Options

These are spot market level based discrete versions of lookback and lookforward options that can be created as combinations of barrier options. The holder of an option that goes into-the-money prior to expiry has a decision to make: should he sell it to lock in a profit enhanced by the remaining time value or continue to hold it anticipating further gains, but risking both the original premium and the profit? Another choice is to sell the option and buy another one at-the-money, but this involves paying for significant time value. There is an alternative using barrier options, which, for a slightly higher initial premium, allows a profit to be locked in and additional profit potential as well. These are called ladder options or either step-up calls or step-down puts depending upon their type.

Example 2   Assume spot USD/JPY is at 100. You could buy a one-rung 100 USD step-up call that would lock-in a value of 5 JPY per USD if the spot market reached 105. It can be synthesized as follows:

1.   Purchase a 100 USD call/JPY put European-style
2.   Sell a 100 USD put/JPY call knock-in at 105
3.   Purchase a 105 USD put/JPY call knock-in at 105

All of these trades would be for equal USD amounts and the same expiry. If spot does not get to 105 during the life of option, 2 and 3 do not knock-in so only 1, the 100 USD call, matters, in this case having a maximum value of 4.99 JPY, as expected. If spot reaches 105, then the other two options knock-in. 1 and 2 form a synthetic forward purchase at 100. This risky position is protected by 3, the 105 put. If spot at expiry is below 105, then it will be exercised yielding the 5 JPY locked-in profit vs. the synthetic forward purchase. If spot at expiry is above 105, then the holder will let the 105 USD put lapse, and a larger profit can be realized by selling the USD in the spot market.

The USD put with the strike at the barrier, 3, is obviously more expensive than an option five big figures out-of-the-money with the same barrier and expiry. Thus, this strategy is more expensive than just the purchase of the European option. However, as it provides a second chance it can be much more valuable. It is usually cheaper than selling the European option and then buying an at-the-money option to remain in a position to profit from further favourable movement. It is much cheaper than the purchase of a lookforward option, which will be described later.

The key to realizing the value lies in selecting the level where the profit locks in. Such considerations are beyond the scope of this chapter, but a technician who thought a particular support or resistance level would be tested might favour the purchase of a ladder option with the level set just inside the chart point. If the chart point holds, then he has locked in some return. If it is broken, then he probably expects that there will be a rapid and significant move. The ladder option would allow him to exploit this opportunity.

It is possible to add additional rungs or steps. Suppose that it was also desired that a total profit of 10 JPY per USD were to be locked in at 110. The synthesis would be:

4.   Sell a 105 USD put/JPY call knock-in at 110
5.   Purchase a 110 USD put/JPY call knock-in at 110

If 110 is never reached, neither 4 nor 5 has knocked-in. If 110 does trade, then 4 offsets 3, and 5 allows the desired 10 JPY per USD to be locked in. As many rungs can be added as is desired. If there are an infinite number of rungs, each one pip apart, then this is equivalent to a lookforward option, which puts an upper bound on the price of a ladder option. By adjusting the strikes of the knock-in options, different variations can be created, such as an option that locks in half of the intrinsic value.

Implicit in the choice of purchasing an at-the-money option is the realization, in the buyer's market view, that spot has a chance of moving out-of-the-money, otherwise they would have chosen to deal in the spot market, and save the premium. Step-down calls and step-up puts are products designed to provide additional profit potential should such an adverse market move occur. If the market moves far enough against the option, the strike can improve. To synthesize the purchase of a step-down call or a step-up put, buy a knock-out option with a barrier at the level to which the strike is to improve, and a knock-in option with both strike and barrier at that level. If the common barrier is not reached within the life of the option, the knock-out option will be exercisable and the knock-in option will not, so the synthesized product will have the original, unimproved strike. If the barrier is reached, the knock-out option lapses, and the knock-in option with the better strike will be activated.

Step-down calls and step-up puts can have more than one step. As an example, the synthesis of a step-down USD call vs. JPY put with a strike of 100, with steps at 95 and 90, is accomplished as shown in the following example:

Example 3   Assume spot is above 95 at inception.

1. Purchase a 100 USD call/JPY put: knock-out @ 95
2. Purchase a 95 USD call/JPY put: knock-out @ 90
3. Sell a 95 USD call/JPY put: knock-out @ 95
4. Purchase a 90 USD call/JPY put: knock-in @ 90

If spot stays above 95, then options 2 and 3 offset each other at expiry, and option 4 is never activated, leaving only option 1, the 100 call, as desired. If 95 trades, but not 90, options 1 and 3 will lapse, and option 4 still hasn't activated, leaving option 3, the 95 call, as required. If spot trades all the way down to 90, then options 1, 2, and 3 have all lapsed, and option 4, the 90 call, has finally been activated, thereby achieving the second step.

This can be extended to as many steps as desired, always by splitting the knock-in option into a long European option and a short knock-out option, and then replacing that European option with a knock-out option whose barrier is at the next step, and a knock-in option with strike and barrier at that step. Each additional step will add to the price of the package, but, if the steps are one pip apart and there are a sufficient number of them, a step-down call is identical to a lookback call, or a step-up put approaches a lookback put. Thus the premium of a lookback option is an upper limit to the price of these products.

As the components of any kind of step options have different strike prices, it is important to make clear which currency amount should remain fixed for all the options. For ladder options, where the pay-off can be a locked-in amount of one currency, the buyer would usually prefer this to be in his home currency if it is one of the pair. Thus a JPY based investor would usually prefer to do equal USD amounts, leaving the pay-off in JPY. A USD based investor would usually prefer to equal JPY amounts, to achieve a USD pay-off. For this reason, for step options, there is a difference between a USD call vs. JPY, which would have equal USD amounts, and a JPY put vs. USD, which would have equal JPY amounts, with strike and step(s) identical. Locking in a JPY pay-off on a USD bullish/JPY bearish strategy is less expensive than locking in a USD pay-off, as the JPY is less valuable in the region where this pay-off occurs. Therefore a step-up USD call is less expensive than a step-down JPY put.

The equivalence that exists for European, American and barrier options, that a put on one currency is the same as a call on the other, breaks down for all kinds of step and ladder options. It is usually easiest to look at the prices of the component options to see which is more expensive. What is important is to recognize that there is a difference, and not let the point get confused between trader, salesperson and client.

(ii) Barrier–European Combinations

There are many popular strategies involving European options that can be adapted to use barrier options in one or both legs. Four will be discussed here: risk reversals, synthetic forwards, spreads, and strangles.

Risk reversals are the purchase of an out-of-the-money option of one type (put or call), and the sale of an out-of-the-money option of the other type, with the same currency pair, maturity and amount. The most popular version is as a zero premium strategy, where the premium of the option sold offsets the premium of the option purchased. When sold to a hedger with an underlying exposure, this is called variously a cylinder, collar, or Range Forward™, and it creates a risk reward profile like a spread. As it offers some profit potential, limited risk and no out-of-pocket cost, it is probably the most frequently used option hedge. Either the put or the call or both can be replaced with a barrier option. As there are four types of barrier calls, and four types of puts, the inclusion of barrier options means that there are now 25 kinds of risk reversals. We will not examine all of them, only the two most popular.

The strike of the purchased option in a zero premium cylinder determines the risk, and its premium determines the upside potential. Using a normal knock-out option in place of the purchased option allows either more protection or more upside potential, or a combination thereof. If the details of the sold option are left unchanged, that premium can finance a nearer strike on the purchased option, thereby providing a more favourable level of cover if the market moves directly against the underlying position. If the strike of the barrier option is left the same as that of the European option it replaces, then its lower premium permits the option sold to finance it to have a more remote strike, increasing the amount by which a favourable spot movement could benefit the underlying position. The variable we have not yet considered is where to set the knock-out level. In a European cylinder, the hedger may select the strike of the option sold at a level at the limit of what they optimistically expect, if the market is favourable. In this way, the option they are selling is one that they consider will be worthless at expiry. If they wish to extend that view to the choice of barrier, they would set the barrier at the strike of the sold option (or just beyond). There is a risk that spot will reach the barrier, causing the protection to disappear, and then move in the other direction, causing greater losses than if it had moved unfavourably from inception. Hedgers who follow technical advice will therefore set the barrier beyond an important level which, if broken, is forecasted to signal the start of a trend. No matter what the hedger's philosophy, once the barrier is reached, it is obligatory to re-examine the hedge, as its characteristics have irrevocably changed.

The other popular variation on a cylinder is replacing the sold option with a reverse knock-in option. Reverse knock-in options have lower premiums than European options, but only slightly if the barrier is not remote. If the strike of the purchased option is

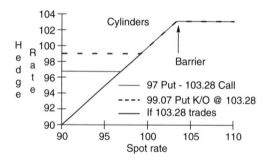

Figure 7.6

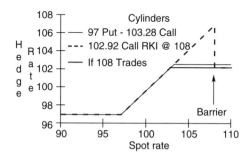

Figure 7.7

not adjusted, then the strike of the reverse knock-in option must be closer. This does not matter until spot reaches the barrier, which will be further away than the European option's strike would have been. Thus, if the hedger is only modestly constructive, which is usually the case for those using cylinders, they gain more profit potential, provided spot does not reach the barrier, which is not a high probability in their market view. This strategy has an advantage over the use of a knock-out option to replace the purchased option in that there is never a situation where the hedger is exposed to unlimited risk.

Hedgers using European options rarely use synthetic forwards, as the standard ones are easier. However, barrier options introduce possibilities not available in the O/R (outright) forward FX market. It is possible to create a knock-out synthetic forward at a level better than the forward. The usual scenario is a hedger has "missed" the market, leaving a position unhedged in the expectation of a favourable move, but the market has not co-operated. They now seek to get a better result than the current O/R forward, and are willing to accept some risk to achieve it. The risk is that the market moves further in the same direction, reaching the barrier and knocking out the synthetic forward, thereby leaving the hedger unhedged at a less favourable spot level than when he initiated the hedge.

A synthetic forward purchase is the purchase of a call financed by the sale of a put with the same strike, maturity and amount. A knock-out synthetic forward purchase at a strike better than the forward is achieved by the sale of a knock-out call struck out-of-the-money and the purchase of a reverse knock-out put at the same strike. A process of iteration is required to find the joint level of the barriers for a given strike level. Reverse knock-out options are quite cheap if the barrier is not too remote, so this can allow for the barrier to be a seemingly safe distance from spot. During the life of the option, if spot never gets to the barrier, then one of the options in the synthetic forward will be exercised, allowing the hedger to unwind his position at a better level than originally available.

Spreads are the purchase of one option and the sale of another of the same type and amount (differing amounts are called ratio spreads). If they have different strikes, but the same expiry, they are called vertical spreads. If they have the same strike, but different expiries, they are called calendar spreads. If both strike and expiry are different, it is a diagonal spread. Buying a vertical spread (the option sold being the one that is less valuable) is a popular way of having the advantages of a long option position but at a lower cost, achieved by accepting a cap on the potential pay-off. The cost can be further reduced by making both options knock-out options. The barriers could be set at the same level, usually at or beyond the purchased option's strike. As it is not too expensive to adjust slightly one of the barriers, it can be tempting for a technically based trader to set the barrier of the sold option just inside some important technical level, and the purchased option's barrier just beyond. If the barrier should hold, then the buyer could benefit from the unlimited profit potential of his long option, uncapped as the sold option had lapsed, all for a price less than a European spread.

Traders expecting a period of range trading consider selling strangles (sale of a put and a call of the same amount and maturity), with the strikes set at the edges of the range. Normally the options sold are out-of-the-money, with the put struck at the bottom of the range and the call struck at the top. However, except for credit and finance considerations, it would make no difference if both options were in-the-money, the premium received would be higher but the pay-off at maturity would be higher as well. Using the in-the-money version, reverse knock-in options can be substituted for both European options. "I expect it will be within the range at expiry" is the view required to expect maximum profit in a European strangle. If the seller's view of the range validity is stronger, i.e. "I expect it will stay within the range until expiry", then he might be willing to set the barriers of each option at the strike of the other. If the barriers are near, then the initial premium is almost as large as the in-the-money European strangle, but if spot trades at neither barrier then there is no pay-off to the buyer, in contrast to the European version where the minimum pay-off is the difference between the strikes. Thus the profit potential to the seller is substantially larger. Larger profit potential occurs only at the acceptance of greater risk. Outside of the range the pay-off to the buyer is the same as the European version, but the initial premium is lower. Even if it is inside the range at expiry, should both barriers be reached during the life of the strangle, then the pay-off will be as large as the European version.

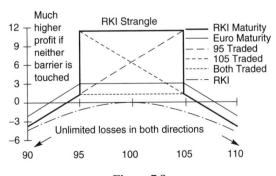

Figure 7.8

7.1.6 Rebates

A rebate is a payment that is received by the buyer of a barrier option if they are not in a position to be able to exercise it. For knock-out options with rebates, if the market trades at the barrier, the buyer will receive a payment, either immediately or when the option would have expired. Rebates on knock-in options are payable if the option never knocks in, which can only be determined with certainty at maturity, therefore the rebate is potentially payable only at that time. Rebates were a part of the early history of knock-out options, speculators buying shares on margin who sold down & out calls against their position, so if they were forced by a margin call to sell the shares they wouldn't be exposed any longer to a rebound in the share price. In order to get the buyer to accept the knock-out feature, it was necessary to offer them a rebate.

Rebates have now acquired a life of their own. As one could buy a barrier option with a rebate, and sell the same barrier option without a rebate, it is possible to create a "naked" rebate. These are usually called one-touch binary options (or one-touch digital options), as they have a pay-off like a binary option, but don't need to finish in-the-money, but merely need to touch the barrier. They are also known as American binary options, as they will exercise it whenever it gets in-the-money. Some market practitioners use the term digital instead of binary. As there is a higher probability of being in-the-money at some time during the life of an option than being in-the-money at maturity, one touch binary options are clearly more expensive than the binary options discussed in the previous chapter.

A rebate payable at maturity can be synthesized by a knock-in "box" spread, all having the same barrier. A box spread is a put spread and a call spread, each using the same pair of strikes. With European options it creates the equivalent of a money market deposit; wherever the market ends up, the return is always the same. By making all of them knock-in or reverse knock-in options all triggered by the same barrier, that fixed payment at maturity is triggered if the barrier is reached. An analytical formula for rebates is provided in Mark Rubenstein and Eric Reiner's *Risk Magazine* article, "Breaking down the barriers", September 1991.

(i) Money-Back Options

A money-back option is a knock-out option with a rebate equal to the initial premium. These are usually normal knock-out options, in which case they cost more than European options. The biggest difficulty in selling options is the premium, and much of the success of the more popular exotic options, such as average rate options and barrier options, can be credited to potential to achieve the same return (under certain circumstances), at a lower premium. The high cost of money-back options has made them relatively rare. To determine the premium to charge for money-back options, divide the premium of the knock-out option without the rebate by (one minus the rebate premium as a portion of the rebate).

Money-back options made with reverse knock-outs are cheaper than European options (provided the intrinsic value at the barrier is larger than premium/rebate). These are not very common yet, but seem to have good potential, as the main disadvantage of buying reverse knock-outs (getting nothing if the market goes too far in-the-money) is mitigated by the return of the premium.

(ii) Exploding Options

Exploding options are reverse knock-out options with a rebate equal to the intrinsic value at the barrier. They can be likened to European options vertical spreads, buying one option and selling another option with the same maturity and for the same amount, but at a strike that is (further) out-of-the-money. Vertical spreads are a popular strategy, but the disadvantage is that if the market gets to the strike of the sold option prior to maturity, the maximum profit is not yet realizable, due to the time value of that option. If the position isn't squared up, in hopes that further favourable movement or simply no movement will permit making the full profit on the spread, a reversal could wipe out the initial gain. An exploding option locks in (if the rebate is paid at maturity), or pays immediately, the maximum profit should the barrier be reached. Obviously, this is a higher probability than being above that level at maturity, so exploding options are more expensive than the equivalent spread. They have found a usefulness in warrant issues, which need to offer a liquidity substitute. Traditionally warrants were American style, allowing the holder to have a choice other than reselling them should they want to realize a profit prior to expiry. This raises the costs of the agent, making their fees higher, etc. If a warrant has an exploding feature, the buyer knows if the market has a good move in his favour, his profit will be locked in or paid immediately, so he need not worry about exercising early.

(iii) One-Touch Contingent Premium Options

A variation on the contingent options discussed in the previous chapter are one-touch contingent premium options. These are the purchase of a European option financed by the sale of a one-touch binary option. As a one-touch binary is more expensive than a plain binary option, the contingent premium, if triggered, is lower. Obviously, there is no reason why the European option strike must also be the barrier that triggers the rebate. There is a whole range of choices, but an interesting one to consider is where the contingent premium is the same as an "at maturity" contingent premium option. The buyer then can take a view as to whether the risk is higher of ending up in-the-money or having touched the necessarily more remote barrier.

7.1.7 Discontinuous Barriers

Most markets close for the weekend, and some event could make the first price on Monday not very close to the last price on Friday, so every barrier option could be considered to have a discontinuous barrier. Sometimes this is made explicit in the terms, usually due to liquidity considerations or to assure verifiability that the barrier was reached. A "fixing" barrier option can only knock in or out if the market level, taken from a specified source at a particular time each day, is at or through the barrier. Market movements in between these times do not trigger the barrier event.

A "fixing" knock-in option is less likely to become a European option than an otherwise identical continuous knock-in, therefore the "fixing" knock-in will have a lower premium. These can be modelled by an approximation where the analytic model is used with a more remote barrier, using a binomial lattice with a number of iterations that is a multiple of the number of days by a Monte Carlo simulation.

Other variations have included options where the barrier only applied during a portion of the life of the option, such as only during the first half, and a barrier that changes as a predetermined function of time. If the barrier is an exponential function of time, there is an analytic solution extant.

7.1.8 Double Barrier Options

A double barrier option has two barriers, one above and one below the current spot market. Reaching either barrier triggers the appropriate action: activation for double barrier knock-ins or disactivation for double barrier knock-outs. If the option is initially out-of-the-money, one of the barriers must be in-the-money, otherwise it is a trivial product, equivalent to a European option for a knock-in, or worthless for a knock-out. If the option is in-the-money at inception, the barrier in the same direction as the strike price could be either in- or out-of-the-money.

The usual equivalence, a knock-out option plus a knock-in option equals a European option, applies to double barriers, so the price of the double barrier knock-out can be found by subtraction. The price of a double barrier knock-in option must be higher than either of the single knock-in options having the same strike and maturity, with its barrier the same as one of the two barriers of the double barrier option, as it is more likely to knock in. The price of a double barrier knock-in option must be lower than the sum of those two single barrier options, as a widely swinging spot market could trigger both, producing a higher pay-off than the double barrier option.

If the barriers are not remote, double barrier knock-in options are even closer to European option prices than reverse knock-in options, and double barrier knock-out options have very low premiums. Thus the more popular strategies involve buying double barrier knock-outs or selling double barrier knock-ins. Buying in-the-money double barrier knock-outs when both barriers are in-the-money can result in a very high potential pay-off compared to the premium spent, although the likelihood of getting any pay-out is quite low. From the dealer's perspective, managing these options is similar to managing a reverse knock-out, except that the chance of hitting the barrier is increased. Accordingly, wider spreads around the theoretical price are observed, especially since fewer participants are active in this product.

7.1.9 Second Market Barriers

Second market barriers, or "outside" barrier options, have a barrier that is triggered by a movement in another market more than the one in which the optional transaction may take place. In common with the currency protected options described in the previous chapter, the premiums of these options are additionally dependent on the parameters of the barrier market and the correlation between the barrier market and the underlying market. These are described in the *Risk Magazine* article (September 1991) by Mark Rubenstein and Eric Reiner, which also includes an analytic model. These would more normally appeal to investors managing multicurrency portfolios, than to commercial transaction hedgers.

7.2 COMPOUND OPTIONS

7.2.1 Definition and Examples

A compound option is an option on an option. As there are two types of options, calls and puts, there are four types of compound options: calls on calls, calls on puts, puts on calls and puts on puts. The underlying option has an amount, strike price and expiry. The compound option also has a strike price and expiry. The compound option's strike price is the premium paid to buy the underlying option. The compound expiry is the date and time by which buyers must decide whether or not to exercise the compound option. It

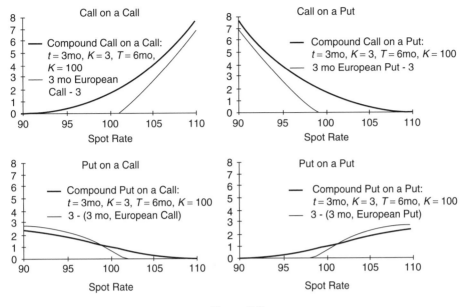

Figure 7.9

must be no later than the underlying expiry. Most compound options are European-style options on European-style options. Calls on options are much more common than puts on options. In that case, even if it was an American-style option on a European-style underlying option, there would be no incentive to exercise early. Why pay the same amount earlier for something that cannot be used until much later?

7.2.2 Geske's Model

After people began comparing the results of the Black–Scholes formula with observed equity options prices, they noted that the implied volatilities of at-the-money options when applied to out-of-the-money options always understated the market prices. A variety of explanations have been put forward, including Jump–Diffusion Processes and Stochastic Volatility. Also, equity in most firms should behave like an option, as the shareholders have limited liability. If the value of a firm's assets is subject to a random process that happens frequently enough, then the value of those assets at some future time will be log-normally distributed. Most firms have debt, which we will assume can be repaid at face value at any time. Thus the shareholders collectively have a "call" on the assets of the firm where the "strike price" is the cost of redeeming the debt. Professor Robert Geske of the Anderson Graduate School of Management at UCLA published a model "The valuation of compound options" (1979) for equity options on the basis of the hypothesis that the equity behaved like an option. This model has made it much easier for participants in a whole range of markets to do compound options, giving him well-deserved recognition. However, as an actual tool for pricing equity options, it is not generally used. A company can have a great deal of influence on the riskiness of its assets, and subject to lending covenants a range of flexibility in its gearing as well. Thus the shareholders could try to maximize the value of their "option" by increasing the volatility or changing the "strike price". This would make it difficult to estimate volatility. However, this behaviour is rare because the shareholding of companies on which equity options are listed is generally widely split, and the management has a relatively small percentage ownership. Management's interest in keeping lucrative jobs frequently overrides their oft-stated objective of maximizing shareholder value, unless their bonus scheme was particularly adapted to co-ordinating their incentives. For increasing the value of the option by increasing the volatility also increases the chance that the "option" will end up out-of-the-money. In this case, out-of-the-money means in the hands of the creditors, which could mean that most of the senior management are out of a job. The exception to this management self-interest dressed up as "prudent management" was the LBO era, where the takeover specialists tried to maximize the value of the option inherently written by purchasers of corporate debt and bank lenders. As these option writers (bondholders) had been used to dealing with previously security oriented managements, they had probably priced the option using too low a volatility (too low a credit spread, or too flexible covenants).

Geske's model used all the same assumptions as the Black–Scholes model: constant volatility, constant interest rates, no dividend on the asset, no transaction costs, etc. Various later work has shown how to relax some of these assumptions in the case of a European option. The volatility need not be constant so long as the average is known. Changing interest rates impact the discounting and the forward price of the asset. The discounting problem can be overcome by using the continuously compounded rate equivalent to the yield of a zero coupon bond maturing at the expiry of the option. The changing rate's impact on the forward price can be corrected for by using the volatility of the forward asset price. (This is made easier if there is a listed futures contract.) A yield on the asset is handled by a change in the drift term. John C. Hull's book, *Options, Futures, and Other Derivative Securities* (1993), shows a compound option model incorporating a yield on the asset.

The particular questions that need to be answered when using a model are: how can the market rates be reflected as inputs to the model? With regard to compound options, given a term structure of rates, of asset yields and of volatility, exactly how can all this be reflected in the model? Certain fairly logical adjustments can be made to the compound option model to allow the three term structures their proper impact upon the final price. This has been implemented in several proprietary exotic option systems and at least one that is commercially available. The rate, yield and volatility in terms associated with the time to expiry of the compound option (T_1) should be the market parameters of that shorter maturity. The rate, yield and volatility in terms associated with the time to expiry of the underlying option (T_2) should be the market parameters of that longer maturity.

The rate, yield and volatility in terms associated with the time between the expiries of the compound option and the underlying option should be the forward–forward market parameters implied between those dates. It is easy to calculate forward–forward rates for continuously compounded rates:

$$_1r_2 = (r_2T_2 - r_1T_1)/(T_2 - T_1) \tag{5}$$

Forward–forward volatilities are less commonly discussed, but they are needed to determine S^*, the level where the market would have to be to make one indifferent between exercising or letting the compound option expire. Volatility is just an annualized standard deviation. Standard deviation squared is variance, and variances are additive. Therefore, the forward–forward volatility is:

$$_1\sigma_2 = \sqrt{(\sigma_2^2 T_2 - \sigma_1^2 T_1)/(T_2 - T_1)} \tag{6}$$

For example, if one-month implied volatility were 10 per cent and two-month implied volatility were 11 per cent, then the forward–forward volatility for one month against two months would be about 11.92 per cent. S^* clearly needs to be found by an iterative process, such as the Newton–Raphson method, which converges quickly thanks partly to the well-behaved nature of the option price as a function of the asset price.

The correlation term in the bivariate normal distribution was modelled as the square root of T_1/T_2, referring to the correlation between the possible asset prices at time of the compound option expiry and the possible final asset prices at the expiry of the underlying option, which is correct if volatility is constant. If there was a period of high expected volatility followed by a period of low volatility, then there would be a higher correlation between the asset prices at those times. Consider purchasing a compound option on a Tuesday, with compound expiry on Friday ($T_1 = 3$ days) and underlying expiry on Monday ($T_2 = 6$ days). If there is no G-7 meeting or other potentially market moving event scheduled for that weekend, then the correlation between Friday's and Monday's possible asset prices should be more like 87 per cent ($\sqrt{0.75}$) than 71 per cent ($\sqrt{0.5}$).

Alternatively, if one contemplated purchasing a compound option on Friday, with compound expiry Monday ($T_1 = 3$ days) and underlying expiry on Thursday ($T_2 = 6$ days), then the correlation could be just 50 per cent ($\sqrt{0.25}$). Other effects besides weekends and holidays can impact, such as the timing of economic releases. Fortunately, these are all reflected in the term structure of volatility. Therefore, the correlation term should be written as $\sigma_1/\sigma_2\sqrt{T_1/T_2}$. If $\sigma_1 = \sigma_2$ then the correlation term collapses back to the way it appears in Geske's paper.

Taking into account the above means of incorporating the information contained in the term structures, the model becomes, when generalized for all four types of compound options:

$$\Phi\Psi Se^{-r_{f2}T_2}N_2[\Phi\Psi a, \Psi d_1; \Phi\sigma_1/\sigma_2\sqrt{T_1/T_2}]$$
$$- \Phi\Psi Ke^{-r_2T_2}N_2[\Phi\Psi(a - \sigma_1\sqrt{T_1})\Psi(d_1 - \sigma_1\sqrt{T_2})\Phi\sigma_1/\sigma_2\sqrt{T_1/T_2}]$$
$$- \Phi ke^{-r_1T_1}N[\Phi\Psi(a - \sigma_1\sqrt{T_1})] \qquad (7)$$

where $\Phi = \{1$ if compound call; -1 if compound put$\}$, $\Psi = \{1$ if underlying call; -1 if underlying put$\}$, $S =$ asset price, $K =$ underlying strike price, $k =$ compound strike price, $S^* =$ asset price on T_1 that makes the underlying option exactly worth k, $N[x] =$ probability of cumulative normal less than x, $N_2[x, y, \rho] =$ probability of bivariate cumulative normal less than x and y for correlation ρ

$$a = \frac{\ln(S/S^*) + (r_1 - r_{f1} + \sigma_1^2/2)T_1}{\sigma_1\sqrt{T_1}}$$

$$d_1 = \frac{\ln(S/K) + (r_2 - r_{f2} + \sigma_2^2/2)T_2}{\sigma_2\sqrt{T_2}}$$

For a means of calculating N_2, see Divgi (1979).

The formula can be interpreted in an intuitive fashion, provided the view is taken from a "risk neutral" world. Take, for example, the case of a compound call on a call. The first term is the value of receiving the asset S at maturity, provided that the compound option was worth exercising ($S_1 > S^*$) and the option ended up in-the-money ($S_2 > K$).

The second term is the cost of paying the premium K at maturity provided again that the compound option was worth exercising and the option ended up in-the-money. The third term is the cost of paying the compound premium k provided that the compound option was just worth exercising. This works because the only random process applies to S. To the extent that one could master the difficulties of calculating cumulative probabilities of a trivariate normal, it could be possible to extend this process to create a model for an option on a compound option, the next step on the road to instalment options, which we will consider later.

When considering options on shares, commodities or bonds, it is clear which is the asset and which is the unit of account. However, for currency options, both are assets and both are units of account. For vanilla options (European- and American-style exercise), there is no practical difference between a DEM call for which one delivers USD to exercise the option and a USD put for which one receives DEM. The Garman–Kollhagen model (European) or Cox–Ross model (American) calculates the premium in USD for a DEM call or in DEM for a USD put. But the premium is paid up front, so, if desired, it can be converted to the other currency at the spot rate. But for compound options, care must be taken, not with the initial premium, but with the compound strike (k). A simple conversion at the outright forward rate for that maturity does not suffice. Take an example of a call on a GBP call (USD put) having a compound strike of 4.5 US cents per GBP. If the forward rate was 1.50, then a certain future cash flow of 4.5 cents could be converted into 3p. However, it is not certain that the compound option will be exercised. If the pound is strong, the holder of the compound option will exercise and pay the 4.5 cents, at a time when that would be worth less than 3p. If the pound weakened, the option would not be exercised. If the compound option seller had sold forward the USD to protect against the phenomena described above, there would be a cost to unwind that hedge. In this example, the USD compound strike is inherently lower than its forward equivalent in GBP. Therefore, the premium for a compound call on a GBP call with a USD compound strike must be higher than a call on the same underlying option with a GBP compound strike of equivalent size.

This difference is straightforward to model. Simply remember the origins of the model. If the compound strike is not in the profit currency (USD for cable or DEM for USD/DEM) but instead is in the "asset", it is necessary to invert the inputs to the model, using one over the spot rate, switching r and r_f. The inverse of volatility is itself. This difference means that there are actually eight kinds of compound options.

7.2.3 Risk Management

(i) Specific Option Hedges

It is tempting for those used to hedging European options to create an analogy to the delta hedging process with which they are already familiar, whereby the underlying option fulfils a role analogous to the spot hedge. Because of the non-linearity of the underlying option price, this is not usually sufficient in the region where there is still some uncertainty whether the compound option will be exercised or not. Clearly, if the underlying option is nearly worthless, then no option hedge is required for a compound call. If the underlying option is much more valuable than the compound strike, then a 100 per cent option hedge will do nicely. In between, however, this doesn't work as well. Any hedge in the underlying option that matches the vega will require a spot hedge to match the net delta.

Given that one option is not a complete hedge, let us consider also whether there are any others that might prove useful in constructing a good hedge, one where the derivatives have a good initial match, and will not rapidly diverge. The compound expiry is normally between the inception date and the expiry date. If it were the same as the day the compound option was purchased, then it would be identical to the underlying option, but with the premium divided into two arbitrary parts. The buyer would not have bought the compound option unless he planned to exercise it. A 100 per cent hedge in the underlying option is a viable but overcautious strategy for the seller of a compound call.

The other extreme case would be a compound option whose expiry was the same as the underlying expiry. Again, the compound becomes identical to a European option. The pay-off for such a compound call on a call would be $(S - K - k)$ which is clearly equivalent to a European call with strike $K + k$. A call on a put where $T_1 = T_2$ is the same as a European put with strike $K - k$. Since paying later is better than paying earlier, and more choice is better than less choice, compound calls become more valuable as T_1 increases for a given T_2. Thus a European option with a strike shifted by k but otherwise identical to the underlying option is a strategy that dominates the pay-off of the compound option. This is less expensive than a 100 per cent hedge in the underlying. In a very illiquid market, it provides a ceiling price above which one should not pay for a compound option.

Another European option to consider is one with an expiry the same as the compound expiry, and with a strike price equal to S^*. An amount of this option equal to the delta of the underlying option when $S = S^*$ and expiry equal to $T_2 - T_1$ provides a very good gamma and theta hedge around the critical point where the compound option is near its strike at expiry. At spot levels further in-the-money, the value of the compound option exceeds the value of this hedge, as the delta of the compound option increases towards 100 per cent of the full amount, whilst the S^* delta weighted hedge is already limited to a 100 per cent delta on a smaller amount. It is easy to see that this strategy provides a floor price to a compound call. The addition of small additional option positions at various strikes so as to track the increasing delta as the underlying option goes further in-the-money can provide an even closer hedge over a wider range of spot prices at compound expiry.

Such a strategy will be destabilized by changes in interest rates or volatility. Any such change will change S^*, creating strike risk. If the volatility shifted enough, S^* might shift by one or two big figures. If spot trends away from S^* then this will not matter, but if it ends up near, this could prove expensive, depending on the way spot moves on the last day.

7.2.4 Extensions

(i) Instalment Options

Instalment options have a schedule of payments which must all be made to have the right to exercise the option at expiry. The buyer can elect to abandon the instalment option prior to any scheduled payment, by giving notice to the seller, and have no future obligation. The economic incentive to abandon the option is created when a "new" instalment option with the same underlying option can be arranged with lower payments than the one about to be abandoned. If the buyer's hedging requirements or market view had changed, then he would prefer to sell the option rather than to abandon it. If he was still interested in the option, yet it was uneconomic not to let it lapse, it is probable that the seller would be quite interested in offering a cheaper instalment schedule, as he would already have the hedge in place.

Like hire purchase, the instalment payments are usually evenly spaced and of equal size. This requires that the pricing model be used in an iterative fashion, starting out with an estimate of the instalment size, setting all instalments except the first one to that amount, and solving for the first payment. If this payment is higher than the other instalments, a higher instalment must be tried, and the process repeated until a figure within an accepted tolerance is achieved. Then any derivatives required for hedging would be calculated. To price an instalment option where the schedule is already specified is easier; there will be some initial payment, which would be lower or higher than the rest of the instalments depending on how the market had changed since the first trade.

When it comes to modelling an instalment option, the most frequent choice is a binomial lattice, though for a low number of instalments an analytic model, requiring numeric integration methods to calculate the multivariate normal probabilities, could be used. The number of iterations would have to be chosen so as to allow an accurate representation of the spacing of the instalments, with sufficient steps between each instalment to have a good approximation of a log-normal distribution. This can raise the total number of iterations quite high, making the model run more slowly than most of the other options in the book. However, as instalment options are a relatively low volume product, this shouldn't seriously affect overall system performance. The nodes between instalments are identical to the intermediate nodes found in a binomial model for a European option. The value of such a node is the discounted probability weighted average of the value of the nodes reached if the market rises or falls. The value of a node where an instalment is due is:

$$\text{Node}_{i,j} = \max(0, e^{-rT/N}(\text{Prob(up)} \, \text{Node}_{i+1,j} + (1 - \text{Prob(up)}) \, \text{Node}_{i+1,j+1} - \text{Instalment}))$$

If the lattice is carried all the way out to expiry, the values of the terminal nodes are $\max(0, \Psi(S - K))$. It is possible to save some iterations if the terminal nodes are set at the last instalment and an analytic model is used to calculate the value of the underlying European option finally purchasable at those nodes, which have a value of $\max(0, \text{European Premium} - \text{Instalment})$. Or Geske's compound option model could be used at the penultimate instalment, possibly further speeding up the computation. It is possible to build binomial trees that reflect the term structure of rates, which is worth doing if there is a steep (or steeply inverted) yield curve.

Instalment options can be combined with bonds to create interesting structures. The instalment dates can be set to match the coupon payments and dates. This could be used to create a currency linked bond that, if the investor were no longer interested in the potential appreciation from the option component (probably because the market had moved in the opposite direction from that required to get any capital gain), then he could elect to begin receiving coupons, and forgo the possibility of a redemption value higher than par.

There is a close relative of instalment options, called pay-as-you-go options. There is a schedule of instalments, but instead of a single underlying option, there is a series of options. Usually the expiry date of each option (except the last one) is also an instalment date. If the buyer decides not to pay an instalment, he forgoes the rest of the options remaining in the series. These first appeared as pay-as-you-go caps, a series of interest rate options having the same strike, providing cover against higher rates. The idea has been applied to foreign exchange to cover the needs of exporters or importers having regular currency flows to manage.

(ii) Chooser Options

A straddle is the purchase of a call and a put, both having the same strike and expiry. At maturity only one will be in-the-money, so the holder will choose to exercise that one. Because they are always worth something at maturity, straddles have high initial premiums. Much of the development of exotic options can be traced to the quest to lower premiums, without lowering the option's utility to some buyers. Chooser options are like straddles, in that the buyer has a choice of having a put or a call, but he must make the choice on a specified date prior to expiry of the underlying. The buyer's self-interest will lead him to choose whichever option is more valuable. If, because of his directional view on the market, he prefers to own the other option, he can sell the expensive one and buy the cheaper one (or if his credit lines permit, do a forward trade to create a synthetic option of the type he wants). Clearly, there is some possibility that the option he chooses will end up out-of-the-money, which means the potential maturity value can be less than a straddle. As it can never be worth more, the chooser must therefore be less expensive than the straddle. Another way to see this is to consider the values on the "choose date" (the date the buyer must choose between the put and the call). On that date the straddle must be more valuable than the more expensive of its two parts. Chooser options are also called "as-you-like-it" options.

Chooser options are most frequently employed when some upcoming event (election, central bank meeting, economic statistic) is expected to have a trendsetting effect on the market, but in an unknown direction. The choose date is selected for immediately after the event, when the outcome will be known. The expiry is set to some later date, allowing time for the market to have moved. A look at historical charts can give an indication of how long previous trends have persisted before a significant reversal. If the event by itself would move the market greatly, then a straddle to the choose date would be a more rewarding strategy. In this age of instantaneous communications, with most markets being subject to continuous professional analysis and significant amounts of capital searching for any market anomaly to achieve a higher return, it is hard to see how such trends could persist. It would either take some less direct linkage for which the effect happens over an extended period of time, or an inertia to the market, perhaps caused by central bank intervention, which will eventually be overcome by market pressures.

From a modelling perspective it is easier to consider that a chooser is a combination strategy, consisting of two products. The holder of a chooser can consider himself long a call to the expiry date, and that he also has an option which allows him to exchange that call for a put. This exchange option is like a compound option (a call on a put), except that the compound strike is a call option rather than a cash payment. If the put has different characteristics than the call, it can be modelled using the same approach as Geske. (UBS extended this idea further by issuing "Presidential Warrants" in 1992 where the choose date was set slightly after the November presidential elections. Warrants are merely transferable certificates representing ownership of options listed on an exchange. At the choose date, the holder of the warrant could pay a premium to receive either a put or a call on a stock market index. Thus it was an option on a chooser. As the compound expiry and the choose date were the same, the model required for pricing was kept simpler than if there were two different dates. As a marketing idea, the product was very appealing. That summer, the stock market was perceived to be worried about the possibility of a Clinton victory, and the polls were showing a tight race developing. However, the outcome was not the one that was most favourable to using a chooser. By the time the election neared, the result was known, and the market had already discounted the effect.)

However, for the special but very common case of the put and call having the same strike and expiry, there is a much easier way of hedging, and therefore pricing, a chooser. The seller of the chooser can be considered to have delivered a call to the buyer, and remains under the obligation to exchange that call for a put on the choose date, if the buyer so chooses. If the underlying market goes up, the buyer will not want to make the exchange, and will keep the call. Therefore, the seller should have bought the call as part of his hedge.

If the market goes down, the buyer will choose to exchange the call for the put. The buyer will be buying a call and selling a put, with the same strike and expiry. This is equivalent to buying the underlying outright forward at the strike price on the delivery date! So, when the market declines by the choose date, the seller finds himself buying the outright forward. Thus the seller has implicitly sold a put expiring on the choose date, with delivery that is later than the customary two business days, two business days after the expiry instead. Such an option can be priced on correctly implemented foreign currency option pricing software, such as is found in most banks; as two business days can vary due to weekends and holidays the European option model can handle different periods between exercise and expiry. As these kinds of options do not trade interbank (although they do have a fair equivalent in the serial options on currency futures, i.e. July or August option expiries on the September futures contract), it is necessary to determine the best available hedge. Three elements define the required put option: expiry, strike and amount. We already have determined that the expiry should be the choose date. Whether the holder of the chooser will pick the put or the call will be determined by which is more valuable. The more valuable one will be the one that is in-the-money. Thus if the outright forward is above the strike on the chooser, then the call is more valuable, so the holder will keep the call, and the implicit put expiring on the choose date will not be exercised. If that forward is below the strike, then he will choose the put, thereby exercising the implicit put. The crossover point is when the forward equals the strike. What spot rate would cause that? The interest rates on each currency are known (and temporarily assumed to be stable). Thus the usual forward vs. deposit arbitrage formula can be used to calculate the strike price of the choose date put. Using continuously compounded rates:

$$K_c = K\mathrm{e}^{((r_f - r)T - (r_{fc} - r_c)T_c)} \qquad (8)$$

where the subscript c refers to that variable on the choose date.

When the holder decides to choose the put, the seller will exercise the OTC put and have to roll the spot position out to the forward date with a swap (buying and selling the put currency, selling and buying the call currency). As the market practice is to do all swaps with the near leg at the spot rate, there will be a positive cash flow at the spot date (as the option was in-the-money, else it would not have been exercised). There will also be a negative cash flow at the forward date. The positive cash flow must be invested to offset the future negative cash flow. Continuing to rely on our constant interest rate assumptions, we conclude that the amount of the choose date put must be equal to the present value of the size of the chooser option, thereby completing our hedge. Since there will be no future profits or losses, the cost of the hedge portfolio is the price of the chooser.

The same logic could have been used, starting with the underlying put and a choose date call, but the price works out the same, thanks to put–call parity. The difference between the two hedging methods is the rhos, or interest rate exposures. If the chooser is hedged with an expiry call and a choose date put, there is some probability that the put will be chosen requiring the seller to borrow the put currency and lend the call currency. Should the interest rates of the put currency rise, or the call currency decline, there would be a loss. However, if the chooser was hedged with an expiry put and choose date call, the same rate shifts would result in a profit. Therefore, the initial rhos can be reduced by using a portion of each hedging method. If the strike price were at-the-money forward, then the appropriate hedge would be a straddle to the expiry date in half the size of the chooser, and a straddle to the choose date of the present value of half the size of the chooser.

Dynamically, the hedge will require some adjustment to maintain low rhos when spot moves. If spot declines, the likelihood of the put being chosen increases, therefore a forward–forward FX position should be taken to anticipate the probable requirement to roll forward the amount of the choose date put that may be exercised. This could also be managed by trading FRAs in each currency, interest rate futures, FXAs, or by adjusting the options position. A change in rates changes the strike price and the amount of the option required at the choose date. This "should" be hedged by trading options, but for small changes, it is more practical to do a spot trade.

Provided the rate changes and spot changes happen at different times there is no problem, the position adjustments required to keep the risk limited are costless. However, if both markets move at the same time, there will be profits or losses. For example, if a rise in the interest rate of a currency made it more attractive, so the spot rate rose, the put on that currency would be less likely to be exercised, so some of the hedges locking in borrowing costs in that currency could be unwound at more favourable rates, producing a profit. In this example, a positive correlation between spot and the "leading" currency interest rates is a source of profits. Of course, the effect on changing the option's strike and amount also needs to be considered for a complete view, but if the choose date is relatively close and the forward is close to the strike, a small shift in the spot rate can cause a big shift in the rhos. An appreciation of this effect on a particular position can be gained through simulation analysis, by observing the P/L changes caused by a matrix of spot and interest rate movements. A rate increase is not always good for a currency. Frequently, if a currency is perceived to be "under attack", any currency weakness is accompanied by an increase in interest rates, as the market anticipates the possibility that the central bank will decide to raise rates to defend the currency.

Observing that correlation affects the hedge performance results in two action points. The pricing, and therefore the model, should be changed to incorporate the correlation. Also, the correlation risk should be measured and managed. There are few direct means of trading correlation, but many products that also produce correlation risk. These should be viewed as an ensemble, with an eye to finding some other product that can produce offsetting correlation risks. This particular type of correlation, spot vs. interest rate (or interest rate differentials), can also be observed in American-style FX options, diff swaps, and interest rate options that are quanted into another currency. As to improving the model, the usual response is, given that choosers are relatively low volume products, it is sufficient to widen out the price to cover the risk. Some banks are reported to have developed models that explicitly factor in a correlation, but these are proprietary, and besides correlation is notoriously unstable, making the value of the effort unclear.

A variation on chooser options, where the seller chooses on the intermediate date whether the buyer has a put or a call, has been modelled, but I have not heard of any trades. The structure would mostly appeal to sellers, but premium would be lower than either the put or the call.

7.3 LOOKBACK OPTIONS

7.3.1 Definition and Examples

Barrier options existed before the analytical model. The compound option model was developed to model an existing feature, the effect of leverage. In the lore of finance, lookback options turned this relationship around. The model was developed first, and not for any commercial purpose. Trading in lookback options was sparked by the existence of the model. It was a model looking for a market, like an answer looking for a question. Actually, the product was frequently discussed, but not in the usual forums. Who has not heard a trader say, "I should have ...", or "I could have ...", usually followed by "I would have ...". The model for a lookback option puts a price on a wish, of a very limited sort.

A lookback call (put) option gives the buyer the right to buy (sell) at the expiry date a fixed amount of the call (put) currency at the lower (higher) of the strike price or the lowest (highest) spot rate that traded during the life of the option. Only if the spot market, at the moment of expiry, is at its extremum low, for a call, or extreme high, for a put, will it not be optimal to exercise. A lookback option is never out-of-the-money. Even if the strike were set out-of-the-money, the instant it was traded, the right to buy or sell would update to the current spot level and become at-the-money. Most lookback options are initially at-the-money, but one that has a recorded low or high that is better than the current spot is exactly equivalent to a new one with that extremum as its strike. Lookback options are therefore described as having strikes that improve, and it is typical that the new strike, if updated, is communicated to buyer by the seller in a timely fashion, to allow any questions to be resolved when the memory of the events is still fresh.

There is a related product, lookforward options, which are cash settled for a value determined as the maximum of zero and, for a call (put), the profit due from buying (selling) a fixed amount of the call (put) currency at the strike price and selling (buying) it at the highest (lowest) spot rate that traded during the life of the option. If the strike price is, as is most common, the initial spot rate, making the lookforward option at-the-money, the option would be exercised unless spot moved out-of-the-money immediately, and stayed there. A more favourable strike price would create an in-the-money lookforward option. Unlike lookback options, it is possible to have an out-of-the-money lookforward option, where the spot market would have to move some distance before there would be any value in the settlement formula. An existing lookback option carries with it some history, not just the strike, but the most favourable settlement rate to date.

There are some parity relationships between lookback and lookforward options. The purchase of a lookback straddle, struck ATM, will have a pay-off of the range that that currency pair trades in during the life of the option, as the lookback call gives the right to buy at the low and the lookback put gives the right to sell at the high. The purchase of a lookforward straddle, struck ATM, also produces the same pay-off, as the lookforward put gives the right to buy at the low and sell at the strike, whilst the lookforward call gives the right to buy at the strike and sell at the high. The purchase and sale at the strike is offset, leaving a profit equal to the range identical to the lookback straddle.

It is possible to synthesize an ATM or an ITM lookforward option with an ATM lookback option of the other type and a synthetic forward trade at the strike. An ATM lookback put gives the right to sell at the high. The purchase of a European call and sale of a European put struck at spot produces an unconditional forward purchase at the strike, which is the inception spot rate. Thus, this portfolio is perfectly equivalent to a lookforward call. Synthesizing an OTM lookforward option from a lookback option is slightly trickier; the lookback option has to be ITM, with the same strike as the lookforward, so that if spot fails to improve the strike, the lookback option merely offsets the synthetic forward, producing the pay-off of an option that stayed out-of-the-money, zero.

Lookback and lookforward options are almost always worth something at expiry, therefore they must have high premiums, obviously higher than European options, as the pay-off will be at least as high, usually higher. This makes them very difficult to sell. The most popular exotic options, barrier and average rate options are cheaper than European options. There is also a psychological reason for their unpopularity. Most professionals in finance are better paid than average, presumably to reward them for their knowledge of the markets. How can such a person justify the paying of an extra high premium for a lookback option that automatically assures his firm of the best price? Where is the value of his market judgement? For whatever reason, lookback and lookforward options are relatively rarely used for hedging, but some have been built into structures marketed for smaller investors.

7.3.2 An Analytical Model

Goldman et al. (1979) derived an analytical model for a European lookback call option using the Black–Scholes assumptions. The formula contains the price of the European option with the lookback option's current strike and what has been described as a "strike bonus" option, that reflects the value of the improvement in the strike and any value at maturity between the final strike and the closer of the original strike or the final spot price. Using the same notation as previously used in this chapter, the formula for a "strike bonus" option can be written as follows:

$$\frac{\Phi\sigma^2}{2\delta}\left(Ke^{-rT}(S/K)^{2\lambda}\mathrm{N}\left(\Phi\left(-d_1+\frac{2\delta\sqrt{T}}{\sigma}\right)\right)-Se^{-r_fT}\mathrm{N}(-\Phi d_1)\right) \qquad (9)$$

where $\delta = r - r_f$.

Whenever spot sets a new relevant extreme, the lookback parameters change. The European option component has a new strike, as does the strike bonus. Mark Garman has pointed out that such formulae are difficult to implement if the foreign and domestic rates should be equal, as there would be a zero in the denominator. However, the price is a continuous function of either interest rate, so the price of a lookback option at a zero rate differential is the limit as the rate differential approaches zero.

From general appearances, the formula for a call looks like a certain amount of hybrid between a knock-in put and a European put, as it has a discounted strike multiplied by a factor similar to one appearing in a knock-in option, times a risk neutral probability minus discounted spot times a risk neutral probability. This makes sense as spot must decline to make the strike bonus portion of a lookback call have a value.

7.3.3 Alternative Models

Due to the similarity between lookback options and structures of barrier options, the same methods have been applied to deal with the same weaknesses in the assumptions. The implementation of any binomial method was thought to be computationally difficult prior to Simon Babbs' or Eric Reiner's work.

7.3.4 Risk Management

(i) Derivatives

The delta of an ATM lookback option, which includes any time that it is setting a new maximum, is equal to its premium. This also applies to puts. If the initial premium is paid in the foreign currency, no delta hedge is required at inception. Once the market begins to diverge from the strike, the delta begins to get closer to that of the underlying European option. In spite of this change, the delta is a continuous function of spot, although the gamma is not. The high price of a lookback option is a product of the potential movement, both down and up. Therefore lookback options have high vegas. Theta will also be high, as the volatility requires time to act.

(ii) Options Hedges

The most frequently mentioned means of hedging a short lookback option is to buy an ATM straddle and roll it to the new strike whenever a new extreme in the spot market improves the lookback's strike. Consider a lookback call: if the spot market never sets a new low, the purchased European call will cover the pay-off. If spot moves down first, the cost of buying a new ATM straddle will be covered by the sale of the previous one, as the put has become more valuable. Eventually, when the low for the whole period had occurred, the call at that strike would cover the full lookback pay-off.

The previous paragraph, like Black–Scholes, ignores transaction costs. In the real world, the straddle strike would only be adjusted when the strike had changed enough to make it worthwhile. The risk of following this strategy is that a sudden drop and immediate rebound would count in improving the strike of the lookback, but would not allow for enough time to adjust the hedge. As this is the opposite kind of gap risk than usually worries barrier option dealers, managing the usually smaller lookback book in conjunction with the barrier book can mitigate the larger risk.

7.3.5 Extensions

(i) Discontinuous Lookbacks

The disadvantage of the high cost of lookback options can be mitigated by limiting the times when the lookback feature is in operation. The liquidity of the underlying market or the need for an independently verifiable measure of the extreme sometimes leads to lookback options that are based on periodic samples, like daily fixings. These variations can be priced using the method described in Simon Babbs' article on binomial pricing of lookback options, which contains an astute method of keeping the tree from becoming too bushy.

A discontinuous lookforward with a relatively low number of fixings is referred to as a "cliquet" or ratchet option. These have been built into multi-year retail equity index products, where the final return is dependent on the appreciation from inception to the highest yearly close. The simplest version of a ratchet option would be one where the cash settlement was based on the better of the spot price at one intermediate date (the ratchet date) and at maturity. This can be viewed as a purchase of an option expiring on the ratchet date, but where the pay-off was deferred until the actual maturity and the purchase of a forward start option, where the strike will be set on the ratchet date at the then current spot market, or the original spot whichever is worse, and expiring at the actual maturity. If the final spot was not as favourable as the intermediate spot, then the forward start option could finish out-of-the-money, and the sole pay-off would be from the European option with the deferred pay-off. If the final spot were more favourable, then the pay-off of the two options would combine to produce the payment for the full movement since inception. The forward start options usually modelled do not have any restriction on the level at which their strike can be set, so this simile may be tricky to implement, but it does show the inter-relatedness of various species of exotic options.

(ii) American Lookbacks

Even though lookback options give the right to deal at an extreme, they aren't necessarily worth their maximum value at maturity. For example, if a lookback call is 10 per cent above its minimum one week prior to expiry, spot could easily decline somewhat by expiry without getting anywhere near the minimum. Selling the lookback option or hedging by selling a European option or dealing in the spot market are all suitable ways of locking in a profit. Eric Reiner has suggested a numerical method of calculating a price for an American-style lookback option, should the buyer not be satisfied with the above methods of realizing a value prior to maturity.

(iii) Shout Options

We have discussed various means of providing lookforward-like features at lesser premiums by discretizing the sampling for the favourable extreme. Ladder options sample at preset levels only, ratchet options sample at preset times. A shout option gives the buyer the right, at one moment of his choosing during the life of the option, to set the then current spot level as the sample point (see Thomas (1993) which describes how to adapt a binomial lattice to model this product).

7.4 EVEN MORE EXOTIC OPTIONS

For a while it seemed that whatever a "rocket scientist" could invent would be sold. Options with formula based pay-offs, like power options or options linking the prices of two unrelated markets seemed about to proliferate. The reaction to publicized losses from derivative products seems to have changed the focus away from novelty for its own sake. Instead the recent thrust seems to be packaging a series of the products described above. This can cut down the exposure to an unfortunate conjunction of the expiry date and an unfavourable market move, although the maximum return is effectively limited as well. These create a different challenge for the modeller, system developer and risk manager, as each trade can involve dozens or maybe even hundreds of component trades. These need to be handled en masse, lest the costs of processing outweigh the potential profits.

7.5 REFERENCES

DuPire, B. (1994) "Pricing and hedging with volatility smiles". *Risk Magazine*, January.

Dvigi, D.R. (1979) "Calculation of univariate and bivariate normal probability functions". *Annals of Statistics*, **7**, no. 4, 903–10.

Geske, R. (1979) "The valuation of compound options". *Journal of Financial Economics*, **7**, 63–81.

Goldman, M.B., Sosin, H.B. and Gatto, M.A. (1979) "Path dependent options: Buy at the low, sell at the high". *Journal of Finance*, December, **34**, 1111–27.

Hull, J.C. (1993) *Options, Futures, and Other Derivative Securities*. 2nd Edition, Prentice Hall International Editions, 417–18.

Rubenstein, M. and Reiner, E. (1991) "Breaking down the barriers". *Risk Magazine*, September.

Thomas, B. (1993) "Something to shout about". *Risk Magazine*, May.

8
Captions and Swaptions

VINCENT LACOSTE

The aim of this chapter is to present a detailed review of the recent literature on interest rates models, with a view to pricing and hedging captions and swaptions. This review completes Chapter 5, "Interest Rate Option Models: A Critical Survey" by Riccardo Rebonato, which presented with great clarity the major techniques and viewpoints of both academics and practioners on the various models and their respective valuation techniques (recombining trees, Monte Carlo simulations, and the numerical resolution of partial differential equations (PDEs)). The present chapter might seem more technical to the reader who is not familiar with stochastic calculus techniques, but we will try to be as clear as possible regarding the practical implications of the models.

8.1 CHANGE OF NUMERAIRE: A GENERAL VALUATION METHOD FOR SWAPTIONS

This section presents a general way of valuing swaptions based on the very efficient technique of change of numeraire developed by Geman et al. (1995). In all of what follows, we use the fact that a swaption is equivalent to a bond option.[1]

8.1.1 Introductory Comments

As noted by Rebonato in Chapter 5, the change of numeraire technique gives a very nice interpretation of the price of a contingent claim. The main idea relies on the property that under the usual no-arbitrage assumption, for every numeraire chosen among the assets traded in the market,[2] there exists a probability which is said to be risk neutral. Under a risk neutral probability measure any price process, expressed in terms of the numeraire, follows a martingale process.

Let us denote by S_t the value at date t of the asset that we want to use as a numeraire. S_t is expressed in a given currency, in dollars for example. We denote by $(P_t)_{t\geq 0}$ the current dollar-value process of a claim in the market, a priori different from S_t. The

Risk Management and Analysis. Vol. 2: New Markets and Products. Edited by Carol Alexander
© 1998 John Wiley & Sons Ltd

S-value of P_t, expressed in the S-numeraire, equals P_t/S_t. Therefore, we call the S-risk-neutral probability, denoted Q_S, the probability under which the process $(P_t/S_t)_{t\geq0}$ is a martingale.

When replacing the numeraire S_t by the value of one dollar invested at date 0 in the saving account, whose value equals $\beta_t = \exp(\int_0^t r_s\,ds)$, where r_s is the risk-free instantaneous rate at date s, we come back to the usual definition of the risk-neutral probability Q,[3] under which any discounted price process $(P_t/\beta_t)_{t\geq0}$ is martingale. Obviously, there is a link between the Q_S probability and the usual risk-neutral probability Q, which is described by the Radon–Nikodým derivative of Q_S with respect to Q. By means of Girsanov's theorem, the relationship between both probabilities can also be explained by a so-called change in Brownian motion (see, for example, Ikeda and Watanabe (1981) for more details).

8.1.2 Technical Properties

Let us assume that we know the stochastic (or deterministic) volatility function of the asset S_t, which we denote σ_t. Under the risk-neutral probability Q, the instantaneous trend of the price process equals the risk-free rate r_t (see, for example, Rogers (1996)). Therefore

$$\frac{dS_t}{S_t} = r_t\,dt + \sigma_t\,dW_t \tag{1}$$

where $(W_t)_{t\geq0}$ is the standard Brownian motion under the probability Q (which means in particular that $E^Q[dW_t] = 0$ and $E^Q[(dW_t)^2] = dt$). A classical arbitrage argument leads to the remarkable property that any discounted price process is a martingale under Q:

$$\frac{P_t}{\beta_t} = E^Q\left[\frac{P_T}{\beta_T}\bigg|\mathcal{F}_t\right] \quad \forall T \geq t \geq 0 \tag{2}$$

where $\mathcal{F}_t$ represents the information available at date t, namely the filtration associated with the Q-Brownian motion W_t.

Considering the equivalent property for the S-numeraire, we have asserted the existence of a probability Q_S for which we get:

$$\frac{P_t}{S_t} = E^{Q_S}\left[\frac{P_T}{S_T}\bigg|\mathcal{F}_t\right] \quad \forall T \geq t \geq 0 \tag{3}$$

where we assume that the information set $\mathcal{F}_t$ is the same for both probabilities Q and Q_S. Comparing equations (2) and (3), we find two alternative expressions for the price process P_t, which should give the same result:

$$P_t = \beta_t E^Q\left[\frac{P_T}{\beta_T}\bigg|\mathcal{F}_t\right] = S_t E^{Q_S}\left[\frac{P_T}{S_T}\bigg|\mathcal{F}_t\right] \tag{4}$$

Considering that an expectation under Q_S can always be calculated as an expectation under Q weighted by the density of Q_S with respect to Q, we get the following equation:

$$E^{Q_S}\left[\frac{P_T}{S_T}\bigg|\mathcal{F}_t\right] = E^Q\left[\frac{P_T}{S_T}\left(\frac{dQ_S}{dQ}\right)_T\bigg|\mathcal{F}_t\right] \tag{5}$$

which implies that

$$P_t = \beta_t E^Q \left[\frac{P_T}{\beta_T} \middle| \mathcal{F}_t \right] = S_t E^Q \left[\frac{P_T}{S_T} \left(\frac{\mathrm{d}Q_S}{\mathrm{d}Q} \right)_T \middle| \mathcal{F}_t \right] \tag{6}$$

This latter equation being true for any claim P_t, we find the necessary expression of the density function $(\mathrm{d}Q_S/\mathrm{d}Q)$:

$$\left(\frac{\mathrm{d}Q_S}{\mathrm{d}Q} \right)_{T|\mathcal{F}_t} = \frac{S_T \beta_t}{S_t \beta_T} \tag{7}$$

Let us remark that it is easy to give an explicit expression for the second member of equation (7), knowing the dynamics of S_t given by equation (1):

$$\left(\frac{\mathrm{d}Q_S}{\mathrm{d}Q} \right)_{T|\mathcal{F}_t} = \exp \left(\int_t^T \sigma_s \, \mathrm{d}W_s - \frac{1}{2} \int_t^T \sigma_s^2 \, \mathrm{d}s \right) \tag{8}$$

Note that this equation only depends on the volatility function of the numeraire S_t, and is independent of its mean and initial value.

As stated previously, Girsanov's theorem gives another nice result related to equation (7): under the probability Q_S, the process denoted W_t loses its properties of Brownian motion. Mainly, the mean of W_t is no longer 0. In fact, we get

$$E^{Q_S}[\mathrm{d}W_t] = E^{Q_S}[\sigma_t] \, \mathrm{d}t$$

However, it is possible to define another process, which we denote W_t^S, defined by

$$\mathrm{d}W_t^S = \mathrm{d}W_t - \sigma_t \, \mathrm{d}t \tag{9}$$

which is a Brownian motion under the probability Q_S. This new process is simply related to the initial W_t by means of an adjustment of the drift. This property implies in particular that the instantaneous variance of the process is unchanged when we go from one probability to another; only the drift terms are adjusted (see, for example, Revuz and Yor (1991) or Ikeda and Watanabe (1981) for more details on Girsanov's theorem and change of probability).

8.1.3 Application to Swaptions

A swaption can be considered as an option on a single underlying instrument, namely the associated swap.[4] Such an assumption is implicitly made by practitioners when they use the Black–Scholes (1973) formula to mark to market their books and derive their deltas. Another way of modelling the swaption consists of considering the underlying as a basket of zero-coupon bonds, which can be priced independently in the market, and have their own volatility structure. This latter approach fits better within the framework of interest rates models which tend to specify the volatility structure of zero-coupon bonds. We will keep our topic very general in this section, consequently we consider that the volatility structure of zero-coupon bonds is described by a function σ, which we do not intend to specify at this stage.

Let us assume that $B_{t,T}$ denotes the value at date t of a zero-coupon bond paying one dollar at date $T \geq t$. The dynamics of $B_{t,T}$ are given under Q by

$$\frac{\mathrm{d}B_{t,T}}{B_{t,T}} = r_t \, \mathrm{d}t + \sigma_{t,T} \, \mathrm{d}W_t \tag{10}$$

where r_t is the risk-free rate at date t, and $\sigma_{t,T}$ is the stochastic (or deterministic) volatility function. $(W_t)_{t\geq 0}$ is the Brownian motion under Q, possibly multidimensional, which would then imply that σ is a vector.

Let us call k the strike of the swaption. The swaption is equivalent to an option on a bond paying k annually until maturity of the swap. Let us call P_t the price at date t of the fixed-coupon bond, whose value equals

$$P_t = \sum_{i=1}^{N-1} kB_{t,T_i} + (100 + k)B_{t,T_N} \tag{11}$$

The price U_0 of the swaption at date 0 (we take, for example, the call case) equals

$$U_0 = \mathrm{E}^Q \left[\max \left(\sum_{i=1}^{N-1} kB_{T,T_i} + (100 + k)B_{T,T_N} - 100; 0 \right) \Big/ \beta_T \right] \tag{12}$$

Let us now denote by ξ the exercise domain, here simply defined by $P_T > 100$. $\mathbf{I}$ stands for the indicatrix function ($\mathbf{I} = 1$ if the option is exercised, and 0 otherwise). Developing the previous expression, we get

$$U_0 = \sum_{i=1}^{N-1} \mathrm{E}^Q[kB_{T,T_i}\mathbf{I}_\xi / \beta_T] + \mathrm{E}^Q[(100 + k)B_{T,T_N}\mathbf{I}_\xi / \beta_T] - \mathrm{E}^Q[100\mathbf{I}_\xi / \beta_T] \tag{13}$$

It is possible to simplify the latter expression by choosing for each expectation in the equation a suitable numeraire. Let us call Q_{T_i} (resp. Q_T) the risk-neutral probability associated with the zero-coupon bond maturing at date T_i (resp. T) as a numeraire. Q_{T_i} is usually called the T_i-forward probability, in the sense that the value of an asset expressed in the numeraire B_{t,T_i} equals its forward price maturing at date T_i. Using equation (7), where S_t is replaced by B_{t,T_i}, and taking $t = 0$, we get the following expression for U_0:

$$U_0 = \sum_{i=1}^{N-1} kB_{0,T_i}\mathrm{E}^Q \left[\frac{\mathrm{d}Q_{T_i}}{\mathrm{d}Q}\mathbf{I}_\xi \right] + (100 + k)B_{0,T_N}\mathrm{E}^Q \left[\frac{\mathrm{d}Q_{T_N}}{\mathrm{d}Q}\mathbf{I}_\xi \right] - 100B_{0,T}\mathrm{E}^Q \left[\frac{\mathrm{d}Q_T}{\mathrm{d}Q}\mathbf{I}_\xi \right] \tag{14}$$

Changing the probabilities in the expectations, we get the final result:

$$U_0 = \sum_{i=1}^{N-1} kB_{0,T_i}\mathrm{E}^{Q_{T_i}}[\mathbf{I}_\xi] + (100 + k)B_{0,T_N}\mathrm{E}^{Q_{T_N}}[\mathbf{I}_\xi] - 100B_{0,T}\mathrm{E}^{Q_T}[\mathbf{I}_\xi] \tag{15}$$

where $\mathrm{E}^{Q_{T_i}}[\mathbf{I}_\xi]$ (resp. $\mathrm{E}^{Q_T}[\mathbf{I}_\xi]$) can be replaced by $Q_{T_i}(\xi)$ (resp. $Q_T(\xi)$), representing the probabilities of the swaption to be exercised, taken under the successive forward probabilities.

8.1.4 Hedging a Swaption

The valuation equation (15) is interesting because it is very general, and it does not depend on the volatility function that is ultimately chosen. Interestingly, it is easy to relate this equation with the Black–Scholes formula which is commonly used to price swaptions:

$$U_0^{\mathrm{bs}} = S_0\mathrm{N}(d_1) - 100B_{0,T}\mathrm{N}(d_0) \tag{16}$$

where the ratios $N(d_i)$ equal probabilities of the option to be exercised, calculated respectively with the numeraire P_t (the underlying fixed-coupon bond), and the zero-coupon bond maturing at date T. $N(d_1)$ is well known to be the δ-ratio of the option, which gives the amount to invest at date 0 in the underlying in order to hedge the swaption.

From equation (15), hedge ratios can be calculated the same way, namely by differentiating both members with respect to infinitesimal price changes in the hedge instruments. In a general framework, we assume that the whole curve of zero-coupon bonds can be traded in the market, which implies that the hedging strategy gives individual ratios for every coupon payment date. Differentiating with respect to B_{0,T_i} (resp. B_{0,T_N}), we deduce from equation (15) that $kQ_{T_i}(\xi)$ (resp. $(100 + k)Q_{T_N}(\xi)$) is the right amount to invest in each individual zero-coupon bond in order to hedge the swaption. Whereas the Black–Scholes formula gives a single ratio for a unique underlying, the general formula diversifies the hedge ratio across maturities.

The discrepancy that is often pointed out between a Black–Scholes model and a more general model of interest rates relies on the way the hedge is performed. Hence, it is important to describe as precisely as possible what affects the ratios in the general case. Naturally, the volatility structure is the only explanatory variable that implies such a discrepancy.

In the Black–Scholes case, the volatility of the bond P_t is assumed to be a constant, which we denote γ. The ratio $N(d_1)$ is known to be different from the money market ratio $N(d_0)$ in the sense that

$$d_1 = d_0 + \sqrt{\gamma^2 T} \tag{17}$$

where $\gamma^2 T$ represents the variance of the log return of P between 0 and T.

Unfortunately, there is no general formula for the ratios $Q_{T_i}(\xi)$, but some specific cases exist. Among these, we find the Vasicek model (and its extended version within the Heath, Jarrow and Morton (1992) framework, which allows for a perfect fit of the initial term structure, see Chapter 5 for more details). Assuming that the volatility structure is time homogeneous implies a decreasing exponential form for $\sigma_{t,T}$:

$$\sigma_{t,T} = \frac{1 - e^{-\lambda(T-t)}}{\lambda} \sigma \tag{18}$$

where λ is the rate of return of interest rates to their mean, and σ is the instantaneous variance parameter of the risk-free rate r_t.

The explicit calculation of the ratios (see El Karoui et al. (1995) and Jamshidian (1989)) have an interpretation in terms of the variance of interest rates very close to the one given in the Black–Scholes case: $Q_{T_i}(\xi)$ (resp. $Q_T(\xi)$) equals $N(d_i)$ (resp. $N(d_0)$) for given real numbers d_i (resp. d_0) which relate to each other as follows:

$$d_i = d_0 + \sqrt{\int_0^T (\sigma_{s,T_i} - \sigma_{s,T})^2 \, ds} \tag{19}$$

where $\int_0^T (\sigma_{s,T_i} - \sigma_{s,T})^2 \, ds$ is the variance of the random variable $\int_T^{T_i} r_s \, ds$. Because the interest rates are Gaussian when $\sigma_{t,T}$ is a deterministic function, the probabilities of the option to be exercised reduce to the probabilities of a suitably normalized Gaussian distribution to reach a given barrier. Consequently, the ratios depend on the usual cumulative function of a normal distribution $N(\cdot)$.

It is important to note that the series $d_0, d_1, \ldots, d_N$ is strictly increasing. This implies in particular that there is no way one could make equation (15) fit the Black–Scholes equation (16) perfectly.[5]

This result clarifies the way unified models drive off the Black–Scholes model for the pricing and hedging of interest rates options: the main issue is the diversification of the hedging portfolio, which is highly dependent on the shape of the volatility structure that is chosen for the zero-coupon bond curve.

Finally, we remark that, within the Cox–Ingersoll–Ross (CIR) framework, it is well known that interest rates are described by non-central χ^2 density functions (see Chapter 5 for more details). Under such a specification, Chen and Scott (1992) found a pricing formula for swaptions, similar to equation (19), where the terms $N(d_i)$ are replaced by χ^2-probabilities of the exercise domain. Under general specifications, numerical procedures are necessary to perform the valuation of the ratios $Q_{T_i}(\xi)$.

8.2 HEDGING SWAPTIONS AGAINST YIELD CURVE SCENARIOS

One could say that three major problems occur when one decides to implement an interest rates model to price a book of swap derivatives. First, the deltas of the book should be set to 0 frequently for all maturities affecting the portfolio. Therefore the prices of the derivatives should take into account the specific risk of each individual zero rate. Another important problem is to mark to market the volatility structure of interest rates. This implies the requirement that the option prices are consistent with implied volatilities quoted in the market. Two questions arise which we will try to answer separately: How do we mark to market the term structure of volatility? How do we deal with the smile effect?

In this section we give some insight into the calibration of a model so that the prices of derivatives actually take into account the cost of delta neutral hedging. We assume that the term structure of interest rates evolves within a domain which can be estimated from historical scenarios.

8.2.1 The Hedging Space

The natural information a risk-dealer would require is to identify precisely the set of yield curves for which his position can be considered as riskless. If, for example, the model is unable to valuate an inverted yield curve, then the portfolio hedged with such a model becomes risky as soon as the curve inverts. The appendix studies the space of deformation of the yield curve in the case of deterministic volatilities. The model then reduces to a Gaussian model of interest rates, for which the volatility term structure is a linear combination of decreasing exponential functions. The yield curve itself evolves within a linear manifold also generated by decreasing exponential functions (see equations (49) and (50) of the appendix for more details). This result emphasizes one of the main properties of interest rates models, namely the fact that the space in which the rates evolve is highly dependent on the space of the volatility structure. The practical implications of this result are extremely important in the sense that one has to decide what to privilege in the calibration of the model: it is virtually impossible to control separately the shape of the future yield curves and the volatility structure of bonds.

8.2.2 Estimation Methods

We now focus on estimation methods based on historical data. We limit our presentation to the class of linear models with a finite set of state variables driving the market. Usually, the first step in data analysis consists of extracting zero-coupon yields. We therefore assume that the set of data consists of observations of zero yields, which we denote by $(Y_{t,T})_{T \geq t}$ (given by $Y_{t,T} = -1/(T-t) \ln B_{t,T}$).

The natural setting for the statistical model is derived from the linear properties we discussed earlier. For every date t, the zero rates $(Y_{t,T})_{T \geq t}$ are assumed to be linearly dependent on n state variables, which we denote by the n-dimensional vector z_t:[6]

$$Y_{t,T} = A(T-t)^{\mathrm{T}} z_t + B(T-t) \tag{20}$$

where $A(T-t)$ and $B(T-t)$ are n-dimensional vectors deterministically depending on $T-t$, and T denotes the transpose operator. This equation (20) is called the static equation of the model, in the sense that it describes the invariant relationship between interest rates and z_t.

The dynamics of the model are given by the stochastic differential equation followed by the state variables z_t:

$$dz_t = (M - \Lambda z_t) \, dt + \Gamma(z_t) \, dW_t \tag{21}$$

where W_t is the n-dimensional Brownian motion, M is a time independent n-vector, and Λ and $\Gamma(z_t)$ are (n, n) matrices. The set of equations (20) and (21) completely defines the statistical framework.

Examples

1. In the Gaussian model, the matrix Γ is a constant matrix, which makes the stochastic differential equation a multi-dimensional Ornstein–Ulhenbeck process. The model therefore reduces to a multi-dimensional Vasicek process (see Langetieg (1980)). Under such a specification, each component of the vector $A(T-t)$ is an exponential function $[1 - e^{\lambda_i(T-t)}]/(\lambda_i(T-t))$, where the parameters $(\lambda_i)_{i=1,...,n}$ are the eigenvalues of matrix Λ in (21).

2. In a more general linear model (see Frachot and Lesne (1996)), Γ depends on z_t in such a way that the instantaneous variance–covariance matrix of z_t, namely $\Gamma^{\mathrm{T}}\Gamma$, depends linearly on z_t:

$$\Gamma^{\mathrm{T}}\Gamma = \alpha z_t + \beta \tag{22}$$

for constant (n, n) matrices α and β. The support function $A(T-t)$ is then the solution of the Ricatti equation:

$$A'(\cdot) = A(0) + \Lambda A(\cdot) - \tfrac{1}{2}A(\cdot)\alpha A(\cdot)^T \tag{23}$$

One can consider that setting α to zero yields to the previous Gaussian case.

Various statistical methods propose consistent estimations of the model described by equations (20) and (21). To our knowledge, all methods are based on maximization of the likelihood function of the model. Unfortunately, the likelihood function cannot be expressed analytically in the general case when Γ depends on z_t. In such a case, indirect inference methods, recently developed in particular by Gouriéroux et al. (1993), are the adequate methods to perform the estimation. The basic idea of this theory is to derive the likelihood function from simulations, and to head towards the true values of the parameters by maximizing the simulated likelihood function. This method has been proven to converge, and it satisfies the usual central limit theorems that allow for the calculation of confidence intervals.

Because of its high computational cost, many authors (see, for example, Chen and Scott (1993) and Geyer and Pichner (1996)) have preferred to discretize the dynamics (21) of z_t by a locally Gaussian process, of the kind

$$z_{t+\Delta t} = (M - \Lambda z_t)\Delta t + \Gamma(z_t) \in_t \sqrt{\Delta t} \qquad (24)$$

where $\in_t$ is a n-dimensional centred normal distribution with variance equal to the identical n-matrix. Such a simplification has the advantage of allowing for the use of a Kalman filter to estimate the quasi-likelihood function of the model.

In the simpler case of a Gaussian model, equations (20) and (21) define a Kalman filter. Therefore, it is easy to perform a robust estimation of the various parameters of the model by maximizing the filter likelihood function (see, for example, Gouriéroux and Monfort (1989) or Harvey (1989) for a detailed presentation of Kalman filters).[7]

8.2.3 Empirical Results

In this subsection we reproduce some empirical results El Karoui et al. (1996) obtained on European swap market data, in order to give the reader an insight into how these models fit with historical observations of interest rates. The method used is the maximization of the likelihood function given by the Kalman filter (20) and (21) when the matrix Γ does not depend on z_t. Therefore the model is a multifactor Gaussian model.

Table 8.1 shows the estimated values of the mean-reversion parameters $(\lambda_i)_{i=1,...,n}$ introduced in equation (48), as well as the volatility parameters allowing for a complete description of the matrix Γ. Confidence intervals are given in parentheses beside the estimated values. For all markets we have studied, n has been chosen equal to 2, except for the Japanese market, and for the British market for the period preceding the exit of the United Kingdom from the EMS in November 1992. In these two special cases, contrarily with the other sets of data, a principal components analysis of the swap interest rates curves shows that more than 95 per cent of the total variance of rates are explained by a single state variable. The subsequent importance of this predominant factor, as well as the bell shape of the residuals, usually typical of the third factor in other economies (see Litterman and Scheinkman (1991) for an earlier analysis of US bond data), led us to reduce n to one.

A remarkable feature of these results is the very tight confidence intervals we get for the parameters λ. These parameters fully describe the hedging space of the model proven to be generated by the functions $([1 - e^{\lambda_i(T-t)}]/(\lambda_i(T-t)))_{i=1,...,n}$.[8] The great stability of the estimated space of deformation is a remarkable empirical property, which has often been pointed out by academics as well as practitioners who performed principal components analysis of yield curves. Consequently, it is interesting to compare the values of Table 8.1 with values directly inferred from fitting the PCA factors with exponential functions. Table 8.2 shows the new λ' parameters we get, as well as the R^2 of the optimal fit. We also show the proportion of the total variance explained by the predominant factors.

Table 8.1

Currency	λ_1	λ_2
FF	0.1519 (0.0044)	1.7708 (0.0409)
ITL	0.0651 (0.0034)	1.8458 (0.0534)
JPY	0.2155 (0.0028)	
UK1	0.2137 (0.0061)	
UK2	0.1998 (0.0142)	1.3725 (0.0999)

Currency	γ_1	γ_2	ρ
FF	2.0223 (0.2088)	7.6653 (0.6362)	−0.6535 (0.0809)
ITL	2.2954 (0.2196)	8.3882 (0.7509)	−0.4441 (0.1101)
JPY	1.0695 (0.1131)		
UK1	2.7887 (0.3686)		
UK2	3.1129 (0.4475)	1.6857 (0.2429)	−0.9339 (0.0290)

Table 8.2

Currency	λ_1'	λ_2'	$1 - R^2$	Total Variance
FF	0.149	1.805	5.71×10^{-4}	99.4%
ITL	0.059	1.846	2.09×10^{-3}	99.2%
JPY	0.215		4.10×10^{-3}	98.4%
UK1	0.214		4.63×10^{-3}	96.9%
UK2	0.288	0.863	4.92×10^{-3}	96.8%

The PCA factors prove to be very well described by exponential functions, and the estimated parameters $(\lambda_i')_{i=1,2}$ are very close to those estimated by maximizing the Kalman filter. This result is very interesting in practice, considering the necessity of having good initial values in order to get a quick convergence of the optimization algorithm of the Kalman filter likelihood function, which is highly non-linear.

In the case of the second period of the British market, this property is not as robust as in the other markets. This is due to the particular shape of the variance–covariance of rates. Figure 8.1 represents the two main PCA factors. The non-monotonic shape of the first factor is due to a non-standard term structure of volatility of interest rates: the variance is higher for the two-year rate than the three-month rate. Figure 8.2 plots the historical standard deviations of zero-rates with time to maturity ranging from 1 month to 10 years.

The same phenomenon was also observed on the term structure of implied volatility of caps and floors. Such a non-standard behaviour, which is inadmissible for one-factor models, can be described within a Gaussian multifactor framework when allowing for a high correlation parameter (−0.93 in Table 8.2) between two different state variables.[9]

8.2.4 Concluding Remarks on Historical Data

The estimation performed in the case of a Gaussian model can easily be extended to non-Gaussian cases using similar estimation methods. A noticeable empirical result that Steven Schaefer presented at the 1995 Cambridge workshop on Mathematical Finance showed that Gaussian models tend to provide a better fit to market data than CIR-type models, which sometimes work poorly in reproducing the historical space of deformation.

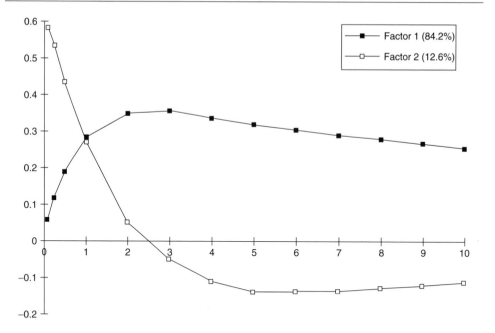

Figure 8.1   PCA factors for the British market (1992–95)

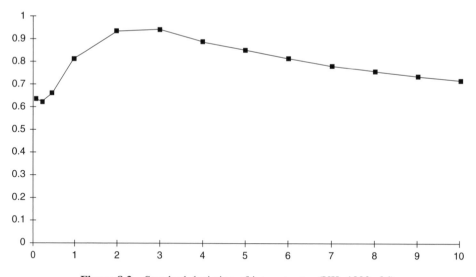

Figure 8.2   Standard deviation of interest rates (UK, 1992–96)

However, the more general linear models (see Frachot et al. (1995)), which combine both characteristics (having a variance that is affine instead of being either constant or proportional to rates), give interesting results. When the model is appropriate, the results are qualitatively analogous to ours: the swap curves are well represented by a small number of factors, and the estimation we get for the parameters defining the hedging space are stable and have good confidence intervals.

This is not always the case for other parameters, such as the volatility parameters, which tend to depend quite highly on the observation period. Assuming that the parameters γ_1 and γ_2 estimated in Table 8.1 are stable is also much too optimistic considering the fact that implied volatilities of interest rates derivatives have their own quotations, and prove to be highly time dependent. The next section presents some ideas on how to deal with such a problem in the context of mark to market of implied volatilities.

Another interesting empirical feature, which has important practical implications, is the great stability of the correlation parameter ρ between the factors. This tends to prove that the market behaves historically with a rather fixed correlation between rates. The comparison of cap and swaption prices depends almost uniquely on the correlation parameter: the state variable whose mean reversion parameter is lower (for example $\lambda_1 = 0.1519$ for the French market) leads to long-term interest rate movements and therefore explains mainly swaption prices, whereas the short part of the curve is led by both variables (for $\lambda_2 = 1.7$, the state variable explains only movements of the yield curve for two or three years). Consequently, captions depend on both variables. Knowing that the parameter ρ tends to be historically stable should therefore have interesting practical implications.

Figure 8.3 reproduces the series of short-term and long-term rates, together with the series followed by the state variables estimated by the Kalman filter (for the French market). This figure illustrates the fact that the variables driving the model are combinations of interest rates, one of the two variables leading predominantly the long-term rate.

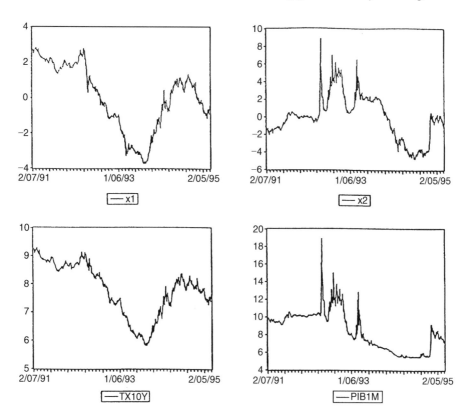

Figure 8.3 Comparison of interest rates and state variables series

8.3 MARKING TO MARKET THE TERM STRUCTURE OF VOLATILITY

There is truly a difficult problem to address, which concerns the mark-to-market procedure of derivative products. The caption and, to a less extent the swaption market is liquid enough to be taken as the benchmark for all risk-dealers. There is no choice but to use implied volatilities to price current positions on derivatives. This viewpoint might be considered as exclusive from the one outlined in the previous section. Indeed, calibrating the model to historical data implies a specific shape of the term structure of volatility, which we denoted by $\sigma_{t,T}$. There is no a priori reason why the market should price the term structure of implied volatility consistently with such historically estimated parameters.

One way to deal with this important issue consists of allowing for market driven parameters in the model. As our empirical results pointed out, the volatility parameters (defining the matrix Γ) tend to be the most unstable parameters. A natural extension of the estimation procedure would be to calibrate these parameters with daily quotations of derivatives products, namely captions, and, in a second step, swaptions.

In this section we intend to describe how to do so using the pricing formulas the model provides for cap options. In the final subsection we present an alternative approach, initiated by Brace and Musiela (1994), who use non-parametric estimation of $\sigma_{t,T}$ from cap prices, and drive off the specific shapes implied by finite dimensional models, without losing the important property of time homogeneity of the volatility structure.[10]

8.3.1 Captions

Captions are strips of caplets. Each individual caplet, maturing at date T, is an option on a δ-Libor[11] rate maturing at date $T + \delta$, which we denote $L(T)$. $L(T)$ is related to zero-bond prices using the following equation:

$$L(T) = \frac{1}{\delta} \left(\frac{1}{B_{T,T+\delta}} - 1 \right) \tag{25}$$

Let us denote by k the strike of the caplet. The payoff function, paid at date T, equals:[12]

$$C_T = \delta \max(L(T) - k; 0) B_{T,T+\delta} \tag{26}$$

which can be written, using bond prices, as

$$C_T = \max(1 - (1 + k\delta) B_{T,T+\delta}; 0) \tag{27}$$

This expression proves that a caplet is nothing other than a put option on a zero bond. It is also an option on a one-period swap (or FRA contract).

Using the change of numeraire technique outlined in Section 8.1, we get the following pricing formula:

$$C_0 = B_{0,T} Q_T(\xi) - (1 + k\delta) B_{0,T+\delta} Q_{T+\delta}(\xi) \tag{28}$$

where ξ denotes the exercise domain, and Q_T and $Q_{T+\delta}$ are the risk-neutral probabilities with respective numeraires $B_{t,T}$ and $B_{t,T+\delta}$.

This formula is equivalent to formula (15) previously exhibited for swaptions, written with a single payment date T_i. At this stage we need to calculate the exercise probabilities

$Q_T(\xi)$ and $Q_{T+\delta}(\xi)$. We give two examples of explicit formulas for the case of Gaussian and CIR models.

(i) Gaussian Assumption

Under the Gaussian assumption, the zero-coupon bond $B_{T,T+\delta}$ is log-normally distributed with variance $v^2 = \int_0^T |\sigma_{s,T+\delta} - \sigma_{s,T}|^2 \, ds$.[13] Formula (28) therefore reduces to a Black–Scholes put formula on the zero bond:

$$C_0 = B_{0,T} N(-d_0) - (1 + k\delta) B_{0,T+\delta} N(-d_0 - v) \qquad (29)$$

where d_0 is given by

$$d_0 = \frac{1}{v} \left(\ln \frac{(1 + k\delta) B_{0,T+\delta}}{B_{0,T}} - \frac{1}{2} v^2 \right) \qquad (30)$$

(ii) CIR Model

In the CIR framework, the dynamics of the short rate under Q are given by

$$dr_t = a(b - r_t) \, dt + \sigma \sqrt{r_t} \, dW_t \qquad (31)$$

As noted by El Karoui et al. (1995), the short rate distributions under both probabilities Q_T and $Q_{T+\delta}$ are non-central χ^2, with respective parameters of non-centrality q_0 and q_1. This property allows for an explicit formula, which was exhibited by Cox et al. (1985):

$$C_0 = B_{0,T} \chi^2(d_0, n, q_0) - (1 + k\delta) \chi^2(d_1, n, q_1) \qquad (32)$$

where $\chi^2(\cdot, n, q)$ is the non-centered χ^2 distribution with n degrees of freedom and parameter of non-centrality q. n, q_0, q_1, d_0 and d_1 depend on a, b and σ.

Using the techniques of time changes and rescaling, introduced independently by Geman and Yor (1993), Maghsoodi (1996) derives an extension of formula (32) in the case of time dependent parameters a, b and σ.

When such formulas are available, the calibration of the term structure of volatility extracted from cap and floor prices is possible as soon as it fits within the parametric shape given by $\sigma_{t,T}$.

It is interesting to consider the way the pricing formula (29) behaves for an at-the-money option. A caplet is said to be at-the-money-forward when its strike rate equals the forward Libor rate at date 0 for the period $[T, T + \delta]$, which we denote L_0^f. L_0^f is given by

$$L_0^f = \frac{1}{\delta} \left(\frac{B_{0,T}}{B_{0,T+\delta}} - 1 \right) \qquad (33)$$

When $k = L_0^f$, the put option on the zero bond priced by (29) is at the money. Indeed $B_{0,T} = (1 + k\delta) B_{0,T+\delta}$. Hence the pricing formula reduces to

$$C_0 = B_{0,T} (N(-d_0) - N(-d_0 - v)) \qquad (34)$$

We can consider that v is a sufficiently small number to allow for a Taylor's development:

$$C_0 \sim B_{0,T} N'(-d_0) v \qquad (35)$$

which means that the at-the-money-forward caplets are proportional to the log variance of bonds, which depends solely on the volatility function $\sigma_{t,T}$.

Using the parametric expression of $\sigma_{t,T}$ given by the model the volatility parameters of the state variables driving the market can be chosen in order to get the best fit of v with implicit volatilities.

Obviously, there is little chance that the term structure of volatility can be exactly replicated in terms of decreasing exponential functions.[14] At this stage, we have to decide what to privilege: either the hedging domain is chosen to be most important, in the sense that the hedging performance will depend highly on its ability to reproduce the historical support of deformations, and then at least the mean-reversion parameters are assumed to be historically estimated; or the information of the derivatives market is considered as more important, in the sense that marking to market the implicit volatility is a requirement that needs to be satisfied.

8.3.2 Non-Parametric Estimation of the Volatility Structure

Consequently, some authors have proposed models of the term structure that allow for a non-parametric estimation of the volatility function. Most of these models (see Brace and Musiela (1994) and Kennedy (1994)) are Gaussian, even though the same ideas could be used in non-Gaussian frameworks.[15] The main idea is to allow for the model to depend on a non-finite set of state variables, namely the continuous set of instantaneous forward rates. Within the Heath–Jarrow–Morton framework, the whole yield curve is assumed to evolve randomly, following a stochastic differential equation given by

$$\mathrm{d}f_{t,T} = \mu_{t,T}\,\mathrm{d}t + \partial_T\sigma_{t,T}\,\mathrm{d}W_t \tag{36}$$

where $(f_{t,T})_{T\geq t}$ represents the instantaneous forward rates at date t, $\mu_{t,T}$ the drift function of the forward rate $f_{t,T}$, and $\partial_T\sigma_{t,T}$ its volatility, which is related to the bond volatility $\sigma_{t,T}$ by a partial differentiation with respect to the maturity argument T.

Considering the dynamics (36) under the risk-neutral probability Q, Heath et al. (1992) proved that $\mu_{t,T}$ is fully described by the volatility function. Put in a slightly different form, this result can be expressed as follows:

$$\mathrm{d}f_{t,t+\theta} = \left(\frac{\partial f_{t,t+\theta}}{\partial\theta} + \sigma_{t,t+\theta}\partial_\theta\sigma_{t,t+\theta}\right)\mathrm{d}t + \partial_\theta\sigma_{t,t+\theta}\,\mathrm{d}W_t \tag{37}$$

where the maturity argument T has been replaced by $t+\theta$, θ representing the time to maturity.

Equation (37) is very important because it proves that under the risk-neutral probability, the drift of a given forward rate $f_{t,t+\theta}$ is partly explained by a volatility bias, and on the other hand is driven by the derivative of the forward rate curve at time to maturity θ.

In the general case, when the volatility function $\sigma_{t,T}$, assumed to be deterministic, is not chosen specifically, the process followed by $\partial f_{t,t+\theta}/\partial\theta$ is not related to $f_{t,t+\theta}$. More precisely, $\partial f_{t,t+\theta}/\partial\theta$ and $f_{t,t+\theta}$ are deterministically related to one another if and only if the instantaneous variance of $\partial f_{t,t+\theta}/\partial\theta$ is proportional to the $f_{t,t+\theta}$ variance, which means

$$\partial_\theta^2\sigma_{t,t+\theta} = \lambda\partial_\theta\sigma_{t,t+\theta} \tag{38}$$

for some constant λ. The solution of equation (38) is an exponential volatility function, and the model therefore reduces to a Vasicek-type model.

The same argument stands for the successive derivatives of $f_{t,t+\theta}$: if the volatility function is not a solution of the differential equation already described in the appendix by equation (47), then the model is driven by an infinite set of variables: $f_{t,t+\theta}$ is driven by $\partial f_{t,t+\theta}/\partial\theta$, which is itself driven by $\partial^2 f_{t,t+\theta}/\partial\theta^2$, which is itself driven by $\partial^3 f_{t,t+\theta}/\partial\theta^3$, etc... knowing that none of these variables is redundant. As a result, the hedging domain of the model is itself going to have an infinite dimension, and is therefore going to be much more general (and richer) than in the case of finite dimensional models.

The very attractive feature of this model is that the formula (29) given previously to price a caplet is still valid under such general specifications of the volatility structure. It is therefore possible to extract the volatility function from market prices, without being obliged to stick to a parametric form. This is why the model can be called *non-parametric*. Such an estimation is done with great care in the last section of Brace and Musiela (1994), using market prices of at-the-money caps and floors.

At this stage, one might think that such a model performs extremely well, being able to reproduce any historical deformation, and allowing for a perfect fit of the term structure of volatility. However, such general properties have inevitably some drawbacks. First, even though equation (15) is still valid, there is no explicit solution for the ratio $Q_{T_i}(\xi)$. This can make the pricing of a swaption uneasy.[16] Considering also the fact that a general model of interest rates becomes necessary when pricing more complex instruments, namely exotics and path-dependent options, consistently with market prices, this model has the drawback of being difficult to implement numerically. Indeed, the fact that an infinite number of stochastic variables is required to replicate the time evolution of the interest rates makes it impossible to use recombining trees or numerical resolution schemes of partial differential equations. As a result, simulation-based methods, or non-recombining trees are the adequate instruments to use.

Another important point to raise is the fact that the model is entirely estimated from derivatives products. Obviously, the non-parametric form of the volatility is going to change daily, according to the changes of the term structure of at-the-money options. The user of the model therefore has to question the possibility of having unstable volatility functions, the model being entirely "market-driven".

8.3.3 Concluding Remarks

In this section we emphasized the mark to market of the term structure of volatility. For the sake of simplicity, we have restricted our presentation to caption prices, for which we have explicit formulas. The same kind of problem arises when extending the arguments to swaptions.

Mainly, our goal was to exhibit the following dilemma: either one chooses to fit the model perfectly with derivatives prices, which is possible within an infinite dimensional model, and in that case the model is entirely driven by the derivatives market, or one prefers to estimate a given number of parameters historically (namely the mean-reversion parameters, for example, in a Gaussian framework), and then ends up fitting a parametric form of the volatility with market data.

8.4 IS THERE A "MARKET MODEL OF INTEREST RATES"?

The previous section studied the problem of marking to market the volatility term structure. However, no insight has been given into the way the models deal with the behaviour of out-of-the-money options. Put another way: How do the models deal with the important issue of the smile effect?

Most practitioners use the traditional Black–Scholes formula to price their book of interest rates derivatives. Daily, volatility parameters are put into the formula, depending on the time to maturity of the options, and how far they are from the money. In such a context, the choice of a unique model to price all the positions at the same time (basically, using the same set of parameters) has a very important impact on the profit and loss of the book, in the sense that most models drive off the Black–Scholes prices, in particular for far-off-the-money options.

The use of the Black–Scholes formula for caplets and floorlets is based on the assumption that Libor rates are log-normal, centred around the forward values extracted from the current zero-coupon curve. Therefore many authors and practitioners have been interested in models where the interest rates are log-normal, rather than Gaussian, as in Vasicek (1977) or squared Gaussian as in Cox et al. (1985). Among these models, one can quote Dothan (1978), Black et al. (1990) and Black and Karasinsky (1991). All these authors propose specifying a given stochastic differential equation for the instantaneous spot rate r_t, such that its distribution is log-normal. As in other models, solutions are given for the zero-yield curve, as well as the bond prices, and numerical implementations are proposed to solve the partial differential equations followed by contingent claims such as caplets and swaptions.

Morton (1988) and Hogan and Weintraub (1993) were the first to show that such models have the very unpleasant feature of allowing for the rates to explode with positive probability, implying zero prices for some bonds, or infinite premium for the Eurodollar futures.

Along those lines, some authors, namely Miltersen et al. (1997) and Brace et al. (1997), have studied the possibility of exhibiting a general model of interest rates, satisfying the regularity conditions and set within the Heath–Jarrow–Morton framework, which would be able to replicate exactly the Black–Scholes formula for caplets and floorlets. The main idea of these two papers consists in assuming that the corresponding Libor rate itself, rather than the continuously compounded instantaneous short rate r_t, is log-normal. Hence the effort is put in satisfying the Heath–Jarrow–Morton assumptions together with log-normal Libor rates, rather than exhibiting the dynamics of r_t.

An important point can be discussed from describing the price of a caplet as the expected value of its discounted final payoff:

$$C_0 = \mathrm{E}^Q \left[\delta \max(L(T) - k) \exp\left(-\int_0^{T+\delta} r_s \, ds \right) \right] \tag{39}$$

where $L(T)$ represents the δ-Libor rate set at date T, the payoff being paid at date $T + \delta$. Introducing the $(T + \delta)$-forward probability defined in (7) by

$$\left(\frac{dQ_{T+\delta}}{dQ} \right)_{T+\delta} = \frac{1}{B_{0,T+\delta} \beta_{T+\delta}} \tag{40}$$

and for which $B_{t,T+\delta}$ is the numeraire, equation (39) reduces to the following:

$$C_0 = B_{0,T+\delta} \mathrm{E}^{Q_{T+\delta}} [\delta \max(L(T) - k)] \tag{41}$$

The important point emphasized by this latter equation is that the price depends on the expectation of the payoff function under the only $(T + \delta)$-forward probability. As a result, the Black–Scholes formula will be recovered if and only if the rate $L(T)$ is log-normal under the probability $Q_{T+\delta}$, and not necessarily under the usual risk-neutral probability Q. In fact, it has be proven that under Q, the Libor rate is led to be a mixture of log-normal and normal distributions: when the Libor is close to 0, its behaviour is well described by a log-normal distribution, and when its value becomes large, its behaviour is better described by a Gaussian distribution.

Let us now assume, for the sake of the argument, that under the probability $Q_{T+\delta}$, the forward Libor rate for the period $[T, T + \delta]$ which we denote by L_t^f given by equation (33), follows the stochastic differential equation:

$$\frac{dL_t^f}{L_t^f} = \gamma_{t,T} \, dW_t^{T+\delta} \tag{42}$$

where $(W_t^{T+\delta})_{t\geq 0}$ is the standard Brownian Motion under probability $Q^{T+\delta}$, and $\gamma_{t,T}$ represents the volatility of the forward rate. Let us note that at date T, we have $L(T) = L_T^f$.

Under such an assumption, the expectation (42) can be calculated explicitly, and we recover the Black–Scholes formula for the caplet:

$$C_0 = B_{0,T+\delta}\delta(L_0^f N(d_1) - kN(d_1 - v_{0,T})) \tag{43}$$

where

$$v_{0,T}^2 = \int_0^T \gamma_{s,T}^2 \, ds \tag{44}$$

and

$$d_1 = \frac{\ln(L_0^f/k) + \frac{1}{2}v_{0,T}^2}{v_{0,T}} \tag{45}$$

In a way, the arguments that led to formula (43) replicate precisely the practitioners arguments who use Black–Scholes formula to price options on Libor rates. The only (and essential) difference is the fact that the dynamics of the forward Libor rates (42) are given under the forward probability rather than under the usual risk-neutral Q probability. At this stage, it remains to prove that the dynamics (42) are consistent with a general model of interest rates, which could therefore be used to price other derivatives. This theoretical work has been done separately by Miltersen et al. (1997) and Brace et al. (1997), who proved the existence of a Heath–Jarrow–Morton model consistent with equation (42). This result is, in a way, extremely reassuring: after something like 20 years of research on interest rates models, academics end up proving that the market has always priced consistently interest rates options, using the simplest and oldest model, namely the celebrated Black–Scholes model!

Indeed, such a unified model, which allows us, by construction, to replicate market prices for any caplet is, to a certain extent, *the* model that all risk dealers have been looking for: the mark to market of volatility can be done by calibrating the function $v_{0,T}$ in equation (44) with implied volatilities. As long as there is no important smile on caps and floors, the model is able to reproduce the prices of out-of-the-money options.

Unfortunately, this implied model, which has been fairly called by Brace et al. the "market model of interest rates", is not easily tractable when pricing derivatives other than options on Libor. In the case of swaptions, equation (15) can be approximated by a closed-formed formula which depends on Gaussian cumulative functions, like in Black–Scholes, but the exact calculation is untractable. Regarding other kinds of contingent claims, as in the previous case of non-finite-dimensional models, numerical problems arise, implied by the non-Markovian structure of interest rates, which makes it impossible to use robust numerical procedures.

Another important feature of the model is that the volatility structure is well defined for actual rates with the δ-compounding period corresponding to the maturity of the Libor rate taken as a benchmark for plain vanilla swaps. Unfortunately, the implied volatility structure for other kinds of rates, namely actual rates with a different compounding period, or even continuously compounded rates, is very complex, and cannot even be defined (for example, in the case of the instantaneous spot rate r_t). These drawbacks are the usual counterpart of the great flexibility of the model regarding the specific pricing problem of captions.

In this final section we have shown that it is indeed possible to build a model which allows for a perfect replication of market caption prices, recovering the Black–Scholes formula. Consequently, the mark-to-market problem can be solved — as long as the implied volatilities of out-of-the-money options do not drive too far away from at-the-money options.

One could argue that there exists a smile effect on interest rates derivatives which makes Black–Scholes fail even on a given set of caplets maturing at the same maturity date. It is truly possible to extract from such a set of prices the implied distribution of rates, as various authors (see, for example, Dupire (1993)) have done for other markets like stocks and foreign exchange rates. From such an analysis we can infer the optimal model, among Gaussian, squared Gaussian, or log-normal, that fits the actual implied distribution.

As a conclusion, the possibilities of choice of a general model of interest rates are very wide, in terms of distributions of rates as well as for the number of degrees of freedom. Each of the models reviewed in this chapter has its advantages, but the constant features are the following: flexibility has a high price in terms of computational tractability; and more fundamentally, a very flexible model, which allows for a rich hedging space of deformation and for an exact mark-to-maket procedure, becomes statistically less and less specific, which implies that the whole set of parameters describing the model becomes essentially driven by the derivatives market.

For end users, the optimal choice might differ: a global risk manager would certainly prefer a finite-dimensional model, with robust historical estimations of constant parameters, whereas a risk dealer would privilege the ability of the model to price his derivatives book consistently with market data. Facing this permanent dilemma, the present academic trend is to consider the most general and flexible arbitrage-free models as theoretical benchmarks, which can be practically (and statistically) approximated by more tractable and simple models (namely finite dimensional and Black–Scholes models) when applied to specific products with specific objectives. However, more progress needs to be made until academics can fully explain market behaviour in a rational way.

8.5 APPENDIX

The set of admissible yield curves is represented by the support of the diffusion of interest rates. It can be proven (see Brace and Musiela (1994)) that in the case of a specified deterministic volatility function $\sigma_{t,T}$ in equation (10), the set of admissible forward yield curves is a linear manifold generated by the successive derivatives of $\sigma_{t,T}$ with respect to its second variable:

$$\text{supp}(f_{t,T})_{T\geq0} = \text{vect}(\partial_T \sigma_{t,T}, \partial_T^2 \sigma_{t,T} \ldots)_{T\geq0} \tag{46}$$

where $f(t, \cdot)$ represents the curve of instantaneous forward rates for maturities ranging from t till the longest maturity traded in the market.

For a general form of the deterministic volatility function $\sigma_{t,T}$, the dimension of the support has therefore no reason to be finite, which means that any continuous function is an admissible yield curve (see Section 8.3 for a detailed discussion of this point). Such a feature looks very attractive at first sight. However, there is a drawback to such a general property: indeed, the dimension of the support equals the minimal number of state variables for which the model becomes Markovian. As is well known, Markovian models are interesting in the sense that they allow easier computational tractability.[17] Consequently, the additional requirement that the model should be driven by a finite Markovian process has often been considered as natural by some authors (see, for example, El Karoui et al. (1996) and Duffie and Kan (1996)).[18] Equation (46) shows that the support of the distribution has a finite dimension if and only if, for a sufficiently large integer n, the nth derivative of the volatility function equals a linear combination of the $n-1$ first ones. Therefore, the function $\sigma_{t,T}$ must the solution of an ordinary differential equation of the following kind:

$$\partial_T^n \sigma_{t,\cdot} = \sum_{i=1}^{n-1} \mu_i \partial_T^i \sigma_{t,\cdot} \tag{47}$$

where $(\mu_i)_{i=1,\ldots,n-1}$ are real numbers. If we restrict the admissible set of $(\mu_i)_{i=1,\ldots,n-1}$, the solutions of such an equation are linear combinations of n decreasing exponential functions (see equation (18)) with exponential parameters solutions of the polynomial equation

$$\lambda^n = \sum_{i=1}^{n-1} \mu_i \lambda^i \tag{48}$$

This gives an exponential form of the volatility which is the classical feature of Vasicek-type models. Hence, $\sigma_{t,T}$ is an element of the linear space generated by a finite number of support functions:[19]

$$\sigma_{t,T} \in \text{vect} \left(\frac{1 - e^{-\lambda_1(T-t)}}{\lambda_1}, \ldots, \frac{1 - e^{-\lambda_n(T-t)}}{\lambda_n} \right) \tag{49}$$

whereas the support of the distribution of instantaneous forward rates is described by

$$f_{t,T} \in \text{vect}(e^{-\lambda_1(T-t)}, \ldots, e^{-\lambda_n(T-t)}) \tag{50}$$

Strictly speaking, these results are valid in the sole case of deterministic volatility structures. However, the same kind of properties stand for other models (see, for example, Duffie and Kan (1996) and El Karoui et al. (1991)). One property that is often considered as an interesting feature is the fact that the hedging space is a linear manifold (see also the recent paper by Björk and Christensen (1996)), which practically means that the relationship between interest rates and the state variables is affine. This is obviously true for Gaussian models, but it still holds for more complex ones, like the celebrated CIR model, which has the advantage of not allowing for negative interest rates. Separately, Chen and Scott (1992), Fong and Vasicek (1991), and Longstaff and Schwartz (1992), among others, proposed their own specifications, which led to multi-dimensional extensions of CIR, which still verify the linear property. This class of models have become so important that they are now well known under the name of "linear models of interest rates" (see Duffie and Kan (1996) and Frachot and Lesne (1996)). Some details about these models were given in Section 8.2.2.

8.6 ENDNOTES

1. We assume that the underlying swap contracts are plain vanilla swaps, written with respect to Libor rates, settled in arrears. Consequently, the floating leg of the swap is at par at every setting date of the Libor rate, which makes the swaption equivalent to a bond option with a par strike.
2. Or, more generally, any attainable asset.
3. We have decided to keep the usual notation Q for the risk-neutral probability associated with the money-market account. Q_β would be more consistent with the notation Q_S.
4. Or, equivalently, the fixed coupon bond paying the swap rate on a regular basis, when identifying the swaption with a bond option.
5. At least when $N > 1$. When $N = 1$, the swaption reduces to a caplet. A suitable choice of the volatility function can then make both equations fit perfectly (see Sections 8.3 and 8.4 for a discussion of this issue).
6. Equation (20) is valid for time homogeneous volatility structures. In such a case the support of the distribution of rates is invariant through time, generated by support functions $A(\cdot)$ depending on time to maturity $T - t$.
7. Let us remark that Kennedy (1997) also uses Kalman filtering to estimate his very elegant model where interest rates are described as elements of a Gaussian random field (see also Kennedy (1994) for a theoretical presentation of the model).
8. This is true for the zero-rate curve $(Y_{t,T})_{T \geq t}$. Equation (50) proved that the forward rate curve is generated by the functions $(e^{-\lambda_i(T-t)})_{i=1,\dots,n}$.
9. In such a case, the high correlation parameter makes the Kalman filter optimization program uneasy, because of the almost singular variance matrix $\Gamma^T \Gamma$. This explains the discrepancies between the parameters in Tables 8.1 and 8.2.
10. An important literature provides various methods, namely forward induction methods, in order to calibrate finite dimensional models to any volatility term structure by allowing for time dependent volatility parameters (see, for example, Hull and White (1990), Jamshidian (1995), and Maghsoodi (1996)). These methods have an obvious practical interest. However, the time homogeneity of the model remains a very critical property to require, since the convergence of statistical estimators depends highly on the stationarity of the interest rate process. Knowing that the limit theorems fail when the process loses its stationary property, one should try to systematically minimize the time heterogeneity (see, for example, El Karoui et al. (1996) for a discussion of this special point in a Gaussian framework), or avoid it (see Brace and Musiela (1994) and Kennedy (1994)).
11. δ stands for the maturity of the Libor rate, usually equal to three or six months.
12. We decided to assume that the payment date of the caplet is T. The payoff $\delta \max(L(T) - k; 0)$, usually paid at date $T + \delta$, is therefore discounted by the T value of the zero bond $B_{T,T+\delta}$ maturing at date $T + \delta$.
13. In the case of a multi-dimensional model, $|\cdot|^2$ stands for the usual norm.
14. Or Ricatti solutions.
15. The next section will study log-normal models.
16. Let us note, however, that analytical approximations are provided by Brace and Musiela.

17. A Markovian model can be dealt with using recombining trees as well as numerical resolutions of PDEs based on explicit or implicit schemes, whereas a non-Markovian model does not allow for any method but simulation-based methods, or exponential trees.

18. Some authors, like Brace and Musiela (1994) and Heath et al. (1992), do not consider this additional requirement as necessary, and use simulation methods to solve both pricing and hedging problems. Brace and Musiela (1994) proposed, in the framework of a non-Markovian Gaussian model, a closed-formed approximation for the swaption formula (15).

19. It is usual to consider only the negative roots of equations (48), which we call $(-\lambda_i)_{i=1,...,n}$. We also limit the presentation to time homogeneous volatility structures, which implies that $\sigma_{t,T}$ only depends on the time to maturity $T - t$.

8.7 REFERENCES

Black, F., Derman, E. and Toy, W. (1990) "A one-factor model of interest rates and its application to Treasury bond options". *Financial Analysts Journal*, 33–9.

Black, F. and Karasinsky, P. (1991) "Bond and option pricing when short rates are lognormal". *Financial Analysts Journal*, July–August, 52–9.

Black, F. and Scholes, M. (1973) "The pricing of options and corporate liabilities". *Journal of Political Economics*, **81**, 637–53.

Björk, T. and Christensen, B.J. (1996) "Forward rate models and invariant manifolds". Working Paper, Stockholm School of Economics, Sweden.

Brace, A. and Musiela, M. (1994) "A multifactor Gauss Markov implementation of Heath, Jarrow and Morton". *Mathematical Finance*, **4**, no. 3, 259–83.

Brace, A., Gatarek, D. and Musiela, M. (1997) "The market model of interest rate dynamics". *Mathematical Finance*, **7**, no. 2, 127–155.

Brown, R.H. and Schaefer, S. (1996) "Ten years of the real term structure". *Journal of Fixed Income*, March, 6–22.

Chen, R.R., and Scott, L. (1992) "Pricing interest rate options in a two-factor Cox–Ingersoll–Ross model of the term structure". *Review of Financial Studies*, **5**, no. 4, 613–36.

Chen, R.R. and Scott, L. (1993) "Maximum likelihood estimation for a multifactor equilibrium model of the term structure of interest rates". *Journal of Fixed Income*, December, 14–31.

Cox, J., Ingersoll, J. and Ross, S. (1985) "A theory of the term structure of interest rates". *Econometrica*, **53**, 385–407.

Dothan, L.U. (1978) "On the term structure of interest rates". *Journal of Financial Economics*, **6**, 59–69.

Duffie, D. and Kan, R. (1996) "A yield-factor model of interest rates". *Mathematical Finance*, **6**, no. 4, 379–406.

Dupire, B. (1993) "Model art". *Risk Magazine*, **6**, no. 9, 119–26.

El Karoui, N., Geman, H. and Lacoste, V. (1996) "On the role of state variables in interest rates models". Working Paper, ESSEC, France.

El Karoui, N., Geman, H. and Rochet, J.C. (1995) "Changes of numeraire, changes of probability measure and option pricing". *Journal of Applied Probability*, **32**, 443–58.

El Karoui, N., Myneni, R. and Viswanathan, R. (1991) "Arbitrage pricing and hedging of interest rate claims with state variables, theory and application". Working Paper, Université Paris VI.

Fong, G. and Vasicek, O. (1991) "Fixed-income volatility management". *Journal of Portfolio Management*, Summer, 41–46.

Frachot, A. and Lesne, J.P. (1996) "Linear models of interest rates". Working Paper, Banque de France, Paris.

Frachot, A., Lesne, J.P. and Renault, E. (1995) "Indirect inference of factor models of the term structure of interest rates". Working Paper, Université de Cergy, Thema.

Geman, H. and Yor, M. (1993) "Bessel processes, Asian options, and perpetuities". *Mathematical Finance*, **3**, no. 4, 349–75.

Geyer, A.L.J. and Pichner, S. (1996) "A state space approach to estimate and test multi-factor Cox–Ingersoll–Ross models of the term structure". Working Paper, University of Economics, Vienna.

Gouriéroux, C. and Monfort, A. (1989) *Statistiques et modèles économétriques*. Economica. Paris.

Gouriéroux, C., Monfort, A. and Renault, E. (1993) "Indirect inference". *Journal of Applied Econometrics*, **8**, 85–118.

Harvey, A.C. (1989) *Forecasting, Structural Time Series Models and the Kalman Filter*. Cambridge University Press, Cambridge.

Heath, D., Jarrow, R. and Morton, A. (1992) "Bond pricing and the term structure of interest rates: a new methodology for contingent claims valuation". *Econometrica*, **60**, 77–105.

Ho, T. and Lee, S. (1986) "Term structure movements and pricing interest rate contingent claims". *Journal of Finance*, **41**, 1011–29.

Hogan, M. and Weintraub, K. (1993) "The lognormal interest rate model and Eurodollar futures. Working Paper, Citybank, New York.

Hull, J. and White, A. (1990) "Pricing interest rate derivative securities". *Review of Financial Studies*, **3**, 573–92.

Ikeda, N. and Watanabe, S. (1981) *Stochastic Differential Equations and its Application*. Kodansha Ltd, Tokyo.

Jamshidian, F. (1989) "An exact bond option formula". *Journal of Finance*, **44**, 205–9.

Jamshidian, F. (1993) "Options and futures evaluation with deterministic volatilities". *Mathematical Finance*, **3**, 149–59.

Jamshidian, F. (1995) "A simple class of square-root interest rate models". *Applied Mathematical Finance*, **2**, 1–20.

Kennedy, D.P. (1994) "The term structure of interest rates as a Gaussian random field". *Mathematical Finance*, **3**, 247–58.

Kennedy, D.P. (1997) "Characterizing Gaussian models of the term structure of interest rates". *Mathematical Finance*, **7**, no. 2, 107–118.

Langetieg, T. (1980) "A multivariate model of the term structure of interest rates". *Journal of Finance*, **35**, 71–97.

Litterman, R. and Scheinkman, J. (1991) "Common factors affecting bond returns". *Journal of Fixed Income*, June, 54–61.

Longstaff, F.A. and Schwartz, E.S. (1992) "Interest-rate volatility and the term structure: a two factor general equilibrium model". *Journal of Finance*, **4**, 1259–82.

Maghsoodi, Y. (1996) "Solution of the extended CIR term structure and bond option valuation". *Mathematical Finance*, **6**, no. 1, 89–109.

Miltersen, K.R., Sandmann, K. and Sondermann, D. (1997) "Closed form solutions for term structure derivatives with log-normal interest rates". *Journal of Finance*, **52**, 409–430.

Morton, A.J. (1988) *Arbitrage and Martingales*, Technical Report 821, Cornell University, New York.

Revuz, D. and Yor, M. (1991) *Continuous Martingales and Brownian Motion*. Springer-Verlag, Berlin.

Rogers, L.C.G. (1996) "Which model for term-structure of interest rates should one use?". Working Paper, University of Bath, UK.

Vasicek, O. (1977) "An equilibrium characterization of the term structure". *Journal of Financial Economics*, **5**, 177–88.

9
Trading Volatility

M. DESMOND FITZGERALD

9.1 INTRODUCTION

Essentially there are two types of derivative trading. The first is position trading where the trades are based on expectations of where prices are going, but are consistent with the current market assumed level of volatility. The other type of trading is based on taking a view on market volatility different from that contained in the current set of market prices. The market forecast of volatility over the life of a derivative is obviously one of the prime determinants of derivative prices. If, therefore, for whatever reason, the trader believes the market forecast of volatility is incorrect, he can put in place trades which will make profits if his forecast is realized. Such trades will be designed to insulate the trader from underlying price movements distinct from those induced by changes in volatility.

However, one has to be very careful when talking about volatility trading to distinguish between different types of volatility and different sources of volatility trading profits. Figure 9.1 illustrates the different types of volatility: historical volatility, implied volatility, and realized volatility. Previous chapters in this book have extensively discussed alternative volatility forecasting procedures using historical information to analyse subsequent realized volatility. Historical and realized volatilities are both measures of observed price volatility. Implied volatility is a measure of how variable option traders expect the underlying asset price to be over the life of the option. Changes in both types of volatility will influence the profitability of an options volatility trade where the position is kept broadly delta neutral. Profits and losses will accrue as underlying prices move and the position is rebalanced to maintain delta neutrality. Profits and losses will also accrue as changes in market prices influence and change option traders' views of likely volatility over the remaining life of an option.

The easiest way to consider these different profits is to identify the precise sources of profit to a delta neutral trade through time. These can be listed as follows.

$$\text{Time decay profit:} \quad \text{Position gamma} \times \frac{(\text{Asset price})^2}{2} \times (\text{Implied volatility})^2$$

Risk Management and Analysis. Vol. 2: New Markets and Products. Edited by Carol Alexander

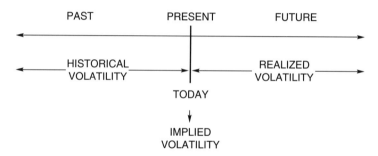

Figure 9.1   Three types of volatility

The realization here is that in simple option models, theta pays for gamma, and the rate of theta profit depends on the implied volatility at which the option was originally sold or purchased.

$$\begin{array}{c}\text{Net profit from} \\ \text{realized volatility:}\end{array} \begin{array}{c}\text{Position} \\ \text{gamma}\end{array} \times \frac{(\text{Asset price})^2}{2} \times \left[\left(\frac{\text{Realized}}{\text{volatility}} \right)^2 - \left(\frac{\text{Implied}}{\text{volatility}} \right)^2 \right]$$

This profit is accounted for by the rebalancing of the position to maintain delta neutrality. If the option position has high gamma, then if daily price changes are significantly different to those needed to cover time decay (changes consistent with original implied volatility), profits and losses on the book will be created. Although this might technically be referred to as gamma trading by derivatives traders, its profitability is still based on realized market volatility.

$$\begin{array}{c}\text{Net profit from changes} \\ \text{in implied volatility:}\end{array} \text{Vega} \times \left[\begin{array}{c}\text{Current implied} \\ \text{volatility}\end{array} - \begin{array}{c}\text{Original implied} \\ \text{volatility}\end{array} \right]$$

This profit is accounted for by the impact of a change in implied volatility on the current price of the option. This could be the result of a volatility term structure effect, or a change in implied volatility occasioned by market developments. The process of attempting to make profits from predicting changes in implied volatility would be termed vega trading.

It should be noted that these two different types of volatility trading are not necessarily independent. An abrupt rise in realized volatility versus original implied volatility (as occasioned, for example, by a market crash) is also highly likely to lead to a reassessment upwards of subsequent implied volatility by market traders. The ability of individual derivatives positions to realize profits from gamma and vega trading, however, is crucially dependent on the average maturity and degree of moneyness of the derivatives book. This is because although the level of vega and gamma are both highest at-the-money, vega and gamma sensitivities are mirror images of each other with respect to maturity. This is well illustrated in Figures 9.2 and 9.3. For at-the-money options it can be seen that long maturity options display high vega and low gamma: short maturity options display low vega and high gamma. By contrast for out-of-the-money options, long maturity options display lower vega and higher gamma, and short maturity options higher vega and lower gamma. Hence designing a position with exactly the combination of vega and gamma exposure desired by a specific trader will be a complex and dynamic process.

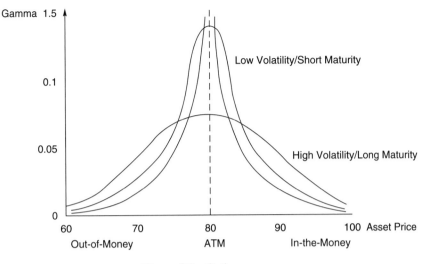

Figure 9.2   Option gamma

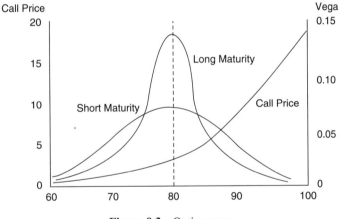

Figure 9.3   Option vega

Certain fundamental points concerning the balance between gamma-based and vega-based volatility trading may be noted, however.

1. If a trader desires high gamma but zero vega exposure, then a suitable position would be a large quantity of short maturity at-the-money options hedged with a small quantity of long maturity at-the-money options.

2. If a trader desires high vega but zero gamma exposure, then a suitable position would be a large quantity of long maturity at-the-money options hedged with a small quantity of short maturity at-the-money options.

3. For either of the previous positions, a significant movement in the underlying asset price could reverse the degree of exposure, and necessitate major rebalancing to restore the original position.

There is one further general point that needs to be mentioned before going on to the technical details of designing volatility trades and that is the implication of using simple option models to calculate vega sensitivities. It is well known that one of the main assumptions underlying the Black–Scholes and related models (including binomial models) is that the asset price process is a constant variance diffusion process. Many commentators have previously pointed out the apparent inconsistency in asking a model based on constant variance to provide risk parameters with respect to changes in volatility. However, for volatility trading the use of such models causes greater difficulties. We have mentioned before that in standard simple models theta pays for gamma, yet there is no mechanism within such models for any payment for vega exposure. This does not affect the pricing of at-the-money options since at-the-money options are linear in volatility across a wide range of models, and linear bets have no value. However, out-of-the-money and in-the-money options are certainly not linear with respect to volatility, and hence it would appear that there should be some trade-off between the level of vega and the level of theta. Hence in practice it would not be too surprising if the pattern of time decay suggested for specific options by a regular Black–Scholes or binomial model was not an accurate predictor of the actual evolution of the option price. Modelling the true impact of vega risk on time decay patterns could significantly improve the expected profitability of volatility term structure trading. We will return to this point below.

Another general volatility point that should be mentioned is the relationship between the best historical forecast volatility and implied volatility, and the relationship between diffusion volatility components and jump volatility components. This is because different volatility assumptions will give rise to different delta and gamma measures, which in turn will have considerable impact upon the dynamic risk management of the position. In essence, the first problem arises because of the unknown nature of the process of determination of implied volatility. We could imagine two extreme cases. The first is one of market efficiency where at-the-money implied volatility is the best forecast of subsequent realized volatility. The second is where the best historical based forecast is indeed the market's forecast, but the market is short volatility to customers. Hence by assigning a suitable margin for the cost of hedging and for expected profit, the final implied volatility is generated. Thus the situation might be as follows.

Historical forecast	12 per cent
+	
Cost of hedging	3 per cent
+	
Required profit margin	1 per cent
=	
Observed implied volatility	16 per cent

If the trader accepted this view of implied volatility generation, then he would also face interesting questions as to which is the "best" volatility estimate to adopt in determining the delta and gamma sensitivities of the position. It would surely not be 16 per cent since this includes a simple profit margin add-on unrelated to market risk. Should it be 12 per cent or 15 per cent? It would appear that using 15 per cent would produce a dynamic hedging strategy that would minimize day-to-day P/L fluctuations, but if the 12 per cent forecast truly explains the realized volatility of the underlying price, then this strategy would not be the *risk* minimization hedge. On the other hand, the risk minimization hedging strategy may induce undue fluctuations in day-to-day P/L, which could cause concerns within senior management about the trading book.

The second hedging question that arises is in the situation where the realized volatility of an asset price process is best described not as that of a diffusion process but as that of a jump-diffusion process. Many observers, for example, of precious metal price processes are of the opinion that a jump-diffusion process is a better description of daily price movements. Now suppose we observed gold price volatility (implied) at 11 per cent, and came to the conclusion that around 6 per cent was attributable to the jump process. We also know that a dynamic hedging strategy (delta-based strategy) cannot hedge P/L fluctuations due to the jumps. Such P/L fluctuations can only be hedged using other option positions. Then the important question arises as to what volatility number should be used to dynamically hedge the position. There appears to be a strong case for saying that since only the diffusion component is dynamically hedgeable, it is only the volatility associated with that process that should be used to define the deltas used in the hedging process. Hence this would imply hedging strategies based on a volatility input of 5 per cent. This could have a very major impact upon the amount of hedging carried out during the progress of a volatility trade.

The fundamental message, therefore, before we talk about the technical details of volatility trading is that the inputs into trading profits and losses can be relatively complex. First, we have to distinguish between volatility profits due to gamma exposure, due to vega exposure, and due to gamma–vega correlation exposure. Second, we have to analyse the term structure and degree of moneyness of trades very carefully to determine the precise structure of gamma and vega sensitivities. Third, we have to be aware that the reliability of the reported vega exposures from simple option models needs to be considered carefully. Fourth, the exact volatility inputs to be used in determining delta and gamma levels for dynamic hedging of volatility positions need to be very carefully analysed. Only after all these matters are considered, should a volatility trade be actually implemented.

9.2 BASICS OF VOLATILITY TRADING

Let us take the simplest type of volatility trading. A trader believes that the current implied volatility in at-the-money options is lower than he expects to be realized over the life of the option. Hence he wishes to acquire a delta neutral, gamma positive position. He does not wish to concern himself with vega exposure because he intends to run the position all the way through to maturity if necessary.

Clearly the simplest trade on day 0 would be to buy a straddle: a combination of an at-the-money call and an at-the-money put with zero delta. This is the position A shown in Figure 9.4. The P/L profile shown in the figure represents the position one day later on day 1. We can easily identify the size of the daily movements up and down that are required to offset the impact of time decay and realize a net profit on rebalancing the position to delta zero one day later. Such price changes are naturally consistent with the original implied volatility at which the option was purchased. In our case, let us imagine at the end of day 1 that the price has moved to a level consistent with point B on the P/L profile. This has obviously generated a significant profit to the simple volatility trade. Assuming the trader is running a pure volatility position, then he will desire to restore his delta neutral position at B by selling five futures contracts.

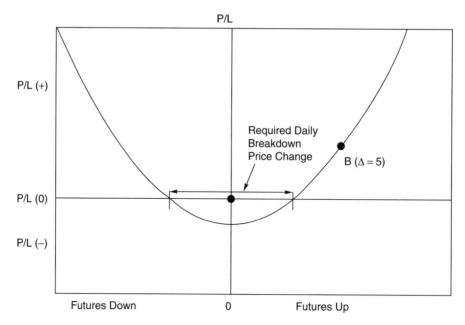

Figure 9.4   Long volatility position (Day 1)

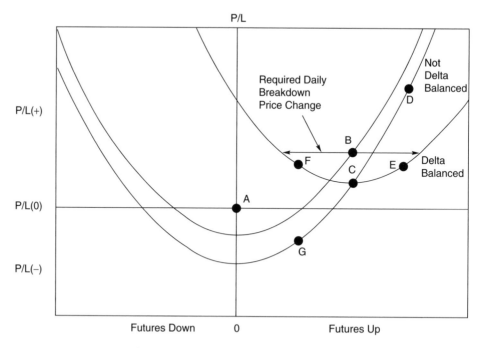

Figure 9.5   Long volatility position (Day 2)

Figure 9.5 shows the result of the rehedged position one day later on day 2. This is the curve marked F-C-E. It is interesting to compare the new hedged P/L profile with the P/L profile resulting from an unhedged position marked G-C-D. However, the important point to note is the changing nature of the volatility trade as a gamma trade. If we examine the required breakeven price change successively on Figures 9.4 and 9.5, then the change is slightly larger on day 2 than on day 1. This is natural because we are now creating a delta neutral position with an in-the-money call and an out-of-the-money put. Hence the overall gamma of the position has diminished, as indeed has the vega exposure. If the trader wishes to maintain the original degree of gamma exposure, then the alternative strategy might be to roll the position up into the current at-the-money straddle. The message here, of course, is that simply delta hedging the original gamma position does not result in an unchanged realized volatility exposure, and the trader needs to think carefully about whether to delta hedge the original position or to establish a new position more in keeping with his original volatility view at the new price level.

Further insights into this trade-off can be garnered by looking at Table 9.1 which shows the P/L of the position for various combinations of price and volatility changes. We can see the interplay of the gamma and vega aspects of volatility changes. The theta of the position is USD 6,000 per day, and it requires a DM rate change up and down of around 1 per cent per day to cover that cost of carry. That equates to an annualized volatility of around 16 per cent. It is also interesting to observe the degree of vega risk with this position, whereby a 1 per cent change in implied volatility would produce a daily profit/loss of USD 16,000. Hence a 1/2 per cent rise in volatility would be enough to offset the impact of time decay even if the asset price failed to move.

However, it is also worth noting the possible impact of correlation between price movements and implied volatility movements. If a 2 per cent price movement up or down convinced the market to raise its implied volatility 2 per cent from 15.8 per cent to 17.8 per cent, then the position would show a realized profit of USD 46,000. Similarly if a zero price change resulted in a reduction in volatility of, say, 1 per cent, the daily theta loss of USD 16,000 would be dramatically increased to USD 28,000.

Any serious volatility trader needs to be fully aware of the potential implications of the correlation between extreme price movements and changes in implied volatilities.

The relationship between the gamma and vega aspects of volatility can be further examined via Figures 9.6 and 9.7 representing the P/L profiles for a 15-day maturity

Table 9.1   Value of long DM volatility position after 1 day*

		Futures Change from 0.5500				
		−0.0110	−0.0055	0	+0.0055	+0.0110
	+2%	301	285	281	286	301
	+1%	287	270	265	271	287
Implied Volatility	0%	272	255	249	255	273
Change From	−1%	258	240	233	240	259
15.8%	−2%	244	225	217	225	245

*Position: Long 100 55   Calls
            Long 100 55   Puts
            Short 2   Futures
Original Cost = USD 255 Thousand

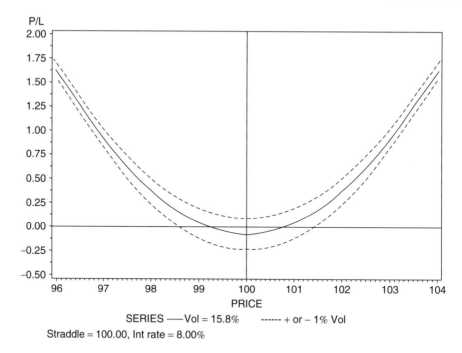

Figure 9.6   Potential P/L for long straddle (calendar days to expiration = 15)

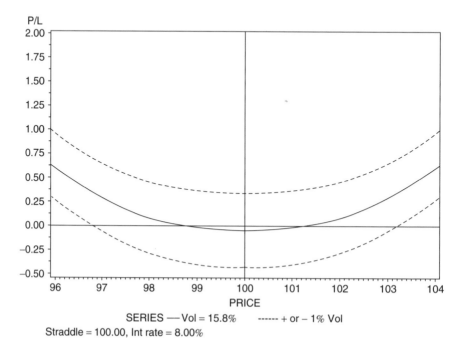

Figure 9.7   Potential P/L for long straddle (calendar days to expiration = 90)

straddle and a 90-day maturity straddle. If we look at the 15-day straddle, we can see the relatively narrow price movement required for a daily breakeven, but additionally the relatively limited impact of a 1 per cent volatility change up or down. The 90-day straddle reveals a much wider breakeven range (lower gamma) but a very much greater responsiveness to a volatility change.

The alternatives to the traditional straddle as pure volatility trades would be various forms of strangle and butterflies. Remember a strangle involves the purchase or sale of a combination of out-of-the-money puts and calls. The butterfly involves any one of three combinations of option positions. We illustrate these via long volatility positions.

Call butterfly: Sell ITM call, buy 2 ATM calls, sell OTM call

Put butterfly: Sell ITM put, buy 2 ATM puts, sell OTM put

Iron butterfly: Buy OTM put, buy ATM put, buy ATM call, buy OTM call

If we now examine Table 9.2, which shows the characteristics of various volatility trades, including the 55 straddle discussed previously, we can immediately see that the positions offer all sorts of combinations of vega and gamma exposures at various prices to the volatility trader. Indeed one useful thing to do for any volatility trader would be to produce a gamma and vega value index for each position: in other words, to identify how much exposure per unit of theta is obtained for each position. Table 9.3 shows these index values.

What is interesting about this table is how different positions give such different bangs for the buck for different risk measures. Thus if we take the short-term volatility positions, we can see how the various straddles and strangles provide virtually the same volatility exposure per dollar of theta, but the out-of-the-money strangle provides by far the largest gamma exposure per dollar of theta. By contrast if we look at the longer-term option positions, the apparently low risk butterfly position provides both the highest vega and highest gamma exposure per dollar of theta. Hence the automatic assumption that straddles provide the maximum "volatility" exposure is not necessarily entirely accurate.

Table 9.2   Characteristics of straddles, strangles and butterflies*

Contract Month	Position			
	55 Straddle	54/56 Strangle	53/57 Strangle	53/55/57 Butterfly
SEP				
Cost	$2550	$1500	$800	$1750
Gamma	0.0030	0.0028	0.0024	0.0006
Vega	$160	$150	$119	$41
Theta	$40	$37	$29	$11
DEC				
Cost	$4925	$3800	$2862	$2063
Gamma	0.0016	0.0016	0.0014	0.0002
Vega	$314	$307	$288	$26
Theta	$19	$19	$18	$1

*Assume DM futures at 0.5500 for both SEP and DEC and that SEP options have one month to expiration.

Table 9.3 Gamma and vega value indexes

	55 Straddle	54/56 Strangle	53/57 Strangle	53/55/57 Butterfly
September				
Gamma	75.0	75.7	82.8	54.5
Vega	40.0	40.5	41.0	37.3
December				
Gamma	84.2	84.2	77.8	200.0
Vega	165.3	161.6	160.0	260.0

The second thing to remember about even relatively simple volatility trades is that they are inherently dynamic. Rarely does a trader manage a volatility position by mechanical delta hedging as discussed earlier. As an example, it is useful to refer to an actual volatility trade carried out in the OEX stock index options. We will follow this trade through in detail.

June 7   The trader's volatility forecast over the life of the July option, with approximately six weeks to go to maturity, was 15.5 per cent. Implied volatility in the July 330–355 strangle was 18 per cent, so the trader sells 2,500 units of this strangle. He is happy with the volatility differential and with a breakeven index range of 322.85 to 362.15, around the current index level of 341.00 — this is something like a 10 per cent range for a six-week period.

					Cash Flow
Sold	2,500	July	330 Puts	2.95	+USD 737,500
Sold	2,500	July	355 Calls	4.205	+USD 1,051,250

The structure of the risk position can be seen in Figure 9.8(a).

June 11   The trader observed quite a significant rise in the market and decided to hedge the call side by buying 2,500 July 365 calls. At the same time he bought some cheap June downside protection with out-of-the-money puts.

					Cash Flow
Bought	2,500	July	365 Calls	2.25	−USD 562,500
Bought	1,045	June	330 Puts	0.62	−USD 64,790
Bought	100	June	325 Puts	0.375	−USD 3,750

The changed structure of the risk position can be seen in Figure 9.8(b).

June 14   The trader seized the opportunity offered by a further rise in the market to close all the put positions, leaving the effective position as short 2,500 July 355–365 call spreads at an effective level of 1.95 (4.205 − 2.25).

					Cash Flow
Bought	2,500	July	330 Calls	1.5625	−USD 390,625
Sold	1,045	June	330 Puts	0.0715	−USD 7,471
Sold	100	June	325 Puts	0.0625	−USD 625

The adjusted risk position is shown in Figure 9.8(c).

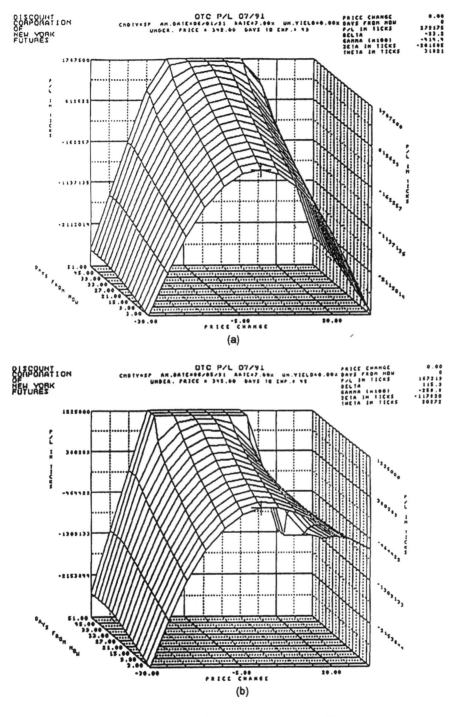

Figure 9.8   P/L profiles for a dynamic volatility trade

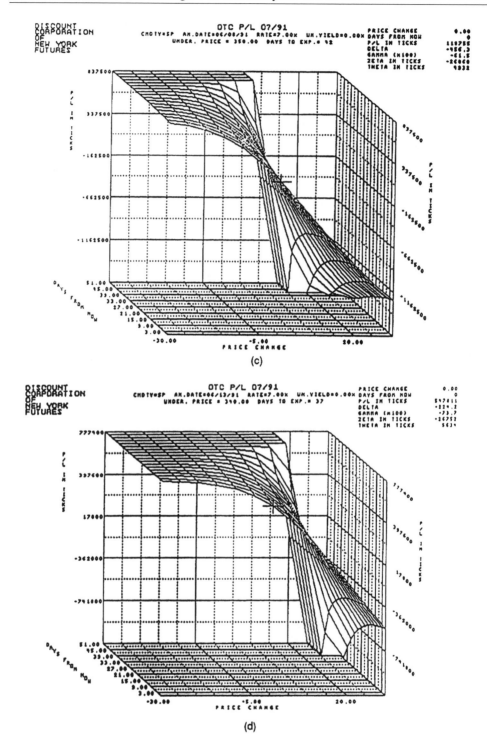

(c)

(d)

Figure 9.8   *(continued)*

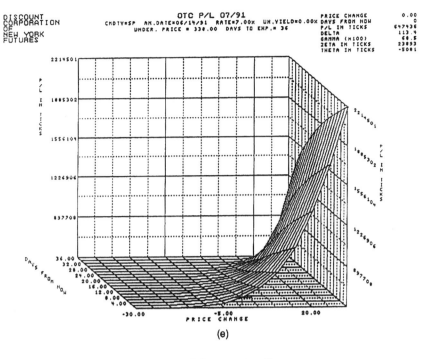

Figure 9.8 *(continued)*

June 16   The trader took the opportunity of a fall in the market to buy back 601 of
             the call spreads at an all-in price of 1.00.

				Cash Flow
Buy	601	July	355 Calls } 1.00	−USD 50,100
Sell	601	July	365 Calls	

The adjusted risk position is shown in Figure 9.8(d).

June 18   The trader on a slight fall in the market bought back 1,899 July 355 calls
             at a price of 1.128 leaving a final speculative out-of-the-money call position
             effectively in the book at zero cost.

					Cash Flow
Buy	1,899	July	355 Calls	1.128	−USD 214,207

The final risk position is shown in Figure 9.8(e). This position was run
through to expiration as a pure punt and expired worthless.

If we now add up the cash flows, we can see that the final position on June
18th was

Net Cash Flow   +USD 500,874
Final Position
Long 1899 July 365 Calls
At Zero Cost

This was clearly a very satisfactory volatility trade, although ironically if the trader had simply held the volatility position through to maturity and done no hedging or rebalancing, the entire premium income would have been retained. The important point to note, however, is that the dynamic nature of the hedging is pretty much independent of delta hedging theory. Also note the willingness of the trader to close and open positions in the reverse direction to apparent trends in the market — the mirror image of normal delta hedging.

This interplay of short and long volatility positions is often referred to in terms of "volatility overlay" strategies. Thus some typical volatility strategies might be:

1. Take advantage of lower expected volatility by selling short-dated strangles. Protect the ends of the position by buying longer-dated strangles. Here the trader should benefit from differential time decay on the shorter-dated options if the market displays low realized volatility, but gets protection from the longer-dated strangles if there is a big market movement. Furthermore if a big market move leads to an increase in implied volatility, the longer-dated options will differentially benefit the trader through higher vega exposure. Typical individual positions and the combined position for this strategy are shown in Figures 9.9(a), (b) and (c).

2. Take advantage of higher expected realized and implied volatility by buying longer-term straddles. Cover some of the cost of running the position by selling at-the-money short-term butterflies. The extreme time decay features of the short-dated butterfly should cover much of the cost of financing the longer-dated straddle position, whilst

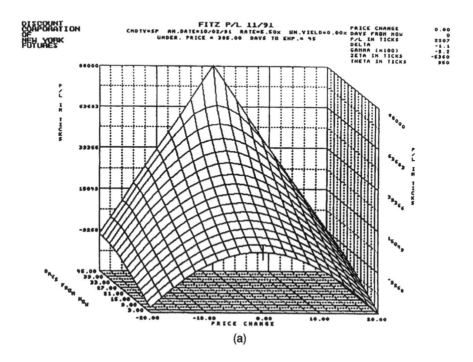

(a)

Figure 9.9 P/L profiles for a volatility overlay strategy

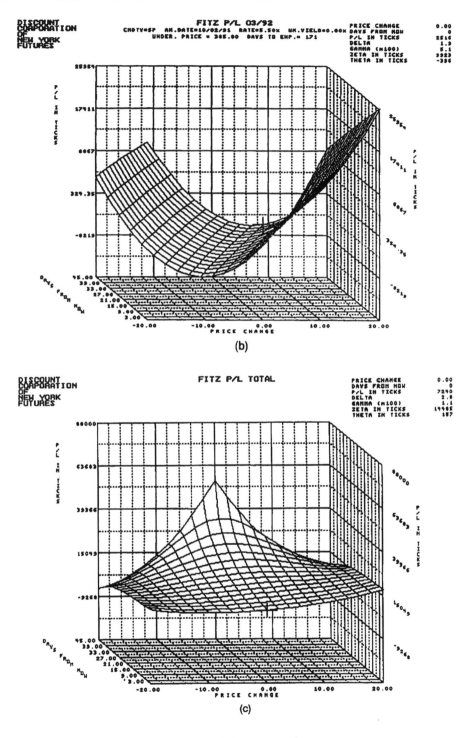

Figure 9.9 *(continued)*

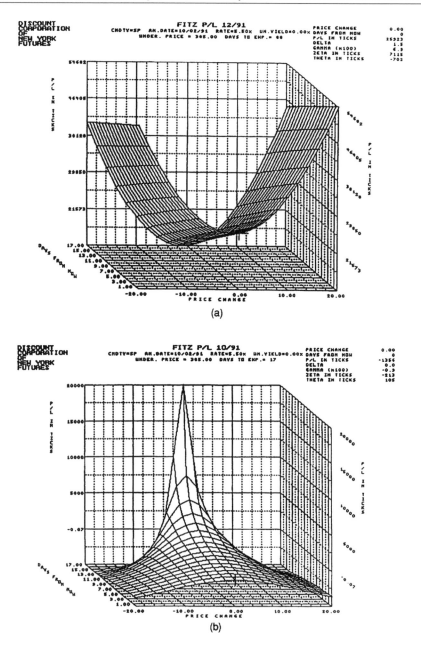

Figure 9.10   P/L profiles for a volatility overlay strategy

retaining many of the benefits of a large price move because of the limited risk characteristics of the butterfly position. Typical individual positions and the combined position for this strategy are shown in Figures 9.10(a), (b) and (c). Note that in this case the pattern of market prices has enabled the trader to generate an extremely attractive combined position.

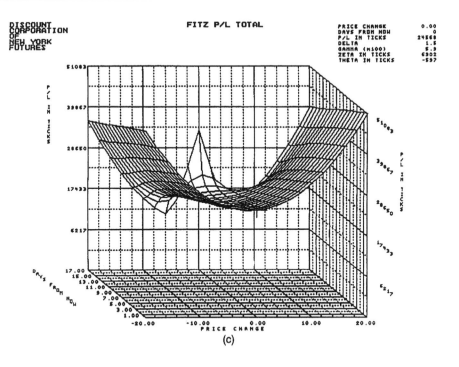

Figure 9.10 *(continued)*

9.3 ANALYSING VOLATILITY PATTERNS FOR TRADING

So far we have discussed the basic principles of volatility trading and how the standard
volatility trades are implemented and managed. The next question is what would determine
an active volatility trader to institute a trade. Clearly the answer is: if his view on realized
volatility or subsequent implied volatility is significantly different to the current implied
volatility. Many volatility traders utilize volatility cones to examine the term structure of
volatilities for individual contracts and identify anomalies. Such volatility cones, which
could be created using historical volatilities or implied volatilities, are designed to illustrate
the mean volatility and appropriate confidence limits for different option maturities. A
typical cone can be seen in Figure 9.11, which is a typical page of volatility analysis from
a major US broker: the diagram marked "Maturity Structure of Volatility" represents the
volatility cone. As can be seen the US Treasury bond volatility term structure shows a
modest tendency to rise from the one-month maturity with a mean of 8.743 per cent to
one year with a mean of 9.622 per cent. The pattern of confidence limits illustrates the
widely different volatilities of volatility at the short end (very high) and the long end
(relative low).

Obviously the intent of cone-based volatility trading is to identify periods when the
implied volatility of the options lies outside the confidence limits for a significant period
of time, and buy or sell volatility accordingly. Obviously the timing of such volatility
trades is important because a 90-day volatility purchased outside the confidence bounds
could easily be inside the confidence bounds as a 60-day volatility, without the volatility
actually changing. Hence there is a need for the trader to monitor the speed of mean

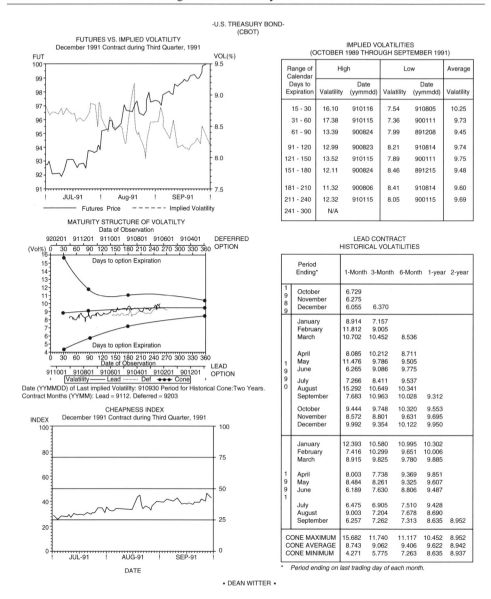

Figure 9.11 (Reproduced by permission of Dean Witter Institutional Futures)

reversion displayed by implied volatility, as well as simply its current relationship to the cone. In the Treasury bond cone in question, we can observe the pattern of implied volatility for the current lead and next to lead contract superimposed on the cone. In this case, although implied volatilities have been trading somewhat cheap to the volatility mean, they are well within the 95 per cent confidence bonds so that no volatility trade is suggested.

To give an illustration of how volatility cones can be used to suggest successful volatility trades, however, we use one of the most famous examples of yen–dollar volatility back in 1988 — old but good as the saying goes. This is actually one of the more renowned volatility trades. Figure 9.12 shows the volatility cone and superimposed implied volatility and 30-day historical volatilities as of 13 June 1988. It will be observed that both implied and 30-day historical volatilities have traded well outside the confidence bounds. Moreover they are sufficiently far outside the current bounds to be still undervalued over the next 30 days. Hence the trader is likely to feel comfortable in buying a straddle. Figure 9.13 shows the classic result: over the next 30 days implied and 30-day historical volatilities trade back towards the mean. The total rise in implied volatility over 30 days was from around 7.5 per cent to 12 per cent, representing a significant volatility trading opportunity. Although trades will not always work out as successfully as this, volatility cones are useful tools for suggesting suitable trades. Similar techniques could be used to study the relationship between volatilities on different assets by superimposing their volatility cones and centring the means of the cones at zero.

The other features that option traders often make use of in designing volatility trades are skews and smiles in the pattern of implied volatilities. Volatility smiles reflect the phenomenon that out-of-the-money options often display generally higher volatility than at-the-money options when implied volatilities are calculated using standard Black–Scholes and binomial models. Figure 9.14 shows a typical volatility smile for DM/USD implied volatility. Note how the shape of the smile becomes accentuated as we move from options with 60–90 days to maturity to 1–7 days to maturity. There is a general consensus among volatility traders that the smile probably reflects the inadequacy of simple standard models to deal with the fat middles and long tails (high kurtosis) displayed by many underlying return distributions. Such distributions are often the result of the underlying distribution being characterized as generated by a jump-diffusion process

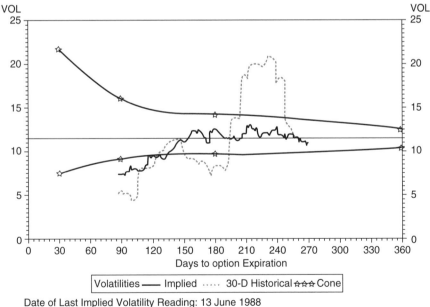

Date of Last Implied Volatility Reading: 13 June 1988
Time Period for Historical Cones: May-1986 through Apr-1988
Source : DCNYF Research Group

Figure 9.12   Maturity structure of September 1988 Japanese yen volatility: implied volatility vs. 30-day historical volatility

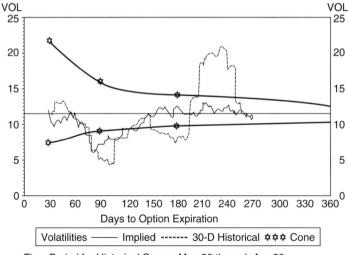

Time Period for Historical Cones: May-86 through Apr-88
Source: DCNYF Research Group

Figure 9.13 Maturity structure of September 1988 Japanese yen volatility: implied volatility vs. 30-day historical volatility

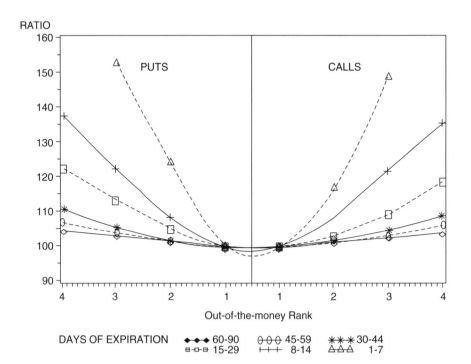

Figure 9.14 Average skewness in DM lead implied volatility (with different days to expiration): 1 January 1990 to 12 November 1991

rather than a pure diffusion process. Mean reversion effects in volatility would also be likely to generate smile effects as discussed earlier in this volume.

Nevertheless although the smile effect may be primarily due to the inadequacy of the model used to derive implied volatilities, it does have an impact on the design of traditional volatility trades. Clearly straddles and strangles will react differentially to movements up and down the smile. For instance, consider a trader purchasing a straddle. Suppose there is then a significant movement upwards in the underlying asset price. Then the call will move into the money and benefit from the increased volatility embedded in the smile, and the put will move out-of-the-money and do the same. Hence the smile effect will boost the profitability to a successful straddle trade considerably. In the case of the strangle, the out-of-the-money call will move down the smile to become at-the-money and suffer from the reduced implied volatility, whilst the out-of-the-money puts will become further out-of-the-money. Although technically they will benefit from the smile, the value is likely to be so small anyway that it will be dominated by the adverse call effects. Hence the strangle will be adversely effected by the smile effect if the market moves substantially. Therefore a low risk volatility trade if the trade expects major market movements might be to sell strangles and buy straddles with the same maturity.

The other volatility phenomenon is that of skewness, meaning differential patterns of implied volatility between out-of-the-money calls and out-of-the-money puts. Figure 9.15 shows a typical pattern of skewness for various FX options — note the skewness phenomenon is often known as a pattern of risk reversal in the foreign exchange options market. Note in Figure 9.15 the extreme pattern of skewness for the peseta/dollar options, where calls display lower and lower volatility as they move further out-of-the-money

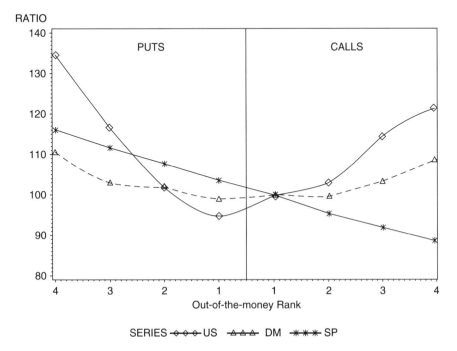

Figure 9.15   Skewness in implied volatility: 24 October 1991

whilst the puts display higher and higher volatilities as they move further out-of-the-money. One can debate the reasons for the existence of this phenomenon. Traders often argue that this pattern of skewness reflects market forecasts of underlying asset price movements: in other words the pattern of peseta skewness suggests the market expects the currency to rise significantly against the dollar. Alternatively one could argue that if there is an underlying jump process, the chances of a jump and its size are greater in one direction than another. In any case clearly different volatility trades will react differently to skewness in the market.

It is important, however, to be careful in interpreting actual patterns of volatility in practice. As an example of this, Tables 9.4 and 9.5 show the volatility pattern after a substantial shift in the FTSE market on 27 May 1994. Table 9.4 shows the patterns of implied volatilities for the June FTSE options, whilst Table 9.5 shows the closing levels of the FTSE and relevant FTSE futures contracts. Remember the implied volatilities are calculated using a standard option model with the cash value of the index as an input since these are options on cash rather than options on futures.

Table 9.4

Assume Index
93.8/yr Div.
UKX

OPTION HORIZON ANALYSIS
JUN OPTIONS ON FT-SE 100 INDEX
MARKET CLOSED TODAY

			TRADE DATE 2966.4				7 DAYS LATER 2966.4 unch				
							Volat=Same			Volat=Same		
OPTION PRICING:	Tickr CALLS			Tickr PUTS			CALLS			PUTS		
STRIKE	Prc	Del	I.Vol	Prc	Del	I.Vol	Prc	Chg	%Chg	Prc	Chg	%Chg
2800	b.int			11.0s	0.13	22.56				5.5	−5.5	−50%
2850	b.int			20.5s	0.22	22.65				12.5	−8.0	−39%
2900	75.5s	0.83	10.20	36.5s	0.33	22.33	71.5	−4.0	−5%	26.0	−10.5	−29%
2950	48.5s	0.58	13.49	58.5s	0.44	22.98	41.0	−7.5	−15%	46.5	−12.0	−21%
3000	27.0s	0.39	14.21	87.5s	0.55	24.99	19.5	−7.5	−28%	75.5	−12.0	−14%
3050	16.0s	0.24	15.78	127.5s	0.64	28.21	9.5	−6.5	−41%	115.0	−12.5	−10%
3100	7.5s	0.13	15.92	172.5s	0.70	32.20	3.5	−4.0	−53%	159.0	−13.5	−8%
3150	3.0s	0.06	15.85	220.5s	0.73	36.73	1.0	−2.0	−67%	206.5	−14.0	−6%
Fri 5/27/94			(21days Expr)			4.88%Fin	Fri 6/3/94		(14days Expr)			4.88%Fin

| OPTION PRICING | T - "Tickr" price M - Trade "Match" volatility | s - "Same" volatility 12.5% (or any other volat.) |

Source: Bloomberg.

Table 9.5

FT - SE 100 INDEX
AS OF CLOSE: FRI 5/27

				1 ⟨GO⟩ FOR YESTERDAY n ⟨GO⟩ FOR n DAYS AGO 0 ⟨PAGE⟩ FOR LATEST				BID/ASK N -- AS REPORTED 5/27 --		
Exchange: London Futures Exchange Red date = option trading									57811 OpenInt	20896 TotVol	Previous Close
Symbol		Last	Chg	Time	High	Low	Tic	OpenInt	TotVol	Close
1) UKX	spot	2966.4	−53.3	11.30	3033.7	2959.0	1024	0	0	3019.7
2) X M4	Jun94	2940.0s	−67.0	Close	3024.0	2932.0	4680	50090	20222	3007.0
3) X U4	Sep94	2953.0s	−68.5	Close	3035.0	2945.0	90	7470	674	3021.5
4) X Z4	Dec94	2964.0s	−67.0	Close			4	251	0	3031.0

Source: Bloomberg.

At first sight, the most observable phenomenon is the high level of skewness between the puts and calls, with at-the-money volatility trading at 24 per cent for the puts and only 14 per cent for the calls. However, observe the pattern of cash and futures prices in Table 9.5. Because of the rapid fall in the market, futures closed extremely cheap relative to cash — indeed cash was at 2,966.4 whilst the June future was at 2,940.0. Since most volatility traders and market-makers use futures rather than cash positions to hedge, then they tend to price the options off the hedging instrument rather than the model prices based on cash. Given the cash index level of 2,966.4, a dividend yield over 21 days of 3.16 per cent and a financing rate of 4.88 per cent, the fair forward would appear to be 2,969.30 compared with the futures price of 2,940.0. By using the fair forward to compute the implied volatilities instead of the futures, the effect is to dramatically increase apparent implied put volatility and decrease implied call volatility.

After adjusting for the effect of mispricing, however, the actual pattern of volatility skews and smiles remains interesting. The usual skew in stock index contracts is declining volatility for out-of-the-money calls and increasing volatility for out-of-the-money puts. This probably represents the observed phenomenon of higher probabilities of extreme jumps on the downside in stock markets. In Table 9.4, however, we observe the reverse: increasing volatility for out-of-the-money calls from around 13.5/14.0 per cent at-the-money to 16 per cent 100 points plus out-of-the-money. By contrast the puts show declining volatility as they go out-of-the-money and increasing volatility as they go in-the-money. If one ignores arguments of market efficiency, then it might be argued that the market is expecting a market reversal (that is, the fall in the index will not continue) and hence is not assigning extra value to the out-of-the-money puts. If, however, one expects a return to the more usual pattern of volatility behaviour, then this could represent an excellent opportunity to sell out-of-the-money call volatility and buy out-of-the-money put volatility, delta hedging the resultant position with index futures.

One final point on volatility analysis that may be mentioned is the role of different types of volatility forecast in the dynamic hedging of these volatility positions once they have been instituted. Elsewhere in this book, the forecasting of volatility and correlation is discussed in great detail. We have already mentioned the distinction between using implied volatilities and historically based forecasts in determining risk sensitivities for volatility positions. We reshow in Table 9.6 some results for straddle trading for the S + P 500 and the Nikkei-Dow, where the hedging is based on a variety of volatility forecast estimates.

The main points to note are that all the volatility trading strategies, including the most naive, are profitable. This is because of the strong tendency in implied volatilities to overreact to asset price changes and then to regress to the mean. Obviously the best strategy in terms of profit is when the hedging is carried out using the subsequent realized volatility (not possible in practice) but note that the profits are not that much larger than for the next best strategies. Nor is there significant evidence that mean reverting volatility models and GARCH type models are any better or worse than naive strategies based on constant or simple historical forecasts. In other words, it may not make too much difference in terms of realized results to volatility trading which volatility estimate is used to determine risk sensitivities.

In practice many traders adopt a much more robust approach to the dynamic hedging of volatility positions. We would, for example, when selling a strangle suggest an *ad hoc*

Table 9.6   Straddle trading*

| | S&P 500 | | | | | | |
	MR	LOG MR	GARCH	EGARCH	HISTORICAL	REALIZED	CONSTANT
gain 1	0.65	0.59	0.62	0.82	0.48	0.48	0.00
gain 2	1.96	3.54	3.21	2.40	3.16	3.29	−0.15
gain 3	2.76	2.30	4.99	0.03	1.09	2.97	1.65
gain 4	2.88	2.52	0.00	2.51	2.13	3.53	2.08
gain 5	0.44	0.60	0.04	0.24	0.89	0.72	1.00
gain 6	4.96	5.44	3.64	4.46	4.62	4.98	3.36
gain 7	3.06	2.58	2.77	2.75	1.81	4.15	1.31
gain 8	2.66	2.61	2.96	2.12	3.95	2.78	2.93
total	19.36	20.18	18.23	15.34	18.14	22.90	12.16
transactions	283	292	262	278	221	243	158

| | NIKKEI | | | | | | |
	MR	LOG MR	GARCH	EGARCH	HISTORICAL	REALIZED	CONSTANT
gain 1	0.13	0.21	−0.26	0.17	0.34	0.40	0.18
gain 2	0.69	0.69	−1.14	1.17	1.27	1.10	1.48
gain 3	0.05	0.05	0.05	0.05	0.27	0.00	0.00
gain 4	9.05	8.62	8.68	9.57	10.68	17.69	5.40
gain 5	8.47	14.36	4.74	13.14	4.76	21.62	11.17
gain 6	28.03	26.94	33.02	29.39	28.22	41.40	37.42
gain 7	30.37	25.10	49.18	25.30	20.16	24.33	20.39
gain 8	21.40	12.85	0.00	13.58	30.02	30.68	28.67
total	98.17	88.83	94.25	92.35	95.73	137.22	104.70
transactions	692.00	779.00	491.00	707.00	643.00	641.00	600.00

*Thanks are due to Jacques Pézier of Credit Agricole-Lazard for this table.

approach whereby no hedging is done until halfway to the at-the-money point, with a full hedge only being created if either the put or the call option becomes at-the-money. For instance, suppose a trader sold a 3,300–3,500 FTSE strangle when the current market is at 3,400. Then a possible dynamic hedging strategy might be no hedging in the range 3,350–3,450, and as the index moves outside this level gradually increase the hedge to a full delta hedge at index levels of 3,300 or 3,500. This hedge strategy seems to work quite well for distributions with high degrees of kurtosis.

9.4 RELATIVE VOLATILITY TRADING

As well as outright volatility trading based on analysis of skews, smiles and the term structure of volatility, there has been considerable interest of late in so-called relative volatility trading. That is, trading anomalies between the volatilities of options defined on different but related assets. Such trades could be between different stock indexes in a single economy (OEX vs. SPX), between different equities (BP vs. SHELL), between different interest rates (sterling vs. Deutschmark) and so on. The methods of analysis would broadly be the same as for standard volatility trades, save that we would attempt to establish confidence bounds on the relative volatility indexes and volatility spreads.

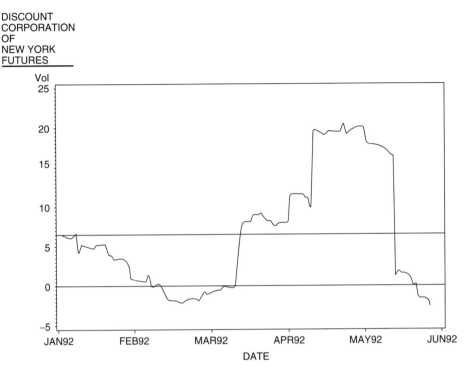

Figure 9.16   03-M sterling vs. EuroDM September 1992 historical (20-day) volatility spread

Figures 9.16 and 9.17 show one of the more famous relative volatility patterns of recent years. They show the relative volatility spread between short sterling and EuroDM September implied volatility in the period up until 18 May 1992. We can observe the peak relative volatilities in April as the first difficulties with sterling's position in the ERM became apparent, and the subsequent decline to a negative spread of sterling volatility over DM volatility in May. This was apparent on both historical and implied volatility calculations, and compared with a normal position spread of around 4 per cent. Hence this appeared to represent an excellent opportunity to buy sterling volatility and sell DM volatility in a hedged position. At the time volatility on sterling was 7.4 per cent with a cheapness index of 12.6, and DM volatility was 8.6 per cent with a cheapness index of 67.9. Remember the cheapness index represents cheapness or dearness relative to the mean of the volatility cone and is centred at 50.0.

Obviously, therefore, the trader will buy short sterling at-the-money straddles and sell DM at-the-money straddles. The aim would be to unwind the position when the current negative volatility spread of −1.2 per cent returns to a positive volatility spread of +4.0 per cent. To construct the trade we want to create equal and opposite exposures to changes in implied volatilities — that is, equal and opposite vegas expressed in a single currency. The risk sensitivities of the options available are shown in Table 9.7. We can see from this table (note the Dean Witter system we are using happens to refer to vega as zeta) that we will have equal dollar vegas if we sell 147 EuroDM September 90.50 straddles and buy 100 Short Sterling September 90.25 straddles. The structure of the trades is illustrated below.

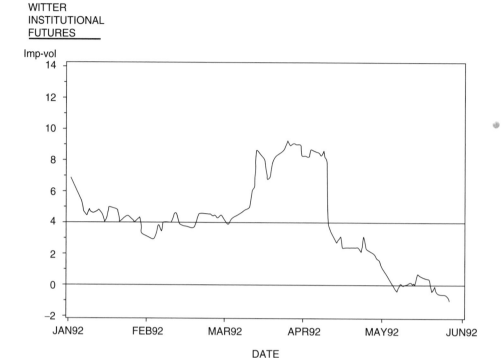

DEAN
WITTER
INSTITUTIONAL
FUTURES

Figure 9.17   03-M sterling vs. EuroDM September 1992 implied volatility spread

Activity: 28 May 1992

1. Establish vega neutral options position, using at-the-money straddles.
    Vega ratio, using common currency:
    (Short Sterling/EuroDM): (USD 92.82/USD 63.28) = 1.47
    Need 1.47 times as many EuroDM as Short Sterling.

    Short Sterling: Buy 100 of the Sep-92 90.25 straddle
    EuroDM: Sell 147 of the Sep-92 90.50 straddle.

2. Make delta neutral.

    Short Sterling: Delta of 1 straddle = 0.20
                            Delta of 100 straddles = 0.20 × 100 = 20
                            Sell 20 Sep-92 futures @ 90.36
    EuroDM: Delta of 1 straddle = 0.06
                            Delta of −147 straddles = 0.06 × −147 = −8.82
                            Buy 8 Sep-92 futures @ 90.54

Note that, of course, the position will have to be rebalanced at regular intervals whilst
the trade is held to keep it neutral with respect to overall rather than relative volatility

Table 9.7

Conversion Rates: May 28, 1992
$/£ 1.8010 DM/$: 1.6338 DM/£: 2.9425

EURODM

(c) 1993 Dean Witter Reynolds Inc.

COMMOD RU	MO/YR (Days) UNDERLYING		09/92 110 90.54		00/0 0 0.00		00/0 0 0.00	
			Call	Put	Call	Put	Call	Put
Date 05/28/92	90.50	Price	0.20	0.16				
		Vol	8.64	8.64				
		Delta	0.53	−0.47				
Int rate 0.00%		Gamma	0.89	0.89				
		Zeta	51.69	51.69				
		Theta	−2.03	−2.03				
Yld rate 0.00%	90.75	Price						
		Vol						
		Delta						
		Gamma						
Gamma × 100		Zeta						
		Theta						
	91.00	Price						
		Vol						
Zeta and Theta in DM		Delta						
		Gamma						
		Zeta						
		Theta						

Zeta of 90.50 EuroDM Straddle
ticks: 4.14   BP: 35.13   DM:103.38 $: 63.28

SHORT STERLING

(c) 1993 Dean Witter Reynolds Inc.

COMMOD RL	MO/YR (Days) UNDERLYING		09/92 112 90.36		00/0 0 0.00		00/0 0 0.00	
			Call	Put	Call	Put	Call	Put
Date 05/28/92	90.25	Price	0.22	0.11				
		Vol	7.42	7.42				
		Delta	0.60	−0.40				
Int rate 0.00%		Gamma	0.97	0.97				
		Zeta	25.77	25.77				
		Theta	−0.86	−0.86				
Yld rate 0.00%	90.50	Price						
		Vol						
		Delta						
Gamma × 100		Gamma						
		Zeta						
		Theta						
	90.75	Price						
		Vol						
Zeta and Theta in BP		Delta						
		Gamma						
		Zeta						
		Theta						

Zeta of 90.25 Short Sterling Straddle
ticks: 4.12   BP: 51.54   DM: 151.66 $: 92.82

Trade Ratio: Zeta Neutrality
Ratio (Short Sterling/EuroDM) (in $): (92.82/63.28) = 1.47
Therefore: Sell 147 EuroDM Sep 90.50 straddles
Buy 100 Short Sterling Sep 90.25 straddles

movements, and most importantly to maintain delta neutrality on both the sterling side and the DM side.

Moving ahead, Figures 9.18 and 9.19 show the movements of the relative volatility during the period through September 1992. It will be observed that by early July 1992, the relative volatility spread has moved back to its long-term mean of 4 per cent and hence the position would be unwound. We show below the results of the trade: remember the P/L reflects a considerable amount of dynamic hedging during the period the trade was held.

Activity: 13 July 1992

Lift trade.

Date	Implied Volatility		Spread = Short Sterling− EuroDM	P/L (USD)
	Short Sterling	EuroDM		
	(cheapness index)	(cheapness index)		
28 May 1992	7.4%	8.6%	−1.2%	0
	(12.6)	(67.9)		
13 July 1992	11.9%	6.1%	+5.8%	78,251
	(46.3)	(34.3)		

This is a classic example of a successful relative volatility trade triggered by apparent anomalies in the volatility spreads in the market.

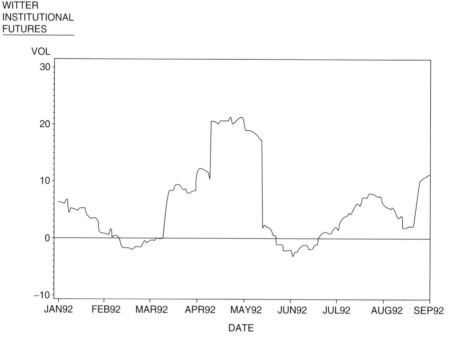

Figure 9.18   03-M sterling vs. EuroDM September historical (20-day) volatility spread

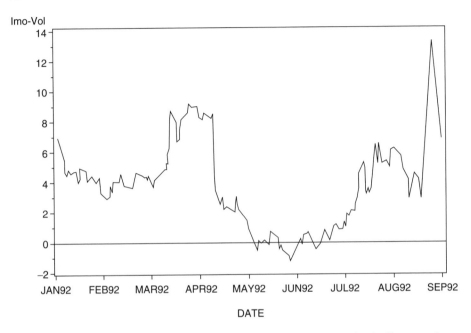

DEAN
WITTER
INSTITUTIONAL
FUTURES

Figure 9.19   03-M sterling vs. EuroDM September 1992 implied volatility spread

In practice, traders try to establish relative volatility confidence limits for many related assets. Figure 9.20 shows a typical relative volatility analysis for British Gas vs. British Telecom on 25 May 1995. This shows relative historical volatilities and relative implied volatilities for the period 4 May 1993 to 25 May 1995, together with the current 95 per cent confidence limits for relative implied volatilities. Currently relative implied volatilities lie around the centre of the bounds, but the analysis would have suggested the purchase of relative volatility earlier in the year. In general, the trader would have purchased British Gas straddles and sold British Telecom straddles in proportion so as to create equal and opposite sterling vega positions. Rather than hedge the delta of each position separately with the stock, the trader is more likely to work out the net market exposure of the entire position and hedge the net sterling delta with FTSE index futures. Individual exposures to British Gas and British Telecom will be monitored on a continuous basis, however.

Many other forms of relative volatility trading can be identified. We give some ideas of types of trades below.

1.   *Stock index vs. stock index*
     The United States has long been trading stock index futures including price-weighted and value-weighted indexes, narrow and broad indexes, and basket indexes. Since many index constituents are common, it may be possible to establish relative volatility

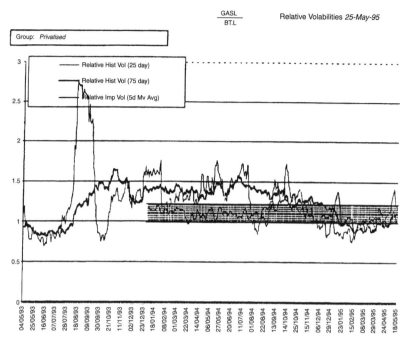

Figure 9.20

bounds to monitor. Typical trades would be the Major Market Index vs. the OEX, a group of basket indexes vs. the OEX or SPX, and so on.

2. *Embedded options vs. traded options*
    Many futures contracts are known to contain embedded options — for instance, one of the most famous is the cheapest to deliver switch option in the US Treasury bond contract. If the implied volatility in the embedded options is significantly different to the implied volatility in the equivalent exchange traded futures options, then a relative volatility trade may be successfully implemented.

3. *Interest rate term structure relative volatility trading*
    A very active area of interest rate research currently is the use of term structure models to ensure consistent pricing of all interest rate products and related derivatives. The prices derived from such models can then be reprocessed through standard Black models, widely used to price caps, floors and swaptions, to determine required patterns of implied volatilities. If these consistent patterns are violated in the market, then relative volatility trading opportunities may well exist.

9.5 SUMMARY

What we have tried to do in this chapter is outline various aspects of volatility and relative volatility trading, and explain on what basis traders in the market institute such trades. It is important to remember that most volatility trading in practice is hardly pure, and may be biased by the trader's directional view. He may choose to hedge more often in one direction than another, or put in protection via options in one place and not in another and so on. Nevertheless there are certain principles which seem to summarize most volatility trading.

1. Traders need to be aware of the crucial difference between gamma (realized volatility) based volatility trading and vega (implied volatility) based volatility trading.

2. Reliance on simple Black–Scholes and binomial models is likely to lead to misguided decisions for the potential profitability of vega based volatility trading.

3. Dynamic hedging strategies for volatility trades depend crucially on the right option model, but hardly at all on the type of volatility forecasting procedure.

4. Sophisticated analysis of skews, smiles and volatility term structures is essential for successful volatility trading.

5. Relative volatility trading may be capable of generating higher risk adjusted profit margins than outright volatility trading.

10

Credit Derivatives

BLYTHE MASTERS[*]

10.1 BACKGROUND AND OVERVIEW: THE CASE FOR CREDIT DERIVATIVES

10.1.1 What are Credit Derivatives?

Derivatives growth in the latter part of the 1990s continues along at least three dimensions. First, new products emerging as the traditional building blocks — forwards and options — have spawned second and third generation derivatives that span complex hybrid, contingent and path-dependent risks. Secondly, new applications are expanding derivatives use beyond the specific management of price and event risk to the strategic management of portfolio risk, balance sheet growth, shareholder value, and overall business performance. Finally, derivatives are being extended beyond mainstream interest rate, currency, commodity and equity markets to new underlying risks including catastrophe, pollution, electricity, inflation and credit.

Credit derivatives fit neatly into this three-dimensional scheme. Until recently, credit remained one of the major components of business risk for which no tailored risk-management products existed. Credit risk management for the loan portfolio manager meant a strategy of portfolio diversification backed by line limits, with an occasional sale of positions in the secondary market. Derivatives users relied on purchasing insurance, letters of credit or guarantees, or negotiating collateralized mark-to-market credit enhancement provisions in Master Agreements. Corporates either carried open exposures to key customers' accounts receivable or purchased insurance, where available, from factors. Yet these strategies are inefficient, largely because they do not separate the management of credit risk from the asset with which that risk is associated.

For example, consider a corporate bond, which represents a bundle of risks, including perhaps duration, convexity, callability and credit risk (constituting both the risk of default and the risk of volatility in credit spreads). If the only way to adjust credit risk is to

---

[*] The opinions expressed in this chapter are those of the author and do not necessarily reflect those of J.P. Morgan or any of its affiliates.

buy or sell that bond, and consequently affect positioning across the entire bundle of risks, then there is a clear inefficiency. Fixed income derivatives introduced the ability to manage duration, convexity and callability independently of bond positions; credit derivatives complete the process by allowing the independent management of default or credit spread risk.

Formally, credit derivatives are bilateral financial contracts which isolate specific aspects of credit risk from an underlying instrument and transfer that risk between two parties. In so doing, credit derivatives separate the ownership and management of credit risk from other qualitative and quantitative aspects of ownership of financial assets. Thus, credit derivatives share one of the key features of historically successful derivatives products, namely the potential to achieve efficiency gains through a process of market completion. Efficiency gains arising from disaggregating risk are best illustrated by imagining an auction process in which an auctioneer sells a number of risks, each to the highest bidder, as compared with selling a "job lot" of the same risks to the highest bidder for the entire package. In most cases the separate auctions will yield a higher aggregate sale price than the job lot. By separating specific aspects of credit risk from other risks, credit derivatives allow even the most illiquid credit exposures to be transferred from portfolios that have, but do not want, the risk, to those that want, but do not have, that risk, even when a job lot auction of the underlying asset itself could not have been transferred in the same way.

10.1.2 What is the Significance of Credit Derivatives?

Even today we cannot yet argue that credit risk is, on the whole, "actively" managed. Indeed, even in the largest banks, credit risk management is often little more than a process of setting and adhering to notional exposure limits and pursuing limited opportunities for portfolio diversification. In recent years, stiff competition among lenders, a tendency by some banks to treat lending as a loss-leading cost of relationship development, and a benign credit cycle have combined to subject bank loan credit spreads to relentless downward pressure, both on an absolute basis and relative to other asset classes. At the same time, secondary market illiquidity, relationship constraints and the luxury of cost rather than mark-to-market accounting have made active portfolio management either impossible or unattractive. Consequently, the vast majority of bank loans reside where they are originated until maturity. In 1997, primary loan syndication origination in the United States alone exceeded US$1.1 trillion, while secondary loan market volumes were less than US$62 billion.[1]

However, five years hence, commentators will look back to the birth of the credit derivative market as a watershed development for bank credit risk management practice. Simply put, credit derivatives will fundamentally change the way banks price, manage, transact, originate, distribute and account for credit risk. Yet, in substance, the definition of a credit derivative given above captures many credit instruments that have been used routinely for years, including guarantees, letters of credit, and loan participations. So why attach such significance to this new group of products? Essentially, it is the combination of the precision with which credit derivatives can isolate and transfer certain aspects of credit risk, rather than their economic substance, which distinguishes them from more traditional credit instruments. There are several distinct arguments, not all of which are unique to credit derivatives, but which combine to make a strong case for the increasing use of credit derivatives by banks and by all institutions that routinely carry credit risk as part of their day-to-day business.

First, the Reference Entity, whose credit risk is being transferred, need neither be a party to nor be aware of a credit derivative transaction. This confidentiality enables banks and corporate treasurers to manage their credit risks discreetly without interfering with important customer relationships. This contrasts with both a loan assignment through the secondary loan market, which requires borrower notification, and a silent participation, which requires the participating bank to assume as much credit risk to the selling bank as to the borrower itself.

The absence of the Reference Entity at the negotiating table also means that the terms (tenor, seniority, compensation structure) of the credit derivative transaction can be customized to meet the needs of the buyer and seller of risk, rather than the particular liquidity or term needs of a borrower. Moreover, because credit derivatives isolate credit risk from relationship and other aspects of asset ownership, they introduce discipline to pricing decisions. Credit derivatives provide an objective benchmark representing the true opportunity cost of a transaction. Increasingly, as liquidity and pricing technology improve, credit derivatives are defining credit spread forward curves and implied volatilities in a way that less liquid credit products never could. The availability and discipline of visible market pricing enables institutions to make pricing and relationship decisions more objectively.

Secondly, credit derivatives are the first mechanism via which short sales of credit instruments can be executed with any reasonable liquidity and without the risk of a short squeeze. It is more or less impossible to short-sell a bank loan, but the economics of a short position can be achieved synthetically by purchasing credit protection using a credit derivative. This allows the user to reverse the "skewed" profile of credit risk (whereby one earns a small premium for the risk of a large loss) and instead pay a small premium for the possibility of a large gain upon credit deterioration. Consequently, portfolio managers can short specific credits or a broad index of credits, either as a hedge of existing exposures or simply to profit from a negative credit view. Similarly, the possibility of short sales opens up a wealth of arbitrage opportunities. Global credit markets today display discrepancies in the pricing of the same credit risk across different asset classes, maturities, rating cohorts, time zones, currencies, and so on. These discrepancies persist because arbitrageurs have traditionally been unable to purchase cheap obligations against shorting expensive ones in order to extract arbitrage profits. As credit derivative liquidity improves, banks, borrowers and other credit players will exploit such opportunities, just as the evolution of interest rate derivatives prompted cross-market interest rate arbitrage activity in the 1980s. The natural consequence of this is, of course, that credit pricing discrepancies will gradually disappear as credit markets become more efficient.

Thirdly, credit derivatives, except when embedded in structured notes, are off-balance-sheet instruments. As such, they offer considerable flexibility in terms of leverage. In fact, the user can define the required degree of leverage, if any, in a credit investment. The appeal of off- as opposed to on-balance sheet exposure will differ by institution: the more costly the balance sheet, the greater the appeal of an off-balance-sheet alternative. To illustrate, bank loans have not traditionally appealed as an asset class to hedge funds and other non-bank institutional investors for at least two reasons. First, because of the administrative burden of assigning and servicing loans; and second, because of the absence of a repo market. Without the ability to finance investments in bank loans on a secured basis via some form of repo market, the return on capital offered by bank loans was unattractive to institutions which do not enjoy access to unsecured financing. However, by taking exposure to bank loans using a credit derivative such as a Total Return Swap (described more fully below), a hedge fund can both synthetically finance the position (receiving under the swap the net proceeds of the loan after financing) and avoid the administrative costs of direct ownership of the asset, which are borne by the swap counterparty. The degree of leverage achieved using a Total Return Swap will depend on the amount of upfront collateralization, if any, required by the total return payer from its swap counterparty. Credit derivatives are thus opening new lines of distribution for the credit risk of bank loans and many other instruments into the institutional capital markets.

This chapter introduces the basic structures and applications that have emerged in recent years and focuses on situations in which their use produces benefits that can be evaluated without the assistance of complex mathematical or statistical models. The applications discussed will include those for risk managers addressing portfolio concentration risk, for issuers seeking to minimize the costs of liquidity in the debt capital markets, and for investors pursuing assets that offer attractive relative value. In each case the recurrent theme is that in bypassing barriers between different asset classes, maturities, rating categories, debt seniority levels and so on, credit derivatives create enormous opportunities to exploit and profit from associated discontinuities in the pricing of credit risk.

10.2 BASIC CREDIT DERIVATIVE STRUCTURES AND APPLICATIONS

10.2.1 Credit (Default) Swaps

The Credit Swap or ("Credit Default Swap") illustrated in Figure 10.1 is a bilateral financial contract in which one counterparty (the Protection Buyer) pays a periodic fee, typically expressed in basis points on the notional amount, in return for a Contingent Payment by the Protection Seller following a Credit Event of a Reference Entity. The definitions of a Credit Event and the settlement mechanism used to determine the Contingent Payment are flexible and determined by negotiation between the counterparties at the inception of the transaction. At the time of writing, the International Swap and Derivatives Association (ISDA) has completed a lengthy project to produce a standardized letter of confirmation for Credit Swaps transacted under the umbrella of its ISDA Master Agreement. The standardized confirmation allows the parties to specify the precise terms of the transaction from a number of defined alternatives. The evolution of increasingly standardized terms in the credit derivatives market is an important development because it has reduced legal uncertainty which, at least in the early stages, hampered the market's development. This uncertainty originally arose because credit derivatives, unlike many other derivatives, are frequently triggered by a defined (and fairly unlikely) *event* rather than a defined

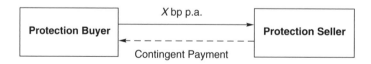

Figure 10.1   Credit (default) swap. *Source:* J.P. Morgan Securities Inc.

price or *rate* move, making the importance of watertight legal documentation for such transactions commensurately greater. It is interesting to note that, due to the benign nature of the credit cycle over the past few years, to the best of the author's knowledge at the time of writing, there have been few, if any, recorded instances of triggered Credit Swaps.

A Credit Event is commonly defined as bankruptcy, insolvency, receivership, material adverse restructuring of debt, or failure to meet payment obligations when due; coupled, where measurable, with a significant price deterioration (net of price changes due to interest rate movements) in a specified Reference Obligation issued or guaranteed by the Reference Entity. This latter requirement is known as a Materiality clause and is designed to ensure that a Credit Event is not triggered by a technical (i.e. non-credit-related) default, such as a disputed or late payment, which would not, presumably, be accompanied by a material price deterioration in the Reference Entity's obligations.

The Contingent Payment is commonly effected by a cash settlement mechanism designed to mirror the loss incurred by creditors of the Reference Entity following a Credit Event. This payment is typically calculated as the fall in price of the Reference Obligation below par (or some other designated reference price or "strike") at some pre-designated point in time after the Credit Event. Counterparties typically wait from one week to three months after default in order to give the Reference Obligation's price time to settle at a new level, or take an average over a similar time period. Typically, the price change is determined by reference to a poll of price quotations from dealers in the Reference Obligation. Since most debt obligations become due and payable in the event of default, plain vanilla loans and bonds will trade at the same dollar price following a default, reflecting the market's estimate of recovery value, irrespective of maturity or coupon. Alternatively, the Contingent Payment may be fixed as a pre-determined sum, known as a "binary" settlement.

Another alternative for the settlement of the Contingent Payment is for the Protection Buyer to make physical delivery of a specified Deliverable Obligation in return for payment of its face amount. Deliverable Obligations may be the Reference Obligation or one of a broad class of obligations meeting certain specifications, such as any senior unsecured claim against the Reference Entity. A key distinction between physical delivery and cash settlement is that, following physical delivery, the Protection Seller has recourse to the Reference Entity and the opportunity to participate in the work-out process as owner of a defaulted obligation. The physical settlement option is not always available since Credit Swaps are often used to hedge exposures to assets that are not readily transferable or to create short positions for users who do not own a deliverable obligation. Of course, assuming perfect liquidity in distressed debt markets, a Protection Seller in a cash settled Credit Swap could replicate a physically settled transaction by buying defaulted obligations through the dealer poll process, but this assumption cannot be guaranteed to hold, particularly for larger transactions.

It is interesting to note that while Credit Swaps can be triggered by a Credit Event defined as narrowly as a default on a single specified Reference Obligation, they are commonly triggered by default with respect to any one of a much broader class of obligations. Similarly, while the Contingent Payment can be determined with reference to a specific instrument, it is also commonly determined by reference to any one of a broad class of qualifying obligations. Thus, while some credit derivatives closely resemble the risks of direct ownership of a specific underlying instrument, others are structured to create more "macro" exposure to a Reference Entity.

Credit Swaps, and indeed all credit derivatives, are almost exclusively inter-professional (meaning non-retail) transactions. Averaging US$25–50 million per transaction, they range in size from a few million to billions of dollars. Maturities usually run from one to ten years and occasionally beyond that, although counterparty credit quality concerns frequently limit liquidity for longer tenures. Reference Entities may be drawn from a wide universe including sovereigns, semi-governments, financial institutions, and all other investment or sub-investment grade corporates. The only true limitation to the parameters of a Credit Swap is the willingness of the counterparties to act on a credit view.

(i) Addressing Illiquidity Using Credit Swaps

Illiquidity of credit positions can be caused by any number of factors, both internal and external to the organization in question. Internally, in the case of bank loans and derivative transactions, relationship concerns often lock portfolio managers into credit exposure arising from key client transactions. Corporate borrowers prefer to deal with smaller lending groups and typically place restrictions on transferability and on which entities can have access to that group. Credit derivatives allow users to reduce credit exposure without physically removing assets from their balance sheet. Loan sales or the assignment or unwind of derivative contracts typically require the notification and/or consent of the customer. By contrast, a credit derivative is a confidential transaction which the customer need neither be party to nor be aware of, thereby separating relationship management from risk-management decisions.

Similarly, the tax or accounting position of an institution can create significant disincentives to the sale of an otherwise relatively liquid position — consider an insurance company that owns a public corporate bond in its hold-to-maturity account at a low tax base. Purchasing default protection via a Credit Swap can hedge the credit exposure of such a position without triggering a sale for either tax or accounting purposes. Recently, Credit Swaps have been employed in such situations to avoid unintended adverse tax or accounting consequences of otherwise sound risk-management decisions.

More often, illiquidity results from factors external to the institution in question. The secondary market for many loans and private placements is not deep, and in the case of certain forms of trade receivable or insurance contract may not exist at all. Some forms of credit exposure, such as the business concentration risk to key customers faced by many corporates (meaning not only the default risk on accounts receivable, but also the risk of customer replacement cost), or the exposure employees face to their employers in respect of non-qualified deferred compensation, are simply not transferable at all. In all of these cases, Credit Swaps can provide a hedge of exposure that would not otherwise be achievable through the sale of the underlying asset. Simply put, Credit Swaps deepen the secondary market for credit risk far beyond that of the secondary market of the underlying credit instrument.

(ii) Exploiting a Funding Advantage or Avoiding a Disadvantage

When an investor owns a credit-risky asset, the return for assuming that credit risk is only the *net* spread earned after deducting that investor's cost of funding the asset on its balance sheet. Thus, it makes little sense for an A-rated bank funding at Libor flat to lend money to an AAA-rated entity which borrows at Libid: after funding costs, the A-rated bank makes a loss but still takes on risk. Consequently, entities with high funding levels often buy risky assets to generate spread income. However, since there is no up-front principal outlay required for most Protection Sellers when assuming a Credit Swap position, these provide an opportunity to take on credit exposure in off-balance-sheet positions that do not need to be funded. Credit Swaps are therefore fast becoming an important source of investment opportunity and portfolio diversification for banks, insurance companies (both monolines and traditional insurers), and other institutional investors who would otherwise continue to accumulate concentrations of lower quality assets due to their own high funding costs.

On the other hand, institutions with low funding costs may capitalize on this advantage by funding assets on the balance sheet and purchasing default protection on those assets. The premium for buying default protection on such assets may be less than the net spread such a bank would earn over its funding costs. Hence a low cost investor may offset the risk of the underlying credit but still retain a net positive income stream. Of course, as we will discuss in more detail, the counterparty risk to the Protection Seller must be covered by this residual income. However, the combined credit quality of the underlying asset and the credit protection purchased, even from a lower quality counterparty, may often be very high, since two defaults (by both the Protection Seller and the Reference Entity) must occur before losses are incurred, and even then losses will be mitigated by the recovery rate on claims against both entities.

(iii) A Note on Terminology

Given that the payout profile of a Credit Swap is option-like, with the Protection Seller receiving a premium in return for taking the risk of having to make a large (although capped) pay-out, terminology is frequently a source of some confusion. Why would an option-like contract be referred to as a swap? In fact, while Credit Swaps certainly share characteristics with option-like products, they should not be confused with what derivatives traders think of as true "credit options"; that is, options on credit-risky instruments, such as a bond or loan, or on credit spreads. In the same way that receiving fixed in an interest rate swap is the duration equivalent of a long (financed) position in a bond, selling protection in a Credit Swap (or, for that matter, being a Total Return Receiver in a Total Return Swap) is the credit risk equivalent of a long (financed) position in a bond. The origin of the "swap" terminology derives from this analogy. It is intended to convey the fact that the Credit Swap (and Total Return Swap) are effectively swaps of positions in credit-risky assets, rather than options on positions in credit-risky assets. The latter are referred to below as "Credit Options" and, just like any other option in which the contingency is a market price development rather than a remote credit event, they derive their value from the expected forward value and volatility of market prices (i.e. credit spreads). If an institution is capable of "pricing" a position in a loan or a bond, by extension, given financing costs (and counterparty charges), it is also capable of pricing a Credit Swap. To price a Credit Option, on the other hand, requires additional information to that required to price a loan or a bond, namely information about volatilities and implied forward credit spreads.

10.2.2 Total (Rate of) Return Swaps

A Total Rate of Return Swap ("Total Return Swap" or "TR Swap") is also a bilateral financial contract designed to transfer credit risk between the parties, but a TR Swap

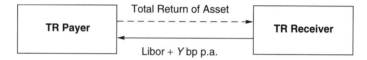

Figure 10.2   Total return swap. *Source:* J.P. Morgan Securities Inc.

is importantly distinct from the Credit Swap in that it exchanges the *total* economic performance of a specified asset for another cash flow. That is to say, payments between the parties to a TR Swap are based upon changes in the market valuation of a specific credit instrument, irrespective of whether a Credit Event has occurred.

Specifically, as illustrated in Figure 10.2, one counterparty (the "TR Payer") pays to the other (the "TR Receiver") the total return of a specified asset, the Reference Obligation. "Total return" comprises the sum of interest, fees, and any change-in-value payments with respect to the Reference Obligation. The change-in-value payment is equal to any appreciation (positive) or depreciation (negative) in the market value of the Reference Obligation, as usually determined on the basis of a poll of reference dealers. A net depreciation in value (negative total return) results in a payment *to* the TR Payer. Change-in-value payments may be made at maturity or on a periodic interim basis. As an alternative to a cash settlement of the change-in-value payment, TR Swaps can allow for physical delivery of the Reference Obligation at maturity by the TR Payer in return for a payment of the Reference Obligation's initial value by the TR Receiver. Maturity of the TR Swap is not required to match that of the Reference Obligation, and, in practice, rarely does. In return, the TR Receiver typically makes a regular floating payment of Libor plus a spread (Y bp p.a. in Figure 10.2).

The key distinction between a Credit Swap and a TR Swap is that the former results in a contingent or floating payment only following a Credit Event, while the latter results in payments reflecting changes in the market valuation of a specified asset in the normal course of business.

(i) Synthetic Financing Using Total Return Swaps

When entering into a TR Swap on an asset residing in its portfolio, the TR Payer has effectively removed all economic exposure to the underlying asset. This risk transfer is effected with confidentiality and without the need for a cash sale. Typically, the TR Payer retains the servicing and voting rights to the underlying asset, although occasionally certain rights may be passed through to the TR Receiver under the terms of the swap. The TR Receiver has exposure to the underlying asset without the initial outlay required to purchase it. Ignoring the important issues of counterparty credit risk and the value of aspects of control over the Reference Obligation, such as voting rights if they remain with the TR Payer, the economics of a TR Swap resemble a synthetic secured financing of a purchase of the Reference Obligation provided by the TR Payer to the TR Receiver.

Consequently, a key determinant of pricing of the "financing" spread on a TR Swap (Y bp. per annum in Figure 8.2) is the cost to the TR Payer of financing (and servicing) the Reference Obligation on its own balance sheet which has, in effect, been "lent" to the TR Receiver for the term of the transaction. Counterparties with high funding levels can make use of other lower cost balance sheets through TR Swaps, thereby facilitating investment in assets that diversify the portfolio of the user away from more affordable but riskier assets.

Because the maturity of a TR Swap does not have to match the maturity of the underlying asset, the TR Receiver in a swap with maturity less than that of the underlying asset may benefit from the positive carry associated with being able to roll forward short-term synthetic financing of a longer term investment. The TR Payer may benefit from being able to purchase protection for a limited period without having to liquidate the asset permanently. At the maturity of a TR Swap, whose term is less than that of the Reference Obligation, the TR Payer essentially has the option to reinvest in that asset (by continuing to own it) or to sell it at the market price. The TR Payer has no exposure to the market price since a lower price will lead to a higher payment by the TR Receiver under the TR Swap.

Other applications of TR Swaps include making new asset classes accessible to investors for whom administrative complexity or lending group restrictions imposed by borrowers have traditionally presented barriers to entry. Recently, insurance companies and levered fund managers have made use of TR Swaps to access bank loan markets in this way.

10.2.3 Credit Options

Credit Options are put or call options on the price of either (a) a floating rate note, bond or loan, or (b) an "asset swap" package, which consists of a credit-risky instrument with any payment characteristics and a corresponding derivative contract which exchanges the cashflows of that instrument for a floating rate cashflow stream. In the case of (a), the Credit Put (or Call) Option grants the Option Buyer the right, but not the obligation, to sell to (or buy from) the Option Seller a specified floating rate Reference Asset at a pre-specified price (the "Strike Price"). Settlement may be on a cash or physical basis.

The more complex example of a Credit Option on an asset swap package described in (b) is illustrated in Figure 10.3. Here, the Put Buyer pays a premium for the right to sell to the Put Seller a specified Reference Asset and simultaneously enter into a swap in which the Put Seller pays the coupons on the Reference Asset and receives three- or six-month Libor plus a pre-determined spread (the "Strike Spread"). The Put Seller makes an upfront payment of par for this combined package upon exercise.

Credit Options may be American, European or multi-European style. They may be structured to survive a Credit Event of the issuer or guarantor of the Reference Asset (in which case both default risk and credit spread risk are transferred between the parties), or to knock out upon a Credit Event, in which case only credit spread risk changes hands.

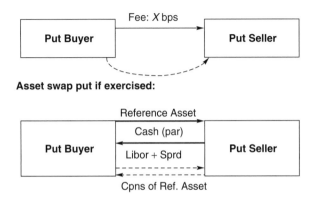

Figure 10.3   Credit put option. *Source:* J.P. Morgan Securities Inc.

As with other options, the Credit Option premium is sensitive to the volatility of the underlying market price (in this case determined only by credit spreads rather than the outright level of yields, since the underlying instrument is a floating rate asset or asset swap package), and the extent to which the Strike Spread is "in" or "out of" the money relative to the applicable current forward credit spread curve. Hence the premium is greater for more volatile credits, and for tighter Strike Spreads in the case of puts and wider Strike Spreads in the case of calls. Note that the extent to which a Strike Spread on a one-year Credit Option on a five-year asset is in or out of the money will depend upon the implied five-year credit spread in one year's time (or the "one by five year" credit spread), which in turn would have to be backed out from current one- and six-year spot credit spreads.

(i) Yield Enhancement and Credit Spread Protection

Credit Options have recently found favour with institutional investors as a source of yield enhancement. In the current buoyant market environment, with credit spread product in tight supply, credit market investors frequently find themselves underinvested. Consequently, the ability to write Credit Options, whereby investors collect current income in return for the risk of owning (in the case of a put) or losing (in the case of a call) an asset at a specified price in the future is an attractive enhancement to inadequate current income. Buyers of Credit Options, on the other hand, are often institutions such as banks and dealers who are interested in hedging their mark-to-market exposure to fluctuations in credit spreads: hedging long positions with puts, and short positions with calls. For such institutions, which often run highly levered balance sheets, the off-balance-sheet nature of the positions created by Credit Options are an attractive feature.

(ii) Hedging Future Borrowing Costs

Credit Options also have applications for borrowers wishing to lock in future borrowing costs without inflating their balance sheet. A borrower with a known future funding requirement could hedge exposure to outright interest rates using fixed income derivatives. Prior to the advent of credit derivatives, however, exposure to changes in the level of the issuer's borrowing spreads could not be hedged without issuing debt immediately and investing funds in other assets. This had the adverse effect of inflating the current balance sheet unnecessarily and exposing the issuer to reinvestment risk. Today, issuers can enter into Credit Options on their own name and lock in future borrowing costs with certainty. Essentially, the issuer is able to buy the right to put its own paper to a dealer at a pre-agreed spread. In a further recent innovation, issuers have *sold* puts or downgrade puts on their own paper, thereby providing investors with credit enhancement in the form of protection against a credit deterioration which falls short of outright default (whereupon such a put would of course be worthless). The objective of the issuer is to reduce borrowing costs and boost investor confidence.

10.2.4 Downgrade Options

A downgrade or anticipated downgrade by the rating agencies will be reflected by credit spread widening in the secondary market, resulting in mark-to-market losses. Certain portfolios may be forced to make mandatory sales. Credit Options can be used to hedge exposure to downgrade risk, and both Credit Swaps and Credit Options can be tailored so that payments are triggered upon a specified downgrade event.

Such options have been attractive for portfolios that are forced to sell deteriorating assets, where pre-emptive measures can be taken by structuring credit derivatives to provide downgrade protection. This reduces the risk of forced sales at distressed prices and consequently enables the portfolio manager to own assets of marginal credit quality at lower risk. Where the cost of such protection is less than the pick-up in yield of owning weaker credits, a clear improvement in portfolio risk-adjusted returns can be achieved.

10.2.5 Dynamic Credit Swaps

One of the difficulties in managing credit risk in derivative portfolios has been the fact that counterparty exposures change with both the passage of time and underlying market moves. In a swap position, both counterparties are subject to counterparty credit exposure, which is a combination of the current mark to market of the swap as well as expected future replacement costs.

Figure 10.4 shows how projected exposure on a cross-currency swap can change in just a few years. At inception in May 1990, prevailing rates implied a maximum exposure at maturity of US$125 million on a notional of US$100 million. Five years later, as the yen strengthened and interest rates dropped, the maximum exposure was calculated at US$220 million. By January 1996, the exposure slipped back to around US$160 million.

Swap counterparty exposure is therefore a function both of underlying market volatility, forward curves, and time. Furthermore, potential exposure will be exacerbated if the quality of the credit itself is correlated to the market; a fixed rate receiver which is domiciled in a country whose currency has experienced depreciation and has rising interest rates will be out of the money on the swap and could well be a weaker credit.

An important innovation in credit derivatives is the Dynamic Credit Swap (or "Credit Intermediation Swap"), which is a Credit Swap with the notional linked to the mark-to-market of a reference swap or portfolio of swaps. In this case, the notional amount applied to computing the Contingent Payment is equal to the mark-to-market value, if positive,

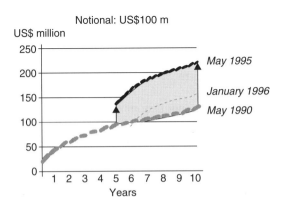

Figure 10.4   The instability of projected swap exposure. The shaded area shows the extent to which projected peak exposure on a 10 year yen/$ swap with principal exchange, effective in May 1990, fluctuated during the subsequent five and a half years. *Source:* J.P. Morgan Securities Inc.

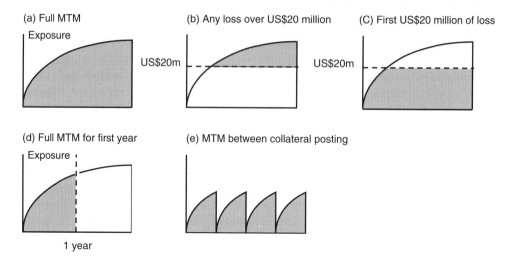

Figure 10.5 Coverage of dynamic credit swaps. These graphs show the projected exposure on a cross-currency swap over time. The shaded area represents alternative coverage possibilities of Dynamic Credit Swaps. *Source:* J.P. Morgan Securities Inc.

of the reference swap at the time of the Credit Event (see Figure 10.5(a)). The Protection Buyer pays a fixed fee, either upfront or periodically, which once set does not vary with the size of the protection provided. The Protection Buyer will only incur default losses if the swap counterparty *and* the Protection Seller fail. This dual credit effect means that the credit quality of the Protection Buyer's position is compounded to a level better than the quality of either of its individual counterparties. The status of this credit combination should normally be relatively impervious to market moves in the underlying swap, since, assuming an uncorrelated counterparty, the probability of a joint default is small.

Dynamic Credit Swaps may be employed to hedge exposure between margin calls on collateral posting (Figure 10.5(e)). Another structure might cover any loss beyond a pre-agreed amount (Figure 10.5(b)) or up to a maximum amount (Figure 10.5(c)). The protection horizon does not need to match the term of the swap; if the Buyer is primarily concerned with short-term default risk, it may be cheaper to hedge for a shorter period and roll over the Dynamic Credit Swap (Figure 10.5(d)).

A Dynamic Credit Swap avoids the need to allocate resources to a regular mark-to-market settlement or collateral agreements. Furthermore, it provides an alternative to unwinding a risky position, which might be difficult for relationship reasons or due to underlying market illiquidity.

Where a creditor is owed an amount denominated in a foreign currency, this is analogous to the credit exposure in a cross-currency swap. The amount outstanding will fluctuate with foreign exchange rates, so that credit exposure in the domestic currency is dynamic and uncertain. Thus, foreign currency denominated exposure may also be hedged using a Dynamic Credit Swap.

10.2.6 Other Credit Derivatives

Like most derivatives, credit derivatives have already evolved into a multitude of structural variations. Occasionally, Credit Events have included an additional requirement of a material movement in equity prices, commodity prices, or interest rates, and so on (a "Hybrid Credit Derivative"). Alternatively, they may be structured so that the Credit Event triggers a substitution of one asset for another rather than a cash payment (a "Substitution Option"). "Basket" Credit Swaps are triggered by a Credit Event not just of a single Reference Entity, but of, say, the *first or second to experience a Credit Event* among a basket of such entities. Credit Spread Forwards allow two parties to take opposing views on the level of a specified credit spread at a specified point in the future — a payment is made (in either direction) by one of the parties to the other depending on the amount by which the spread is wider or narrower than a specified strike at maturity. Similarly, Credit Spread Options are options on forward credit spreads in which one party pays an upfront premium to the other in return for a payment linked to the amount by which a spread is wider than the strike (a Credit Spread Cap or Call) or narrower than the strike (a Credit Spread Put or Floor) at a specified point in time. Credit Spread Options may be written on credit spreads over swap rate benchmarks, such as Libor, or over risk-free yield benchmarks, such as US Treasuries. As described above, Credit Options are put or call options on the price of floating rate bonds, loans or asset swaps, rather than options on credit spreads. A Credit Option on the price of a floating rate instrument is a "pure" credit derivative in which only credit spread risk is exchanged; however, options are also written on the price of fixed rate assets. These "Fixed Rate Bond Options" are a hybrid of both credit and interest rate derivatives in which both risks change hands.

The common denominator among all credit derivatives is their ability to transfer one form or another of credit risk between counterparties in isolation of both other risks and the underlying source of credit risk. This chapter focuses on this key feature and the applications of credit derivatives that arise naturally from it. In what follows, we concentrate primarily on Credit Swaps since these represent the most plain vanilla structure, although in many cases alternative structures could be employed to achieve substantially similar results.

The next section considers the use of credit derivatives in credit portfolio management, particularly in the context of recent innovations in credit portfolio risk modelling.

10.3 A PORTFOLIO APPROACH TO CREDIT RISK MANAGEMENT

10.3.1 Why Credit Has Become a Risk-Management Challenge

Clearly, it would be a mistake to consider the rapid evolution of credit derivatives as an isolated event. In fact, their contribution is best evaluated in the context of other complementary and perhaps mutually reinforcing developments. Credit derivatives have made possible more active trading of credit risks without interfering with other business objectives, such as relationship management. At the same time, market liquidity for secondary loans, high yield and emerging market credits is also improving. However, such sophisticated new tools for trading credit risk are of limited use if not accompanied by a framework within which to evaluate the impact of such transactions on a portfolio basis. In response to increased focus on credit risk management, the past few years have also seen the rapid evolution of more sophisticated techniques for the measurement and evaluation of credit transactions in the context of specific portfolios. Perhaps the most notable of these has been J.P. Morgan's launch of CreditMetrics®,[2] the first readily available portfolio model for evaluating credit value-at-risk. The relationship between credit derivatives and such models is an important one: by combining better credit risk trading tools with more sophisticated methodologies for evaluating credit risk, credit derivatives are making more active credit portfolio management a possibility.

Credit risk may be the key risk management challenge of the late 1990s. In recent years, a booming global economy and healthy credit cycle have created a business environment in which a growing number of institutions are taking on more and increasingly complex forms of credit risk.

Capital market bond issuance increased from US$1.2 trillion in 1996 to US$1.5 trillion in 1997.[3] Moreover, syndicated loans have enjoyed an origination boom (approximately doubling the dollar total for bond issuance in the same period). Only a small fraction of outstanding volumes trade in the secondary bond market while secondary loan trading, although rapidly improving, is even thinner. Even in the United States, where secondary loan markets are most liquid, the difference between volumes transacted in the primary versus the secondary loan markets is remarkable: secondary transaction volumes are little more than 5 per cent of new origination. Elsewhere such statistics are even more skewed. Clearly, banks and institutional investors in competitive lending markets are retaining more credit risks.

Meanwhile, as investors find fewer opportunities in interest rate and currency markets, they are moving towards yield enhancement through extending and trading credit rather than taking outright market exposure. In Europe, for example, the post-EMU world will likely see participating government bond markets become credit markets. Recently, as in the 1980s, the high yield and emerging market sectors have grown significantly, and new forms of credit risk are finding their way to the institutional capital markets as asset securitization is spreading globally.

Moreover, an increasingly varied array of institutions is intermediating and extending credit. Global credit markets have experienced a significant inflow of funds from mutual funds, pension plans, hedge funds, and other non-bank institutional investors. Similarly, corporates, insurance companies and their reinsurers are taking on increasing credit exposures through commercial contracts, trade receivables, insurance, and derivatives activities. Many of these are troublesome to manage because they do not derive from standardized or marketable credit instruments. Moreover, the proliferation of complex financial instruments has created uncertain and market-sensitive counterparty exposures that are significantly more challenging to manage than traditional instruments such as bonds. Credit derivatives have, for the first time, made the active management of such exposures a possibility.

At the same time, credit spreads across the credit spectrum have become compressed on both an absolute basis and relative to most historical comparisons. Institutions are increasingly vulnerable not only to a potential turn in the credit cycle leading to default-related losses, but also to mark-to-market losses caused by a reversion in credit spreads towards historical levels. Meanwhile, many institutions are experiencing constraints on regulatory and/or economic capital, and, following recent high-profile risk-management mishaps, there has been intensified focus on risk monitoring and controls. Common sense dictates that, if businesses are demanding better performance in terms of return on economic capital, management must have a solid grasp of all forms of risks being taken to achieve this. Consequently, as credit exposures have multiplied and become more complex, the need for more sophisticated risk measurement and management techniques for credit risk has also increased. Of course, more active credit risk management could be achieved by more rigorous enforcement of traditional credit processes such as stringent underwriting standards, limit enforcement, and counterparty monitoring. Increasingly, however, risk managers are also seeking to quantify and integrate overall credit risk within benchmark value-at-risk statements that treat exposure to both market and credit risks consistently. Moreover, having identified credit risks, risk managers are becoming increasingly inclined to take actions to manage them.

10.3.2 The Need for a Portfolio Approach to Credit Risk

A portfolio approach to credit risk analysis has two aspects. First, exposures to each obligor are restated on an equivalent basis to produce integrated statements of credit risk across the entire institution, irrespective of the underlying asset class. This is particularly useful when combined with a risk-management strategy that makes use of credit derivatives to transfer credit risk independently of the underlying instruments in a portfolio. Thus, both the methodology used to assess risk and the tools used to take action to manage risk are uninhibited by asset class barriers. Second, correlations of credit quality across obligors are taken into account. Consequently, portfolio effects — the benefits of diversification and costs of concentrations — can be properly quantified.

Until relatively recently, portfolio managers had very little to say in quantified terms about the concentration risk in their credit portfolios, since it is only in the context of a portfolio model that concentration risk can be evaluated on anything other than an intuitive level. Concentration risk arises from an acceleration in the expected loss of a portfolio due to increased exposure to one credit, or groups of highly correlated credits (perhaps in a particular industry or location). The problem can be mitigated only through diversification or transactions such as credit derivatives that hedge the specific risk of the concentrated exposure. On the whole, financial systems have historically proven to be very robust in the face of isolated credit failures. By contrast, correlated credit deterioration has been the specific cause of many occurrences of financial distress (consider agricultural loans in the US mid-west, oil loans in Texas, the Latin American debt crisis, and so on). A portfolio approach to credit risk analysis allows portfolio managers to quantify and stress-test concentration risk along many different dimensions such as industry, rating category, country, or type of instrument. Traditionally, credit limits have been the primary defence against unacceptable concentrations of credit risk. Fixed exposure limits may be intuitive, but are somewhat arbitrary in that they do not recognize the relationship between risk and return. A more quantitative approach would make credit lines a function of marginal portfolio volatility (that is, an *output* of the portfolio management model rather than an *input* to it).

Another important reason to take a portfolio view of credit risk is to more rationally and accountably evaluate and prioritize credit extension decisions and risk-mitigating actions. For example, rightly or wrongly, financial markets currently indicate a widespread perception of diminished risk due to credit, as illustrated by the historically tight level of credit spreads. In this environment, the bank lending marketplace has become increasingly competitive. As a result, good customer relationships have often become synonymous with heavily concentrated exposures as corporate borrowers command smaller bank groups and larger commitments from relationship banks. Yet banks are often caught in a paradoxical trap of their own making whereby those customers with whom they have developed the most valued relationships are precisely the customers to whom they have the least capacity to take incremental risk. Bank portfolio managers have begun to harbour suspicions that they may be vulnerable to a turn for the worse in global credit cycles and that current levels of spread income may not justify the concentration of risks being accumulated. Such concerns cannot easily be evaluated nor systematically reflected in pricing and credit extension decisions in the absence of a portfolio model. In a portfolio context, the decision to take on ever higher exposure to an obligor will meet with ever higher risk — risk that grows geometrically with the concentration on that obligor. If relationship demands the extension of credit to a customer to whom the portfolio is overexposed, then a portfolio model allows the portfolio manager to quantify (in units of undercompensated risk) exactly the extent of envisaged investment in relationship development. Consequently, the risk–return trade-off of concentrated lending activity can be better managed. Conversely, the portfolio manager can rationally take increased exposure to underconcentrated names. Indeed, such names may be *individually* risky yet offer a relatively small marginal contribution to overall *portfolio* risk due to diversification benefits. In this context, the ability of credit derivatives to assume and shed risk on a purely economic basis has become increasingly valuable.

Finally, by capturing portfolio effects, recognizing that risk accelerates with declining credit quality, and treating credit risk consistently, regardless of asset class, a portfolio credit risk model can provide the foundation for rational risk-based capital allocation and rational pricing of both cash credit instruments and credit derivatives. Such a model is equally appropriate for economic and regulatory capital purposes, but, as we shall see, differs fundamentally from the capital measures currently mandated for bank regulation by the Bank for International Settlements (BIS).

10.3.3 The Challenges of Estimating Portfolio Credit Risk

Modelling portfolio credit risk is neither analytically nor practically easy, presenting at least two significant challenges. The first problem relates to the remote probability of large losses in credit portfolios, combined with the limited potential for upside capital appreciation. Illustrated in Figure 10.6, this produces skewed return distributions with long, fat tails that differ significantly from the more normally distributed returns typically addressed by market value-at-risk models. Because of this feature, to understand the risks of credit portfolios completely requires that the nature of these tails be explored, a computationally onerous exercise.

The second problem is empirical. Unlike market portfolios where the data necessary to compute correlations are readily available, correlations in credit portfolios cannot easily be directly observed. Consequently, credit quality correlations must either be derived

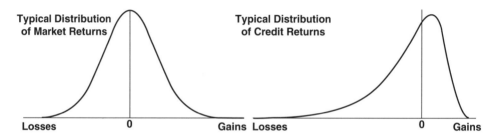

Figure 10.6 Comparison of distribution of market returns and credit returns. *Source:* J.P. Morgan Securities lnc.

indirectly from other sources, such as equity prices, or tabulated from historical data at a relatively high level of aggregation (e.g. treating all A-rated obligors identically).

(i) Unexpected Versus Expected Losses

The *expected* loss calculation is, in one sense, the most straightforward aspect of portfolio theory. That is, the ability to estimate credit quality and the expected size of losses given changes in credit quality, allows the risk manager to price, and reserve for, expected loss. Summing across all credit states, the probability of loss multiplied by expected size of loss equals expected loss. If there were no further uncertainty relating to possible credit losses, then computing expected loss would be the extent of the risk-management problem: predictable credit losses year after year would be no more than a budgeted expense. *Risk*, however, entails not just an estimated possibility of loss but also the *uncertainty* of loss, namely the chance that the estimate of expected loss may be incorrect. Unexpected loss measures the potential for error in the estimate of expected loss. Typically, this has been estimated as a function of portfolio volatility; for example, if unexpected loss is deemed that level of loss which is, say, 95 per cent likely not to be exceeded, then in a normal distribution this would be 1.65 standard deviations distant from the portfolio mean.

(ii) Characteristics of Credit Risk Distributions

It turns out that while it is difficult to estimate *expected* credit portfolio values, it is harder still to predict *unexpected* loss, or *uncertainties* around these values. This is because the distribution of credit-related losses is heavily skewed, with the result that meaningful probabilities of loss can occur many standard deviations distant from the expected level. Because of this, modelling the full distribution of portfolio values requires a great deal of information beyond simple summary statistics such as the mean and standard deviation (volatility). Without a full specification of the portfolio value distribution, it is not possible to compute the percentile levels necessary to describe risk in credit portfolios. By considering every possible combination of credit states across every obligor in the portfolio, the full distribution of a credit portfolio can be constructed mechanistically; however, this is computationally complex for portfolios of more than a few obligors. One approach, adopted in CreditMetrics, is to estimate the portfolio distribution by a process of simulation which reduces the computational burden by sampling outcomes randomly across all possibilities. Once the portfolio distribution has been approximated in this way, it is possible to compute percentile levels and summary statistics that describe the shape of the distribution.

(iii) The Importance of Diversification

Intuitively, two loans held to maturity will have a default correlation much lower than their corresponding equity price correlation (due to the low likelihood that two extremely remote events will occur simultaneously). For the layperson, a natural conclusion to draw might be that the benefits of diversification in a credit portfolio are not significant precisely because default correlations are so low. But this is not a correct conclusion. The implication of very low default correlations is that the systematic risk in a credit portfolio is small relative to the non-systematic or individual contribution to risk of each asset. Non-systematic risk is hedgable or diversifiable risk. The greater the component of non-systematic risk, the greater the benefits of diversification, and vice versa. The problem can be viewed another way. Indices provide great hedges of risk in equity portfolios because most equity portfolios are sufficiently diversified to resemble the market. However, because a portfolio of debt of those same names is unlikely to be sufficiently diversified to resemble the market, this same type of index hedge will not work in debt portfolios. The portfolio management consequences of a full characterization of credit risks are thus not insignificant: it takes many more names to fully diversify a credit portfolio than an equity portfolio, but when those diversification benefits are achieved, they are considerable. An inadequately diversified portfolio, on the other hand, can result in significantly lower return on risk ratios than would seem intuitively obvious. Absent cash market alternatives, the case for proactive management of credit risk using derivatives is compelling.

(iv) The Importance of Liquidity and Active Risk Management

Credit exposure has sometimes been modelled as analogous to a portfolio of short, deep, out-of-the-money put options on firm assets, an insight first suggested by Robert Merton.[4] The analogy is intuitively sound given the limited upside and remote but large downside profile of credit risk. This "short option" analogy allows us to draw some insights into the consequences of illiquidity in credit portfolios. In equity portfolios, it has been argued, independence of daily returns allows time to diversify risk. If credit portfolios are similar to a portfolio of out-of-the money puts, then it can be argued that as the market declines (credit quality deteriorates) the "delta" equivalent of that portfolio increases and the portfolio becomes more leveraged (riskier). Consequently, any persistent serial correlation in credit returns, as suggested by the historical tendency of one downgrade to be followed by another, can cause poor performance to increase volatility and create accelerating portfolio riskiness. An ability to rebalance the portfolio in response to credit deterioration is the only effective way to materially offset this effect. The consequences of illiquidity and the absence of active risk management in credit portfolios are therefore more severe than in market risk portfolios.

Taking a quantitative approach to portfolio concentration risk does not, of course, necessitate the use of credit derivatives as a portfolio management tool. However, where existing positions are illiquid for whatever reason, credit derivatives offer a new solution to reducing exposure, or at least to quantifying the trade-off of *not* reducing exposure.

10.3.4 Assessing Credit Risk on a Portfolio Basis: Methodology

The application of modern portfolio theory to credit risk measurement continues to evolve rapidly and has had little standardization to date. As the first readily available portfolio model for evaluating credit value-at-risk, the following discussion focuses on CreditMetrics methodology, recognizing that it is not necessarily the only approach to the problem. The purpose here is to illustrate how such analysis may be integrated with a portfolio risk management strategy incorporating the use of credit derivatives in a fashion that allows the user to identify, prioritize, and ultimately evaluate or "price" the opportunities presented by credit derivatives.

CreditMetrics employs a three-step process to compute individual and portfolio credit value-at-risk. First, it computes the exposure profile of each obligor in a portfolio. Where the portfolio incorporates instruments such as derivatives whose credit exposure is a dynamic function of underlying market moves and the passage of time, this requires some preprocessing to estimate the exposure profile of each instrument. Secondly, it computes the volatility of each instrument caused by credit events (including upgrades, downgrades, and defaults). Likelihoods derived from a transition matrix are attributed to each possible credit event. Each event results in an estimated change in value (derived from credit spread data and, in default, recovery rates). Each value outcome is weighted by its likelihood in order to create a distribution of value across each credit state, from which expected value and volatility (standard deviation) of value are computed. Finally, taking into account correlations between each of these events, the model combines the volatility of the individual instruments to give an aggregate portfolio volatility. Recently, there have been significant developments in the field of default and migration correlation estimation. As a result, some of the difficulties encountered in the direct estimation of historical correlations due to the small historical sample set have been avoided by inferring such information from equity price correlations.[5]

As a measure of symmetrical dispersion about the expected portfolio value, portfolio volatility is not an accurate measure of risk in a skewed distribution. The standard deviation measure cannot, for example, capture the fact that the maximum upside might be only one standard deviation above the average, while meaningful occurrences of loss can be many standard deviations below the average. Consequently, CreditMetrics includes a simulation engine that estimates the entire distribution of a credit portfolio and computes percentile levels. These reflect the likelihood that the portfolio value will fall below a specified level, e.g. that the likelihood of its falling below the first percentile level is 1 per cent.

In the next section we go on to discuss the practical applications of a portfolio approach to credit risk measurement, many of which identify opportunities for specific credit derivative transactions.

10.3.5 Practical Applications of Portfolio Methodology Using Credit Derivatives

(i) Prioritizing Risk-Reducing Transactions (Selling Exposure or Buying Credit Protection)

Decisions to buy, sell or hold an exposure should be made in the context of an existing portfolio. The relevant calculation is then not the stand-alone risk of that exposure but the *marginal* increase to the portfolio risk that would be created by adding that exposure to it. Marginal risk refers to the difference between the total portfolio risk before and after the marginal transaction. If the new transaction adds to an already overconcentrated portion of the portfolio, then the marginal risk is likely to be high. If the new transaction is diversifying (or in the extreme is actually hedging a position), then the marginal risk may be quite small or even negative. The importance of calculating the marginal risk is that it captures the specific characteristics of a particular portfolio. It would not be unusual for a given credit to be considered risky in one institution's portfolio but of considerably lower risk in another institution's portfolio. Mechanically, a marginal risk statistic can be calculated using either standard deviations or percentile levels. The point is the same: to show the change in total portfolio risk upon the addition of a new transaction.

Thus, marginal credit value-at-risk analysis may be used to direct and prioritize risk-mitigating actions, and as such it is a useful tool for identifying opportunities for the use of credit derivatives to restructure a portfolio's composition. To illustrate, Figure 10.7 shows marginal risk versus size of exposures within a typical credit portfolio.

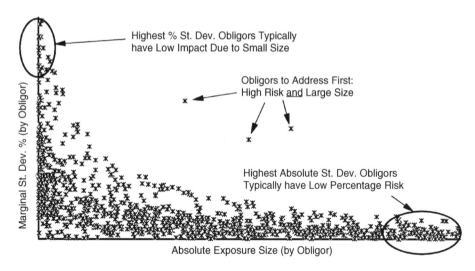

Figure 10.7   Risk versus exposure size. *Source:* J.P. Morgan Securities Inc.

When considering risk-mitigating actions, it is useful to prioritize transactions that have the greatest impact on the *absolute* amount of portfolio risk (which appear in the lower right-hand corner of Figure 10.7) since this prioritizes exposures that are both a relatively high contribution to portfolio risk on a percentage basis and a relatively large exposure amount. In practice, such outliers may be the result of fallen angels, whose now excessive exposures were appropriate when originated, or simply relationship-driven concentrations. Where relationship is a driving concern, purchasing protection via a credit derivative is often preferable to an outright sale of the asset.

(ii) Risk versus Return: A Numerical Example

Portfolio analysis highlights where an asset may contribute differently to the risk of distinct portfolios and yet yield the same returns in either case. Consequently, it is easy to imagine a situation in which two managers identify two credit risks of the same maturity, yield, and credit quality, but — because of the composition of the two portfolios — the risk of *both* portfolios is reduced by the swap. This is often accomplished most easily using credit derivatives and, moreover, without a loss in return: the financial equivalent of a free lunch. The importance of identifying the contribution of each asset to portfolio risk is obvious. The risk of credit assets is largely due to concentrations particular to the portfolio. Thus, opportunities may exist to restructure the portfolio to reduce risk with no change to profitability.

The following example shows measures of portfolio value-at-risk due to credit taken from a hypothetical 20-obligor portfolio of assets with various maturities, ratings, and exposure amounts. In Figure 10.8, the plots of marginal portfolio risk against exposure size identify "asset 15" as the highest marginal contributor to overall risk. Asset 15 happens to be a B-rated, US$3.26 million, two-year position.

In fact, as the largest risk contributor to the portfolio, asset 15 makes up 4.83 per cent of the portfolio value, but 23.77 per cent of the portfolio standard deviation. The solution? Selling or buying credit protection against asset 15 would reduce portfolio risk

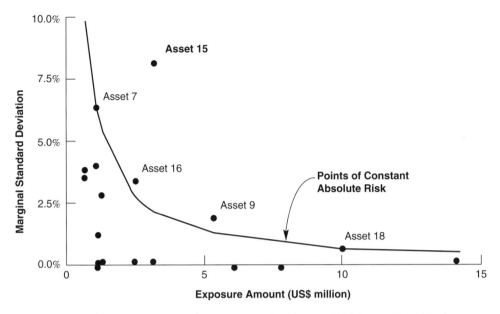

Figure 10.8   Marginal risk against exposure size. *Source:* J.P. Morgan Securities Inc.

by 23.77 per cent. However, this leaves a reinvestment problem, so as an alternative we should compute the impact of substituting this asset for another. We choose a hypothetical substitute asset that has identical stand-alone statistics (i.e. is a B-rated, US$3.26 million, two-year position). Having the same credit rating, this can reasonably be assumed to yield the same return as asset 15. Importantly, however, the new asset is assumed to have a *zero* correlation with the rest of the portfolio. The effect of this substitution is to reduce portfolio standard deviation by 7 per cent. Given that the portfolio yield is unaffected, the portfolio Sharpe Ratio (ratio of excess return to risk) improves accordingly, by $7.5 = (1/0.93 - 1)$ per cent.

The analysis illustrates how marginal risk measures can be used to suggest transactions that will generate better returns for the risks being taken or, alternatively, to take less risk for the returns being generated. However, many sources of credit risk are not associated with liquid or readily transferable instruments. Consequently, when overconcentrated or undercompensated risks are identified within a portfolio, such as that presented by asset 15, the portfolio manager is often constrained from simply being able to sell that exposure or replace it with another. Similarly, when seeking to diversify away concentration risks, such as when seeking that substitute for asset 15, the portfolio manager is frequently constrained by the limited availability of diversifying assets. Clearly, the credit derivatives provide the portfolio manager with an important new means to shed illiquid existing exposures and source diversifying new ones.

(iii) Risk-Based Credit Limits

Traditionally, credit risk limits have been based on intuitive but arbitrary exposure amounts, which is unsatisfactory because resulting decisions are not properly risk-driven. Consequently, the next step beyond using risk statistics for prioritizing transactions is to

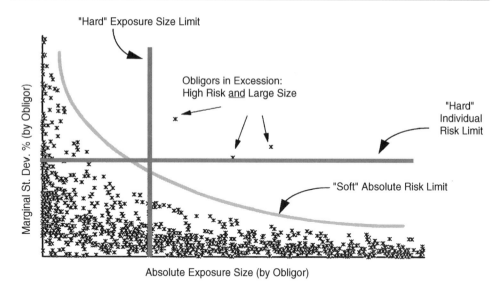

Figure 10.9   Risk-based limit-setting. *Source:* J.P. Morgan Securities Inc.

use them for limit-setting. Just as it is best to address exposures with the highest level of absolute risk first, it makes sense to set credit limits according to the absolute contribution to portfolio risk. This would correspond to a limit resembling the curve defined by the boundary of non-outlying scatter points in Figure 10.7, as illustrated in Figure 10.9. Such a limit would prevent the addition to the portfolio of any exposure that increased portfolio risk by more than a given amount, rather than the more traditional approach of limiting absolute exposure size (a vertical line) or individual riskiness (a horizontal line).

Figure 10.10 illustrates how marginal risk statistics can be used to make credit allocation decisions sensitive to the trade-off between risk and return. Part (a) reflects how marginal contribution to portfolio risk increases geometrically with exposure size of an

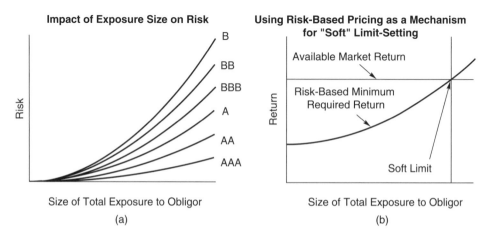

Figure 10.10   Exposure targets based on risk–return trade-off. *Source:* J.P. Morgan Securities Inc.

individual obligor, more noticeably for weaker credits. Consequently, as illustrated in part (b), proportionately more return is required with each increment of exposure to an individual obligor to maintain a constant balance between risk and return. The marginal risk of the obligor is shown by the curve labelled "risk-based minimum required return". This represents the set of points at which the return on risk is constant — the curvature of this line reflects the fact that as exposure size and hence portfolio risk increases, a proportionately greater return is required to maintain a constant risk–return trade-off. The horizontal straight line represents the available market return for the obligor, as reflected, perhaps, in the premium available for a Credit Swap on that name. Areas to the right of the intersection between the two lines represent situations in which the portfolio manager might rationally decrease exposure, because doing so would more than proportionately reduce risk relative to the loss in return. Areas to the left of the intersection represent situations in which the portfolio manager might increase exposure because doing so would more than proportionately increase return relative to the increase in risk. The vertical line marking the point of intersection is thus effectively the "soft" risk-based target for exposure to the obligor, given available market pricing, the portfolio targeted risk–return balance, and the relationship between the obligor and the existing portfolio. The appeal of a limit that is an output of a model which is sensitive to both risk and return is unmistakable.

(iv) Risk-Based Capital Allocation

To assess the risk a firm takes by holding a credit portfolio requires an understanding of the risk of that portfolio with regard to what this implies about the stability of the organization. Essentially, in this framework risk is measured in terms of its threat to shareholder capital: if a firm's liabilities are constant, then it is taking risk by holding assets that are volatile. Risk-taking capacity is not unlimited and must be allocated as a scarce resource. For example, if a manager found that there was a 10 per cent chance of a decline in portfolio value occurring in the next year which would be severe enough to cause organization-wide insolvency, then he would likely seek to decrease the risk of the asset portfolio. For a portfolio with a more reasonable level of risk, the manager cannot add new exposures indiscriminately, since eventually the portfolio risk will surpass the "comfort level". Thus, each additional exposure utilizes a scarce resource, which is commonly thought of as risk-taking capacity or "economic capital".

Consequently, as an indicator of economic capital, a percentile level seems quite appropriate. Using, for example, the first percentile level, economic capital could be defined as the level of losses on the portfolio that, with 99 per cent certainty, will not be exceeded in the next year. Such a measure would be sensitive to obligor credit quality, would reflect the risk of portfolio concentrations, and would allow uniform treatment of risk, irrespective of the underlying instrument.

(v) Regulatory Capital Allocation

Finally, in predicting that credit derivatives will change the way in which institutions measure and manage credit risk, it is necessary to assume that banks in particular will not continue to face the disincentives to portfolio risk management currently caused by regulatory capital requirements.

The risk-based approach to economic capital allocation described above contrasts starkly with the so-called risk-based capital framework currently mandated for bank regulation under the Bank for International Settlements (BIS) accord. Under the current BIS rules, the required capital reserve for a portfolio of credit positions residing in the banking book (as the vast majority do) is a simple summation of the capital for the portfolio's individual transactions. In turn, each transaction's capital requirement depends on a broad categorization of the obligor (rather than credit quality), on the transaction's exposure type (e.g. drawn loans versus undrawn commitments), and, for off-balance-sheet exposures, on whether the transaction's maturity is more or less than one year. Moreover, as described more fully below, there are very limited opportunities for banks to offset capital requirements where exposures have been hedged using credit derivatives because the current guidelines require virtually complete offset of risks with a lower risk-weighted counterparty (irrespective of credit quality) in order to recognize any capital relief. The weaknesses of this structure, such as its one-size-fits-all risk weight for all corporate loans and its inability to distinguish between diversified and undiversified portfolios, are increasingly apparent to regulators and market participants. Particular concern has been paid to the uneconomic incentives created by the regulatory regime and the inability of regulatory capital adequacy ratios to accurately portray actual bank risk levels.

If regulatory capital ratios were used only as originally intended, namely as supervisory tools measuring minimum prudent capitalization levels in the context of a more thorough regulatory review of a bank's risks, then the issue of regulatory capital calculations would be immaterial. Banks would report the required ratios but continue to manage their businesses so as to optimize *economic* capital utilization. However, perhaps because regulatory capital ratios are one of the few standardized public risk measures for banks, they are closely monitored by a number of observers including the public rating agencies as an indicator of a financial institution's stability and hence credit quality. Consequently, the management of regulatory capital ratios has become as much of an imperative as the management of economic capital for those banks that are focused on maximizing shareholder value.

Increased credit derivative activity by both dealer and end-user banks has highlighted the need to reform the bank regulatory capital framework and over the next few years will likely contribute to bringing such reform to the front of the regulatory agenda. The point is a simple one: if discrepancies continue to exist between economic and regulatory measures of risk, then banks, once equipped with tools such as credit derivatives, will either be forced to avoid entering into economic transactions because of their adverse effect on regulatory capital, or compelled to enter into uneconomic transactions because of their beneficial effect on regulatory capital.

By contrast, the appeal of the internal models approach described above is illustrated by the analogy of a parent dividing a pie between two squabbling children. As the knife moves to and fro over the pie, each child protests at the size of its share. To resolve the problem, the parent gives the knife to one child, but tells them both that once the division is made, the other may choose which piece to eat. The analogy illustrates the point that, by enforcing a system that is inherently unbiased, the regulator is able to supervise without interfering with the efficient allocation of resources.

In response to these concerns, both banks and bank regulators are looking for insights into credit risk models such as CreditMetrics that generate expected losses and a probability distribution of unexpected losses and would close the gap between economic and regulatory capital measures, thereby encouraging proactive credit risk management and promoting the further growth of credit derivatives.

10.4 REGULATORY TREATMENT OF CREDIT DERIVATIVES

Over the past year, US and European bank regulators have responded to the rapid increase in credit derivatives use by banks by publishing supervisory guidance including guidelines on appropriate regulatory capital treatment. These include papers from the following:

- Federal Reserve Board (SR 1996-17, 12 August 1996 and SR 1997-18, 13 June 1997)
- Office of the Comptroller of the Currency (OCC Bulletin 96-43, 12 August 1996)
- Federal Deposit Insurance Corporation (FIL-62-96, 15 August 1996)
- Bank of England ("Discussion Paper: Developing a Supervisory Approach to Credit Derivatives", November 1996, and "Credit Derivatives: Amended Interim Capital Adequacy Treatment", 5 June 1997)
- Securities and Futures Authority (Board Notice 414: Guidance on Credit Derivatives, 17 April 1997)
- Commission Bancaire (Credit Derivatives: Issues for Discussion on Interim Prudential Treatment", June 1997; and "Traitement Prudential des Instruments Dérivés de Crédit", 18 April 1998)
- OSFI (Policy for Credit Derivatives. Statement no. 1997–04, 31 October 1997)

The existence of such guidance encourages many users by reducing uncertainty surrounding the potential legal and regulatory treatment of such new products.[6] Moreover, the regulatory guidelines broadly agree that credit derivatives are a viable tool to manage credit risk and approve their use to reduce credit exposure within asset portfolios. In certain circumstances, recognizing the economic effect of buying credit protection, the guidelines also allow for required regulatory capital relief.

However, credit derivatives, in combining certain features of traditional credit products, which are subject to one capital regime (the "banking book"), of traded instruments, which are subject to a quite different capital regime (the "trading book"), and of derivative contracts, which are subject to yet a third capital regime ("counterparty risk capital"), present a significant challenge to any "one-size-fits-all" solution to regulatory capital treatment. Indeed, some of the regulators' suggested solutions have served to highlight the shortcomings of all three approaches.

None the less, some of the regulatory papers cited above are extremely helpful in providing a broad discussion of the issues rather than a narrow prescriptive approach. Moreover, the emergence of credit derivatives in conjunction with more sophisticated internal credit risk models has stimulated a debate that may ultimately lead to reform of the regulatory treatment of credit risk as a whole. The following discussion provides a very broad summary of the regulatory capital treatment of simple banking book transactions in some jurisdictions. Users should consult with their own advisers as to the appropriate regulatory capital treatment of specific transactions in their own jurisdiction.

As off-balance-sheet transactions, credit derivatives need to be translated to an on-balance-sheet equivalent for regulatory capital purposes. When a bank sells protection in a TR Swap or Credit Swap, the guidelines require that the bank's position is treated as if it had written a standby letter of credit or guarantee (collectively known as "direct credit substitutes"). These are translated to on-balance-sheet equivalents with a conversion factor equal to 100 per cent of the notional of the contract. Risk-weighting then proceeds according to the weighting of the Reference Entity (0 per cent for an OECD sovereign, 20 per cent for an OECD bank, and 100 per cent for corporates).

When a bank buys protection in a TR Swap or Credit Swap to hedge an underlying asset, the bank can, in certain circumstances, achieve the same capital relief as if it had purchased a guarantee from its counterparty. Although different regulators apply different standards and some are more specific than others, broadly speaking the transaction will have to achieve a significant degree of risk transference to achieve capital relief; for example, by exactly matching the maturity and seniority of the underlying asset. Provided there is no material mismatch between the underlying asset and the protection purchased, this would result in a reduction in the risk-weighting of the underlying asset to a level equal to that of the Protection Seller, if lower than that of the Reference Entity (i.e. from 100 per cent to 20 per cent for corporate default protection purchased from an OECD bank). Under current regulations, as with guarantees, no such relief would be available for a bank buying protection from a 100 per cent risk-weighted entity (including, in the United States, all corporates and non-bank securities dealers), even if this entity were AAA-rated. Similarly, where the degree of risk transference is considered inadequate due to a mismatch in maturity, seniority, or the Credit Event definition, then the arrangement may not be considered an effective guarantee and no capital relief, rather than partial capital relief, will be allowed.

This treatment clearly creates a significant disincentive for banks that are Protection Buyers seeking to simultaneously manage economic risk and regulatory capital. Despite the fact that hedged positions represent a very small residual risk (since the hedging bank can only lose if its counterparty *and* the underlying Reference Entity default), the bank would be required to hold capital against at least 20 per cent, and possibly 100 per cent (if selling risk to corporates), of the notional contract sizes. Banking book capital treatment clearly presents even more severe problems for dealer banks accumulating large portfolios of mostly hedged positions as a function of their intermediation business. This problem may be somewhat alleviated for dealers and larger, more sophisticated banks that maintain a trading book.

Assets in trading accounts are subject to the BIS-mandated market risk capital rules. Under these rules, capital is required to be held for counterparty risk, general market risk (usually zero for a credit derivative which does not embody market risk), and specific risk. As with all derivatives, the amount of counterparty risk capital required to be held will depend on a conversion factor that is equal to the current exposure to the counterparty on the contract, if positive, plus an add-on, which is determined by reference to maturity and underlying risk type. Although no factors have yet been developed for credit derivatives specifically, the conservative approach adopted by the Federal Reserve requires the use of equity swap factors for investment grade exposures and commodity add-ons for others. Applying the logic that the use of equity add-ons should be a conservative treatment for debt positions since debt is senior to equity in the capital structure of the firm, other regulators, including the Bank of England, have required equity add-ons to be used for all credit derivatives. Risk-weighting proceeds according to the weighting of the swap counterparty (0 per cent for OECD sovereigns, 20 per cent for OECD banks, 50 per cent for corporates).

Table 10.1 Specific risk factors for trading book assets (standardized approach)

Category	Remaining Maturity	Weighting Factor	Old "Conversion Factor" Equivalence
Government	N/A	0.00	0.00
Qualifying	6 months or less	0.25	3.125%
	6 to 24 months	1.00	12.5%
	Over 24 months	1.60	20%
Other	N/A	8.00	100%

As with general market risk, there is a provision for banks to elect either to adopt the standardized approach to specific risk or to use their own internal models. However, specific risk calculations performed using internal models are floored at 50 per cent of the standardized approach. Therefore, until or unless this requirement is dropped, the standardized approach will remain important, even for institutions employing sophisticated internal portfolio credit risk models. Table 10.1 illustrates standardized specific risk factors which vary by the category of the underlying instrument and by maturity. These differ most notably from the older banking book risk-weightings in the case of "qualifying" debt positions. Qualifying positions include OECD bank debt and OECD corporate debt if investment grade or of equivalent quality and issued by a corporate with instruments listed on a recognized stock exchange. For qualifying debt positions, the risk factors equate to weightings of 3.125 per cent for positions with tenure of six months or less, 12.5 per cent for positions with tenor of more than six but no more than 24 months, and 20 per cent for positions with tenor of over 24 months. Non-qualifying debt carries a factor equivalent to 100 per cent, and OECD government debt has a factor of 0 per cent. This is most significant in that the market risk capital rules treat open exposures to investment grade corporates significantly more favourably than exposures held in the banking book.

The guidelines set out by the Federal Reserve for the treatment of credit derivatives in the trading book under the standardized approach (SR 97-18) envisage some netting of specific risks in long and short positions, but only in the case of "matched" positions, defined as those with identical maturities, reference assets, and structures. The requirement for identical structures means that a loan or bond may only be hedged with a Total Return Swap of identical maturity referencing that specific asset, but not with a Credit Swap, even one with identical maturity and referencing that specific asset. In addition, Total Return Swaps and Credit Swaps may only be offset by identical transactions, but not by each other. Offsetting positions which do not meet the necessary requirements to be considered matched do not achieve any capital relief but require capital to be held against the specific risk of either the long or the short position, whichever is greater. Given the additional requirement to hold capital against counterparty risk, this treatment can result in *increased* capital requirements.

In summary, current guidelines suggest that the use of credit derivatives to hedge risks can, in certain limited circumstances, enable banks to free up regulatory capital, although not yet in a manner remotely consistent with the true reduction in economic risk. It is hoped that the development of more sophisticated internal models for credit risk measurement may stimulate a more flexible approach to regulatory capital that involves less restricted use of internal models, initially at least in the trading book but eventually also in the banking book.

10.5 BALANCE SHEET MANAGEMENT: SYNTHETIC SECURITIZATION

In 1997, credit derivatives entered the mainstream of global structured finance as they were put to use for the first time in a number of large, high profile securitizations of assets which cannot as easily be managed using more traditional techniques. By combining credit derivatives with traditional securitization tools, structures can be tailored to meet specific goals with much greater efficiency, such as providing regulatory capital relief, preserving a low funding cost advantage, and maintaining borrower and market confidentiality.

Consider a portfolio of bank loans to corporates. Traditional securitization techniques for such a portfolio would involve the creation of a collateralized loan obligation (CLO). In a CLO, the originating bank would assign or participate its loans to a special purpose vehicle (SPV), which in turn would issue two or more classes of securities to investors. Typically, the originating bank would retain much of the economic risk to the pool of loans by purchasing the most junior (equity) tranche of the SPV securities. The extent to which the transaction would achieve regulatory capital relief for the bank would depend on the size of the retained first loss position. According to the low level recourse rules governing securitizations in the United States, a retained first loss piece of 8 per cent or greater would result in no capital relief, and smaller retained first loss positions would result in a proportionate reduction in required capital.

While a CLO can achieve a number of goals, including regulatory capital relief, financing of a loan portfolio and off-balance-sheet treatment of the portfolio for GAAP purposes, it has some inefficiencies. For example, for a bank that enjoys the advantage of low cost of unsecured financing, the cost of funding usually achieved by such transactions is unattractive. Thus, in seeking to manage regulatory capital, the bank is effectively forced to accept an inefficient financing cost. Moreover, transferring the legal ownership of assets to the SPV via assignment requires borrower notification and consent, introducing the risk of adverse relationship consequences. The alternative of participating loans to the vehicle will normally cause the vehicle's overall rating to be capped at that of the originating bank with adverse consequences for the overall cost of funding. Structures that avoid this particular problem can be structurally and legally complex and require extensive rating agency involvement. Finally, CLOs cannot be readily applied to loans that are committed but undrawn, such as revolving credit lines, or back-stop liquidity facilities.

As alternatives to traditional CLOs, transactions are being developed that make use of credit derivatives to transfer the economic risk but not the legal ownership of the underlying assets. For example, in several recent transactions, the credit risk of loans on the originating bank's balance sheet has been transferred to an SPV via the sale of credit-linked notes rather than the assignment or participation of the loans themselves. In such structures, credit derivatives can be used to achieve the same or similar regulatory capital benefits of a traditional securitization by transferring credit risk synthetically. However, as privately negotiated confidential transactions, credit derivatives allow the originating bank to avoid the legal and structural risks of assignments or participations and maintain both market and customer confidentiality. Other, more innovative, structures have exploited the unfunded, off-balance-sheet nature of credit derivatives (as opposed to funded credit-linked notes) to allow a bank to purchase the credit protection necessary to mimic the regulatory capital treatment of a traditional securitization while preserving its competitive funding advantage. Such structures have the advantage of being equally applicable to the exposure of both drawn and undrawn loans.

Thus, credit derivatives are stimulating the rapidly growing asset-backed securitization market by stripping out and repackaging credit exposures from the vast pool of risks that do not naturally lend themselves to securitization, either because the risks are unfunded (off balance sheet), because they are not intrinsically transferable, or because their sale would be complicated by relationship concerns. In so doing, by enhancing liquidity and bringing new forms of credit risk to the capital markets, credit derivatives achieve the financial equivalent of a "free lunch" whereby both buyers and sellers of risk benefit from the associated efficiency gains.

10.6 INVESTMENT CONSIDERATIONS

10.6.1 Filling Gaps in the Credit Spectrum

Maintaining diversity in an investment portfolio is challenging. Figure 10.11 examines the issuance history and maturity schedule of existing corporate bonds and loans and reveals that some US$20 trillion of issuance would be required over the next 10 years to maintain current funding levels in international bonds and syndicated loans. Meanwhile, as Figures 10.12 and 10.13 illustrate, the new issue profile of credit instruments exhibits significant concentration both by maturity and by rating category. Similar concentrations can be illustrated by geographical and industrial sectors. In a more specific example of the concentration observed in liquid bond markets, the Lehman Aggregate Corporate Index

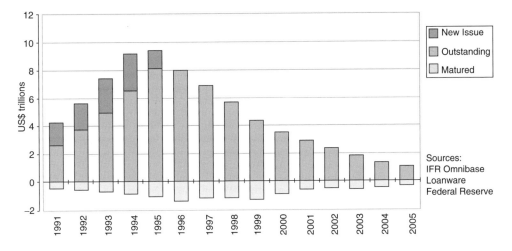

Figure 10.11 Issuance history and maturing schedule of international bonds and syndicated loans (does not include domestic government bonds, or US domestic market). *Source:* J.P. Morgan Securities Inc.

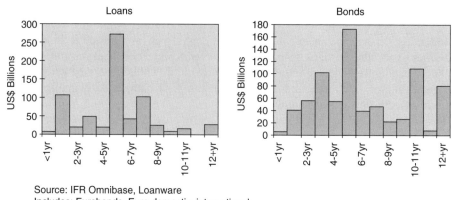

Source: IFR Omnibase, Loanware
Includes: Eurobonds, Euro domestic, international
Excludes: Domestic governments and US domestic

Figure 10.12   Maturity profile of new issuance, 1996. *Source:* J.P. Morgan Securities Inc.

recently had the following composition:

Ford Motor Credit	1.95 per cent
Associates Corp.	1.50 per cent
Ford Capital BV	0.49 per cent
Ford Motor Co.	0.44 per cent
Total Ford-related credits:	4.38 per cent

A large insurance company with assets under management of US$25 billion benchmarked to this index would be required to own US$1.09 billion in assets of Ford and related entities, a number that is probably 300 per cent of the average net income of an insurance company of this size. It does not take a sophisticated model to question this scale of concentration risk.

It should be no surprise, then, to discover similar concentrations in the portfolios of institutional investors and banks that are constrained by the inability to source a diversified pool of investible credit assets. Credit derivatives are being used to address this problem by providing exposure to names that are not otherwise available in the cash market. Under-leveraged credits that do not issue debt are usually attractive, but by definition exposure to these credits is difficult to find. It is rarely the case, however, that no economic risk to such credits exists at all. Trade receivables, fixed price forward sales contracts, third-party indemnities, deep in-the-money swaps, insurance contracts, and deferred employee compensation pools, for example, all create credit exposure in the normal course of business of such companies. Credit derivatives now allow intermediaries to strip out such unwanted credit exposure and redistribute it among banks and institutional investors who find it attractive as a mechanism for diversifying investment portfolios. Gaps in the credit spectrum may be filled not only by bringing new credits to the capital markets, but also by filling maturity and seniority gaps in the debt issuance of existing borrowers.

10.6.2 Transcending Asset Class Barriers

The ability to source credit risk in one market and redistribute it in another also allows both investors and issuers alike to benefit from discrepancies in credit pricing across asset class

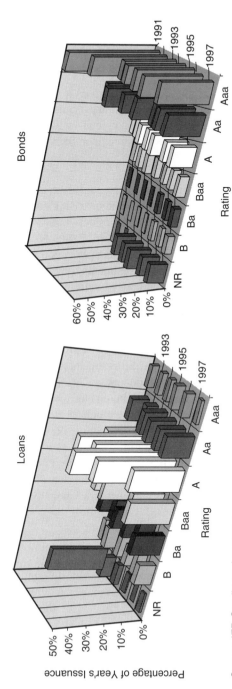

Figure 10.13   Rating profile of new issuance, 1991–97. *Source:* J.P. Morgan Securities Inc.

Source: IFR Omnibase, Loanware
Includes: Eurobonds, Euro domestic, international
Excludes: Domestic governments and US domestic

barriers. For example, an insurance company seeking to reinsure event risk might find that the cost of reinsurance is significantly higher than their current cost of borrowing from the capital markets in surplus note form. A key distinction between purchasing reinsurance (contingent funding) and surplus note issuance (current funding) is the current balance sheet impact. As an alternative, the insurance company can create a Contingent Capital Note. This structure embodies a credit derivative whereby, for a premium somewhat in excess of the current spread to Treasuries yielded by its surplus notes, the insurance company purchases the right to substitute its own surplus notes for Treasuries currently held in a trust vehicle (a "substitution" option). The trust finances itself via the issuance of securities to investors who are satisfied if the spread to Treasuries on the securities exceeds that available on surplus notes. The insurance company is satisfied because it has procured contingent, off balance sheet funding at a cost substantially below that offered in the reinsurance markets.

There are numerous similar opportunities to be found in the credit markets today. All of these arise from situations in which the same default risk trades at different prices in different market-places due to persistent discontinuities between the supply of and demand for a given credit risk in one market versus another. Examples include discrepancies between pricing in the loan markets and bond markets; between taxable and tax-exempt markets; between investment grade and sub-investment grade markets; between capital markets and reinsurance markets; between funded and unfunded assets; between long-term and short-term assets; between domestic and overseas markets, and so on. To arbitrage relative value in these situations traditionally required the existence of a liquid repo market or some other mechanism via which it was possible to short one asset against a long position in another. Credit derivatives significantly expand the universe of arbitrage opportunities because they introduce the possibility of shorting credit instruments in a cash-settled form without the risk of a short-squeeze.

Also worthy of note in this context are Credit-Linked Notes which, unlike Credit Swaps, are funded balance sheet assets that offer synthetic credit exposure to a Reference Entity in a structure designed to resemble a synthetic corporate bond or loan. Credit-Linked Notes are frequently issued by SPVs (corporations or trusts) which hold some form of collateral securities financed through the issuance of notes or certificates to the investor. The investor receives a coupon and par redemption, provided there has been no Credit Event of the Reference Entity. The vehicle enters into a Credit Swap with a third party in which it sells default protection in return for a premium that subsidizes the coupon to compensate the investor for the Reference Entity default risk.

The investor assumes credit risk of both the Reference Entity and the underlying collateral securities. In the event that the Reference Entity defaults, then the underlying collateral is liquidated and the investor receives the proceeds only after the Credit Swap counterparty is paid the Contingent Payment. If the underlying collateral defaults, then the investor is exposed to its recovery regardless of the performance of the Reference Entity. This additional risk is recognized by the fact that the yield on the Credit-Linked Note is the sum of the return on the underlying collateral and the premium on the Credit Swap.

To tailor the cash flows of the Credit-Linked Note it may be necessary to make use of an interest rate or cross-currency swap. At inception, this swap would be on-market, but as markets move, the swap may move into or out of the money. The investor takes the swap counterparty credit risk accordingly. Credit-Linked Notes may also be issued on an unsecured basis by a corporation or financial institution. In this case the investor assumes risk to both the issuer and the Reference Entity to which principal redemption is linked.

10.6.3 Recovery Rate

Investments in conventional debt instruments are normally subject to an indeterminate recovery rate after a default. It is possible to structure credit derivatives so that the recovery rate is fixed at inception, introducing the possibility of tailoring transactions to reflect a recovery rate view. Formulating a recovery rate expectation is an integral component of any credit decision, but one that previously could not be isolated from the investment decision.

The following example elaborates. A bank would take exposure to a credit at the senior unsecured level at a spread of 40 bp. Another bank with existing exposure would sell this credit at the same spread. However, the first considers the likely recovery rate for the credit to be 50 per cent, while the second considers it to be 70 per cent.

The two institutions may enter into a Credit Swap in which the contingent payment is fixed at 50 per cent rather than at the floating recovery rate of senior unsecured debt, as usually determined by dealer poll of a Reference Obligation after default. The second bank, the Protection Buyer, might be prepared to pay up to $40 \times 50/30$ bp. or 67 bp for the fixed recovery contract, since it offers more protection than the floating recovery contract given the bank's recovery rate expectation of 70 per cent (50/30 is the ratio of expected losses upon default in the fixed versus the floating recovery transaction). Conversely, the first bank is happy to receive any premium over 40 bp for the 50 per cent fixed recovery transaction since in its view this is equivalent to the floating recovery transaction. A transaction completed at, say, 55 bp would leave both institutions happy given their divergent recovery rate views.

10.6.4 Term

Traditionally, it has been difficult, or even impossible, for investors to tailor the term of investments to meet their own needs as opposed to those of borrowers. Credit derivatives, however, offer negotiable maturity profiles. Consequently, investors are able to extract relative value for developing focused views on the term structure of credit risk.

For example, consider an eight-year exposure to a corporate that has no shorter term debt outstanding. The predominance of investors limited to terms inside three years and the absence of shorter term debt than eight years means that the term structure of credit spreads for the name is likely to reflect a tighter spread for the first three years and a wider spread for the last five years than would be expected on the basis of default probabilities alone. In other words, the term structure reflects a technical imbalance between the supply of and demand for shorter term versus longer term paper. The situation is illustrated in Figure 10.14.

Using a Credit Swap, it is possible to decompose an eight-year position into a three-year position and a forward-starting five-year position. Thus, an investor limited to a three-year term is able to take the first three years of risk, while another investor with greater flexibility and who has appetite beyond three years is able to take the last five years of risk. Both investors are satisfied since the forward investor is able to focus exposure in the area in which it offers most value for this view, while the shorter term investor is able to generate exposure to a name that was not otherwise available in the cash markets.

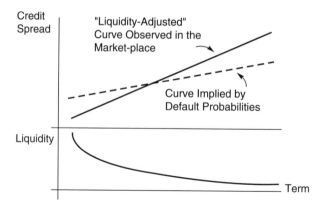

Figure 10.14 Liquidity-adjusted credit spreads. *Source:* J.P. Morgan Securities Inc.

10.7 COMMON PRICING CONSIDERATIONS

10.7.1 Predictive or Theoretical Pricing Models of Credit Swaps

A common question when considering the use of Credit Swaps, as either an investment or a risk-management tool, is: How should they correctly be priced? Credit risk has for many years been thought of as a form of deep out-of-the-money put option on the assets of a firm. To the extent that this approach to pricing could be applied to a Credit Swap, it could also be applied to the pricing of any traditional credit instrument. In fact, option pricing models have already been applied to the credit derivatives for the purpose of proprietary "predictive" or "forecasting" modelling of the term structure of credit spreads.

A model that prices default risk as an option will require, directly or implicitly, as parameter inputs both default probability and severity of loss given default, net of recovery rates, in each period in order to compute both an expected value and a standard deviation or "volatility" of value. These are the analogues of the forward price and implied volatility in a standard Black–Scholes model.

However, in a practical environment, irrespective of the computational or theoretical characteristics of a pricing model, that model must be parameterized using either market data or proprietary assumptions. A predictive model using a sophisticated option-like approach might postulate that loss given default is 50 per cent and default probability is 1 per cent and derive that the Credit Swap price should be, say, 20 bp. A less sophisticated model might value a credit derivative based on comparison with pricing observed in other credit markets (e.g. if the undrawn loan pays 20 bp, and bonds trade at Libor + 15 bp, then adjusting for liquidity and balance sheet impact, the Credit Swap should trade at around 25 bp). Yet the more sophisticated model will be no more powerful than the simpler model if it uses as its source data the *same market information*. Ultimately, the only rigorous independent check of the assumptions made in the sophisticated predictive model can be market data. Yet, in a sense, market credit spread data present a classic example of a joint observation problem: credit spreads imply loss severity given default, but this can only be derived if one is prepared to make an assumption as to what they are simultaneously implying about default likelihoods (or vice versa). Thus, rather than encouraging a more sophisticated theoretical analysis of credit risk, the most important contribution that credit derivatives will make to the pricing of credit will be in improving liquidity and transferability of credit risk and hence in making market pricing more transparent, more readily available, and more reliable.

10.7.2 Mark to Market and Valuation Methodologies for Credit Swaps

A question that often arises is: Do Credit Swaps require the development of sophisticated risk modelling techniques in order to be marked to market? It is important in this context to stress the distinction between a user's ability to mark a position to market (its "valuation" methodology), and its ability to formulate a proprietary view on the correct theoretical value of a position, based on a sophisticated risk model (its "predictive" or "forecasting" methodology). Interestingly, this distinction is recognized in the existing bank regulatory capital framework: while eligibility for trading book treatment of, for example, interest rate swaps depends on a bank's ability to demonstrate a credible valuation methodology, it does not require any predictive modelling expertise.

Fortunately, the valuation of Credit Swaps is relatively straightforward, and related to an assessment of the market credit spreads prevailing for obligations of the Reference Entity which are *pari passu* with the Reference Obligation, or similar credits, *with tenure matching that of the Credit Swap, rather than that of the Reference Obligation itself.* For example, a five-year Credit Swap on XYZ Corp, in a predictive modelling framework, might be evaluated on the basis of a postulated default probability and recovery rate, but should be marked to market based upon prevailing market credit spreads (which, as discussed above, provide a joint observation of implied market default probabilities and recovery rates) for five-year XYZ Corp obligations substantially similar to the Reference Obligation (whose maturity could exceed five years). If there are no such five-year obligations, then a market spread can be interpolated or extrapolated from longer and/or shorter term assets. If there is no prevailing market price for *pari passu* obligations to the Reference Obligation, then adjustments for relative seniority can be made to market prices of assets with different priority in a liquidation. Even if there are no currently traded assets issued by the Reference Entity, then comparable instruments issued by similar credit types may be used, with appropriately conservative adjustments.

10.7.3 Risk Equivalence of Total Return Swaps and Credit Swaps for Valuation Purposes

A further common question is: Are there fundamental distinctions between Credit Swaps and Total Return Swaps for valuation purposes, based upon a concern that default products involve a new and problematic underlying risk (default risk)?

TR swaps are normally referenced to an asset that is widely traded, and for which market prices are readily available. Consequently TR Swaps are easily marked to market, based upon the market value of the specific Reference Obligation. It is sometimes thought that Credit Swaps, on the other hand, transfer default risk only, rather than market price risk, and therefore sit more naturally alongside traditional credit instruments which are not so easily or so often marked to market. This implies that there is no visible market price for default risk.

However, both Credit Swaps and TR Swaps typically reference recognized financial assets, whether bonds, loans or otherwise, whose market price embodies precisely this same risk. Consequently, they can be treated as equivalent instruments for many risk management purposes. The reason for this is that, evaluated on a mark-to-market basis, the transactions are identical. Consider a five-year Credit Swap referenced to obligations of XYZ Corp, and compare it with a one year TR Swap referencing a five-year obligation of XYZ Corp (the "matching TR Swap"). At inception of both transactions, five-year obligations of XYZ Corp are trading at Libor plus 25 bp. If a party were to seek to unwind the Credit Swap after one year, the unwind cost should exactly equal the final mark-to-market payment due under the matching TR Swap at that time. Suppose XYZ Corp has deteriorated so that its four-year obligations are trading at Libor plus 40 bp. Ignoring transaction costs, to unwind the Credit Swap would require the payment by the Protection Seller to the Protection Buyer of the "in-the-money" amount equal to the present value of 15 bp running for the four remaining years of the life of the contract. Similarly, to unwind the TR Swap will require a change-in-value payment equal to the decline in value of what is now a four-year obligation of XYZ Corp, with an initial value of Libor plus 25 bp and a final market value of Libor plus 40 bp, namely the present value of 15 bp running for four years. Thus the Protection Seller in a Credit Swap and the TR Receiver on a TR Swap have equivalent spread risk on a mark-to-market basis. It is only in the case that a Credit Swap, or for that matter a TR Swap, is referenced to a Reference Obligation or Reference Entity for which market prices are not readily available that neither instrument can be readily marked to market.

10.7.4 Relative Value Analysis of Credit Swaps

From the investor's perspective, credit derivatives may add value simply by providing access to credit exposure in a form that would not otherwise be available. However, where credit derivatives exist in parallel with alternative investments offering essentially similar risks, the prospective investor needs to ascertain the relative value in a credit derivative position in order to justify its use over other more traditional or more liquid assets.

This section presents a simple valuation methodology that does not require a complex or "black-box" theoretical model.

Consider an example of a corporate credit that has liquid eight-year maturity public debt outstanding. These bonds trade at a spread of 65 bp over Treasuries which, given interest rate swap spreads of 35 bp, can be asset-swapped to a floating rate of Libor plus 30 bp. A bank that is hedging a credit position might offer a spread of 40 bp per annum for default protection in a Credit Swap. Since the Credit Swap pays the investor a spread that is 10 bp wider than the spread to Libor of the same default risk in bond form, it can be argued that the Credit Swap offers better value. Provided that the investor feels this 10 bp premium is sufficient to compensate for the potential added illiquidity of purchasing a Credit Swap over a public bond, this is an attractive investment.

Clearly, for investors with a hold-to-maturity investment horizon this liquidity decision is easier than for shorter term traders. In the developing Credit Swap market illiquidity premiums are eroding and are currently considered to be at or inside 5–10 bp per annum for investment grade credits in normal contract sizes of up to US$50 million and with maturities inside five years.

It is often asked whether the correct comparison in the preceding analysis is with the bond's spread to Libor or its spread to Treasuries. This issue is resolved by considering the fact that a Credit Swap is an unfunded transaction in which no initial cash outlay is required. If an investor were to attempt to replicate an unfunded investment in a cash bond, then that position would require financing. The cost of secured financing of a bond position is reflected in the cost of repo. On average, repo financing may be achieved for corporate assets at approximately Libor flat. Thus, after financing, the borrower's net spread income is the spread to Libor rather than the spread to Treasuries. Secured financing is chosen here because it least reflects the credit quality of the borrower and therefore is the appropriate benchmark for Credit Swap valuation for the market as a whole rather than for a specific entity. Hence the most obvious benchmark pricing comparison for a Credit Swap is the equivalent asset swap spread.

As implied in Section 10.2.1(ii) above, a specific investor will tailor this analysis to reflect his own cost of balance sheet usage. Thus, for the entity that charges for balance sheet at Libor plus 10 bp the Credit Swap in the example offers 20 bp (40 − (30 − 10)) more net spread income than the bond, and for the investor charged Libor minus 10 bp for balance sheet, relative value is zero (40 − (30 + 10)).

Another common question is: Why might the hedging bank pay a spread of 40 bp for default protection for a credit that trades at a spread of 30 bp? The rationale for this arises from considering the possible origins of the risk being transferred. If the cost of the next best alternative for reducing exposure, or the cost of not hedging at all, is greater than the 10 bp premium, then the seller will rationally incur this cost.

10.7.5 Counterparty Considerations

In a Credit Swap the Protection Buyer has credit exposure to the Protection Seller contingent upon the performance of the Reference Entity. If the Protection Seller defaults, then the Buyer must find alternative protection and will be exposed to changes in replacement cost due to changes in credit spreads since the inception of the original swap. More seriously, if the Protection Seller defaults *and* the Reference Entity defaults, the Buyer is unlikely to recover the full default payment due, although the final recovery rate on the position will benefit from any positive recovery rate on obligations of *both* the Reference Entity and the Protection Seller.

Counterparty risk consequently affects the pricing of credit derivative transactions. Protection bought from higher rated counterparties will command a higher premium. Furthermore, a higher credit quality correlation between the Reference Entity and the Protection Seller will lead to a lower premium; protection purchased from a counterparty against a Reference Entity is less valuable if a simultaneous default on the two names has a higher probability.

The problem of how to compute and charge for counterparty credit exposure is in large part an empirical one, since it depends on computing the joint likelihood of arriving in different credit states, which will in turn depend on an estimate of credit quality correlation between the Protection Seller and Reference Entity which cannot be directly observed. Significant efforts have been undertaken in the area of default correlation estimation, which also has important applications in credit portfolio risk management, as discussed in Section 10.3.4.(iii).

The following expression describes a simple methodology for computing a "counterparty credit charge" (CCC), as the sum of expected losses due to counterparty (CP) default across N different time periods, t, and states of credit quality (R) of the Reference Entity (RE) from default through to AAA. Given an estimate of credit quality correlation, it is possible to estimate the joint likelihood of the Reference Entity being in each state, given a counterparty default, from the respective individual likelihoods of arriving in each state of credit quality. Since loss can only occur given a default of the counterparty we are interested only in the default likelihood of the counterparty. However, since loss can occur due to changes in the mark to market (MTM) of the Credit Swap caused by credit spread fluctuations across different credit states of the Reference Entity, we are interested in the full matrix of credit quality migration likelihoods of the Reference Entity.

Typically, the counterparty credit charge is subtracted from the premium paid to the Protection Seller and accounted for by the Protection Buyer as a reserve against counterparty credit losses.

$$CCC = (100 \text{ per cent} - \text{recovery rate}_{cp})$$

$$* \sum_{t=t_0}^{t_N} \sum_{R=\text{Def}}^{\text{AAA}} \text{Prob}_{\text{Joint}} \left\{ CP_{\text{In Default}}, RE_{\text{Rating}=R} \right\} * Op_{\text{Rating}=R}$$

where

CP = counterparty
RE = Reference Entity
N = number of time periods, t
R = rating of the Reference Entity at time t
Op = price of an option to replace a risky exposure to RE in state R at time t with a riskless exposure,
  i.e. when RE has defaulted, value is $(100 \text{ per cent} - \text{recovery rate}_{RE})$
  i.e. when RE has not defaulted, value is $(100 \text{ per cent} - \text{MTM of Credit Swap},$ based on credit spreads)

10.8 CONCLUSION

The use of credit derivatives has grown exponentially since the beginning of the 1990s. Transaction volumes have picked up from the occasional tens of millions of dollars to regular weekly volumes measured in hundreds of millions, if not billions, of dollars. While no published figures are available, most informal estimates of total outstanding market volume suggest a number in excess of US$200 billion. Banks remain among the most active participants, but the end-user base is expanding rapidly to include a broad range of broker-dealers, institutional investors, money managers, hedge funds, insurers and reinsurers, as well as corporates. Growth in participation and market volume is likely to continue at its current rapid pace, based on the unequivocal contribution that credit derivatives are making to efficient risk management, rational credit pricing and ultimately systemic liquidity. Credit derivatives can offer both the buyer and seller of risk considerable advantages over traditional alternatives and, both as an asset class and a risk-management tool, represent an important innovation for global financial markets with the potential to revolutionize the way that credit risk is originated, distributed, measured, and managed.

10.8.1 Credit Derivatives and Portfolio Management

It is no coincidence that the use of credit derivatives has emerged simultaneously with the development of increasingly sophisticated credit portfolio models. The recent launch of

J.P. Morgan's CreditMetrics with the support of a large group of co-sponsors provided the first readily available benchmark model for evaluating credit value-at-risk in a full portfolio context. This technology allows portfolio managers to quantify concentration risk arising from large exposure to one credit or to groups of highly correlated credits in a particular industry or location. Traditionally, arbitrary credit line limits have been the primary defence against concentrations of credit risk. By contrast, the CreditMetrics approach makes credit allocation decisions sensitive to risk and return (that is, an output of the portfolio management model rather than an input to it). The approach allows portfolio managers to identify those credits contributing most significantly to portfolio risk and evaluate replacing them with other, less correlated, and hence less risky, exposures.

Such advances in the application of modern portfolio theory to credit portfolios have revealed powerful arguments for more active credit risk management. For example, loans have a lower default correlation than their corresponding equity correlation (due to the low likelihood that two remote events will occur simultaneously). The implication of low default correlations is that the systematic risk in a credit portfolio is small relative to the non-systematic or individual contribution to risk of each asset. The greater the component of non-systematic risk in a portfolio, the greater the benefits of diversification, and vice versa. To view the problem another way, indices provide good hedges of risk in equity portfolios, but not in debt portfolios: it takes many more names to fully diversify a credit portfolio than an equity portfolio, but when those diversification benefits are achieved, they are considerable. An inadequately diversified portfolio, on the other hand, can result in significantly lower return on risk ratios than would seem intuitively obvious. The conclusion? Given the opportunity, portfolio managers should actively seek to hedge concentrated risks and diversify with new ones.

The evolution of better models for credit risk *measurement* and better tools for credit risk *management* are mutually reinforcing: traditionally, without the tools to transfer credit risk, it was not possible to properly respond to the recommendations of a portfolio model. Conversely, without a portfolio model the contribution of credit derivatives to portfolio risk–return performance has been difficult to evaluate. However, as such technology becomes more widespread, as the necessary data become more accessible, and as credit derivative liquidity improves, the combined effect on the way in which banks and others evaluate and manage credit risks will be profound. Banks will adopt a more proactive approach to trading and managing credit exposures with a corresponding decline in the typical holding period for loans. It will become more common to observe banks taking exposure to borrowers with whom they have no meaningful relationships and shedding exposure to customers with whom they do have relationships to facilitate further business. Such transactions will occur both on a one-off basis and increasingly via the use of large bilateral portfolio swaps, which in a sense are simply a less radical and more effective solution than a bank merger to the problem of a poorly diversified customer base. Banks will increasingly have the ability to choose whether to act as passive hold-to-maturity investors or as proactive, return-on-capital driven originators, traders, servicers, repackagers, and distributors of the loan product. Ironically, this process will resemble the distribution techniques employed by those institutions that have been disintermediating banks in the capital markets for years. It also seems inevitable that greater transaction frequency and the availability of more objective pricing will prompt a movement towards the marking to market of loan portfolios.

10.8.2 Other Implications

While it is true that banks have been the foremost users of credit derivatives to date, it would be wrong to suggest that banks will be the only institutions to benefit from them. Credit derivatives are bringing about greater efficiency of pricing and greater liquidity of all credit risks. This will benefit a broad range of financial institutions, institutional investors, and also corporates in their capacity both as borrowers and as takers of trade credit and receivable exposures. Just as the rapidly growing asset-backed securitization market is bringing investors new sources of credit assets, the credit derivatives market will strip out and repackage credit exposures from the vastly greater pool of risks that do not naturally lend themselves to securitization, either because the risks are unfunded (off balance sheet), because they are not intrinsically transferable, or because their sale would be complicated by relationship concerns. By enhancing liquidity, credit derivatives achieve the financial equivalent of a "free lunch" whereby both buyers and sellers of risk benefit from the associated efficiency gains.

It is not surprising, then, to learn that credit derivatives are a group of products which, while innovative, are coming of age. When they first emerged in the early 1990s, credit derivatives were used primarily by derivatives dealers seeking to generate incremental credit capacity for derivatives counterparties with full credit lines. Since then they have evolved into a tool used routinely by commercial and investment banks and other institutional investors in the course of credit risk management, distribution, structuring and trading, with liquidity beginning to rival or even exceed that of the secondary loan trading market in the United States and the asset swap market in Europe. Most recently, corporate risk managers have begun to explore the use of the product as a mechanism for hedging their own costs of borrowing, as well as managing credit exposures to key customers.

At the end of 1996, estimates of market volume (none of them official) suggested global annual notional volumes between US$50 and US$100 billion, up from perhaps one-tenth of this amount one year earlier. By mid-1997, anecdotal evidence suggests that this figure has escalated to exceed US$250 billion. While these numbers are tiny relative to the size of the global credit markets and other derivatives markets (both measured in trillions of dollars), today, credit derivatives remind many of the nascent interest rate and equity swap markets of the 1980s — a product whose potential for growth derives from both enormous need and an enormous underlying market-place. For risk managers, credit derivatives are a flexible tool to restructure the illiquid components of credit portfolios. For institutional investors, they represent a new asset class which may be engineered to meet the demands of the investor and extract relative value.

10.9 GLOSSARY

Contingent Capital Note. A security normally issued from a special purpose vehicle or trust collateralized with Treasuries in which a company pays a premium from the outset for the right, at any time during a specified period, to substitute its own notes for the Treasuries.

Contingent Payment. The payment made by the Protection Seller in a Credit (Default) Swap. Usually computed using one of four settlement mechanisms:

- *Recovery Linked Cash Settlement*: usually calculated as the fall in price of a specified Reference Obligation below par, as established by polling the prices provided by reference dealers.

- *Final Work-Out Value*: a cash settlement equal to the losses incurred by creditors of the Reference Entity based on the actual work-out value of either a specified Reference Obligation or a broader class of obligations of the Reference Entity, as established in the bankruptcy proceedings.

- *Binary Cash Settlement*: a predetermined fixed amount, usually expressed as a percentage of the notional amount.

- *Physical Delivery*: the full notional amount in exchange for delivery of the Deliverable Obligations.

Credit Event.   Determined by negotiation between the parties to a Credit (Default) Swap. Typically, public information of a receivership, bankruptcy, insolvency, winding up, material adverse restructuring of debt or failure to meet payment obligations. Often coupled with a Materiality requirement.

Credit (Default) Swap.   A bilateral financial contract in which one counterparty (the "Protection Buyer" or "Buyer") pays a periodic fee, typically expressed in basis points per annum on the notional amount, in return for a Contingent Payment by the other counterparty (the "Protection Seller" or "Seller") after a Credit Event of the Reference Entity. The Contingent Payment is designed to mirror the loss incurred by creditors of the Reference Entity in the event of its default. The settlement mechanism depends on the liquidity and availability of Reference Obligations.

Credit Option.   Put or call options on the price of either (a) a floating rate note, bond or loan or (b) an "asset swap" package, consisting of a credit-risky instrument with any payment characteristics and a corresponding derivative contract which exchanges the cashflows of that instrument for a floating rate cashflow stream, typically three- or six-month Libor plus a spread.

Credit Spread Option.   A bilateral financial contract in which the Protection Buyer pays a premium, usually upfront, and receives present value of the difference between a floating spread between the yield of the Reference Obligation and some benchmark yield (usually Treasuries or Libor) and the Strike Spread, if positive (a Credit Spread Cap or Call), or alternatively if negative (a Credit Spread Floor or Put).

Credit-Linked Note.   A security, normally issued from a collateralized special purpose vehicle, which may be a company or business trust, with redemption linked to the occurrence of a Credit Event. Credit-Linked Notes may also be issued on an unsecured basis directly by a corporation or financial institution.

Deliverable Obligations.   The obligations specified as deliverable under the terms of a physically settled Credit Swap. These may be either the Reference Obligation or any one of a broad class of qualifying obligations issued or guaranteed by the Reference Entity (e.g. any senior unsecured claim in respect of borrowed money against the Reference Entity).

Dynamic Credit Swap or Credit Intermediation Swap.   A Credit Swap with a dynamic notional which for a fixed fee provides the Protection Buyer with a Contingent Payment that matches the mark to market on any given day of a specified derivative (or other market-sensitive instrument).

Materiality.   A significant price deterioration in a specified Reference Obligation, net of price fluctuations due to interest rate movements, following the occurrence of at least one of the other components of a Credit Event, such as a default or bankruptcy.

Reference Entity.   A specified entity which may be a sovereign, financial institution or corporate; or one among a basket of such specified entities.

Reference Obligation(s).   Typically, a public security or securities issued by the Reference Entity; alternatively, loans or other financial obligations (including swaps, trade receivables, indemnification letters and so on).

Substitution Option.   A bilateral financial contract in which one party buys the right to substitute a specified asset or one of a specified group of assets for another asset at a point in time or contingent upon a Credit Event.

Total (Rate of) Return Swap.   A bilateral financial contract in which the total return of a specified asset is exchanged for another cash flow. One counterparty (the "TR Payer") pays the total return (interest plus fees plus price appreciation less price depreciation) of a specified asset, the Reference Obligation, and (usually) receives Libor plus a spread from the other counterparty (the "TR Receiver"). Price appreciation or depreciation may be calculated and exchanged at maturity or on an interim basis.

10.10 ENDNOTES/REFERENCES

1. *Source:* Loan Pricing Corporation. *Gold Sheets*, 1998, Vol. IV.
2. CreditMetrics is a registered trademark of J.P. Morgan & Co. Incorporated. It is written with the symbol® on its first occurrence in this chapter and as CreditMetrics thereafter.
3. *Source:* IFR Omnibase.
4. Merton, R. (1974) "On the pricing of corporate debt: the risk structure of interest rates". *The Journal of Finance*, **29**.
5. The assumptions and mathematics required to estimate default correlations from equity price correlations are complex and beyond the scope of this chapter. The interested reader is referred to J.P. Morgan (1997) *CreditMetrics — Technical Document*, and Merton, R. (1974) "On the pricing of corporate debt: the risk structure of interest rates", *Journal of Finance*, **29**. Conceptually, if liabilities are assumed fixed and default is defined as occurring instantaneously when asset values fall below liabilities, then the volatility of asset levels as inferred from equity price behaviour should directly predict the chance of default by any firm. By extension, these asset volatilities will also drive the joint default probability between any pair of firms. A positive correlation between asset returns (as implied by equity prices) would therefore in turn imply some expected positive correlation in credit quality migration.
6. In this regard, a paper by the Financial Law Panel (1997) "Credit Derivatives: The Regulatory Treatment, A Guidance Notice", and an opinion commissioned by ISDA from Robin Potts, Q.C. (1997), of Allen and Overy, "Credit Derivatives: Opinion", 24 June, also reduce uncertainty by making a strong case that under UK law, credit derivatives are not entered into by way of "insurance business", are not contracts of insurance, and are not void under waging or gaming laws.

Index